THE COURTESAN'S REVENGE

THE COURTESAN'S REVENGE

Harriette Wilson, the Woman who Blackmailed the King

Frances Wilson

ff

faber and faber

by the same author

LITERARY SEDUCTIONS

First published in 2003
by Faber and Faber Limited
3 Queen Square London WC1N 3AU

Typeset by Agnesi Text Hadleigh
Printed in England by Mackays of Chatham, plc

A CIP record for this book
is available from the British Library

ISBN 0–571–20504–6

2 4 6 8 10 9 7 5 3 1

For Anthony and Anne

Contents

List of Illustrations

Acknowledgements

In the notes he wrote for *Nana*, his novel about a courtesan in Second Empire Paris, Zola imagined 'a whole society hurling itself' at her body, 'a pack of hounds after a bitch, who is not even on heat and makes fun of the hounds following her'. This might also describe the life of Harriette Wilson, whose unguarded pursuit by the leaders of the British aristocracy, the army, the government and opposition made her the most desired, and then the most dangerous, woman in Regency London.

As a courtesan, Harriette Wilson belonged to a sexual underworld whose existence is rarely admitted to in the lives of the nineteenth century's great men, and as a blackmailer all but a few of her letters have been destroyed. So erased from the annals of history had she become when my interest in Harriette Wilson began that she threatened to remain for me the figure of fantasy she had been in her lifetime. I owe the fact that I have found such rich material to the help and support of many people. Julian Loose, my editor, encouraged the project from the very start, as did all those at Faber and my agent, Lisa Darnell. Their enthusiasm was a great motivator, particularly at the beginning when Harriette (as I call her for simplicity's sake, her name having changed so often in her career) was stubbornly refusing to show in the books and boxes of letters which were piling up around me like pillars. Working with Faber is a great pleasure.

My research would still be continuing were it not for the generosity of the Leverhulme Trust. I am enormously grateful to Michael Holroyd, Michèle Roberts and Professor Rachel Bowlby for supporting me in my application for a Leverhulme Fellowship, and to my colleagues in the English Department at Reading University for covering my teaching in my absence. I would also like to thank the staff at The British Library, The British Museum Print Room, the Colindale Newspaper Library, Durham University Library Archives and Special Collections, the Guildhall Library, the London Library, Special Collections at London University Library, New York Public Library, Berkshire County Records, Buckinghamshire County Records, Camden Local Studies and Archives Centre, Derbyshire

Record Office, Dorset Record Office, the Family Records Centre, the Hampshire Record Office, Hampton Court, the Hertfordshire Archives and Local Studies, London Metropolitan Archives, the Public Records Office at Kew, the Public Record Office of Northern Ireland, and Westminster Public Archives. Thanks are due to Virginia Murray for permission to reproduce letters from Harriette Wilson in the John Murray Archive, to The Honourable Henry Lytton Cobbold for permission to reproduce letters to Sir Edward Bulwer Lytton kept in the Hertfordshire Archives and Local Studies, to Durham University Library for permission to reproduce letters from the Earl Grey Papers, and to the Duke of Beaufort for permission to reproduce letters from the Badminton archives. I am most grateful to Margaret Richards for her kindness in taking me through the Somerset letters at Badminton, and for her subsequent help. Vital information was generously given to me about the background of the Cheney family by Michael Capel Cure, and of the Proby and Storer families by Peter Fullerton.

For permission to reproduce the pictures in the plate section, I would like to thank the British Museum, the National Portrait Gallery, *Country Life* and the Hulton Getty Picture Collection. Except where shown otherwise, the illustrations are reproduced, by kind permission, from copies in a private collection. All illustrations in the text are reproduced, by kind permission, from copies in a private collection.

Many others have enabled this book come to fruition and I am in the debt of Mike Bott, Professor Cedric Brown, Jill Burrows, Angus Cargill, Ann Carey, Juliet Carey, Simon Carey, Adina Carlson, Stephen Colclough, Ron Costley, Dan Cruickshank, Ben Dean, Jean Debney, Edward and Bridget Dommen, Ophelia Field, Edmund Grey, John Gurnett, the Earl of Harewood, Dr Christine Kenyon Jones, Frances Henderson, Christopher Hibbert, Alastair Laing, Nick Peacock, William Proby, Dr Jane Ridley, Jill Tovey, Kate Ward, Rollo Whately, Ann Woodley, and Andrew Wordsworth. Dr Adam Smyth was an excellent research assistant. My greatest thanks go to William St Clair for reading and commenting on the drafts, and for his willingness to discuss my ideas and share his own.

My parents never ceased to lend me their support, from researching, proof-reading, and reference hunting to photocopying and babysitting. It is to them that this book is dedicated.

Across the broad continent of a woman's life falls the shadow of a sword. On one side all is correct, definite, orderly; the paths are strait, the trees regular, the sun shaded; escorted by gentlemen, protected by policemen, wedded and buried by clergymen, she has only to walk demurely from cradle to grave and no one will touch a hair of her head. But on the other side all is confusion. Nothing follows a regular course. The paths wind between bogs and precipices. The trees roar and rock and fall in ruin. There, too, what strange company is to be met – in what bewildering variety! Stone-masons hobnob with Dukes of the royal blood – Mr Blore treads on the heels of His Grace the Duke of Argyll. Byron rambles through, the Duke of Wellington marches in with all his orders on him. For in that strange land gentlemen are immune; any being of the male sex can cross from sun to shade with perfect safety . . .

VIRGINIA WOOLF, 'HARRIETTE WILSON'

CHAPTER 1

Mayfair

Harriette Wilson's *Memoirs* omit both time and place; there are no addresses given, no locations described, no elections, diseases, or wars. 'Dates make ladies nervous and stories dry,'[1] she wrote. Her scandalous book liberates us from established order and event and presents instead a form of utopia where great men wait in the rain for courtesans, gold watches are left by lords beneath pillows, and the French Revolution passes over the heads of the English aristocracy without stirring so much as a hair. But time and place are essential to an understanding of Harriette Wilson because she could not have existed anywhere other than Mayfair, in the heart of London, at any time other than the dawn of the nineteenth century: her story would simply not have been possible. Mayfair was in Harriette Wilson's very being; she was as vital a part of its body as the Church of St George in Hanover Square or the Dog and Duck at the foot of Hertford Street. So grounded were the events of her life in the streets of her childhood that it is tempting to think that she owed her refusal to be put down, her scorn of authority, her insolent wit and bawd and insistence on pleasure above all else, to the ghost of the annual spring carnival that gave its name to her kingdom and on whose site, on 22 February 1786, she was born. Harriette Wilson was the May fair's spirit incarnate, its Queen of Misrule.

St George's, Hanover Square, *Views of London*

One hundred years before her birth, Great Brookfield, where the fair laid down its roots, was a meadow. It lay on the far side of Piccadilly, which ancient artery stretched out of the clutter of Soho and reached westwards, past St James's Church, past taverns, courts, and stable yards, past Clarendon House and Berkeley House and up to the toll gate at Hyde Park Corner. Here the paved road ended with such abrupt rudeness that the edge of a cliff or even the edge of the world might have been reached. Leaving behind the stench and smoke of the city, Piccadilly now fell into pastures, hamlets, and isolated farms; herds and herdsmen, brick kilns and dung hills speckled the landscape. Great Brookfield lay where London became Middlesex, and every May Day holiday for sixteen days revellers poured here from the Strand, Lambeth, Spitalfields, and Charing Cross and from the surrounding villages of Kensington, Hampstead and Marylebone. Here they sang, danced and drank, saw fire-fighters and rope-dancers, midgets and albinos, giants and mermaids, bearded women and obese men, mock executions, jugglers, wild beasts and performing animals. It was a fortnight of drunkenness, debauchery and disobedience.

But as the eighteenth century rolled by, the land over which the May fair spread itself became the most coveted in the country and the open pastures were gradually eaten up by a body of muscular streets and squares that were finer and more handsome than any other part of London's swelling corpus. Only the name adopted by the new village and the names of the roads that now rippled over the old farmland, 'Farm Street', 'Brook Street', 'Hill Street' and 'Mill Street', revealed its humble origins. 'When do you come?' Horace Walpole asked a friend in 1759. 'If it is not soon, you will find a new town. I stared today at Piccadilly like a country squire; there are twenty new stone houses; at first I concluded that the grooms that used to live there, had got estates and built palaces.'[2] In the 1760s the Earl of Coventry moved into one of the Piccadilly palaces, and his first act as a resident was to get rid of the fair, which moved itself eastwards to Bow.

London had never felt more magnificent; it was the largest city in Europe and Mayfair, enclosed to the north by Tyburn Road (now Oxford Street) to the south by Piccadilly, to the east by Swallow Street (now Regent Street) and to the west by Tyburn Lane (now Park Lane) was the jewel in its crown. The titled and the super-rich moved westwards here from

Covent Garden, Soho, St Giles in the Fields, Leicester Fields and Golden Square to build their piles. It soon contained, Sydney Smith believed, 'more intelligence, human ability, to say nothing of wealth and beauty than the world ever collected in so small a place before'.[3] Years of intermarrying had turned the 'people of fascination' into one incestuous tribe and here they all lived, an extended family of dukes, earls, admirals and generals, cheek by jowl with drapers, breeches-makers, hosiers, fishmongers, coal merchants and stocking-cleaners.[4]

In its transformation from fields to fashion, Great Brookfield became Shepherd Market, Mayfair's commercial centre. Behind the old Dog and Duck Inn lay a pond shaded by willows and surrounded by a gravel walk; here crowds gathered to send spaniels after ducks and place wagers on the winner. The noise of splashing, flapping, barking, quacking and cheering from the garden drowned out the other market activities. In one of the houses overlooking the pond, Harriette's newborn cry broke into the flickering light of a freezing black night. Or perhaps her first breath pierced the watery sunlight of the steely February dawn. She says she was born at 'ten minutes before 8 o/c' but we do not know if this event took place at the start or the close of the day. It seems appropriate, however, that the scene take place in semi-darkness as she would live her life in the shadows. She was raised in the full glare of Mayfair when it felt itself the centre of the world, but along with the city's other Cyprians and Great Impures, as the courtesans were called, she lived in its twilight realm. In her youth she was 'as familiar in the streets as the bill of the play or the walking advertisement of a lottery office',[5] but Harriette can never come fully into focus for us; despite the blaze of her prose she will always remain a figure of myth. She formed the fantasies of her age and slid back, when her role was over, into the city's dusk.

Harriette's birth followed a bitter winter. Yellow crocuses could be seen speckling the city's parks and the songs of the hedge sparrow, thrush, chaffinch, skylark and yellowhammer could be heard. February 1786 was a month of violent storms, brisk west winds, frost, fog and ice. The winter sun forcing its fingers through the blanket of smog gave the city an artificial, orange glow as though you were looking at it through a Claude glass. On her first night the temperature fell to well below freezing and there was thick ice on the panes. She was delivered by Dr Merriman, a

3

local apothecary who delivered each of her siblings and who in later years would sell her a pennyworth of Spanish liquorice over the counter of his shop. General Burgoyne's play, *The Heiress*, was performed that evening in Covent Garden; Mayfair was at its fullest since before Christmas, the aristocracy having returned to town from their country seats, ready to continue the business of government. It is doubtful that there was great jubilation at Harriette's birth: she was the sixth girl born in just over eight years to her mother, Amelia Dubouchet, who was no more than twenty-four years old. Another daughter to keep until she could keep herself or be married off, another dowry to find.

The child was baptized Harriot Dubochet in the fashionable Church of St George, Hanover Square. All month the sky had been overcast, with piercing winds and sleet pelting at the windows, and the nineteenth of March, the third Sunday in Lent, was the first fine day. It is reported to have been 'fair, still and pleasant', with snow on the open plains, seagulls crying over the Thames, bees buzzing round crocuses, brown and brimstone butterflies, flowers on the apricot and almond trees, and the dwarf daffodil in bloom. Perhaps the family walked the by now familiar route to St George's (where all the Dubouchet children were baptized) along Curzon Street, across Berkeley Square, over Bond Street and down George Street, with Amelia carrying the bundle in her arms. As all the Harriets in the parish register are transcribed 'Harriot', we cannot know whether this was the spelling the Dubouchets wanted for their daughter's name, or whether it was her own choice to go for the seemingly more sophisticated 'Harriette'.

One of the mysteries of Harriette's life is why she exchanged her father's Swiss name for that of 'Wilson'. Courtesans tended to use names other than that of their family, but why might Harriette, who was proud of her paternal heritage and liked her French Christian name, trade in Dubouchet, with its air of glamour (and subliminal echoes of debauchery), for a name as solidly, unromantically English as Wilson? Harriette seems never to have known a man called Wilson whose wife she could have passed for. Nor can we be sure when the change took place, whether it was an immediate act on leaving home or a decision reached several years later. Julia Johnstone, her former friend and fellow courtesan, said that Harriette dropped her father's name out of respect for him as long as he lived in

England. While Harriette scoffed at this remark, it is true that when John Dubouchet returned to his native Canton de Berne, she signed herself 'Du Bochet' once more. But his departure coincided with her own retirement, and she may have reverted to her former name because she was no longer a professional courtesan. Whatever the circumstances, it was assumed by all except those who watched her grow up that Wilson was Harriette's real name and the name also of her infamous sisters.

Harriette says in her *Memoirs* that she was born in Queen Street, a more prestigious address on the other side of the market, but the family did not move there until she was five years old. The house in which she began her life, 2 Carrington Street, has now been pulled down to make room for a mansion block and a car park, but rate records show that there were thirteen houses in the road, and maps show a stable yard at the end. It was not glamorous in comparison with Curzon Street, where the Earl of Chesterfield had built his great pile, or Charles Street or Berkeley Square, but it would have been a handsome house: the antiquarian Samuel Carte had lived there; so too had Kitty Fisher, the most popular courtesan of the mid-eighteenth century, 'the most pretty, extravagant, wicked little whore that ever flourished'.[6] Kitty Fisher was painted by Reynolds and Gainsborough, racehorses were named after her, a fall in the park became national news and she was immortalized in the nursery rhyme 'Lucy Locket dropped her pocket, Kitty Fisher found it.' When Casanova came to London he sought her out, but as he offered only ten guineas for an hour of her time, she turned him down. Tales circulated about her placing the fifty-pound note the Duke of York had paid for the pleasure of her company between two pieces of bread and eating it. Immensely rich, Kitty Fisher could choose the best accommodation. She died aged twenty-nine, two decades before Harriette was born, but there were residents who remembered the gilded butterfly who came to and fro in her sedan chair, and their encounters with her, actual or imaginary, had solidified into neighbourhood myth.

The players in Harriette's story all lived within shouting distance of her childhood home, in a few select streets and squares, but Harriette inhabited the half-world of the *demi-mondaine* with its own hierarchy and rules. She was in the peculiar position of being at the same time Mayfair's most and least visible character. She never moved too far from home;

Harriette became the courtesan not of strangers but of those she grew up around; her neighbours, the cousins and companions of childhood friends. She was not received in society but her familiarity with the aristocracy gave her the misplaced sense of belonging she carried throughout her life, and her air of superiority. She never doubted that she was the equal of those whom Byron called the 'twice two thousand, for whom earth was made';[7] she is never found bowing and scraping and is endlessly mocking of male egotism, describing her evenings with the Duke of Wellington, when he was the nation's hero, as something like sitting up with a corpse. She never doubted the brilliance of her conversation; it is her own luminous remarks her *Memoirs* record for posterity; the trivial tittle-tattle of others is brilliantly impersonated and sent up. Nor did she adopt airs; she rather played, with great pride, the anarchic, anti-authoritarian, carnival queen and enjoyed mobilizing this version of herself against the Establishment figures she lived among.

Nor did she have any vanity about her, but rather a quiet, solid confidence in her appeal. Some contemporaries confirm Harriette's acceptance of her own attractiveness; Julia Johnstone, who had no cause to flatter her rival, admitted to being 'fascinated by Harriette's lovely features', and concedes that in her youth Harriette had been 'superlatively lovely'.[8] Harriette seems never to have been painted in the style of a goddess like the endlessly reproduced Emma, Lady Hamilton, or to have been mythologized as were other courtesans by the leading artists of the day. Lord Yarmouth, the model for the gruesome Lord Steyne in Thackeray's *Vanity Fair*, was at one point keen that Harriette and her sisters should all sit to Sir Thomas Lawrence for a large family picture, which he would then place in his private collection, but regrettably this never happened.[9] Harriette was considered too notorious for her image to be displayed on the public walls of private homes, but she was painted in miniature for discreet enjoyment and many knew her from popular prints. These prints represent her as having dark, curled hair, strong eyebrows, white skin, deep brown eyes, a good straight nose and a small neat mouth. It is the eyes to which the viewer is drawn. Sir Walter Scott, who met her once, never forgot Harriette's 'good eyes',[10] and years later, when they were 'sunken' and the 'crow's feet' were 'wide-spreading beneath' them, Julia Johnstone conceded that those once famous eyes still 'gleamed with faded lustre through her long dark eyelashes'.[11] Harriette had a large bosom, small waist and little hands and feet, all that was considered admirable in a woman's body. And yet her more obvious feminine charms seem not to have constituted her allure.

Walter Scott remembered her as 'a smart saucy girl',[12] 'ugly' but 'remarkably witty'.[13] One cannot help feeling that, for some, Harriette's wit undid not just her beauty but also her femininity, hence Scott's remark that she had 'the manners of a wild schoolboy'.[14] Scott's observation picks up on Harriette's androgyny, as does the compliment paid to her by Lord Ponsonby, who 'used to say of me that my advantage over other *sweet fair ones* was that besides my pretty bosom and effeminate qualities, softness of temper etc, I really was "an *excellent fellow*"'.[15] Other of her lovers also called her 'little fellow' and to all of them she was known as 'Harry'. She called herself a 'tom boy' and Julia Johnstone called her a 'masculine heroine', quoting a remark made of her that she 'would make an excellent sailor's wife, she swears such good round oaths'.[16]

Harriette Wilson had sex appeal, an elusive quality that manifested itself in her energy, smell, smile, gestures, gait and, most importantly, the force of her personality. She was 'courted', Walter Scott believed, 'for her mental [rather] than [her] personal accomplishments . . .'[17] and *The English Spy* agreed: 'She was, when at her zenith, always celebrated rather for her *tact* in love affairs, and her talent at *invention*, than the soft engaging qualifications of the frail fair, which fascinate the eye and lead the heart captive with delight: her conversational powers were admirable; but her temper was outrageous, with a natural inclination to be satirical: – to sum up her merits at once, she was what a *connoisseur* would have called a bold, *fine* woman rather than an engaging *handsome* one.' Harriette, it was concluded, resembled more Bellona, the Roman goddess of war, than she did the Venus de Medici, the ideal of classical sexuality.[18]

Because she valued herself so highly, Harriette generated respect and admiration. It was always, she insisted, a pleasure for people to meet her.

CHAPTER 2

John and Amelia Dubouchet

There were many fantasies about the origin of Harriette Wilson. One rumour supposed her the offspring of a market porter and herb vendor; another declared her the child of a shoemaker turned Methodist lay preacher, yet another claimed she was the daughter of an eminent Lincolnshire farmer.[1] Julia Johnstone said that Harriette's father had been a captain who kept them all in near poverty on his meagre commission and an article in *The English Spy* suggested that he was the son of the wit and statesman, the Fourth Earl of Chesterfield, by his mistress, Elizabeth Dubouchette.[2] Most recently it has been supposed that John Dubouchet, being Swiss, was a watchmaker.[3]

But the myths circulating about Dubouchet are put in the shade when compared with his own yarns, and Harriette would inherit her father's gift for story-telling. A handsome raconteur with brilliant white teeth, a Swiss accent, and eyebrows that, Harriette said, 'used to frighten us half out of our senses',[4] Dubouchet saw himself as the dashing hero of a swash-buckling adventure. Finding domestic life restrictive and dull, he regaled his daughters with tales of his misspent youth. He was 'a scholar' who hailed from Vevey, a small town by Lake Geneva in the Canton de Berne. His family was 'the most respectable in Switzerland' and his ancestors, so he said, 'distinguished themselves in the politics of Europe'. 'I could furnish

Crib designed by Sheraton, *The Book of Decorative Furniture* my readers with an account of the former feats, armorial bearings, etc., of the late Barons Du bochet,' Harriette wrote, 'but that I should be afraid of sending them to sleep, and therefore I briefly proceed to inform them that my grandfather was the worse tempered man in all the Canton and my father . . . at the age of thirteen left his parents' roof in search of adventures, never to return. His two brothers followed his example and were not afterwards heard of. My father joined a recruiting party journeying towards Holland, who refused to take him into their service on account of his extreme youth. Charmed, however, with the beauty of his countenance, and his intelligent discourse, they supported him on his journey and suffered him to partake of their meals.'[5]

Dubouchet's beauty continued to attract notice in high places and his daughters heard how he became secretary to a colonel of a Swiss regiment and seduced the colonel's mistress, how the colonel discovered the lovers in each other's arms and how, in the subsequent duel, Dubouchet killed first the colonel and then the guard who tried to arrest him; how in his escape to 'half the known world' his charm and appearance once again enabled him to triumph. On his way to England his ship sank but, an expert swimmer, he swam to shore; in Portugal he became a professor of algebra, maths, German, French, fencing and dancing. After dazzling his students he arrived in London and became acquainted with General Burgoyne (whose play, *The Heiress*, entertained London society on the night of Harriette's birth) whom he then accompanied, as private secretary, to America, where Burgoyne was fighting the Revolutionaries. At the time that the General was disgraced and captured by the Americans, Dubouchet had the good fortune to be drinking Burgundy many miles away, and thus to be spared either imprisonment or the shame of association with the humiliating defeat.[6] On his return to England he ran away with the fourteen-year-old Amelia.

Harriette could not remember if her father was working when he wooed her mother – it is most likely, given his future record, that he was not. Nor did she know how her parents met, but 'it is certain', Harriette wrote, 'that he had art, and wit, and beauty enough to induce her to elope with him'.[7] Her mother agreed to a 'private' marriage with the thirty-four-year-old foreigner and she kept her changed status secret for several months afterwards.

It is unlikely that Harriette knew much about her maternal past. She told very little in her *Memoirs* and very little seems to have been told to her. Amelia Dubouchet's life was the sort that could have gone in several directions and as it was it went in none; her achievement was to produce daughters who refused to live as she had done. She was born in 1762, the illegitimate child of a schoolgirl named Gadston who had been seduced and abandoned by a country gentleman named Cheney. This was all she knew about her heritage, or all she told her children. Harriette spoke only once in her *Memoirs* of Amelia's half-brother, General Robert Cheney of the Guards, who by chance, between fighting in Holland and dealing with the Irish Rebellion, lodged with the Dubouchets when they lived in Queen Street. Cheney, who had been aide-de-camp to George III, was ignorant that his landlady was his sister and thus unaware, in the years to come, of his avuncular relation to the courtesan all London spoke about.

Miss Gadston's seducer, also called Robert Cheney, became Sheriff of Derbyshire in 1765. He had four sons, all of whom were distinguished soldiers.[8] Their uncle was the MP and respected essayist Isaac Hawkins Browne; son of the Isaac Hawkins Browne who was for Dr Johnson, 'one of the first wits of this country'.[9] This is the same Hawkins Browne who is parodied by Mary Crawford in the seventh chapter of Jane Austen's *Mansfield Park*. Through her mother's relationship with the Cheneys, Harriette was directly attached to the solid core of eighteenth-century English cultured society, but the Cheney sons and the Dubouchet daughters knew nothing of the others' existence.

The baby Amelia was left by her mother in Mayfair, in the care of a young married couple called Cook. Miss Gadston then bought herself a passage to America, taking with her a hundred-pound bill sent to her in a letter from Cheney. 'Take that,' he wrote, according to Harriette, 'the wages of shame, and never let me hear from you more.'[10] Harriette Wilson's grandmother was indeed never heard of again.

John Cook and his wife had lived in their three-storey house at 23 Queen Street since 1756, when the street plan of Mayfair was largely laid out and Shepherd Market, only ten years old, was still being plagued by the May carnival. Harriette's previous biographer calls her the daughter of a stocking-mender,[11] but Cook, who divided his business with Amelia and

Dubouchet after they married, was a stocking-cleaner, and the two trades were considerably different. Stocking-mending, like other needle trades such as mantua- and dressmaking, was one of the few trades open to women. As with all women's work it was hardly possible to make a living from the paltry wages. Harriette was disparaged as a mere stocking-mender even during her lifetime, and repeatedly stated that she 'should be proud of possessing such useful talents, and have always been ashamed of my deficiency in the proper, feminine occupation of needlework'.[12] Stocking-cleaning was an industry of a different kind; John Cook was not a worker but an employer, with 'a very extensive business amongst the first nobility'.[13] It was a profitable business too, when sartorial elegance was considered of the utmost importance and white and pale-blue stockings were worn by all gentlemen. Not only were the streets mud baths ('New London is no less entombed in mire than old London,' noted a traveller in the 1760s) but one hundred tonnes of horse manure were deposited on the cobbles each day, making it impossible to suppose that you might ever arrive at your destination with your legs and footware unsoiled. A gentleman would thus need to change his stockings several times a day and Cook, Harriette estimated, was making over £1,000 a year, at a time when the average yearly income of a lord was £8,000, a baronet £3,000, a knight or esquire £1,500, a gentleman £700, and a shopkeeper, farmer, or clergyman under £200.[14] Cook was bringing in enough to enable him to have nothing to do with his business, which operated in his outhouse, to pay high rates for a well-furnished home, to rent at least two other Mayfair houses, and to have servants wait on his family. He took on another business as well, and in 1792 Cook established himself as a coal merchant in premises at 8 Park Street, off Grosvenor Square.

Amelia lived with the Cooks, who seem to have been a childless couple, until she was five and a neighbour, the recently widowed Lady Ferrars, took 'a fancy' to her and 'begged permission to incur the sole charge of the child for a few years'.[15] Amelia was treated by her patroness 'in every respect as a daughter'; she shared the countess's bed and enjoyed her influence and instruction.[16] A few years later, Lady Ferrars married Lord Frederick Campbell, the third son of the Fourth Duke of Argyll. Until she was fourteen, Amelia was mixing in polite company. She had developed into a handsome young woman with strong brown eyes, a pale, clear skin, white teeth, 'a nose such as sculptors might have sought elsewhere in vain' and 'dark, polished, and silky' hair.[17]

Had she made a respectable marriage to a professional man, Amelia might have cast off the stigma of her illegitimacy and grown plump on a life of leisure. In choosing instead to throw in her lot with Dubouchet she displayed the kind of recklessness Harriette admired. Lady Campbell, when she discovered the marriage, disowned her charge, horrified at Amelia's 'binding herself, thus clandestinely, to a wild, rakish foreigner, whom nobody knew',[18] and Mrs Cook's health apparently never recovered. Mr Cook, realizing that the best he could do for Amelia would be to give her a good start in married life, took a house for the couple in Mount Street, which ran from Berkeley Square to Park Lane, where it looked on to the tree-lined reservoir in the huge green expanse of Hyde Park.

John Cook gave Amelia and her husband half of his stocking-cleaning business. Dubouchet was embarrassed by the trade but Amelia, Harriette said, 'possessed too much real pride to be ashamed of any honest way of bettering the condition and prospect of her children'.[19] As stockings began to be sent to the common wash and the era of Jacobinism replaced aristocratic breeches with democratic pantaloons ('Those damned breeches were the ruin of my poor sister, the Queen of France,' the Archduchess Christine complained), business suffered. Silk stockings were still worn with enough regularity at court and by aristocrats to give the Dubouchets some sort of an income, but money was tight and Dubouchet was increasingly extravagant, becoming, Harriette said, something of a 'bon vivant' and developing a 'predilection for expensive dinner-parties'.[20] With the help of Cook and some of his influential customers, Dubouchet established himself as a coal merchant, leaving Amelia to supervise what was left of the stocking-cleaning. His work involved attending for 'an hour or two, in a morning, at a coal-wharf in the city' after which 'we saw no more of him'.[21]

Harriette was brought up surrounded by silk stockings. Delivered by valets, they were washed, dyed pale blue, green or pink, treated for stains and hung to dry in the outhouse. They were then collected and returned to their owners. She would always like stockings on men. Worn with skin-tight knee-high leather breeches they added to a daring form of clothing, revealing every aspect of the male anatomy from the waist downwards.

When she became a celebrity, Harriette's preferences in male attire held more sway in some circles than the dictates of the dandy Beau Brummell, and when it was heard that Harriette Wilson commended silk stockings, white waistcoats and straight hair, this was how the young bucks dressed, regardless of the recent changes in fashion.

The Dubouchets' was an unhappy marriage. 'It was impossible for two minds or dispositions to be more widely different, or more unlikely to agree than my parents,' Harriette wrote. While conceding that the 'tameness of married life . . . but ill suited my father's ardent spirit'[22] – and she would sympathize with him in this – Harriette's loyalty lay with her mother, abandoned, worn out, and washed up. 'My poor mother,' she recalled, 'as she counted the tedious hours of his absence, which afforded her time for reflection, almost to madness, deeply repented of her thought-less disobedience, to her more than parents.'[23] What Harriette says about the influence of her parents' marriage on the future she would choose for herself has about it a directness that contrasts with the irony and evasion that otherwise defines her literary style. 'My dear mother's marriage had proved to me so forcibly, the miseries of two people of contrary opinions and character, torturing each other to the end of their natural lives, that, before I was ten years old, I decided, in my own mind, to live as free as air from any restraint but that of my own conscience.'[24]

Despite her observations of their relationship, Harriette idealized her parents. 'My mother's beauty was that of mind and spirit alone,' she wrote. 'It was not earthly . . . so pale, so still, and so expressive. In the whole course of my life, I never saw my mother anxious, even one instant, unless for others; and yet I have nursed her in the bitter pangs of child bearing, and have often seen her tortured with bodily pain.'[25] Her father she loved 'almost romantically'. It reveals a great deal about Harriette that while she championed her mother she eroticized her father. What drove her was a horror of becoming Amelia, but while she consciously avoided re-enacting those choices her mother had made, John Dubouchet was Harriette's sex-ual ideal: good-looking, irresponsible, idle, remote. She was always drawn to men who lived hard and fast, the self-destructive types who gambled their futures on the throw of a dice or a night with a whore, and when she married, her husband's history was as shadowy and mysterious as her father's had been, and as fabulously reconstructed.

CHAPTER 3

Queen Street

Lady Campbell eventually forgave Amelia her marriage and stood god-mother to the Dubouchets' first child, who died aged two. Their second daughter, Jane, was born in the spring of 1779. Jane, whom Harriette would call her 'Diana' in her *Memoirs*, never married, staying in love 'with a very stupid brother of a very stupid lord' for twenty years.[1] She was musical and the only one of the children whose education was properly attended to; it was Jane who taught Harriette to read. Two years later, in 1781, John and Amelia moved with their family from Mount Street to Carrington Street. Here a third daughter was born who was christened Amelia and known as Amy. Fanny, who arrived the following year, was Harriette's favourite sister. Mary, dubbed 'Paragon' – 'very sharp, very dark, very clever'[2] – came next, following a winter that was so cold that trees froze and split. Harriette's play-mate as a child, Mary was possibly the only one of the girls to have a con-ventional marriage and children born within wedlock. Harriette followed, and soon after her birth, appearing roughly at two-yearly intervals, came Sophia, the second and last daughter to die in infancy; John Emmanuel; Charles Frederick; another Sophia; George; Julia; Rose; Charlotte, and finally, Henry Cook, named after Amelia's adoptive parents.

Rates records show that the year in which Charles Frederick was born, 1791, John Cook swapped houses with John Dubouchet. The Cooks'

The May Queen, *The Gem*

house on Queen Street was larger and this must have been a major reason for the move, but it was also here that the stocking business was based and as her step-parents grew older, Amelia's role in managing the cleaning became more prominent. Queen Street was in a prime position, running between two other smart addresses, Curzon Street and Charles Street. Number 23, where the growing Dubouchet girls would sit all day at the window and watch the young men saunter past, was at the Curzon Street end of the road. At the other end and on the opposite side was a dairy with a large golden cow in the window; girls in poke bonnets would appear from the door to sell milk from buckets. Their new neighbours were Dr Merriman, the apothocary, Lord Craven, Lord Lucan, Lord Whitworth, the Dowager Countess of Granard, Captain Hadfield, and the Bishop of Oxford and Throckmorton. Beau Brummell later moved there too, as did Lord Frederick Campbell, after Amelia's patroness, Lady Campbell, was burned to death in 1812 at a fire in their country house.

It looks as though John Cook gave Amelia and her husband everything he had and more besides; rate records show that Dubouchet had the lease on another house in Queen Street between 1788 and 1793, which was let to tenants. This was presumably a gift from Cook and it provided the family with an extra income until Dubouchet took up as a coal merchant, a year before the second Queen Street lease came to an end. Living in Queen Street was more expensive than living in Carrington Street; the Cooks' house was rated at £24 a year rather than the £17 the Dubouchets paid for the smaller house, but it was in a smarter, more exposed, road. Carrington Street had no titled residents; it was a dead end and so no one walked through. It led only into and out of the market, which would be frequented by servants rather than their masters.

The household in Queen Street was tough, busy and energetic. Harriette had no solitude as a child; the sisters slept in two adjoining rooms at the top of the house where they squabbled, cold-creamed their freckles, and divided themselves into gangs. When the space got too small they would feed the crows from the roof or go to the local parks. Growing up as a middle sister and with an ever increasing number of demanding, mostly female, siblings taught Harriette to be rivalrous and competitive. As an adult, she resisted forming close and trusting connections; she disliked the demands of intimacy, the commitment, weakness and exposure it entailed, and preferred the company of men to that of women. 'The fact is', Harriette later wrote, 'I was never much amused in ladies' society. I ought not to confess this, perhaps; but I never happen to be so fortunate as to meet with pleasant women.'[3]

Harriette was an ambitious child, and the focus of her drive was to better anything done by Amy, her elder sister. Amy Dubouchet was 'a fine dark woman with a Siddonian countenance and a masculine spirit',[4] which description could also fit Harriette, likewise compared with the actress Sarah Siddons, likewise seen as boyish. Even Harriette's wit seems to have been developed to rival Amy's; in a throwaway remark Harriette described her sister as 'really very funny, however spitefully disposed towards me',[5] and it was Amy's company that was sought by the wits of the day, Luttrell and Nugent. Amy appears also to have been musically gifted and 'an excellent linguist, speaking the French, Spanish and Italian languages with the greatest fluency'.[6] Harriette and Amy would not have suffered such enmity were they not both jockeying for the same position; they were too similar – in profession, appearance, temperament and character. Harriette gives little space in her *Memoirs* to the rise of her sister, whose fame as a courtesan preceded her own. All we are told about Amy is that she was a miser, and yet the parties she threw were for years the focal point of what would become known later in the century as the *demi-monde*. Amy seems to have been every bit as popular as Harriette, although she courted less controversy and kept a lower public profile. Throughout their lives the two sisters circled cautiously around one another, never getting too near or moving too far away, neither one shifting her gaze from the other.

Fanny, the second of Harriette's sisters to become a courtesan, was the peacemaker, loved by everyone and sufficiently different from Amy or Harriette to present no threat or challenge to either. Harriette was to Fanny as the fiery Elizabeth Bennet in Jane Austen's *Pride and Prejudice* was to her elder sister Jane. Harriette's refrain was that Fanny, with 'that laughing dark blue eye of hers' was the most beautiful of them all, 'the most popular woman I ever met with. The most ill-natured and spiteful of her sex could never find it in their hearts to abuse one who, in their absence, warmly fought all their battles, whenever anybody complained of them.'[7] Julia Johnstone described gentle Fanny as 'a poor timid, good-natured thing, incapable of doing either harm or good, she scarcely knew the distinction between virtue and vice, when she did good, it was from accident, when she committed evil, it was from want of knowing better, and she had a vacant, see-saw way of thinking that everything happened for the best'.[8]

Amelia, permanently pregnant, raised her family while she ran the business; John Dubouchet, rarely there, beat his daughters when he was irritated. Aged five, Harriette tore up one of his mathematical problems to make a fly-trap and sooner than apologize she let her father birch her until she was senseless. She recalled being 'thrown on the bed and whipped, till my body was disfigured from head to foot', all the time hearing from behind the door the desperate cries of her mother. Harriette was stubborn and maddening, she recalled, and concedes that her father 'acted from principle, for he was not habitually cruel to children'.[9] However much she apologized for her father's violence, fear of Dubouchet played a major part in Harriette's running off when she did.

As soon as she could read, Harriette 'began teazing everybody for books'. Her birth coincided with that of the romantic novel, which she scorned but her sisters brought home from the circulating libraries by the dozen. Nor could Harriette 'endure story books about naughty boys and girls, &t'.[10] Her childhood reading suggests that she was being bred as a lady; the books she re-read were *Gil Blas, The Vicar of Wakefield* and *The Speaker,* an anthology of extracts taken from popular plays, essays and prose, compiled with the aim of educating the youth of Warrington in taste and elocution. *The Speaker* contained, Harriette recalled, 'scraps of Shakespeare, and other great authors, which delighted me, especially Cardinal Wolsey's speech [which] . . . I read . . . over and again, and asked Diana the meaning of every line.'[11] *Gil Blas*, Alain-René Lesage's great comic work of seventeenth-century France, was the book Harriette returned to throughout her life and knew 'by heart'.[12] It became her ambition to write the female *Gil Blas* much as Charlotte Lennox had written the *Female Quixote.* A picaresque novel, *Gil Blas* tells the story of a rogue who has many adventures, including joining a band of robbers, who becomes a corrupt politician and is rewarded by being made a lord, living a life of luxury and ease. Harriette's affection for the novel tells us a good deal about her; Byron, who was obviously much influenced by the picaresque, says that men liked the book but women hated it because it lacked the sentimentality which is their only empire. But Harriette had no real interest in sentimentality, always preferring the variety and surprise of the picaresque, and it was the spirit of adventure she enjoyed so much in *Gil Blas* that she later recaptured in her *Memoirs*.

'Morning, noon and night,' she recalled of her early teens, 'I heard nothing but the softness of Tom Sheridan's hand, the brightness of Berkeley Craven's eyes etc etc.'[13] Her sisters talked endlessly of their 'conquests, the kiss that Tom Sheridan had given Fanny, the appointment that Paragon had made to walk with Ned Jess, etc.' Fanny read aloud every evening the love letter she had received from one of her Swiss cousins until Harriette could stand it no more and stuffed it under the lid of a meat pie she was taking to the baker. She pronounced herself 'disgusted' with her sisters' conversation and their 'desire to be followed and made love to in the streets', and was thus made to feel like a 'spy amongst them, and only because I could not enter into their feelings'. She was naturally shy, Harriette says, and she repeats this claim throughout her life. She seems to have been the type whose shyness was eased in a crowd, who felt happiest performing and most vulnerable when the public mask was removed. She was teased by her sisters for being a 'tell-tale brown, straight-haired figure of fun', and believed herself to be 'ugly and in every way uninteresting'.[14] Harriette presents her subsequent development into an accomplished flirt not, as it had been with Amy and Fanny, as the result of an awakened sex drive, but as one of the predicaments of the Romantic movement: the natural, innocent self threatened with corruption by pressure from the artificial world of codes and manners. 'Now, I will ask my readers whether it be possible for a child to listen for months and years together, to a set of gay young girls, for ever raving on their love, their lovers, their sensations, without having her curiosity just a little bit excited? At length I began to look slyly under my bonnet at these lovers they all made such a fuss about, and as soon as I took the trouble to curl my hair, I was beset with a host of admirers, who sent me messages, and pretty copies of verses by our maid servant, for I appeared much older than I really was.'[15] Another version of Harriette's reception at this time is given in a letter to *The Times* written in 1825. The writer, signing himself 'An Old Rake' and claiming that Harriette will know who he is, recalled 'a little dirty girl, whose name was

Du Bouchet, who was five and twenty years ago a regular *tramp* in St James's Street'. The child was, he recalled, 'bunch backed with a shuffling gait', which description does little to account for Harriette's rise to sexual celebrity.[16]

She had decided by the age of ten that she was not going to follow the same path as her mother and might have absconded sooner had Amelia, aware of the 'admiration' Harriette 'excited in the street', not sent her away to the Ursuline Convent in Rouen to keep her out of harm's way.[17] Harriette had been at school for a while prior to this and returned home when she was eight years old, it being clear to all that she 'could only learn what struck my fancy and nothing that any person might wish to drive into my head'.[18] The Dubouchets were proud and could afford it and so they sent their girls to boarding schools, but the education Harriette received there was little better than that of the daughters of artisans or poor tradesmen who went to local day schools. The staple diet of reciting the Lord's Prayer and the catechisms and learning the basics of writing and arithmetic was of no real use to Harriette, who could read already and whose father was a mathematician. She may have picked up her French, which was fluent if imperfect, from the Ursulines, but again she could have learned this at home, her father being from the French-speaking region of Switzerland.

Her journey to the Convent of St Ursula with John Dubouchet (spiced up in her own account with a tale of attempted seduction during the crossing) was the first time that Harriette had been out of London ('I was, however, disappointed in the pleasure I expected to derive from a first view of the country'[19]) and she was to be the school's first and only English pupil. During her two-year sojourn, the convent failed to influence her religion, education or virtue; the Abbess found the new pupil 'too ignorant even for the third and lowest class . . . so I was an outcast, and I used to amuse myself with drawing horses and cows on my slate' while the other pupils diligently took dictation.[20] Harriette continued to be delinquent. She teased, misbehaved and generally bemused the nuns, making no friends and learning nothing.

She returned home to Queen Street in 1800, her schooling complete, to find that Amy and Fanny 'had both ran off; – one with Mr Trench, the other with Mr Woodcock'.[21]

CHAPTER 4

Courtesans

How did John and Amelia feel about the departure of Amy and Fanny? Were they proud or ashamed that two of their daughters were now kept women? Did the actions of the Dubouchet girls mean a move up or a slide down the social scale for the family?

Harriette does not record her father's reaction to the fall – or the rise – of Amy and Fanny, but his dry insistence that her own schooling now finished and being 'nearly fourteen years of age', Harriette must, 'instead of eating the bread of [her] younger brothers and sisters',[1] earn her own livelihood, suggests that John Dubouchet wanted Amy and Fanny out of his pocket and did not much mind how they went about it. 'From the heedless mode of education', wrote the radical tailor Francis Place on the virtue of the daughters of tradesmen, 'and the want of correct notions of propriety in their relatives, want of chastity in girls . . . was common.' What Place calls 'debauchery' in young women such as Amy and Fanny was not considered too disreputable.[2] Girls in their early teens were considered adult and able to support themselves at the same time as they were still regarded, until they married, as the property of their fathers. Francis Place recalled that several of his father's friends got rid of their daughters by selling them to rich men in the West Indies. All classes of family used their daughters for barter; daughters have been traded, taken, given,

Draped Bed, *The Book of Decorative Furniture*

bought and sold the world over for centuries. It was assumed that girls would be exchanged for money one way or another, whether in or out of the marriage bed, and either way Dubouchet would benefit from his daughters' value. It seems that he made it impossible for Amy and Fanny to stay at Queen Street and that they opted for Mr Trench and Mr Woodcock as alternatives to working long, dreary hours for next to nothing.

Courtesans and prostitutes could be clearly distinguished. Although some prostitutes rose to become courtesans and some failed courtesans turned to prostitution, there was generally little crossover between the two and there was nothing to compare between the lifestyles. Courtesans were idolized figures who belonged to the elite, but London was teeming with prostitutes. A police magistrate, Colquhoun, calculated that there were 50,000 prostitutes in the city in 1793, when London had a population of 1 million. The courtesan lived in comfort and dressed in the finest fashions while most prostitutes lived in poverty and plied their trade, so Francis Place observed, in 'ragged dirty shoes and stockings and some no stockings at all . . . their gowns were low round the neck and open in the front, those who wore handkerchiefs had them always open in front to expose their breasts . . . but numbers wore no handkerchiefs at all in warm weather, and the breasts of many hung down in the most disgusting manner, their hair among the generality was straight and "hung in rat tails" over their eyes, and was filled with lice, at least was inhabited by considerable colonies of insects. Drunkenness was common to them all.'[3] As a child in 1785, Place was apprentice to a leather breeches-maker in the Strand, all of whose daughters were prostitutes of various types. 'At the time I was sent to him, his eldest daughter was and had been for several years a common prostitute. His youngest daughter who was about seventeen had genteel lodgings where she was visited by gentlemen, and the second daughter, who was a fine handsome woman, was kept by a captain of an East India ship, in whose absence she used to amuse herself as such women generally do.'[4] These girls had few options. If they could not sell their labour as domestic servants or in the few trades such as haberdashery that were not the exclusive preserve of men, they had nothing to sell but their bodies. And once a woman's reputation had been lost, her chances of ever gaining respectable employment were more or less over. They belonged to the city's 'twenty thousand miserable individuals of various classes who rise up every morning without knowing how, or by what means they are to be supported, during the passing day; or where, in many instances, they are to lodge on the succeeding night'.[5]

The Dubouchet daughters were faced with different but equally limited choices, which boiled down to marriage or teaching, neither of which would protect them from poverty. When Harriette anticipated a probable future incarcerated as a schoolmistress in a chilly establishment for young ladies, it was a life spent without ever 'having loved and been beloved' which she found unimaginable. She and her sisters preceded the later nineteenth-century insistence that women were without sexual instincts or drive, martyrs to the cause of procreating the species. John and Amelia Dubouchet had married for love and however grim the consequences of their choice, nothing erased for Harriette the liberality of the act. Did the courtesan pursue sensuous pleasure for its own sake or was her object the acquisition of wealth? What made her a suspicious and troublesome figure was that neither goal was acceptable and to pursue both was a violation of the sexual and economic order.

Prostitution was a trap into which women fell, whereas a courtesan could expect to have a career including perks, promotions, pay rises and a certain amount of job security. A courtesan could charge from £50 to £500 where a prostitute might be paid a few shillings, and that for giving what a mistress or a wife would give for free. Courtesans were sought after rather than soliciting their clients; a few became the wives of their protectors – the highest promotion of all – while others received lifetime annuities from those men by whom they had been abandoned, thus enabling them to face retirement without anxiety. As well as an income, all could expect to receive from their 'protectors' a furnished home with servants, a wardrobe, and jewels of the highest order.

Courtesans were purchased by the rich for their style, reputation and conversation; their companionship went well beyond sex. The company of certain courtesans was so coveted that they received banknotes simply for playing cards. Courtesans sold relationships as opposed to anonymous single encounters and they flourished at times when the economy was strong. Prostitutes operated outside society, but the courtesan belonged to an elaborate courtly culture of manners, obligation and discretion. It was for 'her tact in love affairs' that Harriette Wilson was 'celebrated';[6] the courtesan's loyalty, like that of any respected courtier, could be depended on. She was a status symbol, a sign of wealth and style. Harriette complained once of a guardsman who 'insisted on falling in love with me, merely to prove himself a fashionable man'. Courtesans were in vogue at a time when the cut of your coat either made or broke your reputation. Beau Brummell boasted that he had repaid a debt by walking down St James's with his arm linked through that of the man to whom he owed money; such was the power of being seen with the right people. Courtesans were women with whom to be seen; an acquaintance with one of the leading Cyprians of the day finished many a young man's education. 'It was the fashion for young men to procure letters from any celebrated demirep', the courtesan Julia Johnstone wrote, 'and shew them amongst friends, boasting of their success.'[7] Courtesans had their clothes, coaches and companions chronicled in the papers under headings such as 'Cytherian Intelligence'; the very names 'Cytherian', 'Cyprian' or 'Paphian' showing how these figures were draped in classical splendour.

None the less, courtesans were also known as Great, High or Fashionable Impures, oxymoronic terms that coupled the untouchable and the elevated with what was dirty and contaminating. 'High Impure' captured precisely the ambivalence of the courtesan, her position as somewhere between the classical icon, raised above the common people, and the low, sensuous germ-spreading body. Men were as likely to catch syphilis from a courtesan as from a prostitute and any children born of the relationship, despite being given the honour of their father's name, were generally acknowledged only so long as the relationship survived, at which point it fell to the mother to ensure that they were clothed and fed. Like the courtesans Mrs Armistead, Fanny Murray, Harriet Powell, Nancy Parsons, and her own sister, Lady Sophia Berwick, Harriette remained childless all her life. She was almost certainly infertile; it is hard to imagine how she could have avoided pregnancy had she not been, and most of her lovers went on to have children with other women.[8] Venereal disease and abortion could induce sterility,[9] but infertility has always been common among women and in many cases this must have been a blessing. Pregnancy and child-rearing could only interrupt a courtesan's career. Early nineteenth-century contraception consisted of withdrawal, douching after intercourse, sponges that absorbed semen and condoms made of sheep gut which were tied with a ribbon at the open end and rinsed out for future use. None of these methods was foolproof.

For all their exclusivity, courtesans belonged to a massive sex industry that was so much an accepted part of the culture that since the middle of the eighteenth century Jack Harris, son of a good Somerset family, had published *Harris's List of Covent Garden Ladies*, a kind of *Which?* guide to the flesh of the town. *Harris's List* continued to run for thirty years after his death in 1766. The names of around a hundred and fifty women were listed in alphabetical order, each followed by a brief description of her person, merits and price. Harris had emissaries throughout London looking for eligible women to include in his pages, agreements with madams to 'place into High Keeping' any of the women he procured, and contracts with aristocratic clients to provide fresh new 'tits'. Higher-class prostitutes sought to be included by Harris; it was clearly good for business.

In her *Memoirs*, Fanny Murray – forced into prostitution aged thirteen after being seduced and abandoned by Jack Spencer, grandson of Sarah, Duchess of Marlborough – recounts how in 1746 Harris had put her on his list and improved her fortunes.[10] She became mistress to George II and thus, having ensnared a coveted royal, she reigned over the *demi-monde*. Harris's description of Fanny Murray illustrates the acreage between the marketing of an available courtesan and the untouchable status she attained having once been purchased: 'Perfectly sound in wind and limb. A fine Brown girl rising nineteen years next season. A good Side-box piece, she will show well in the Flesh Market and wear well. May be put off with a Virgin at any time these twelve months. Never common this side of Temple Bar but for six months. Fit for High Keeping with a Jew Merchant . . . If she keeps out of the Lock she may make her Fortune and Ruin half the Men in Town.'[11]

Harris's List was by no means the first publication of its kind; nor was it alone in the field. Information about courtesans was available in a variety of forms to satisfy public curiosity, all of which made them seem more fictitious than actual. In 1779, a two-volume book of anecdotes appeared called *Nocturnal Revels, Sketches and Portraits of the Most Celebrated Demi-reps and Courtesans of the Period*. The next year saw the publication of 'Characters of the present most Celebrated Courtezans', in which thirteen women, all courted by high society, were described. Three years later, the *Rambler* magazine contained a list of 'The most Fashionable Votaries of Venus', including a group of courtesans known as 'the Avians': Sarah Adcock, 'the Goldfinch'; Mrs Irvine, 'the White Swan'; Gertrude Mahon, 'the bird of Paradise'; Polly Greenhill, 'the Greenfinch', and Mrs Corbyne, 'the White Crow'.

The Dubouchet girls were never included in lists of this sort. They began their careers at the top. They were well known among their clientele and so did not need to advertise, and nor were they ever without protectors for long enough. Harriette was 'so much sought after', she wrote, 'both by young and old, there could have been no necessity for me to tramp the streets, nobleman hunting'.[12] Harriette and her sisters were also too expensive; women in *Harris's Lists* were charging £1 for services rendered while Harriette Wilson would charge £50 for an introduction alone.

The ambivalent position of the kept woman and the problem of whether she was moving 'up' in the world or 'down', was 'in' the world or 'out' of it, independent of her lover or condemned to him, was personified by Maria Fitzherbert, whose relationship with the Prince of Wales made her one of the central women in English society. Twice widowed and a Roman Catholic, she was wooed by the Prince when he was a young man. Refusing what she considered the vulgarity of being his mistress, she agreed to a secret marriage in 1785. He was certainly aware, and perhaps she was too, that their union was null and void due to the Royal Marriage Act of 1772, which rendered invalid any marriage by an underage royal undertaken without the king's consent. So Mrs Fitzherbert was married in the eyes of God but not according to the law; she was at the same time a future queen, a commoner, a wife and a whore. Having never been strictly wed she could not be divorced; nor was she 'unwed' from him when her husband married another. And she stayed in this limbo for the rest of her life.

Mrs Fitzherbert was at the top of the peculiar pecking order in which women of unofficial status were arranged. This hierarchy was every bit as subtle and complex as that of the English class system. There were steadfast mistresses who lived off royal lovers but would never be called courtesans; there were celebrity courtesans, such as Kitty Fisher and Nancy Parsons, who were also royal mistresses; courtesans such as Mary Anne Clarke, who was a royal mistress and a popular agitator; high-class prostitutes who were not courtesans but neither were they streetwalkers; actresses who were courtesans of a kind; professional kept women who did not see themselves as courtesans but strictly were; serial mistresses who were not courtesans but were seen as such; courtesans who were not mistresses but were seen as such. Courtesans with their own property were above those in rented houses; those living in Somerstown were beneath those who lived in Mayfair. The courtesan Fanny Temple, William Hickey recalled in his *Memoirs*, 'inhabited an excellent house in Queen Anne Street, and had besides neat lodgings in the country, pleasantly situated near the waterside just above Hammersmith, and kept her own chariot, with a suitable establishment of servants'.[13] She had reached the very top of her profession.

And what of the life Harriette turned her back on, that of respectable wife? What might have become of her had she not found her way into the *demi-monde*? Her sister Mary ('Paragon') can be used as a template for one of the alternatives Harriette refused. As a young woman, Mary broke the heart of Sir Harcourt Lees, after which she married a Mr Boroughs, whose uncle, Sir Richard Boroughs, was an Irish contractor who lived in Grafton Street. They had several children, raised according to the principles of family affection suggested by Rousseau, and lived quietly in London. Mr Boroughs was not wealthy but respectable. The Dubouchet family's good connections would ensure that, despite being tradesman's daughters and having notorious sisters, it was possible for those Dubouchet girls who wished to do so to make good marriages. Mary entered the middle classes when she became Mrs Boroughs. She would have received polite visits from neighbours, done nothing out of the ordinary, employed a handful of servants and never been thought of again.

What kind of life would an irreverent, adventurous and energetic girl who hated boredom and disliked female company have led as a spouse, visiting somebody's wife or waiting for somebody's wife to visit her? What role was there in conventional life for a woman of character, like Harriette Wilson? It is unlikely that she would have married well enough to enable her to use her wit and character to the full, as the society hostesses Lady Melbourne or Mrs Armistead, the wife of Charles James Fox, had done. And more typical of society wives anyway was Kitty, Duchess of Wellington, whose diary entries as a young bride record the deadening monotony of her days:

July 31st 1809
I fear indolence is again creeping about me. I am fatigued by a regular course of insignificant occupations & dissatisfied with myself when idle.

August 2nd
Ill & idle. I have nothing to say to this languid day.

August 5th
Much as yesterday, languid and dawdling.

August 6th
Too late for church.

August 7th
Very shamefully late. This will never do. Finished my accounts of the week.

August 8th
Still too late.

August 10th
I am tired. This unvaried life fatigues but must be endured.[14]

Wellington at least married for love, or might have done had his marriage not taken place twelve years after his initial proposal. Otherwise unions tended to be dictated by what Thackerary called the 'grim workings of marriage capitalism', where two estates were joined together in the names of two people who barely knew one another.

'Chastity in woman', Dr Johnson observed, 'is all important because the whole of property is involved in it', and so long as this was the case there was a role for the society courtesan. The attitude of most wives to their husbands' infidelities is expressed by Lady Frances Shelley in her diary of 1807: 'There is one rule from which I have never deviated during the whole course of my married life. I have made it a point never to interfere in any way with my husband's mode of life; and I never kept him from the society even of persons whose conduct I would not admire . . . In this I feel sure that I acted wisely.'[15] When the young Queen Victoria asked the older Lord Melbourne why so many marriages crumbled, he explained that 'a gentleman hardly knows a girl till he had proposed, and then when he has an unrestrained intercourse with her he sees something and says, "This I don't quite like."' Melbourne's mother-in-law, Lady Bessborough, put it differently: 'In the way Girls are often married, hardly knowing their

Husbands or what marriage is, how many there must be who would gladly separate, and still more gladly chuse again, if they could do so without ruining their characters.'[16] Upper-class marriages were permissive, but divorce was rare, scandalous, complicated and expensive; women lost their children and their reputation. Husbands of unhappy partnerships could of course find solace in the *demi-monde*; wives had to be more discreet.

Courtesans were in the unusual position of being able to take on a variety of sexual partners while at the same time increasing their marketability; they became part of a reverse sexual economy whereby rather than losing their value along with their virginity, with each distinguished lover they had they saw their price and appeal increase. Thus were they able to avoid becoming middle-class wives while improving their chances of marrying – if they so chose – into the aristocracy. They were able to live in a style they would not otherwise have known, to experience an independence otherwise not available to women of their backgrounds, while gaining a level of celebrity they would never otherwise have achieved. But they never lost their curious social ambiguity. Growing up as the daughters of a tradesman in Mayfair, the Dubouchet girls had always occupied a liminal position. Did they, as courtesans, move up or slide down the social ladder? In a sense they stayed exactly where they already were, neither in nor out.

Amy and Fanny did not in fact run off with Mr Trench and Mr Woodcock at the same time. Amy was 'the first to set us a bad example', Harriette recorded. 'We were all virtuous girls when Amy, one fine day, sallied forth, like Don Quixote, in quest of adventures. The first person who addressed her was Mr Trench, a certain short-sighted pedantic man, whom most people know about town. I believe she told him that she was running away from her father. All I know for certain is, that when Fanny and I discovered her abode, we went to visit her, and when we asked her what on earth had induced her to throw herself away on an entire stranger whom she had never seen before, her answer was "I refused him the whole of the first day; had I done so the second, he would have been in a fever."'[17]

Amy did not stay long with Mr Trench. He sent her back to school to complete her education, settled £100 a year on her for life, gave her a fifty-pound note with which to go shopping and never saw her again; off Amy ran with General Madden, recently returned from leading the

15th Foot in Portugal. Fanny left home with Mr Woodcock shortly afterwards, and she stayed with him – in a fairly loose sense – for seven years. She took his name but there was another Mrs Woodcock as well, and it was with his legitimate wife that Fanny's protector lived. He died in 1807, leaving Fanny with three children and no further income. 'Everybody was mad for Fanny,' Harriette said, 'and so they had been during Mr Woodcock's life; but it was all in vain. Now there was a better chance for them perhaps.'[18] Fanny was soon under the protection of Lord Yarmouth, son of the indomitable Lady Hertford, mistress of the Prince of Wales.

When her father wanted Harriette out of the house, it was Amelia, with her thirteenth child Rose still not yet weaned, who helped her to get a respectable job. Raised by pillars of the Establishment and anxious to maintain, as far as she could, her family's good name, Amelia found her daughter a situation as a music mistress at an elegant girls' boarding school in Bayswater, on the north side of Hyde Park. Here Harriette remained for three months before running home one night after the French mistress, happening to see Harriette's breast uncovered, exclaimed that she had 'strongly suspected that [it was] not the bosom of a virgin'.[19] John Dubouchet, unmoved by the insult, offered Harriette no option but to find another position and this time she accepted a post as teacher and music mistress to the pupils at Ketridge House, a girls' school in Newcastle upon Tyne. She undertook the journey in the mail coach with her friend and neighbour Tom Sheridan, who was going to join his regiment in Edinburgh. Tom had dark hair, a sallow complexion and dreadful health. And he was the only son of the most popular playwright of the age.

Tom Sheridan was typical of the men who would surround Harriette Wilson. While other courtesans were kept by weighty politicians and statesmen, she initially attracted handsome, charming lightweights with little application, the playboy offspring of considerable parents. Tom's schoolmaster described him as having 'great acuteness, excellent understanding, wit, and humour, but not a particle of knowledge'.[20] His wit made him the idol of his schoolfriends. Told by his father to take a wife, Tom replied, 'Yes Sir, but who's?' Told by his father that he would be cut off with a penny, Tom asked whether he might have the penny now.

On the journey north, Tom suggested that he and Harriette establish a correspondence. 'If I had not wished to act rightly, I should not have gone to Newcastle,' Harriette replied, 'as I found no lack of admirers in London, who wished to get me under their protection',[21] but other remarks she made imply that she did not act rightly during the two days and one night they were together. 'I will not trust myself in a hackney coach with you,' Harriette told Tom at a later date, after he tried to kiss her. 'There was a time', he replied, 'when the very motion of a carriage would . . .'[22] Before she was deposited at Ketridge House, Tom Sheridan agreed to send Harriette love letters with which she could torment Fanny.

Consider the change about to take place in Harriette's life as the coach left London and began its onerous journey. She was used to being at the heart of a city that did not stir before ten o'clock in the morning, when the shops began slowly to open and the milkmaids to knock on the doors. 'Not a single drum – not a cart are seen passing,' Louis Simmonds wrote of London mornings. 'The first considerable stir is the drum and military music of the Guards, marching from their barracks to Hyde Park, having at their head three or four negro giants, striking, high, gracefully, and strong, the resounding cymbal.' She was used to the day then falling silent once more until three or four o'clock when she would see the fashionable world emerge briefly to shop and pay visits before disappearing to dress, to then re-emerge between six and eight o'clock for dinner and the theatre. At this point the city would rise up and resound with the creak of coach wheels and the clack of hoofs, and Harriette would watch 'a multitude of carriages, with two eyes of flame staring in the dark before each of them, shake the pavement and the very houses, following and crossing each other at full speed. Stopping suddenly, a footman jumps down, runs to the door, and lifts the heavy knocker – gives a great knock – then several smaller ones in quick succession – then with all his might – flourishing as on a drum, with an art, and an air, and a delicacy of touch, which denote the quality, the rank, and the fortune of his master.' Silence would follow while the inhabitants of these great establishments absorbed what mysterious entertainment was on offer, and then the 'great crisis of dress, of noise, and of rapidity' ensued once more, 'a universal hubbub; a sort of uniform grinding and shaking, like that experienced in a great mill with fifty pair of stones; and if I was not afraid to exaggerate, I should say that it came upon the ear like the fall of Niagara, heard at two miles distance!'[23] This was the night world to which Harriette aspired.

She arrived at Ketridge House to be offered a 'small beer, which was very small indeed' and some 'uninteresting little Dutch cheese', neither of which could tempt her.[24] Harriette now rose at six in the morning and, perched on a seat so far from the fire that she grew numb with cold, she tried to sew buttonholes in shirts. Her pupils, most of them older than herself, began to 'croak . . . their vile French in my ears, in their broad Scotch accents'. At other times, 'nailed to my chair, by the side of the pianoforte', she would sit, 'from nine to three every day, while the whole school in turn practised their dull lessons out of tune and out of time'.[25] The school was silent save for chanting of verbs and militaristic roll calls; Tom Sheridan's flirtatious letters were Harriette's only entertainment. He said that she looked like the actress Sarah Siddons, a white-skinned and black-eyed beauty, and suggested that she go on the stage. This gave Harriette some hope; she loved the theatre and even if she had not seen Mrs Siddons perform, the great actress's likeness was reproduced all over London.

Instinctively anti-authoritarian, Harriette was as ill-suited to teaching as she was to learning; she needed to work but hated institutions and would no more be told what to do than a miser would part with his purse. She survived Ketridge House for six months before returning to face her father's wrath. She never again worked for somebody else or saw the inside of a school. When she reappeared in Queen Street, Amelia Dubouchet was about to give birth to her fourteenth child, a daughter called Charlotte.

Back home again, Harriette stuffed a cushion into her dress and performed Falstaff to Tom Sheridan. While he thought the tones of her voice well adapted to tragedy, he agreed that she also had a 'turn for low comedy'.[26] It was always as a comedian that Harriette would shine. She was a smart mimic and irreverent observer, ever alert to the humour of a situation. There is no doubt that she would have been a success on the stage; she had a gift for entertaining. She was the kind of woman whose wit increased with the decline of her virtue and as such she belongs to a strong tradition of female wits. 'I am sorry to say', the bluestocking Elizabeth Montagu wrote, 'the generality of women who have excelled in wit have failed in chastity; perhaps it inspires too much confidence in the possessor, and raises an inclination in the men towards them, without inspiring esteem; so that they are attacked and less guarded than other women.'[27] Witty women 'make a shipwreck of their reputation, and sometimes of their virtue', Thomas Browne believed. Harriette was not a wit in the eighteenth-century sense of the term; she was not learned, rational, verbally concise. She was a satirist, what we might call today a 'good laugh'; her personality was a reaction against seriousness and anxiety. John Dubouchet, however, 'fell into a violent passion' at the prospect of his daughter's having a career in the theatre (actresses being no better than prostitutes), 'and declared he would rather see me in my grave'.[28] As it was, Harriette's career did eventually take off in the theatre, but in the auditorium rather than on the stage.

Her father's veto left Harriette with little option but 'to teach the verbs "avoir" and "être" from fifteen to fifty years of age, and then to retire withered and still more forlorn to a work house . . . What chance on earth have I of marrying a man of polished refinement? . . . who will scale the walls of any of these high dried academies, to propose marriage to me?'[29] These ideas 'tormented' her for three months. In a final attempt to placate him, Harriette prepared John Dubouchet's favourite dish for supper. It was ready by ten o'clock that night, at which time she was expected to go to bed, but in order to prevent the food being spoiled she sat up watching it until he returned. Furious at Harriette's disobedience, Dubouchet boxed her ears and Harriette, indignant and hurt, determined to leave home. She planned her escape with typical pragmatism, looking no further than the end of the road. Harriette combined driving ambition with the desire to employ minimum effort. At 16 Charles Street, a few doors down from the home of Beau Brummell, stood a large, handsome house fronted by obelisks, whose prospect faced Queen Street. Here lived Tom Sheridan's friend the Honourable Berkeley Craven, whose bright eyes had so engaged Amy and Fanny. 'I loved no one amongst those who sought to seduce me, but the Cravens were our near neighbours, and old acquaintances, and they were gentlemen,' Harriette reasoned. She later said that it was Berkeley Craven with whom she ran away, and rumour agreed with her. He had clearly also been her lover, but it was Berkeley's elder brother on whom Harriette now cast her own bright eye: 'I was less afraid of them than any other men, so I became the mistress of Lord Craven.'[30]

It was the winter of 1800, and Harriette had stepped over to the far side of the sword.

Harriette Wilson viewing Lord Craven while sailing at Brighton, *Memoirs of Harriette Wilson*

CHAPTER 5

Lord Craven

Ashdown Park, isolated and austere, a magnificent paean to order and tranquillity set high on the Berkshire Downs, was built by the First Baron and Earl of Craven in the latter half of the seventeenth century and consecrated to the woman he adored, Elizabeth of Bohemia, 'The Winter Queen'. Its peculiar situation, the perfect symmetry of its bays, the hipped roof, dormers, balustrade, towering chimney stacks and light chalk and grey walls give it the appearance of a Dutch doll's house. Its interior is organized around a spectacular staircase, which reaches from hall to attic, and from the roof you can see for miles around. *Highways and Byways in Berkshire* describes the road to Ashdown from neighbouring Lambourn as running, 'for the most part, between precipices of solitary downland as cannot be surpassed. No Northern or Western mountain pass is more lonely.'[1] A 1716 drawing by Leonard Knyff (plate 7) shows Ashdown looking every bit the polite town house, standing square and proud in the midst of black woodland, which stretches as far as the eye can see. Four avenues, straight as rods, lead out of the inky thicket. A 1743 painting by James Seymore features in its foreground the Fourth Baron with his hunt and hounds, standing before a forest of medieval density, out of which can be seen gleaming, far away, the winnowing top of Craven's House.

Here, at the dawn of the nineteenth century, the spangled curtain goes up on the first act of Harriette Wilson's new life. It was to Ashdown that William Craven, Seventh Baron and First Earl of the second creation, brought his young mistress. Lord Craven's parents had honeymooned here the winter after their marriage, and it was at Ashdown that the Cravens' two elder daughters were born. But the house was not much in use now; apart from his Charles Street residence, Lord Craven had other Berkshire estates at Hamstead Marshall and Enborne, as well as Coombe Abbey in Warwickshire and Winstantow, West Felton, and Onibury in Shropshire. Ashdown Park, almost on the Wiltshire border, was not so near to London as Hamstead Marshall; it would have been a long day's travel for Harriette and the Earl, rattling west through the pastures of Knightsbridge in a carriage and four.

Craven left London with a girl of little experience, less wardrobe, and no reputation to lose. She was a 'tom-boy, childish looking creature'[2] who had misbehaved at home and then at school, and apart from her time in the French convent and at Ketridge House had always moved against the crush of the city and lived among the babies, stockings and babble of Queen Street. Harriette was, in her own words, 'never one for ruralising'. She disliked being cut off from the world; in her *Memoirs* she always positions herself at the hub of activity and describes herself as part of a crowd; the occasions she goes pastoral are comical in their self-conscious pursuit of Romantic solitude. She had no knowledge of country life, no particular liking for landscape, none whatever for trees, and no interest at all in the blood sports that were celebrated throughout the comfortless interior. 'The year, as well as the century, with a few exceptions, has taken its leave in a very mild manner,' the *Gentleman's Magazine* recorded that month; 'the temperature of the air has been unusually warm and bland, and its vivifying powers are apparent under various forms amongst the vegetable tribes.' Harriette Wilson, urban to the core, would remain unmoved by this felicity. But she was a great and determined walker, able to exhaust most of her companions. Striding through fields, leaping across fences and springing over puddles was how she got rid of her excess energy. Harriette lived in her body and loathed inactivity; she would walk to feel the rush of adrenalin rather than to admire the foliage. She would have stridden through Ashdown Woods and farther afield, to White Horse Hill and

Weathercock Hill, returning to the house with her skirts caked in mud, her hair tangled and cheeks glowing.

The Cravens were known to Jane Austen and her family. Harriette's Lord Craven was patron to Tom Fowle, the ill-fated fiancé of Jane's adored elder sister Cassandra; Tom Fowle's father had married Jane Craven, a relation of the Earl, and was rector of Lord Craven's living at Hamstead Marshall (following his death, Jane Austen's brother, James, was offered, and refused, the vacancy). Once they could afford to marry, Tom Fowle and Cassandra Austen had hopes of also receiving a living from Lord Craven. It was while serving as Craven's private chaplain in his regiment that Fowle died of yellow fever in the West Indies, thus leaving Cassandra to a life of spinsterhood.

It is from the novelist that we know of Harriette's whereabouts in January 1801. Harriette, concerned in her *Memoirs* with character and anecdote rather than biographical detail and preferring to write about conversation rather than its absence, elided the period she spent in the wilds of Berkshire and wrote only of living with Craven in Brighton. Lord Craven, Austen wrote to Cassandra, has 'a Mistress now living with him at Ashdown Park', and while this 'little flaw' was to the sisters 'the only unpleasing circumstance about him',[3] Harriette found more to complain of. Lord Craven was a 'dead bore' who 'used to draw cocoa trees, and his fellows, as he called them, on the best vellum paper . . . Here stood the enemy, he would say; and here, my love, are my fellows; there the cocoa trees, etc. . . . All these cocoa trees and fellows, at past eleven o'clock at night, could have no peculiar liking for a child like myself, so lately in the habit of retiring early to rest.'[4]

Craven's problem, so far as Harriette was concerned, was that he was hopelessly unfashionable. She was a fashion-conscious teenager, embarrassed by his lack of style. Any sexual attraction she had felt towards him – and there seems to have been little – dissolved when he greeted her in bed wearing an 'ugly cotton night cap', a custom Harriette assumed must be unusual or all women would have their 'illusions . . . destroyed on the first night of their marriage!'[5] She and Craven, Harriette recalled, neither 'suited nor understood each other',[6] but once a woman had lost her character there was no going back. Harriette was stuck in a draughty house in the heart of a forest surrounded by a fleet of suspicious and sceptical servants. Some of the undermaids would have been her own age or younger and resented her airs. The older servants, those who had looked after Craven all his life, would have found his young mistress absurd; knowing as she did nothing about His Lordship's culinary likes or dislikes and making no particular efforts to please him or even to be polite. Harriette, it can be imagined, would have enjoyed pulling the bell cord and placing her orders, the thrill of her new-found authority making up for the lack of desire she felt for Craven and the sudden hush that had fallen over her life.

If, as Harriette wrote, 'by going from my father to Lord Craven' she had made a 'bad speculation',[7] what kind of gamble was taken by the man into whose hands she firmly placed herself? William Craven was thirty years old, a lieutenant colonel in the 40th Foot and for the last two years he had been aide-de-camp to George III. He was educated at Eton but did not follow his father on to Oxford; instead he became a professional soldier, joining the Berks Militia aged sixteen and paying the largest sum that had ever been paid to join the 84th Foot Regiment. He rose steadily through the ranks, serving in the Flanders campaign in 1794 and in the West Indies from 1795 to 1796; in the year that he died, Craven became a general.

His life had been spent in masculine environments. His mother, the former Lady Elizabeth Craven, was a famous beauty, traveller and dramatist whose lifestyle generated almost non-stop scandal. She separated from her husband and left the family home when young Craven was away at school and since then he had barely been out of military service. He might well have found it hard to amuse or to strike common ground with an ill-educated, stubborn child, 'all animal spirits' as Julia Johnstone recalled, who had flirted with his friends and his younger brother and was now taking her first steps in the *demi-monde*. But Craven seems not be have been so dreary as Harriette Wilson would have us think, at least as far as his choice of women was concerned.

Later in 1801, his regiment was posted to Brighton and Harriette left the seclusions of Ashdown to join her protector in the second most exciting town in England. Butter-coloured and handsome, Brighton was next only to Mayfair for style. Harriette might at last be able to improve her wardrobe, discarding the few dresses she had brought with her when she ran away from Queen Street, and thus begin to look the part of a woman of fashion.

Brighton's population that year was 7,514; it was rapidly evolving from a fishing village to a substantial regal resort. The Prince of Wales was erecting globes on the roof of his increasingly eccentric Pavilion and importing boat-loads of chinoiserie to drape the interior. His palace, like the town itself, was everything King George III's court was not: indulgent, excessive, intelligent, witty and outrageous. Brighton had become the alternative to London. It was new, with the same gleam of fresh paint as Mayfair and peopled by much the same clientele. Craven's uncle, the Earl of Berkeley, had a palace on the Steyne along with the Duke of Marlborough; Lord Egremont had a splendid Brighton house and Mrs Fitzherbert was having her house built next to the Pavilion. When the Prince was in town, the Mayfair circle uprooted and redistributed itself here; His Highness never ate supper with fewer than sixteen companions and liked to have a continuous succession of fresh faces around him.

Harriette was home from home. Craven settled her west of the Pavilion, in one of the grand and airy mansions on Marine Parade. Here she could gaze towards France, where the Revolution had recently deposited packet-loads of aristocrats on the Brighton shores. The war with France was currently suspended, but neither party expected it to remain so. In expectation that it would soon break out again, defence camps lined the south coast. But only once was the Prince of Wales's regiment, the 10th Dragoons, or Hussars, disturbed from their women and cards by a message that the enemy had landed, and then they found it was all a hoax, another of the Prince's practical jokes. Thus the officers' routine began once more; 'At one o'clock', *The Times* of July 1796 reported, 'they appear to hear the word of command given to the subaltern guard; afterwards they toss off their brandy, dine about five, and come about eight to the theatre.'

Craven's main interest on the south coast was in sailing his yacht, the *Griffin*. Harriette, loathing anything too quiet, claims that during this time she began to wonder about the Prince of Wales's nightcap and wrote to introduce herself:

I am told that I am very beautiful, so, perhaps, you would like to see me; and I wish that, since so many are disposed to love me, one, for in the humility of my heart I should be quite satisfied with one, would be at the pains to make me love him. In the mean time, this is all very dull work, Sir, and worse even than being at home with my father: so, if you pity me, and believe you could make me in love with you, write to me, and direct to the post-office here.[8]

It was Harriette's habit to send introductory notes to prestigious men and it is in keeping with her spirit and ambition that she might write to the Prince; a prince was the ultimate accolade for a courtesan. She tells us that he was amused by her letter and asked to meet her in London, to which she replied:

Sir

To travel fifty-two miles, this bad weather, merely to see a man, with only the given number of legs, arms, fingers, etc., would, you must admit, be madness, in a girl like myself, surrounded by humble admirers, who are ever ready to travel any distance for the honour of kissing the tip of her little finger; but if you can prove to me that you are one bit better than any man who may be ready to attend my bidding, I'll e'en start for London directly. So, if you can do anything better, in the way of pleasing a lady, than ordinary men, write directly, if not, adieu Monsieur le Prince.

I won't say Yours,
By day or night, or any kind of light;
Because you are too impudent.[9]

It is unlikely that these are the actual letters written by Harriette to the Prince. The letters she quotes in her *Memoirs* tend to be inferior versions of the ones she sent; her first drafts were always faster and fresher than anything she copied, revised or recalled and so we can suppose that the letters received by the Prince of Wales were more impudent, more charming than this. Did Harriette have a liaison with the Prince? He was unlikely to have turned her offer, or any offer, down but what affair took place cannot have been momentous. At the time of Harriette's letters, he had just reunited with his adored 'wife', Mrs Fitzherbert, who had been put to pasture during his preference for Lady Jersey, his marriage to Princess Caroline, and the birth of his daughter. And anyway, the Prince was less attracted to coltish youth than he was to maternal women, as corpulent as himself but older and more worldly. He preferred being cosseted in an ample and comforting bosom to running circles around a nubile young Cyprian.

Harriette's bid to seduce the Prince revealed astonishing self-assurance. She had no doubt that she was able to entertain and satisfy the First Gentleman of Europe. At the age of fourteen she was an accomplished coquette who had succeeded with an earl; she began her profession at the top. What her letters also reveal is her skill at self-promotion and this was a vital ingredient in her rapid rise through the *demi-monde*. She operated a publicity machine as effective as any we see today. Harriette's present problem was how to get rid of Craven and move on to better things. To increase her fame and thus fortune, her next protector had to be carefully selected. Craven, too dull and reclusive, had done nothing to promote his mistress's charms. He preferred hiding Harriette away or taking her sailing to parading her on his arm or showing her off in his box at the theatre. Harriette needed to see and be seen; she needed admiration because it is contagious, jewels that would suggest her worth, dresses in which to display herself, and competition which would increase demand and raise her market value.

She needed a powerful lover who would introduce her to the world, display her and deck her in diamonds; someone who could make her a sexual celebrity.

CHAPTER 6

Frederic Lamb

———

Throughout her career Harriette insisted that she was the courtesan of only one man at a time, which determination to appear virtuous in part explains her amnesia when it comes to dates. No matter how 'depraved' she was, she never sank so low, she said, as to move on to a new lover while she was still enjoying the purse of the old.[1] 'I must declare that the idea of the possibility of deceiving Lord Craven, while I was under his roof, never once entered into my head,' she wrote.[2] But Harriette also knew that virtue never paid the bills and that no enterprising courtesan would leave the warmth of one bed without ensuring for herself the superior comfort of the next. And it would not have been possible for her to get through the number of men she did without a considerable amount of overlap taking place.

According to her *Memoirs* the man Harriette selected – or rather, the man who elected – to supplant Lord Craven was his friend, the Honourable Frederic Lamb. 'Frederic Lamb was my constant visitor, and talked to me of nothing else . . . [He] was then very handsome; and certainly tried, with all his soul and with all his strength, to convince me that constancy to Lord Craven was the greatest nonsense in the world.'[3] Lamb became Harriette's 'shadow', following her around Brighton while Craven attended to his military duties, begging her to share with him what little he had, going mad, she wrote, for desire of her.

Library Bookcase, *The Book of Decorative Furniture*

Lamb soon left Brighton to join his own regiment, the 15th Foot, in Hull, after which Craven returned to Marine Parade to be immediately told 'by some spiteful enemy' of Harriette that she had been, 'during the whole of his absence, openly intriguing with Frederick Lamb'.[4] Refusing for one moment to countenance Harriette's innocence, Craven immediately terminated their arrangement. What reason did Craven have to believe in Harriette's loyalty? What he saw was a determined girl who had used him to escape from her father and was now using someone else to help her escape from him. 'This', Harriette noted on reading Craven's acid farewell letter, 'is what one gets by acting with principle', and she reassured herself that what she had lost meant nothing to her. 'I hate his fine carriage, and his money, and everything belonging to, or connected with him. I shall hate cocoa as long as I live; and, I am sure, I will never enter a boat again.'[5]

By happy coincidence, according to her own account of events, the day after being discarded by Craven, Harriette received a letter from Lamb begging her to join him in Hull. 'My case was desperate; for I had taken a vow not to remain another night under Lord Craven's roof.' Craven asked his servant to secure for Harriette a place in the mail coach which would take her to her new protector. 'It is impossible to do justice to the joy and rapture which brightened Frederic's countenance, when he flew to receive me, and conducted me to his house, where I was shortly visited by his worthy General Mackenzie, who assured me of his earnest desire to make my stay in Hull as comfortable as possible.'[6] Frederic Lamb's first mistake was to not reimburse Harriette for the fare, a slight for which he was never forgiven.

If Harriette became Frederic Lamb's mistress in late 1801, he would have been nineteen and she fifteen. He had just returned from Glasgow, where, alongside his brother William (with whom Harriette was also rumoured to have been involved), he had been studying philosophy under the distinguished Professor Millar. Having thought of nothing for two years but the work of David Hume and Adam Smith, both Frederic and William were anxious for adventure. William later confessed that during this year he too fell 'into the power of a lady of no very strict virtue and was entirely devoted to her. Morning, noon and night I was at her house or pining after the moment when I should be there. All my hours were passed in attending upon her, in flattering her vanity by exposing myself in public with her, in gratifying her fancies and obeying her caprices.'[7]

Frederic Lamb might seem an odd choice of protector for Harriette to make at this stage of her career. On paper he did not appear to have the necessary credentials to raise her profile. Not only was he comparatively poor, but he was the third son of a new viscount with an Irish title as opposed to being, like Craven, the eldest son of an ancient English name, and the Melbournes lacked the *gravitas* of the Cravens. Harriette stressed that while she loved beauty in a man, she 'estimated high breeding before it. In short, though my father was a tradesman, it would not be in my power or in my nature to love the greatest beauty on earth until I had convinced myself that he had the habits of the very first society. Added to this, it were a thing devoutly to be wished that he should be no less well born than well bred.'[8] Frederic Lamb would challenge Harriette on both these points. His great-grandfather had been in business and his family, which lacked the finer points of social refinement, was fuelled by ambition and new money. Peniston Lamb, the First Lord Melbourne and Frederic's father, was a man of little substance and large fortune. Like the Sixth Lord Craven, Melbourne lived in the shadow of his legendary spouse. He entered the world 'as a young man to become the pray of harpies and scoundrels, and speedily added many of the vices of his companions to his own colourless personality'.[9] Any blood relationship Melbourne was rumoured to share with five of his six children was not taken seriously and was of little personal concern, but he was, it was remarked, as fond of them as if they were his own. Having produced a legitimate male heir Lady Melbourne's duty was considered done. Not much liking his clever wife, Lord Melbourne was not much interested in who else did. During a parliamentary career spanning forty years, he spoke only once; he had the literacy level of a child ('I should be happey in seeing my love every minnit, with sending you a thousand kisses,' he wrote to the courtesan Mrs Baddeley), and his own daughter described him as seeming to appear 'drunkish' even when nothing more than a glass had passed his lips.

What character he had, Harriette Wilson liked. She had a fondness for fools and Lord Melbourne, known as 'the paragon of debauchery', had a fondness for courtesans. Rumour had it that Melbourne had also been one of Harriette's lovers and it was she who gave him his greatest obituary.

Melbourne was, she wrote, 'a good man. Not one of your stiff-laced, moralising fathers, who preach chastity and forbearance to their children. Quite the contrary; he congratulated his son on the lucky circumstance of his friend Craven having such a fine girl with him.'[10] In the fictitious world she created, Harriette 'recorded' a conversation between Melbourne and Frederic Lamb which she could never have heard but which, as a piece of dramatic dialogue, shows how entertaining a mimic and amusing a raconteuse she was:

'No such thing,' answered Frederic Lamb [on Melbourne's assuming that Harriette Wilson was besotted with his son]; 'I am unsuccessful there. Harriette will have nothing to do with me.' – 'Nonsense!' rejoined Melbourne, in great surprise; 'I never heard anything half so ridiculous in all my life. The girl must be mad! She looks mad: I thought so the other day, when I met her galloping about, with her feathers blowing and her thick dark hair about her ears.'

'I'll speak to Harriette for you,' added his Lordship, after a long pause; and then continued repeating to himself, in an undertone, 'Not have my son indeed! Six feet high! A fine, straight, handsome, noble young fellow! I wonder what she would have!'[11]

A second son could not expect much from life, but as the third son in his family, Frederic could hope for nothing. The Melbourne title and what was left of its fortune would all go to Peniston, the eldest; Lady Melbourne, preferring her second son William, reserved for him her principal adoration and ambition, which left Frederic dependent on his wits to carve out a name for himself. But wits he had; Lady Melbourne raised her children to be great. It was she who set the tone of the household and her own brilliant mind, intellectual scepticism, boundless social energy and ruthless drive soon became recognized Melbourne family attributes. She was what Sheridan called 'an admirable PROSE woman', and her boys, David Cecil writes, were likewise 'vital, sensual, clever, positive and unidealistic'.[12] The social code of the late eighteenth and early nineteenth century *grande-monde* was uncompromising; tough wit and loose morals, an open purse and a closed heart, and even by these unforgiving standards William, Frederic and George Lamb – with whom Harriette would certainly have an affair – were considered coarse by their Whig cousins. They whored, drank, swore, gambled, 'ate greedily and were liable suddenly to go to sleep and snore'.[13] They had a 'splendid talent for living . . . they entered with zest into every pleasure . . . Born and bred citizens of the world, they knew their way about it by a sort of infallible instinct. And they had an instinctive mastery of its social arts.'[14] Frederic, a contemporary observed, saw 'life' much as his mother did – 'in the most degrading light, and he simplifies the thing by thinking all men rogues and all women [whores]'. Twenty years later, when he was an established diplomat, it was observed how 'living abroad and seeing a great variety of people . . . has given [Frederic] a sort of rude polish which his brothers want. He is less like an animal, does not roll about and snore as they do. At meals the real Lamb breaks out, but at other times he is civil, gentleman-like, and gentle.'[15]

Lady Melbourne had no time for sentiment or romantic love; she was once described as not being able to see a happy marriage without breaking it up. She saw relationships in terms of property and not people. In her dry opinion, the only difference between a woman of fashion and a woman of pleasure was breeding, and the spectacular rise of her family proved her point. Frederic might well have been named after his putative father, the Duke of York; the Prince of Wales, the Duke's elder brother, sired Lady Melbourne's next son, George (named in his honour), and Lord Egremont was assumed to be the father of both William Lamb and Emily, her eldest daughter. It was rumoured that Egremont purchased Lady Melbourne from Lord Coleraine for £13,000, which sale earned Lord Melbourne a commission. 'There was hardly a young married lady of fashion', Egremont wrote to Lord Holland, 'who did not think it almost a stain upon her reputation if she was not known as having cuckolded her husband; and the only doubt was who to assist her in the operation.'[16] William Lamb described his mother as 'a remarkable woman, a devoted mother, an excellent wife – but not chaste, not chaste', and Lady Melbourne's select lack of chastity secured the viscountcy for her husband and the careers of her sons.

At the time of Frederic's birth in 1782, the Melbournes' London home was in Piccadilly on the site now occupied by Albany. Frederic was raised primarily in Brocket Hall, the family seat in Hertfordshire, out of the way of his mother who was turning the town house into a Whig power base (an exercise that cost fifty thousand pounds and employed the most fashionable decorators in the country), and he was then sent to Eton. In 1791, Lady Melbourne agreed to swap houses with the Duke of York, who preferred the grandeur of her white and gold palace to his own plainer establishment in Whitehall. It did not take long for the new Melbourne House to become established alongside Devonshire House and Holland House as the place where some of the most significant political discussions of the late eighteenth century took place.

So when Harriette Wilson cast out her line and drew in Frederic Lamb she hooked a member of the most prominent and influential Whig clan in the country. He was, 'by birth, at the centre of everything of interest in literature, politics, or the intellect'.[17] There was no one with whom Frederic was not acquainted, no drawing room or club to which he was not welcome. He was *fashionable* and this is what Harriette needed; he would, she hoped, establish her in London rather than hide her away in a hunting lodge, and by his side she would have access to the life of the *haut ton*. Frederic Lamb could also educate her. His obituary would later praise his 'vigourous understanding' and 'great quickness', and remember him for being 'well versed in business and public affairs . . . a very sensible and intelligent converser and correspondent. He took a deep and lively interest in politics . . . [and] was insatiably curious about all that was going on.'

Lamb was a cool, urbane intellectual. Craven was a soldier with no cultural or political interests. Craven could teach Harriette nothing about who was in and who was out, who said what to whom and which novels and poems were causing a stir. He wanted her to be a cheerful, loyal and agreeable companion and Harriette wanted to be more than this. And, most importantly, Craven could teach her nothing about being a courtesan. Courtesans need training. William Hickey remembered his first meeting with the courtesan Emily Warren in 1776, when she was 'an unripe and awkward girl, but with features of exquisite beauty'. Emily was taken off the streets by 'that experienced old matron Charlotte Hayes, who then kept a house of celebrity in King's Place' and here Hickey, who was a constant visitor, watched her 'under the tuition of the ancient dame, learning to walk, a qualification Madame Hayes considered of importance, and in which her pupil certainly excelled, Emily's movements and air being grace personified, and attracting universal admiration whenever she appeared abroad.'[18]

Until she met Frederic Lamb, Harriette had not expected to entertain her lover; she assumed that it was *his* responsibility to please *her* and it was Craven's failure to do so that sealed his fate. What Lamb taught Harriette was that if her ambition was to be the companion of the most powerful men in the country, she had to appear a woman of the world herself. The society Harriette courted was so thoroughly infused with the political spirit that the line between politics and pleasure had long dissolved: social life and political life, political and sexual intrigues, amounted to the same thing, the great Whig hostesses were political beings, drawing-room and dinner-party talk was merely a continuation of the Commons debates. Harriette did not have a political bone in her body (any stirrings of sympathy she had were anyway towards the Tories), and so she could never wield the same power as a courtesan such as Mrs Armistead, who went on to marry the Whig politician, Charles James Fox. Harriette saw her lack of interest in politics as a strength as opposed to a failing: politics she found dull and she would hate to appear a bore. But she needed to be politically informed.

Lamb recognized at once Harriette's qualities and the importance of her being noticed in the highest circles; she says that it was he who encouraged her to write to the Prince of Wales.[19] They became engaged, Harriette wrote, she took his name and he called her his 'little wife' but he continued to encourage her flirtations; it reflected well on him to be seen as the tutor and protector of an admired young woman. What Lamb saw in Harriette was an exuberant, still-unformed girl, ready to be moulded into any shape he pleased. This suited Harriette perfectly. Not only had the schooling she received left her ignorant but one of the appeals for her of a courtesan's life was the access it gave her to self-improvement.

Educating women was an area in which Lamb and his elder brother excelled. 'Oh those Lambs,' Lady Caroline said of her husband, William, 'how they do enlighten one's mind.' The early years of her marriage to William, Caroline Lamb described as being a continual process of instruction and edification: she was introduced to philosophers, historians, classicists, and often before breakfast. Frederic took on much the same role with Harriette, but this was their arrangement and both parties enjoyed the respective roles of master and pupil:

He sometimes passed an hour in reading to me. Till then, I had no idea of the gratification to be derived from books. In my convent in France, I had read only sacred Dramas; at home, my father's mathematical books, Buchan's Medicine, Gil Blas, and the Vicar of Wakefield, formed our whole library . . . Fred Lamb's choice was happy – Milton, Shakespeare, Byron, the Rambler, Virgil, etc. I must know all about these Greeks and Romans, said I to myself. Some day I will go into the country quite alone, and study like mad. I am too young now.[20]

'I never saw a girl except yourself [Harriette recalled Frederic telling her] possessing unbounded liberty from the age of fourteen, without a single friend, or anything better to guide her than her own romantic imagination, who yet contrived to grow wiser every year, to reflect, to read, and to improve her mind, in the midst of such flattery as you are surrounded by.' Fred Lamb did actually say all this, but I do not tell my reader that I was vain enough to believe about half of it; for, though, I had bought my books to be ready, in case a fit of reading should happen to come over me, yet I must confess that, hitherto, I have not had a call . . .[21]

Once in London, Lamb established Harriette in a less than reputable house in Duke's Row, in the suburb of Somerstown, under the eye of her sister Fanny's old nurse. Here he 'suffered' her to pass her 'dreary evenings alone, while he frequented balls, masquerades, etc.' Frederic, Harriette assumed, 'contrived to enjoy all the luxuries of life' while keeping her 'in extreme poverty', certain that she would not leave him because she had already proved her natural fidelity by resisting his advances when she was living under Lord Craven's protection in Brighton.[22] Any glamorous notions Harriette entertained about being protected by Lamb were disappointed. 'I [can]not but feel provoked', Harriette recalled, 'at the idea of a young man going about the world, always laughing, and showing off the character of a fine, good-tempered, open-hearted, easy, generous, sailor-like fellow, and who yet could take me from a rich man, to leave me starving at Somers-town, as he had done, without once making me the offer of a single shilling . . .'[23]

But Harriette was making a name for herself. Hearing of her reputation, several men were asking for an introduction and the Mayfair procuress, Mrs Porter of Berkeley Street, was approached for this purpose by General Walpole. Walpole was twenty years older than Harriette and from solid aristocratic stock. He had recently left a successful army career to become a supporter of Fox in the House of Commons; his mother was daughter of the Duke of Devonshire and his father was Lord Walpole of Wolterton. Harriette was unimpressed. He seemed to her nothing more than an ancient and comic old man, and having accepted his introductory fee she sent her elderly landlady to meet him in her place. The impostor covered her wrinkled face with a veil which she lifted only after the General had been introduced to the beautiful Harriette Wilson. Walpole was furious and left the establishment immediately, but Mrs Porter continued to receive requests to meet the wild young woman who was creating such a stir in Somerstown.

Duke's Row is a short road on the south side of what was then called the New Road and is now called Euston Road. The New Road had been built as London's first bypass forty years earlier, to divert drovers travelling from the west to Smithfield Market from herding their cattle and sheep along Oxford Street and through Holborn. The Duke of Bedford, whose land the road cut through, objected to the dust and, finding no sympathy in Parliament, he upgraded a track running from the back of his mansion into a road for his own use. Duke's Row was part of this private route. On the north side of the New Road, five minutes' walk from Harriette's lodgings, was a fifteen-sided building three storeys high, called the Polygon, where four years before Mary Wollstonecraft had died of fever after giving birth to her daughter, also called Mary. In the year that Harriette's career would begin its downward slope, Mary Shelley, as this motherless child was now called, would publish a novel called *Frankenstein*. Five minutes' walk south-east of Duke's Row lay the Foundling Hospital and ten minutes' south was the British Museum. Harriette was living on the margins of Bloomsbury; the area of London also inhabited by Isabella Knightley in Jane Austen's *Emma*, and whose air she defended against the aspersions of the hypochondriacal Mr Woodhouse:

No indeed – we are not at all in a bad air. Our part of London is so very superior to most others! You must not confound us with London in general, my dear sir. The neighbourhood of Brunswick Square is very different from almost all the rest. We are so very airy! I should be unwilling, I own, to live in any other part of the town; there is hardly any other that I could be satisfied to have my children in; but we are so remarkably airy! Mr Wingfield thinks the vicinity of Brunswick Square decidedly the most favourable as to air.[24]

Beau Brummell, when invited to dinner in Bloomsbury, replied that he would attend if his coachman could find his way there.

At the time of Harriette's birth, the land between St Pancras churchyard and the British Museum was open country extending to Paddington, Primrose Hill, Chalk Farm, Hampstead and Highgate. But a new, middle-class neighbourhood was fast developing as Harriette watched. 'The immense accumulations of building that have lately taken place on this side of the metropolis are apparently beyond credibility,' wrote a London historian of Bloomsbury in 1807. 'In 1803, all the new houses between Russell and Bloomsbury Squares were erected; and most of the large tract, formerly known by the name of the Long Fields, have [sic] been covered with magnificent houses since 1801.'[25]

Bloomsbury was a burgeoning bourgeois suburb and Somerstown was a working-class one, populated with prostitutes and émigrés from the French Revolution. There was very little on either side of the New Road to interest Harriette, save her love of walking. It was during one of her expeditions north of Duke's Row that she met Julia Storer and formed one of her few female friendships.

CHAPTER 7

Julia Johnstone

Julia Storer was born on 11 August 1777, probably in St James's Palace where George III held his London court and her mother was maid of honour to Queen Charlotte. While there is a question mark over whether Harriette rose or fell to her position of celebrity, there is no doubt that when Julia first took her place in the salons of the *demi-monde* she was on her way down. Julia Storer belonged at the heart of the English Establishment and had it not been for what she would call her '*faux pas*', her story would have been entirely different. She grew up in the royal household under the gaze of the King, but following her descent into the underworld she is as hard to see as Euridice.

The voice Julia left to posterity lacks charm or warmth; she comes across as disappointed, moralizing and unforgiving. But she was also Harriette's friend and a successful courtesan in her own right, which suggests that she cannot have been entirely without appeal. Harriette presents Julia as having been ordinary, but she had the courage to rebel and when she was forced to cross to the shady side of the sword, Julia did so with determination. There was nothing ordinary about Julia's life, and there was a great deal more at stake in her fall than there had been in Harriette's.

One of her first cousins, Elizabeth Chichagov, fell in love with and married a Russian admiral before sailing off to live happily in St Petersburg;

George Cruikshank, '*Alteration*'

nothing so dramatic had happened before to a woman in Julia's family. Other cousins lived quieter lives. A letter from Lady Sarah Lyttelton to her brother, Robert Spencer, describes a meeting with Julia's relations at a soirée hosted by her aunt, Lady Carysfort, in 1811:

There were but very few steady people there, and one card table, where Papa risked his shillings, while Mama and Lady Carysfort, I and her daughters, sat amusing ourselves as we could . . . I delight in those girls; they are so thoroughly right and respectable, and, besides, have such warm, good hearts, and good educations, and their conversation is just what pleases me . . . They are not very pretty, and rather cold to strangers – that is, entirely without coquetterie [sic] or vanity – so that I dare say they will remain the 'Lady Proby's' for ever.[1]

Had she stayed on the right side of the sword, Julia would have been presented at court aged seventeen or eighteen along with the other debutantes before embarking on the exhausting round of balls, parties, dinners and breakfasts that comprised the London season. This would have marked her entry into adulthood, society and conspicuous virtue. As a debutante, she would have worked hard during her first two seasons to meet an eligible peer or son of a peer to whose country estate she would retreat following her marriage, and from which she would emerge in May for the next London season to begin the rounds of depositing and collecting calling cards at the homes of other married ladies. How would 'a woman of very violent passions', as Harriette described Julia, 'combined with an extremely shy and reserved disposition', have coped with this life? She saw herself as neither witty nor bright – 'My mother-wit is not much,' Julia admitted, comparing herself with Harriette[2] – and she would not perhaps have shone as a hostess in London circles. Julia would have raised her children quietly and seen her daughters well matched in marriage during their first season, some time after which her body would be buried with that of her lord and the fact of her death recorded in stone.

Her parents were the Honourable Elizabeth Proby, daughter of the First Lord Carysfort, and Thomas, second son of Thomas Storer of Belle Isle, Jamaica, and Golden Square, London. Julia's mother was brought up in Elton Hall, the family seat in Huntingtonshire; a charming manor house built around a fine fifteenth-century tower, extended over the centuries and surrounded by acres of parkland. Through Julia Storer's maternal grandmother, Elizabeth Allen, the Probys also had extensive estates in Ireland from which Lord Carysfort took his title when he was created Baron in 1752. John Joshua Proby, Julia's uncle, married another Elizabeth, the daughter of the eminent statesman George Grenville and sister of Lord Grenville and the First Marquis of Buckingham. John Joshua Proby was given an earldom. His and Elizabeth Proby's paternal grand-mother had been Jane Leveson-Gower, daughter of the First Baron Gower, which connected Julia's family to a fine aristocratic line and made her the niece of Lord Granville Leveson-Gower and, most importantly, of his sister, the Duchess of Beaufort, whose son would become a vital player in Harriette Wilson's life.

The Storers had grown rich from slavery and for generations Julia's paternal collaterals in Jamaica had married into other ex-patriot colonial families. Julia's uncle was Anthony Morris Storer, the fashionable man about town and antiquary who left his fabulous library and collection of prints to Eton College. From childhood Anthony Morris Storer had been great friends with the Earl of Carlisle, Byron's guardian, and as an adult he was intimate with Charles James Fox, George Selwyn, Lady Craven and the other leading characters of the eighteenth-century scene. On his death in 1799, he left to his nephew, Anthony Gilbert Storer, his house at Purley Park near Reading, his Jamaican estates, and an income of £8,000 a year – the equivalent today of half a million pounds. Julia Storer received a bracelet.

Thomas Storer died 'in embarrassed circumstances' in 1792, at his family's Belle Isle home. Julia said she never saw him, but as the eldest of four children, the youngest of whom, Anthony Gilbert, was born when she was five, she must have had some recollection of her father being around. She was educated at a boarding school near Eton and a convent in the South of France. Aged thirteen, she returned to the royal household to have her schooling completed by a governess, after which she waited for her presentation at court and first London season.

Julia had developed into an unhappy, uncomfortable figure whose features, Harriette Wilson said, 'were not regular, nor their expression particularly good'.[3] The one sketch of her that survives (plate 6), drawn to be a frontispiece to her *Confessions*, shows an attractive woman, with a nice figure, fair skin, almond eyes, dark, curled hair and rosy lips. Harriette says she had pretty arms, hands and feet but that her teeth were crooked. Growing up in the suffocating etiquette of George III's 'cheese-paring' court seems to have affected quite severely the children of King and courtiers alike. Along with the Prince of Wales and his ducal brothers, who reacted to their father's bourgeois domesticity by spending and whoring on a fabulous scale, Julia loathed the 'gloom' of St James's, which had about it all the excitement of a rainy Sunday afternoon. Sitting down in the presence of the King was forbidden, even for heavily pregnant women; palace food was unappetizing, and socializing each week consisted of a continuous round of stiflingly formal Levees and Drawing Rooms.

Before long Julia declared herself against 'the starched and stately manners of the Anglo-Germanic school' represented by the court and for 'freedom and independence'. In her account of what happened next, she suggests that she fell out with her mother over her refusal to learn German and that she burst out of St James's like a diver gasping for air. 'What a fortune is my mother's,' she exclaimed as she packed her bags, 'such a one will never do for me.' Having made up her mind to leave for ever, Julia bade the Honourable Elizabeth farewell and sped away. 'Adieu daughter,' came the reply, and never again were the twain to meet.[4]

Julia's carriage rolled down Piccadilly and some fifteen miles out of London before arriving at Hampton Court Palace on the banks of the Thames:

Another palace, thought I, pray heaven it prove less gloomy than the one I have turned my back upon . . . I was handed out of the carriage by a military officer; the sight inspired me with unusual pleasure, a hussar's cap and feather gives such fillip to the spirits of a young miss in her teens . . . In a very elegant drawing room I found a lady of superior cast, looking sour as a crab, and surrounded by a family of smiling young cherubs . . . the duenna looks of Mrs Cotton (for such was her name) made me freeze: in about an hour, Colonel Cotton was announced, a tall handsome man, below the middle age, advanced and took me by the hand.[5]

It is an important part of her story that Julia be seen as 'abandoned to the care of strangers'. Unlike Harriette, she would take no responsibility for her fall. Julia claimed that she lived with Colonel and Mrs Cotton as one of their children, but according to Hampton Court records the Honourable Mrs Storer had a suite of her own in the Palace, numbers 19 and 27, where she retired when not needed at St James's. The Cottons themselves do not appear on the Palace records before 1797, by which time Julia was twenty years old and already the mother of several children, and then Colonel Cotton occupied suite 21, almost next to Mrs Storer's rooms, until his death in 1843. Harriette Wilson recalls Julia's saying that she had been wooed by Beau Brummell – whose father had suite 17 – when they were both growing up at the palace, and she also recounts a story told by Julia about living at Hampton Court with her mother and hiding Cotton under her bed. So it seems as if Julia may not have been living with the Cottons at all and may not even have left home when she found herself confronting the icy Mrs Cotton and melting in the arms of her husband.

Whatever the circumstances of her introduction to Colonel Cotton, 'At the age of sixteen I fell victim to my own inexperience, and the impassioned solicitations of a man, one of the handsomest and most accomplished of the age.'[6] And on a stone staircase at Hampton Court, Julia Storer's descent began. 'Let no one condemn me,' she wrote later of the loss of her virtue, 'who has not been placed in a similar situation; neglected from my childhood by those who ought to have nurtured my infant mind; abandoned to the care of strangers at the most critical period of a young girl's existence; with a warm and grateful heart; and passions, though not wild as the wave, certainly too strong for me to keep under control without the advice of a friendly mentor – I must have been more than mortal to have withstood temptation.'[7] Julia's experience – unhappiness, seduction, ostracism – is described by all courtesans (apart from Harriette Wilson) in their memoirs.

In one of Harriette's more dramatic tableaux, she tells of Julia, nine months pregnant and attempting to conceal her condition, going into the first stage of labour as she curtsied to Queen Charlotte. Mrs Cotton, only now noticing the critical nature of Julia's state, called her a 'monster' and a 'wretch' and left her to deliver her son alone, which Julia duly did. Harriette says that Mrs Storer then hurried her daughter away to the country leaving Julia's brother to fight a duel with Cotton; Julia says that far from protecting her, Mrs Storer 'received the news of my disaster with the greatest apathy and contented herself with writing me a note to say I must expect no further assistance, but live upon my own small fortune of

£4,000 left by a relative. My brother was at the time abroad, and consequently the duel was an imaginary one of Miss Wilson.'[8] Julia, love-sick, wrote to her Colonel threatening to kill herself if he abandoned her; he declared his devotion, and the two were reunited.

Julia had been brought up under strict regulations. No unmarried woman under thirty with a reputation to keep could, under any circumstances, be alone with a man unless chaperoned; no member of a family stained by scandal could be received at court. By becoming pregnant, Julia had brought ruin not only upon herself but on the Storers' unblemished reputation. 'I was truly sensible of the value of all I had lost,' she wrote of her '*faux pas*'. 'The world is very uncharitable! Man may commit an hundred deviations from the path of rectitude, yet he still can return, every one invites him; in sober truth he gains an *éclat* by his failings, that establish him in the Ton, and make him envied, instead of pitied or despised. But woman, when she makes one false step . . . becomes a mark for the slow-moving finger of scorn . . .'[9]

The birth of one bastard child might have been forgiven by the Storers, had Julia disappeared abroad with a suitable companion for the duration of the pregnancy and given the baby up for adoption. But the chances of being received into society again were slim. In 1820, the Duke of Devonshire gave a ball in the hope of welcoming back into the world his transgressive cousin Harriet, who gave birth to a daughter out of wedlock but was now the wife of a respectable aristocrat. While the ball was attended by most of the town the Duke failed in his task; Harriet was ceremonially cut by all.

Julia's pregnancy was on full display. Rather than save what reputation she had left by adopting a life of public shame, she became Cotton's mistress. Disowned by her mother and brother, she and the Colonel took for themselves and their child the name Johnstone, most likely from her aunt, Elizabeth Johnstone of Anchovy Valley, Jamaica. Cotton then found for her a cottage near Primrose Hill, a rural village north of the New Road, where she lived in seclusion for nine years and raised an ever increasing brood of young Johnstones. Colonel Cotton would visit her twice a week, striding over the fields to the back of the house so as to avoid being seen. Harriette wrote that the scandal cost him his regimental position, but it seems that it was only Julia's name that suffered. Colonel

Cotton did not leave the 10th Dragoons until 1799, when Julia was twenty-two, and then it was he who tendered his resignation, selling his colonelcy on to George Leigh (the husband of Augusta, Byron's adored half-sister). The 10th Dragoons being the most fashionable regiment, Cotton was able to pocket the profit and at the same time buy himself a less expensive position elsewhere.

It was while Julia Johnstone was living in Primrose Cottage that she met the dazzling Harriette Wilson and emerged from retirement once more to face the world. The year was 1803, and Harriette was living in Duke's Row, trapped between the lower-class dreariness of Somerstown and the middle-class dreariness of Bloomsbury. 'There was a very elegant-looking woman residing in my neighbourhood,' Harriette wrote,

in a beautiful little cottage, who had long excited my curiosity. She appeared to be the mother of five extremely beautiful children. These were always to be seen with their nurse, walking out, most fancifully dressed. Everyone used to stop to admire them. Their mother seemed to live in the most complete retirement. I never saw her with anybody besides her children. One day our eyes met: she smiled, and I half bowed. The next day we met again, and the lady wished me a good morning. We soon got into conversation. I asked her, if she did not lead a very solitary life? 'You are the first female I have spoken to for four years,' said the lady, 'with the exception of my own servants; but,' added she, 'some day we may know each other better. In the meantime will you trust yourself to come and dine with me today?' – 'With great pleasure,' I replied, 'if you think me worthy that honour.' We then separated to dress for dinner.[10]

Harriette wasn't an entire stranger to Julia, who had admired her from afar. 'Do you believe', Julia told her, 'that I should have asked you to dine with me, if I had not been particularly struck and pleased with you? I had, as I passed your window, heard you touch the pianoforte with a very masterly hand, and therefore I conceived that you were not uneducated, and I knew that you led almost as retired a life as myself.'[11]

Harriette returned to the cottage that evening and noted her new friend's fine taste: a harp, a piano, needlework, her firescreens ornamented with extracts from Thomas Moore's melodies; even Julia's handwriting was beautiful. There was 'something dramatic' about Julia, Harriette observed; her life was arranged like the scene of a play. She lived in antici-pation of guests who never came; her dress was studied and fashionable, her lifestyle was graceful, her lamps were soft, her rooms were perfumed, and nothing ever happened to disturb this appearance of perfection. Julia was without doubt 'one of the best mannered women in England, not excepting those of even the very highest rank', Harriette thought. But all the same, 'she is not a bad woman – and she is not a good woman, said I to myself. What can she be?' Mr Johnstone arrived as they were sitting down to dinner. 'He was a particularly elegant handsome man, about forty years of age. His manner of addressing Mrs Johnstone was more that of an humble romantic lover than of a husband.'[12] Following supper, Harriette played with the children in the nursery, dressing their dolls and teaching them to skip.

There are very few occasions in which Julia Johnstone's *Confessions* seem credible and the account she gives of meeting Harriette Wilson is one of them. Julia dismisses out of hand what she calls Harriette's 'very romantic unaccountably well got up tale, that I, whom you say had not spoken to anybody but my servants for four years and was the mother of five children, should at one glance of your basilisk features throw aside years of discretion and maternal retirement and plunge into familiarity with a heedless and giddy girl, whose face was as familiar to all on the streets as a bill of the play or the walking advertisement of a lottery office.'[13] What Julia tells us is that Colonel Cotton was introduced to Harriette through Tom Sheridan, and that the two women first met when Cotton brought Harriette and Tom to Primrose Cottage for dinner one Sunday. 'I do not deny', Julia recalls, with a generosity not typical of her, 'that I was actually fascinated by your lovely features and arch vivacity; and as the Colonel told me you had never made a faux-pas with any other than Fred Lamb, whose name you then bore, I imagined your case and my own to be very similar and I became sympathetically attached to your fate.'[14] Julia was always anxious to prove that her profession was the result of a moment of weakness while Harriette was born a whore.

The two women soon formed a partnership in which Julia lent the class and Harriette the sex appeal. 'We were as friendly as two sisters,' Julia wrote, 'and every evening when Fred Lamb left her alone, which was four out of six, she came to me, danced to my music, romped with my children; she was all animal spirits, and I believe nothing could have made her grave for an hour but the loss of her beauty.'[15] Before long Julia had been introduced to Harriette's sister Fanny. The three women became 'sworn friends'. 'Most people believed that we were three sisters,' Harriette wrote. 'Many called us the Three Graces. It was a pity that there were only three Graces! – and that is the reason I suppose, why my eldest sister, Amy, was cut out of this ring, and often surnamed one of the Furies.'[16] Amy, meanwhile, was entertaining Julia's uncle Lord Proby.

Shortly after she met Harriette, Colonel Cotton, Julia says, wrote to her through his attorney terminating their arrangement. She was alone for the first time in her life. The Johnstone boys were sent to boarding schools; the girls were given a small annuity and left to their mother to dispose of. 'As for me, I was left to shift as I thought proper,' Julia wrote and she moved from Primrose Cottage to share with Harriette a furnished house near Bedford Square. She took the first floor and Harriette had the ground floor.

It was late 1803 when Harriette and Julia Johnstone moved into their Bloomsbury house, with the rent, bills, food, servants and carriage all paid for by Harriette's glamorous new protector.

CHAPTER 8

The Marquis of Lorne

George William Campbell, the raffish, urbane and coolly insouciant Marquis of Lorne, heir to the Dukedom of Argyll, was 'without exception', Frederic Lamb told Harriette Wilson, 'the highest-bred man in England'.[1] His aunt was Lady Frederick Campbell, who had raised Amelia Dubouchet as her own child. By the time he housed Harriette in Bloomsbury, Lorne had squandered most of his great inheritance and nearly ruined his family. Lamb saw no danger in encouraging Harriette's interest in the Marquis, underestimating not only her ambition but also her appeal.

Lorne was exactly Harriette's type: ten years her senior, his title placed him right at the top of the aristocratic pecking order. He was rich, decadent, debauched and popular. He had none of Lamb's sense of financial responsibility, none of the steady dullness of Craven. Lorne was hard living, hard drinking, a dandy and cynic, a believer in 'nothing good or noble or elevated'.[2] He was also beautiful – 'His expression', Harriette thought, 'is one of the finest things in nature',[3] and Harriette was always drawn to classical perfection. Lorne was a Member of Parliament with no interest in politics, no concern for the future, no reverence for the past. He was extravagant in the mould of John Dubouchet, and Harriette was excited by Lorne in an entirely new way. 'The sensations which Argyle [*sic*]

Entrance to Zoological Gardens, Regent's Park, *Views of London* had inspired me with, were the warmest, nay, the first of the same nature I had ever experienced.' Harriette had a habit, in her *Memoirs*, of calling her lovers by the titles they would subsequently inherit.

The Duke of Argyll had consistently bailed his eldest son out, selling farms to pay his gambling debts, emptying the coffers to finance his liaisons. In 1796, £23,900 4s 1d had to be borrowed from the rent roles of the Argyll estate on the Marquis's behalf; £30,000 worth of Lorne's debts were settled but more than £3,000 was still owing. Over the next few years Lorne's creditors swallowed up £2,466 of the Argyll rents annually.

In 1804, the year in which Harriette became Lorne's mistress, his father concluded that the principal cause of his son's 'misfortunes' was gambling. Lorne was, like many of his contemporaries, addicted to the green baize tables and the Duke of Argyll was not the only father anxious about the effect of his offspring's compulsion on the family estates. Lord Lyttelton also anticipated the day that 'the rattling of a dice box at White's may . . . shake down all our fine oaks', and many a fortune was lost and won in the clubs of St James's. Lord Holland regularly had to meet the phenomenal sums lost at Almack's by his son, Charles James Fox, and those in Fox's circle were half ruined by the securities they provided for him.

The degree of Lorne's disengagement from responsibility, the sheer scale of his retreat into hedonism and his disregard for money, suggests that he was an extreme example of that type produced by Regency England, the aristocratic dandy who lived like a butterfly, only for a day. 'His manner is remarkably simple and unaffected', Lady Holland observed of Lorne, 'and tho' his abilities are not of the most brilliant order, yet he does not appear in the least deficient. He has in his disposition an uncommon share of indifference, almost to apathy. And tho' in possession of every requisite for happiness, it does not appear that he enjoys anything.'[4] Lord and Lady Holland spoke of Lorne as 'talent thrown away'. He had 'natural abilities and a good education' but became, as he grew older, 'insignificant, from nonchalance and indolence'.[5] He held the dukedom for thirty-five years but is barely mentioned in any history of the Dukes of Argyll. There is little to say about the Sixth Duke, or as the Eighth Duke says of his uncle, George, 'I have, unfortunately, nothing very favourable to record.' He drank, whored, won and lost at cards and died leaving several offspring, none of whom were legitimate. 'From sheer carelessness, idleness, and want of purpose in life,' his nephew wrote, Duke George 'did nothing but dilapidate his great inheritance.'[6] Lorne's contributions to the development of the family seat at Inveraray Castle were considered by his father to be typically foolish: 'Your idea of appropriating so much room to Wine Cellars and Kitchen, shew you mean to keep a good table to set up the wine merchant business, but these places will be much better applied to the accommodation of housekeeper and butler, with dining and sitting rooms for upper and lower servants.'[7] The Fifth Duke recommended marriage to his son, 'which if you can find a woman to your mind would keep you at home'.

Lorne was born on 22 September 1768, at Argyll House on a site now occupied by the London Palladium. He was christened by the Archbishop of Canterbury; King George III and his brother the Duke of Gloucester stood by as sponsors. When he was twenty-one, Lorne spurned the opportunity of marrying Lady Charlotte Villiers, the eldest daughter of Lord Jersey, after which she married Lord William Russell, brother of the Duke of Bedford, and commenced on a prolonged affair with Lorne, conducted under her husband's nose. Lorne was still involved with 'Lady W—', as Harriette called her, when he began his arrangement with Harriette. Women had thrown themselves at the Marquis of Lorne since he was an adolescent; Harriette's forwardness was nothing new to him. They had friends in common but Harriette didn't wait to be introduced. Knowing something of Lorne's reputation and fed up with the low profile she received under Lamb's protection, Harriette wrote to him, 'merely to say that if he would walk up to Duke's Row, Somerstown, he would meet a most lovely girl'.[8] Lorne, ever in need of entertainment, was unlikely to spurn such an invitation, and in Harriette's account of their courtship he answered her letter with one equally flirtatious: 'If you are but half as lovely as you think yourself, you must be well worth knowing; but how is that to be managed? Not in the street! But come to No. 39 Portland Street, and ask for me.' 'No!' Harriette replied. 'Our first meeting must be on the high road, in order that I may have room to run away, in case I don't like you', to which request the Marquis conceded, with the addendum that he would come 'on horseback; and then, you know, I can gallop away'.[9] The

Marquis did not gallop away and was charmed by Harriette's 'sunny face of joy and happiness.' 'And for my part,' Harriette wrote of their subsequent meeting, 'I had never seen a countenance I had thought half so beautifully expressive. I was afraid to look at it, lest a closer examination might destroy all the new and delightful sensations his first glance had inspired in my breast. His manner was most gracefully soft and polished. We walked together for about two hours.'[10] Harriette returned after midnight, according to Julia Johnstone, bringing with her a fifty-pound note and a diamond ring.

Lorne and Harriette agreed to walk together again the next day, pacing out from the turnpike at Somerstown past hawthorn and elm, stinking ditches and swampy ponds, up through Marylebone Fields to the Jew's Harp House, a popular tavern, tea house and pleasure garden which looked across to the hills of Hampstead and Highgate. Here they refreshed themselves with cider. Harriette returned home to debate with her conscience. 'I cannot, I reasoned with myself, I cannot I fear, become what the world calls a steady, prudent, virtuous woman. That time is past, even if I was ever fit for it. Still, I must distinguish myself from those in the like unfortunate situations, by strict probity and love of truth. I will never become vile . . . when I am ill used, I will leave my lover rather than deceive him . . .'[11]

'My dear mother would never forgive me,' Harriette concluded, 'if I became artful',[12] so she confessed all to Frederic Lamb and found that rather than being jealous at the thought of her flirtation with the most eligible bachelor in the country, he enjoyed the rivalry and encouraged her to drink with Lorne in the same place every day. Anticipating meeting the Marquis that night at Lady Holland's, Lamb joked about asking him publicly 'what he thinks about the air about the turnpike at Somerstown'. Lamb was so secure of Harriette's affections that he supposed it was Lorne and not himself being made a fool of. 'I must not deceive this man,' Harriette vowed as she realized how much Lamb trusted her. 'And the idea began to make me a little melancholy.'[13]

Harriette's being able to make Lord Craven and Frederic Lamb believe unquestioningly in the happiness she felt in their company and the fidelity she practised when apart was testament to her skill from the outset as a courtesan. Until he read her *Memoirs*, Craven presumably remained ignorant of the degree to which he bored her, still thinking himself the most interesting man she had ever met. And Lamb no doubt supposed himself the most generous and fascinating of all Harriette's protectors. Harriette combined a natural anarchistic charm with a cultivated masquerade of flattery. The blind adulation she showed for her current protector disguised how much he might irritate her; there were very few of her conquests who weren't sent up, ridiculed or mocked by Harriette to her sisters, future lovers or friends.

The ubiquitous Tom Sheridan acted as a pander between Harriette and Lorne, appearing at one point at Duke's Row with a letter from the Marquis that begged forgiveness for having to break an engagement to walk with her in order to have dinner with the Prince of Wales. 'I would write to her again and again,' Lorne told Sheridan, who reported it to Harriette, 'but that, in all probability my letters would be shown to Frederic Lamb, and be laughed at by them both.'[14] In her *Memoirs*, Harriette dresses up this part of her story with an account of Tom Sheridan's imminent demise. 'Death had fixed its stamp on poor Sheridan's handsome face,' she wrote. ' "I must go to the Mediterranean," poor Sheridan said. To die! thought I, as I looked on his sunk, but still very expressive dark eyes . . . He parted my hair and kissed my forehead, my eyes, and my lips. "If I do come back," said he, forcing a languid smile, "mind let me find you married, and rich enough to lend me an occasional hundred pounds or two." He then kissed his hand gracefully, and was out of sight in an instant.'[15] Dramatic and engaging though this scene is, Sheridan's consumption did not kill him until 1817. But, as Harriette continually reminds her readers, she cannnot be responsible for the task of combining the correct event with the correct date; the historical order of things is of less significance to her than their emotional impact.

Encouraged by Sheridan, Harriette continued to walk with Lorne for a month while she was still under the protection of Lamb, and only once, she claimed, did she allow the Marquis to kiss her, after which she reprimanded him and decided it was time to part. 'At the first, I was afraid I should love you,' Harriette says she wrote in her farewell letter,

and, but for Fred Lamb having requested me to get you up to Somerstown, after I had declined meeting you, I had been happy: now the idea makes me miserable.

Still it must be so. I am naturally affectionate. Habit attaches me to Fred Lamb. I cannot deceive him or acquaint him with what will cause him to cut me, in anger and for ever. We may not then meet again, Lorne, as hitherto: for now we could not be merely friends: lovers we must be, hereafter, or nothing. I have never loved any man in my life before, and yet, dear Lorne, you see we must part. I venture to send you the inclosed [*sic*] thick lock of my hair; because you have been good enough to admire it. I do not care how I have disfigured my head, since you are not to see it again.[16]

She felt torn, Harriette said, between the feelings of Lorne, which were increasing by her neglect of them, and those of Lamb, which were 'increasing, as all men's do, from gratified vanity'.[17] Harriette played her cards right: Lorne, never having been rejected before, began to sit on the fence by Duke Street in the hope of catching a glimpse of Harriette as she set out on one of her trips. He became the butt of jokes, not only at the hands of Lamb but also from other friends, Horace Beckford and Sir John Shelley, who, Lamb reported to Harriette, scoffed at Lorne's public humiliation. Harriette, rather than laugh with Lamb when she heard these stories, felt remorse. Eventually, with Lamb out of town and no longer able to stand the tension, Harriette invited herself to dinner at Argyll House. 'Are you really serious?' Lorne asked, breathless with gratitude in Harriette's report of the event. 'I dare not believe it. Say, by my servant, that you will see me, at the turnpike, directly, for five minutes, only to put me out of suspense. I will not believe anything you write on this subject. I want to look at your eyes, while I hear you say yes.'[18]

The meeting took place, the supper was had, and Lorne at last, 'after having gone through all the routine of sighs, vows, and rural walks . . . saw me blooming and safe in his dismal chateau in Argyll Street'.[19] Lamb, when Harriette told him of her triumph and of her imminent departure, was incandescent with rage and muttered something between clenched teeth about true love making you blind to the imperfections of another. But, 'Then who, with love, first love! beating in their hearts,' Harriette reasoned, 'could think of Frederic Lamb?' 'Did I ever tell you I was in love with you?' Harriette asked him. 'Indeed, it was your vanity deceived you, not I. You caused me to lose Lord Craven's protection, and therefore, loving no man at the time, having never loved any, to you I went. I should have felt the affection of a sister for you, but that you made no sacrifices, no single attempt to contribute to my comfort or happiness. I will be the mere instrument of pleasure to no man. He must make me a friend and companion or he will lose me.'[20]

Lamb did not take well to losing his pupil and possession, and continued to pursue Harriette for several years after she left him. 'His passions were the most ardent,' Harriette recalled, 'and he would grind his teeth in bitterness of wounded pride if you did not happen to be affected with the same ardour.' He could be violent and Harriette grew afraid of him. He would return from the Continent, where he was beginning his diplomatic career, and seek her out as though she were his 'humble slave, any day of the week'.[21]

When Harriette left Frederic Lamb for the Marquis of Lorne, her star was ascending. Her Somerstown days were over, she was returning to the West End of London as the courtesan of a leader of fashion, she was newly equipped with a better wardrobe, better jewels and better carriage than Amy had ever seen. Through Lorne's admiration, she had been given the official stamp of approval.

Harriette was eighteen and would never be so happy again.

CHAPTER 9

Sir Arthur Wellesley

Harriette's only problem with Lorne was that he had no intention of leaving Lady Charlotte Russell, his mistress of over a decade, and she disliked having his affections divided between herself and another. Lorne dealt with the situation pragmatically; after sharing Lady Charlotte's box at the opera, he would share his bed with Harriette back at Argyll House. In the early days Harriette would squabble with the Marquis and he continued to wear tokens given to him by Lady Charlotte, a habit Harriette thought 'a dead bore'. 'One night,' she writes, 'I plucked the rose from his breast, another time I hid the chain, and all this, to him, seemed the effect of pure accident: for who, with pride and youth and beauty, would admit that they were jealous?'[1] The world knew of Lorne's affair with Lady Charlotte; the *demi-monde* knew of his affair with Harriette Wilson, and the Marquis crossed effortlessly from sun to shade.

Harriette soon became pragmatic too. She saw that there were benefits to be gained from her peculiar situation that went beyond the pleasure of obliterating a rival. 'If, thought I, this man is not to be entirely mine, perhaps I shall not be entirely his.'[2] It was typical of Harriette to temper pain and humiliation with large doses of practicality, and she threw herself into spending Lorne's money and enjoying the attention she generated as his courtesan. As in all cases of instant celebrity, timing was everything.

Cadiz Mortar, *Views of London*

The right dress worn on the right night, the right phrase caught by the right ear, the laws that dictate who is to wake up and find themselves famous have always been arbitrary, dependent on the mood of the moment. In Harriette's case it was the continuing presence of Lady Charlotte Russell that was to be the making of her, giving her the impetus she needed to make herself the most desirable *demi-mondaine* on the circuit. Her efforts to make one man jealous catapulted her to social visibility, to a level unattainable by those without a husband, a title or a seat in Parliament, and otherwise achieved only by Beau Brummell. Had Lorne been possessive of Harriette she would never have been able to establish herself so thoroughly or become so sought after. Being under the protection of the Marquis, she was in the perfect position to generate desire; she was, strictly speaking, unavailable. It was now that she began to dress in her trademark white muslin and to ensure that she was seen everywhere. A certain guarantee of exposure was to attend the opera, and for one hundred guineas she took for the season a box at the Haymarket, which she shared with Julia and Fanny.

The King's Theatre was one of the most superb in Europe. Fashionable society and *demi-mondaines* together congregated at the opera; the price of tickets, at one guinea a head for a seat in the gallery as opposed to the one shilling it cost to sit on the bench to see a play, meant that opera audiences were more select than those found at the theatre. A box for the season could cost as much as a thousand guineas and here the city's courtesans were displayed alongside hostesses such as Lady Melbourne and Lady Jersey.

The notion of an attentive and appreciative audience was alien to the culture of the playhouse. English theatre audiences were notorious for interrupting the performance with shouts, songs, witticisms and abuse, and for breaking into fights. And while opera-goers could expect less hostility, they were hardly involved in the performance at all. While the singers struggled to be heard below, those in the boxes would entertain their friends, beckon to one another, generate and pass on gossip, comment on fashions and hairstyles and make love. While the dandies paraded their clothes and snorted derision, those in the gallery would shout at them to sit down and be quiet. A new foyer was built at the Haymarket Theatre in the hope that 'in this more remote haunt, the elegant beau may indulge in his promenade with less interruption to the Audience and to the Artists on the Stage'.[3]

The playhouse was associated with vice, and prostitutes and courtesans were certain to be found there. Brothel-keepers used the theatre to display their latest recruits. Covent Garden was described in the 1790s by the *Theatrical Guardian*, as 'little less than a public brothel' and the next century Walter Scott wrote of London audiences, 'One half come to prosecute their debaucheries so openly that it could degrade a bagnio.'[4] The design of the King's Theatre took into account these multiple roles. The Round Room, in which the audience would congregate after the performance, was 'a circular vestibule, almost lined with looking-glass, and furnished with sophas, in which female loveliness is not only seen but reflected'.[5] So significant was this room in Harriette's life that the original title for her *Memoirs* was 'Sketches from the Round Room at the Opera House'.

Harriette's box was her own theatre. It gave her maximum visibility and here she held her salon and presented herself to the waiting world. 'The lighting of the theatre is better adapted for being seen than for seeing,' wrote Prince Pückler-Muskau. 'In front of every box hangs a chandelier which dazzles one very offensively, and throws the actors into the shade.'[6] As a centre of gossip, the theatre enabled her to generate enough of a flurry to become the talk of the town. 'I ran up three times to the opera, but she did not make her appearance,' the young Marquess of Worcester told the Duke of Leinster.[7] 'Everybody is talking about you,' Lord Frederick Bentinck told Harriette. 'Two men, downstairs, have been laying a bet that you are Lady Tavistock. Mrs Orby Hunter says you are the handsomest woman in the house.'[8] Julia Johnstone, pregnant again, was not doing so well:

Poor Julia, all this time, did not receive the slightest compliment or attention from anybody . . . in vain did we cry her up and puff her off, as Lord Carysfort's niece, or as an accomplished, elegant, charming creature, daughter of a maid of honour: she did not take. The men were so rude as often to suffer her to follow us, by herself, without offering their arms to conduct her to the carriage. She was, in fact, so reserved, so shy, and so short-sighted, that, not being very young, nobody would be at the trouble of finding out what she was.[9]

Even the attention paid to her by Beau Brummell was – Harriette sadly noted – 'no longer the effect of love'.[10]

According to Julia, it was she who introduced Harriette to fashionable society:

I well remember the time when [Harriette] teased me into taking a box at the opera-house for the season. We could ill afford it. I had introduced her to a good deal of respectable society, chiefly males indeed; which was owing to my brother, an officer in the army . . . He forgave me for being led astray by Cotton, because I had left him. He lodged at the Russell Coffee-House, and made our house what he termed, 'his head-quarters', so that every morning we had a military levee. He tried in vain to bring my mother and me together, but she was not to be persuaded. I was sorry for this, as it would have been the means of restoring me to respectability.[11]

It is most unlikely that Julia's brother would have had any contact with his fallen sister, let alone flaunted his relationship with her. Julia's '*accouchements*' continued to take place 'regularly once in eleven months'.[12] She was penniless, living in a house with the courtesan of the Marquis of Lorne, and the only women who visited them were the Dubouchet sisters.

Flanked in her box by the beautiful Fanny and well-connected Julia, with Amy and a 'host of beaux' in her own box close by, Harriette nodded, smiled and teased her fan (passing her glance over that of Lorne, seated with his mistress), while queues would gather around her door, waiting their turn to be introduced. Here London's leaders of fashion, the wits and the dandies, sought her out and having these arbiters of taste surround her made it possible for Harriette to reach the very top of the courtesan's market. Her circle included Lord Alvanley, Beau Brummell, Lord Kinnaird, Berkeley Craven, and the inseparable George Nugent and Henry Luttrell, known as 'the Albanians'. Nugent was the younger son of the Marquis of Buckingham and cousin to Julia Johnstone; Julia's aunt, the former Elizabeth Grenville, was Buckingham's sister. Luttrell – 'Everybody knows Luttrell,' explained Harriette – was the bastard son of the Earl of Carhampton, a friend of Byron, a great conversationalist and a composer of epigrams and light verse. His poems 'Advice to Julia, a letter in Rhyme' and 'Mayfair' were popular satires of high society. Nugent and Luttrell were more in Amy's camp than Harriette's, which tells us something about the quality of Amy's company, but Luttrell became 'father-confessor-general' to all three sisters.

It was in her box, under the furtive gaze of her protector, that Harriette avenged herself on her faithless lover and 'learned to be a complete flirt'.[13]

Her reconstruction of opera nights are among the most authentic aspects of her *Memoirs*.

Our box was soon so crowded that I was obliged to turn one out as fast as a new face appeared. Julia and Fanny left me to pay a visit to the enemy, as Luttrell used to call Amy. Observing me for a moment, the Duke of Devonshire [then the Marquis of Hartington] came into my box, believing that he did me honour.

'Duke,' said I, 'you cut me in Piccadilly today.'

'Don't you know,' said the thick-head, 'don't you know, belle Harriette, that I am blind as well as deaf, and a little absent too?'

'My good young man,' said I, out of all patience, '*allez donc à l'hôpital des invalides*: for really, if God has made you blind and deaf, you must be absolutely insufferable when you presume to be absent too. The least you can do, as a blind, deaf man, is surely to pay attention to those who address you.'

'I never heard anything half so severe as la belle Harriette,' drawled out the Duke.

Luttrell now peeped his nose into my box, and said, dragging in his better half, half-brother I mean, fat Nugent, 'A vacancy for two! How happens this? You'll lose your character, Harriette.'[14]

In Julia's account of the night in question, the Duke of Devonshire 'merely nodded to her, then addressed himself to me.'[15]

From one night at the opera, Harriette could plan her week ahead, making appointments with admirers to ride out in Green Park, Hyde Park or St James's, to attend dinner parties, to walk up to Primrose Hill or Marylebone Fields, to visit the pleasure gardens at Ranelagh or Vauxhall. The Three Graces became a formidable force, making fools of their followers, and Harriette was the ringleader, endlessly laying traps and playing tricks in a way that would have thrilled Fanny and Julia, who were quieter and more respectful of potential suitors. For example, Lord Burghersh, whose advances at Covent Garden under the jealous eye of Lorne Harriette had encouraged, met with the trio in Hyde Park, where fashionable society gathered at five o'clock each day, and was given a letter by Harriette which he slipped away, 'with a look of gratified vanity, believing, no doubt, that it was one of my soft effusions on the beauty of his eyes'. 'For the post,' Harriette said, nodding, as they turned to leave him, the Three Graces bursting into a loud laugh.

Hyde Park in the late afternoon was as exclusive a club as any on St James's. According to Captain Gronow, 'the men were mounted on such horses as England alone could then produce, and the carriage company consisted of the most celebrated beauties . . . You did not see in those days any of the lower or middle classes of London intruding themselves in regions which, with a sort of tacit understanding, were then given up exclusively to persons of rank and fashion.'[16] The Fashionable Impures used their open carriages every bit as much for display as their opera boxes. It was at the theatre and in the park that the wives of the *grande-monde* and the courtesans of the *demi-monde* mixed, neither world touching the other.

After the opera, Amy and Harriette held court at separate ends of the Round Room. Amy, Harriette said, would fix herself near enough to her sister to try to charm some of her admirers into her own camp. Lorne, from the side of Lady Charlotte, would look on, and whisper something to Harriette as he passed, confirming their arrangement later that evening. Following the Saturday night performance, the Three Graces would attend Amy's regular cold chicken and champagne suppers, held at the house she shared with General Madden at York Place. Madden, having distinguished himself in the army, sold his commission in the 12th Dragoons in May 1802 and temporarily settled back to London high life, devoting himself to his great friend the Margravine of Anspach, formerly Lady Craven, and to the former Amy Dubouchet. Amy was less devoted; when Madden was away, either abroad or staying with the Margravine at Brandenburg House, she enjoyed an assortment of intrigues including an affair with William Ponsonby and a relationship with the MP Hart Davies in which he paid her generously for the honour of patting her arm. Amy used the 'patting' money to pay for the season's opera box, and the plaintive, bleating voice in which Hart Davies, patting away, would ask Amy if 'that feels nice' became another source of hilarity between Harriette, Julia and Fanny.

Amy's champagne parties, despite being 'merely a tray supper in one corner of the drawing room', so Harriette complained, had become a focal point for demi-reps and 'half the fashionable men in town'. Dandies, aristocrats, MPs, ambassadors, foreign dignitories and their friends would fill the house to the point that many had to spend the evening in the passageway and others in the parlour, cut off by the crowds from the room where the rivalrous queens of the *demi-monde* were holding court. On entering the room, Julia recalled, 'the beaux all crowded near Harriette; but as the evening advanced, they generally formed a sober circle round me'.[17] It is unlikely that anyone attending Amy's parties found themselves sober as the evening advanced, or that Julia's conversation provided anything like the entertainment of Harriette's merciless mockery. Seeing one night a guest, 'the gay Montagu', snorting with laughter at the comments of almost everyone with whom he spoke, Harriette decided to test 'his wonderful luck in addressing himself to witty persons'.

I asked him if he had heard the excellent story about Amy and Harry Mildmay?

'No, but pray tell it me directly: it must be so very excellent.'

'Listen then,' said I, and I began to laugh and to say, 'You must know Amy met Mildmay in the park', and I then went on with a few unconnected words, affecting suitable action, and to be half dead, or quite choked with laughter. So far from repeating anything like a story, I did not connect two words of sense together; and, if I had, we were in such a noisy neighbourhood I could not have been heard; yet Montagu, with equal reason, once more gave full play to his risible faculties, and appeared quite delighted with my story . . . declaring that it was the best thing he had ever heard in his whole life.[18]

While Harriette had been incarcerated in Somerstown, Amy had established herself as a central attraction and now the elder sister had to deal with the triumphant reappearance of the younger. What could Amy do? If she did not invite Harriette to her suppers, then all those men who came only on Harriette's account would stay away also, and if she did invite her, she risked her sister being the centre of attention and Harriette's making a fool of her, both of which were genuine threats. Harriette was bent on embarrassing Amy, never missing an occasion to reveal how much her sister liked black pudding ('sometimes toad-in-the-hole, or hard dumplings; but black pudding takes the lead'[19]) or how the fetching lisp Amy was trying to pass off as a lifelong handicap had never been noticed at home.

Harriette's and Amy's feud became a problem to those who enjoyed the company of them both, among whom was Luttrell. In an attempt to get the sisters to be civil to one another, he 'undertook to draw up a little agreement, stating that since public parties ought not to suffer from private differences, we were thereby requested to engage ourselves to bow to each other in all societies, going through the forms of good breeding, even with more ceremony than if we had liked each other, on pain of being voted public nuisances and private enemies to all wit and humour'.[20]

Amy, Fanny and Harriette were regularly invited to dinner parties where the company, as Sir Walter Scott put it, was fairer than honest. The sisters would together entertain a dozen men. The relationship between the siblings was a source of fascination to their admirers. Walpole observed that the main appeal of Lorne's mother and aunt, Elizabeth and Maria Gunning, when they first arrived in London from Ireland was not that they were each attractive but that they were together beautiful; it was the fact that there were *two* of them that made them so instantly celebrated. In Harriette's case there were three of them, and when Sophia was old enough to join her sisters, there were four Dubouchet girls out on the town; there may even have later been six.[21] Harriette's rivalry with Amy, together with their similar looks and temperaments, added to their appeal; attractive women at war with one another have long been a source of erotic fantasy.

In the autumn of 1805 Nelson was killed in the battle of Trafalgar. He bequeathed his mistress, Lady Hamilton, to the care of the nation, but the nation did not want her and she went the way of other discarded courtesans, ending her days in a French boarding house. Harriette, who had been under Lorne's protection for over a year, was about to become the courtesan of the next English national hero. Lorne had left London for his annual visit to Inveraray, the last he would make before the death of his father and his acquisition of the Dukedom. Harriette's and Amy's lifestyles were getting them both into debt and Lorne's absence left Harriette bereft of ready cash. 'I do not understand economy, and I am frightened to death at debts,' she sighed in anticipation of his departure; 'I shall want a steady sort of friend of some kind, in case a bailiff should get hold of me.'[22] Harriette appears to have been abandoned by Lorne at this point and replaced in his affections by Amy, who became for some time the favourite 'sultana' of the Marquis, whose name she took.[23] Harriette reportedly never forgave her sister.[24]

Thus it was that when Mrs Porter – unfazed by her mocking of General Walpole the previous year – got back in touch with her, Harriette did not again refuse to meet her admirer. Mrs Porter had received a visit from an old customer, a brilliant Irish soldier called Sir Arthur Wellesley, just returned home from nine years in India. He wanted to meet the young woman whose name he had heard mentioned so often in the clubs of St James's, where Harriette's friends lounged about all day, and he offered Mrs Porter and Harriette one hundred guineas each for an introduction.

In Harriette's comic reconstruction of her meetings with Wellesley there is the usual confusion of dates and titles. Their relationship had to be hushed up, she wrote, because he was already – in 1805 – 'the wonder of the world!!', the 'terrific' Iron Duke, 'the most talked about man in Europe!' Harriette's Wellesley struts about in full military regalia, including the Order of the Bath medal he has not yet received, and she calls him the Duke of Wellington, the title he would inherit only after his victories in the Peninsular War in 1814. When Harriette knew Wellesley he was a regular soldier who had not been in society for years and was unheard of except by those few who were interested in the battle of Assaye.

Born in Ireland in 1769, the same summer that saw the birth of Napoleon in Corsica, Wellesley was the third of five sons. Sent to school in England in 1781, he was, in his own words, 'a dreamy, idle, and shy lad'[25] whose passion was his violin and whose poor health held him back from those playing fields of Eton on which he later claimed the battle of Waterloo had been won. Neither scholar nor sportsman, Wellesley was lonely, awkward and solitary. 'I vow to God I don't know what to do with my awkward son Arthur,' his mother complained.[26] Skipping university, he went straight from school into training for a military career. In 1793 Wellesley proposed to and was refused by Kitty Packenham, the daughter of Lord Longford. The humiliating effect of this rejection on his character cannot be overestimated. He became cool, determined and laconic; he burned his violin and turned his back on Ireland for ever. He told Kitty that should she change her mind, his would 'still remain the same'; Kitty stayed unmarried during his years in India, and on his return home the correspondence between the two picked up once more. Suddenly Wellesley found himself, through the pressure of her friends and the pull of his sense of honour, renewing his proposal to Kitty and, having been accepted, preparing to spend the rest of his life with a woman he had not seen for twelve years and who had greatly changed from the blushing twenty-two-year-old with whom he had fallen in love: 'She has grown ugly, by Jove,' he muttered to his brother, Gerald, who was to conduct the ceremony. The unhappy union took place in April 1806, and sixteen years later Wellington wrote to his confidant, Mrs Arbuthnot, 'I married her because they asked me to do it & I did not know myself. I thought that I should never care for anybody again, & that I should be with my army &, in short, I was a fool.'[27] He never settled down into domestic life. Wellesley was always most at home surrounded by soldiers.

He sought out Harriette Wilson in the tense months before he married; he was thirty-six, handsome, tanned, with unfashionable short hair and a large, hooked nose, but the toll of India had made his complexion sallow. Harriette tended to dislike professional soldiers and she found Wellesley, as she had found Craven and General Walpole, a bore; 'He groaned over me by the hour,' she complained. Her view of him would have been no different had he at this point been the national hero; Harriette mixed with aristocrats and leaders because they were rich, not because she found them interesting; she had no doubt that she was the better company. She disliked seriousness and talking politics or war – for this reason she never became the established courtesan of a statesman – and Wellesley, permanently preoccupied with military matters, would have failed to attract her however celebrated he was. Harriette's representation of Wellesley in her *Memoirs* was humiliating to him because it associates him with a notorious woman, but also because it brings an idol down to earth. She never sent up anyone's sexual prowess; she was courteous to this extent. Instead, Harriette shed her old lovers of dignity by more subtle means: 'Men are more hurt at being painted weak, silly creatures than gross blackguards,' she reasoned. She impersonated her clients and there was no question, contemporaries admitted when her *Memoirs* came out, that she had not caught the voices and mannerisms of her whole circle. These details were retained in her memory for up to twenty years. Harriette's imitation of the future Duke of Wellington captured precisely his abrupt speech, his paternalism and peculiar humour, as well as the awkwardness he felt around women. His biographer Elizabeth Longford concedes that 'the taciturnity broken by rather naive gestures of homage sound perfectly authentic'.[28]

He bowed first, then said –

'How do you do?' then thanked me for having given him permission to call on me; and then wanted to take hold of my hand.

'Really,' said I, withdrawing my hand, 'for such a renowned hero you have very little to say for yourself.'

'Beautiful creature!' uttered Wellington, 'where is Lorne?'

'Good gracious,' said I, out of all patience at his stupidity, – 'What come you here for, Duke?'

'Beautiful eyes, yours!' reiterated Wellington.

'Aye, man! They are greater conquerors than ever Wellington shall be; but, to be serious, I understood you came here to try to make yourself agreeable?'

'What, child! Do you think that I have nothing better to do than to make speeches to please ladies?' said Wellington.[29]

Arthur Wellesley became Harriette's 'constant visitor' and 'a most unentertaining one, Heaven knows! . . . In the evenings, when he wore his red ribbon, he looked very like a rat-catcher.'[30]

Wellington called on me, the next morning before I had finished my breakfast. I tried him on every subject I could muster. On all, he was impenetrably taciturn. At last he started an original idea of his own . . .

'I wonder you do not get married, Harriette!'

(Bye-the-bye, ignorant people are always wondering.)

'Why so?'

Wellington, however, gives no reason for anything unconnected with fighting, at least since the convention of Cintra; and he, therefore, again became silent. Another burst of attic sentiment blazed forth.

'I was thinking of you last night, after I got into bed.'

'How very polite to the Duchess,' I observed. '*Apropos* to marriage, Duke, how do you like it?'

Wellington, who seems to make a point of never answering one, continued, 'I was thinking – I was thinking that you will get into some scrape, when I go to Spain.'

'Nothing so serious as marriage neither, I hope!'

'I must come again tomorrow, to give you a little advice,' continued Wellington . . .

I am glad he is off, thought I, for this is indeed very up-hill work. This is worse than Lord Craven.[31]

Harriette's most memorable vignette is the story of Wellington, just back from Spain where he had 'won a mighty battle', thundering on her door in the pouring rain at midnight and being refused entry by Argyll, dressed as an old servant and affecting to have no idea who the caller was.

'Come down, I say,' roared this modern Blue Beard, 'and don't keep me here in the rain, you old blockhead.'

'Sir,' answered Argyle, in a shrill voice, 'you must please to call out your name, or I don't dare to come down, robberies are so frequent in London just at this season, and all the sojers, you see, coming home from Spain, that it's quite alarming to poor lone women.'

Wellington took off his hat, and held up towards the lamp a visage which late fatigue and present vexation had rendered no bad representation of that of the knight of the woeful figure. While the rain was trickling down his nose, his voice, trembling with rage and impatience, cried out, 'You old idiot, do you know me now?'[32]

In Harriette's version of her relationship with Arthur Wellesley, he continued to pursue her for at least the next nine years. He would turn up at her house and, on finding it full of suitors, promptly bolt; he would call out to her from his carriage when he was Ambassador to Paris and she was living there also, and murmur 'little fool' before kissing her with masculine force.

The suggestion that Wellesley's affair with her began after his marriage to Kitty seems to be no more than a ploy to embarrass him, just as her anecdotes are constructed for the purposes of entertaining her reader. It is highly unlikely that Harriette saw Wellesley after April 1806. He confided in Mrs Arbuthnot, to whom he always told the truth, that 'he had never seen [Harriette] since he had married tho' he had frequently given her money when she wrote to beg for it'[33] and, as Elizabeth Longford points out, late 1808 to spring 1809, the months during which Harriette claims to have 'consoled' Wellesley, may have been a bad time in his marriage but was an even worse time to be seeking consolation from a courtesan.

In 1808 Arthur complained to his elder brother Richard, the First Marquis Wellesley, of his 'whoring'. The Marquis had also visited Harriette Wilson, 'to tell me', she mocked, 'what a great man he was and how much he had been talked of in the world'.[34] His marriage to the French actress by whom he first sired five illegitimate children was breaking down in bitter circumstances, and Lord Wellesley was now keeping company with a Cyprian called Sally Douglas whom he could not keep faithful despite the gift of an elegantly furnished house, a silver dinner service, a carriage and copious quantities of precious stones. Arthur Wellesley thought it was his brother's fornications rather than his indolence that had kept him out of high office and that he would be better off castrated. The domestic lives of historical figures, Arthur now believed, should be whiter than white.

In early 1809 the country was caught up in the scandal of another avenging courtesan, Mary Anne Clarke, who was being tried in the House of Commons for allegedly selling commissions in the army which she gained through the influence she wielded over her protector, the Duke of York. Mrs Clarke shimmered and sparkled during the proceedings, the Duke was profoundly embarrassed, and Arthur Wellesley – whose name had been mentioned – sat through the trial feeling, along with most of the Commons, increasingly nervous. Harriette, following the events with the rest of the country, could note with interest the way in which a courtesan was able to bring parliamentary proceedings to a standstill.

At the same time as the Clarke trial, Lady Charlotte Wellesley, the wife of Henry, Arthur's youngest brother, ran off in a hackney coach with Arthur's best cavalry officer, Lord Paget, Marquis of Anglesey, future hero of Waterloo. This freed his abandoned wife, Lady Caroline Paget, to run off with the Marquis of Lorne. The scandal evoked by these high-profile divorces and remarriages was tremendous. 'The people in the streets talk of it – even the mob,' wrote Paget's brother-in-law, Lord Graves, in desperation.[35] European travellers sending home their descriptions of London society could scarely believe such a thing. With both his brothers publicly involved in broken marriages and his own marriage clearly unhappy, Arthur Wellesley could not afford to have his name linked to London's most popular Impure.

Shortly after Arthur Wellesley wed Kitty Packenham in 1806, Amy, now abandoned by Lorne, was considering an offer to take the name of a great favourite of the Wellesleys, Captain Benjamin Sydenham. Sydenham had originally been a lover of Julia's, but she 'wearied of his bold impertinence, and happily Amy succeeded in entangling him in her net'.[36] William Wellesley, another of his brothers, wrote to Arthur, amused to hear that the virtuous and loyal Sydenham 'was discovered viewing Blenheim the other day with a whore – they went by the names of Mr and Mrs Thompson – O the profligacy of the Age!!!'[37] The captain reasoned that it would simplify his and Amy's situation if she were to become Mrs Sydenham rather than Mrs Madden or Mrs Thompson, and, after a certain amount of negotiation and reshuffling, Amy did so, moving in the process from York Place to the captain's own West End house. Amy's relationship with Sydenham consolidated the bond between the Dubouchet girls and the Wellesleys.

Captain Sydenham, called by Harriette 'Colonel', had served under Arthur Wellesley in the war against Tipu Sultan and been aide-de-camp to Richard Wellesley when he was Governor General of India. Sydenham's devotion to duty, knowledge of imperial military and political life, and sharp intelligence quickly brought him into the Marquis's inner circle and in August 1805, when the Govenor General left his post and returned to England, Sydenham accompanied him.

When Benjamin Sydenham arrived in London in 1806 as the secretary and general 'minion' of Lord Wellesley, he had little money or experience of English politics and society.[38] But he was acutely intelligent and well read ('Amy tries his patience . . . with his passion for books; she is always taking them out of his hand, and making him look at her attitudes before the glass, or her attempts at the shawl dance,' Harriette reported[39]), and attractive and sharp enough to win over Amy Madden from the contending bids of Counts Beckendorff and Palmella. The former was the Russian Ambassador, whose sister Madame, later Princess, de Lieven, was the most influential woman in high society. ('It is not fashionable', Madame de Lieven said, 'where I am not.') The latter was the Portuguese Ambassador, whose annuity of £200 a year Amy accepted before disposing of him for Sydenham. Beckendorff and Palmella were both richer and more glamorous figures than their rival.

For several years Mrs Sydenham led 'a pure, virtuous, chaste and proper life',[40] even ending her parties several hours earlier, to suit the temperament of her lover. Harriette was to follow suit.

CHAPTER 10

Lord Ponsonby

———

In May 1806 in Sloane Street Harriette saw a stranger riding on horse-back with a Newfoundland dog by his side and she fell violently in love. 'I have never enjoyed one hour's health since,' she wrote in her *Memoirs*. 'Now, however, I look on all my past bitter suffering caused by this same love, which many treat as a plaything and a child, and which I believe to be one of the most arbitrary ungovernable passions in nature, as a wild dream, remembered by me merely as I recollect three days of delirium . . .'[1] The stranger was 'a very god!', Harriette told Amy; he was her 'fate', she told Fanny. 'Though he treated me ill and for ever destroyed my heart's affection,' she wrote twenty years later, 'I would compare him with no mortal.'[2] He was 'not the sort of man . . . that generally strikes the fancy of a very young female; – for he was neither young nor at all gaily dressed. No doubt he was very handsome; but it was that pale expressive beauty, which oftener steals upon us, by degrees, after having become acquainted, than strikes at first sight.' Harriette thought about her hero constantly, comparing him favourably with every other man she knew or met. 'If I could but touch with my hand, the horse he rode, or the dog he seems so fond of, I should be half wild with joy!' she believed.[3]

In the hope of seeing the stranger again, Harriette started to walk more often in the neighbouring parks. He always appeared after six o'clock; he

'Lord Ponsonby's meeting with Harriette at her own house', *Memoirs* was sometimes throwing stones in the water to coax his dog to swim, he was sometimes riding, but 'he always turned his head back, after he had passed me . . . whether he admired, or had, indeed, observed me, or whether he only looked back after his large dog, was what puzzled and tormented me. Better to have been merely observed by that fine noble-looking being, than adored by all the men on earth . . . thought I.'[4] One evening, sitting down to dinner with Fanny and Amy, Harriette 'felt a kind of presentiment come over' her, 'that if I went into Hyde Park at that moment, I should meet this stranger'. Off she went in her bonnet and shawl, accompanied for some of the way by a mocking Lord Alvanley. The park was empty, and after walking up and down for nearly an hour, she gave up hope and began home, meeting on the way an impoverished old woman. Wanting to give her some money but having none about her, Harriette ran after a gentleman she slightly knew and borrowed from him half a crown. Turning back to give the coin to the pauper, Harriette 'came immediately in contact with the stranger, whose person had been concealed by two large elms, and who might have been observing me for some time. I scarcely dared encourage the flattering idea.'[5] The horseman rode by, and Harriette thought she saw him blush.

It was Julia who identified him. One night he was at the opera, sitting in a nearby box. 'I have met him in society when I was a girl,' Julia said, 'but I was intimate with a girl to whom, when young, he proposed. Her wedding clothes were made; she used to sleep in my room, with his picture round her neck. She adored him beyond all that could be imagined of love and devotion, and, within a few days of their proposed marriage, he declared off. His excuse was that his father refused his consent. For many years . . . my friend's sufferings were severe; her parents trembled for her reason. No one was permitted to name her former lover in her presence. She is now Lady Conyngham.' The stranger, Julia confirmed, had since married 'the loveliest creature on earth'. He was Lord John Ponsonby, 'the handsomest man in England'.[6]

The 'sly, voluptuous and most luxurious' John Ponsonby was the eldest son of William Brabazon, First Baron Ponsonby, and Louisa Molesworth, daughter of Viscount Molesworth.[7] He succeeded his father in 1806, the year in which he also succeeded with Harriette Wilson. His grandparents were John Ponsonby, second son of the First Earl of Bessborough, and

Lady Elizabeth Cavendish, of the great Devonshire family. He was the cousin of Lady Caroline Lamb and therefore related by marriage to Frederic Lamb as well as to the Duke of Argyll. The Ponsonbys were a great sprawling clan who had virtually ruled Ireland since Cromwell gave Sir John Ponsonby an estate near Kilkenny; as staunch Whigs they kept the State provided with a steady flow of politicians, churchman and soldiers. Of John Ponsonby's four brothers, Richard was Bishop of Derry, and William was the celebrated major general who led the charge of the Union brigade on d'Erlon's corps at Waterloo and was killed by French lancers. His sister Mary married Charles, Second Earl Grey, future Whig Prime Minister.

Ponsonby's beauty, of which he was vain, was legendary. It was rumoured that as a young man he travelled through France at the height of the Revolution and was seized by the mob, strung up by his neck, and left hanging from a lantern. Seeing him there, a crowd of women protested that he was too handsome to die, whereupon he was cut down and carried home to be nursed back to health.

He was born at the family estate of Bishopscourt in County Kildare, in 1771. His father intended for him a political career, in keeping with family tradition, and he duly stood as MP for Tallaght in 1793 and for Dungarvan, in the Irish House of Commons, in 1798. Ponsonby's reserve and dislike of public speaking made parliament an unsuitable place for him: 'It is all I can do', he once said, 'to find nerve for "yes" or "no" when there is a question in the House, and that is in a whisper.'[8] He could relax only when slightly drunk and several descriptions suggest that under the influence of alcohol his character changed from taciturnity to easy charm. In 1826, the year after Harriette's *Memoirs* were published, Ponsonby became a diplomat.

Ponsonby's letters reveal him to be stubborn and opinionated and he was considered by his peers to be too indolent to take on a profession. The few memories of Ponsonby to survive present him as being something of a maverick. Harriette said that 'his humour exactly suited mine'[9] and he seems to have been the type to enjoy her irreverence. In 1826, *en route* to Argentina as Ambassador, he caused havoc by wearing only his underwear on deck. In Constantinople six years later, he was asked to give a speech to the Sultan which to be translated into Turkish by the Chief

Dragoman. A great number of dignitaries were present, standing in rows and holding banners and flags; with gravity and dignity Ponsonby unrolled his prepared script, and began to read, slowly counting 'one, two, three, four, five, six . . .' until he had reached 'fifty', 'occasionally modulating his voice as if he desired to make an impression upon the minds of his hearers, putting emphasis upon some numbers and smiling with satisfaction and pleasure when he reached the higher numbers of twenty to fifty. Of course, his excellency knew that the Sultan, his ministers, and the officials of the Court were not acquainted with the English language. On concluding, he turned to the interpreter and motioned him to speak.' After the Sultan had expressed his thanks, Ponsonby 'commenced to count from sixty upwards, pausing now and then on particular numbers, which by his voice and gesture, it would appear he desired especially to impress on His Imperial Majesty's mind'.[10] This same Sultan, ensuring that he was greeted with respect, had a low arch built at the entrance of his reception room which required visitors to enter on their hands and knees. Ponsonby did what was expected of him, but parted his coat tails and crawled backwards, presenting His Imperial Majesty with the ambassadorial behind.

Harriette's version of meeting Lord Ponsonby has about it the same self-conscious air of romance as the tale of her initial encounter with Julia Johnstone. Harriette liked to picture herself as the wanderer alone in nature, spying a kindred spirit and making a connection so immediate and so deep that few words were necessary to consolidate the bond. Her relationship with Ponsonby takes up more space in her *Memoirs* than any other affair related so far, and it strikes an entirely different note. Through love of Ponsonby, she sanctifies herself; with Ponsonby she became 'angelick Harriette'. Her love for him was doomed, eternal, as good as fiction. She equates her love for Ponsonby with her feelings for Fanny; the only person she loved more was her mother.[11] For the first time in her life, Harriette began to regret the 'unfortunate situation she had fallen into', fearing that her profession might make Lord Ponsonby think less of her. She lost interest in society and started to reflect on various sacrifices she might make or virtuous deeds she could perform in the hope of Ponsonby respecting her memory after her death. Ponsonby was sanctified too; Harriette presented nothing hypocritical or cruel in his treatment of her. At least, her portrait of him revealed little of what she really felt about his behaviour. Lord Ponsonby was to go down in posterity as her perfect man and their affair would be recorded as one perfect love: this was Harriette's revenge. She punished Ponsonby's treatment of her by painting him as the love-sick consort of the most notorious siren of the age. Her description of him was limp and lifeless enough to render him impotent.

Meanwhile, sitting in her opera box with Julia, Harriette found her heart was sinking fast. It had never occurred to her that the stranger might be married; he always looked so alone and unloved, so unbearably *sad* (a melancholic appearance, she later realized, that was due to the slow demise of his father). 'I resolved now to make no kind of advances to become acquainted with Lord Ponsonby; but on the very next evening, I indulged myself in passing his house at least fifty times. I saw and examined the countenances of his footmen, and the colour of his window curtains: even the knocker on his door escaped not my veneration.'[12] His wife, Fanny, was the youngest daughter of the formidable Lady Jersey, mistress to the Prince of Wales during his marriage to Princess Caroline. Lady Ponsonby was therefore the sister of the Lorne's mistress, Lady Charlotte. Fanny, 'beautiful beyond all description . . . an engaging, affectionate, gentle person' was treated by Ponsonby with 'affected contempt and brutality'.[13] Married at fifteen, Lady Ponsonby was deaf from scarlet fever. She spent her days playing with a mouse who lived in the wainscot. When her husband met Harriette Wilson, Fanny had just trained the mouse to eat from her hand.

Ponsonby and his wife left town for the summer and shut up house. Although 'half the fine young men in town were trying to please' her, Harriette went into mourning, and hung around outside Ponsonby's door in Curzon Street, hoping for signs of renewed life. One day, several months later, a letter arrived:

I have long been very desirous to make your acquaintance: will you let me? A friend of mine has told me something about you, but I am afraid you were then only laughing at me . . . I hope, at all events, that you will write me one line, so say you forgive me, and direct it to my house in town.[14]

Putting aside all anguished thoughts of poor Lady Ponsonby, Harriette answered:

For the last five months I have scarcely lived but in your sight, and everything I have done or wished, or hoped, or thought about, has had a reference to you and your happiness. Now tell me what you wish.[15]

Ponsonby's reply enclosed an exquisite watch. Their correspondence continued, and the happiness Harriette felt during this time was 'the purest, the most exalted, and the least allied to sensuality, of any I have ever experienced in my life'. Eventually the couple met: 'I heard the knock, and his footsteps on the stairs, and then that most godlike head uncovered, that countenance so pale, so still, so expressive, the mouth of such perfect loveliness, the fine, clear, transparent dark skin.'[16] She wept; he comforted her; they talked all night, her head on his breast. He told her he had first seen her two years ago when she lived at Somerstown, and that he was there when she first came out at the opera. She was spoken of by everyone, and being shy he feared her notoriety. When he saw her again, however, walking in the park, she looked so natural and unaffected and wild that he forgot that side of her life; and when he saw her give money to the old lady what he said was too flattering for Harriette to repeat. She longed to kiss him but he refused. 'No, not tonight! I could not bear your kiss tonight. We will dream about it till tomorrow.'[17]

As ever with Harriette, the stylistic monotony of the Ponsonby episode is occasionally relieved by a whiff of familiar cynicism – 'I am sure my readers are growing as tired of this dismal love story as I am'[18] – and a characteristic wink. 'Heavy work, ma'am, all this love and stuff, says my fair reader of sixty, taking off her spectacles . . . and my young reader does not like playing second fiddle, which is my own reason for hating novels.'[19] Left to her own devices, she would have preferred to leave out 'this love of mine, altogether', but her editor insisted on it. 'Nevertheless I will make shorter of our second night.'[20] True to her word, the second night is passed over swiftly. 'And then! – yes, and then, as Sterne says, – and then, – and then, – and then, – and then, – and then we parted.'[21] The nuts and bolts of the rest of their affair are hardly described. During their time together, 'my life produced very few anecdotes which I can recollect worth relating; for I had neither eyes, nor ears, nor thoughts, but for Ponsonby'.[22]

Harriette and Ponsonby 'seldom contrived to separate before five or six o'clock in the morning, and Ponsonby generally came to me as soon as it was dark. Nor did we always wait for the evening to see each other, though respect for Lady Ponsonby made us ever, by mutual consent, avoid all risk of wounding her feelings; therefore, almost every day after dinner, we met in the park, by appointment, not to speak, but only to look at one another.'[23] She could feel Ponsonby's arrival in his wife's opera box without having to look up; the air, Harriette said, 'suddenly became purer'.[24] Often, at the end of an evening together, 'finding it so difficult to separate', Harriette would drive to the House of Lords with him and wait in his coach half the night just for the pleasure of one last kiss, and accompany him back to his venerated front door. One night Ponsonby came late to Harriette's rooms and rather than wake her, he slipped a pearl ring on her finger and left a note under her pillow reading, *'Dors, cher enfant, je t'aime trop tendrement pour t'éveiller.'* Harriette began to think herself 'in the land of fairies!'[25] She shone, as lovers do, in his company, recalling that 'though I have never been called agreeable in all my life, I am convinced that I was never half so pleasant or so witty as in Ponsonby's society'.[26]

In order to make herself 'rather more worthy' of her protector and to 'improve [her] powers of consol[ation] and charming away all his cares',[27] Harriette used the time they were apart to continue the educational process begun by Frederic Lamb. When Ponsonby was away one time, she set off with her maid to the Castle Inn at Salt Hill, on the Bath road. Here she proposed to study: 'The word study sounded very well, I thought, as I pronounced it.' Unpacking her trunk of books, Harriette

sat down to consider which of them I should begin with, in order to become clever and learned at the shortest notice. Let me see! What knowledge will be likely to make me most agreeable to him? O! politics. What a pity that he does not like something less dry, and more lively! But no matter! And I turned over the leaves of my History of England, for George the Second and George the Third, and I began reading the Debates in Parliament. Let me consider! continued I, pausing. I am determined to stick firm to the opposition side, all my life; because Ponsonby must know best; and yet it goes against the grain of my late aristocratical prejudices, which, by-the-bye, only furnish a proof how wrong-headed young girls often are.[28]

She tried to make a 'little Whig' of herself and read a speech of Charles James Fox. 'This man, thought I, when I had finished his speech, appears to have much reason on his side; but then all great orators seem right, till they are contradicted by better reasoners.' But finding that all her instincts were Tory ('Opposition is such a losing game! And then I have a sneaking kindness for my king'), Harriette decided that 'out of respect for Lord Ponsonby' she would 'stand neuter in regard to politics'.[29] Shakespeare, who she would love reading all her life, was too beautiful to be considered study, so she settled down to a history lesson. 'The Greeks employed me for two whole days, and the Romans six more: I took down notes of what I thought most striking. I then read Charles the Twelfth, by Voltaire, and liked it less than most people do; and then, Rousseau's Confessions, then, Racine's Tragedies, and afterwards, Boswell's Life of Johnson. I allowed myself only ten minutes for my dinner.' Her work was interrupted by the arrival of the Pitcher family, who, 'having once taken a fancy to my society, I had no chance but returning to town as fast as possible'.[30]

Back in London the pattern of Harriette's days otherwise continued much the same, but she remained faithful to her lord. On one occasion, Lamb appeared at her house at ten o'clock in the evening. Being told by Harriette's servant that it was too late to visit, he none the less admitted himself. He talked to her first of his feelings and then 'grew desperate, and proceeded to very rough, I may say brutal, violence, to gratify his desires against my fixed determination'. In self-defence, Harriette pulled his hair until it came out by the roots; in retaliation, Lamb put his hand on her throat, 'saying, while he nearly stopped my breath and occasioned me almost the pangs of suffocation, that I should not hurt him another instant. He spoke this in a smothered voice and I did in truth believe that my last moments had arrived. Another moment would have decided the business; but he, thank God, relinquished his grasp at my throat. He is, however, mistaken if he believes I have ever forgotten the agony of that moment.'[31]

Harriette refers again to this event in one of her few surviving letters, reminding Ponsonby in years to come that she was 'nearly choaked' by Lamb *'pour vos beaux yeux* rather than be unfaithful to you'.[32] Panicking about his reputation after his attack, Lamb quickly spread around Harriette's friends a breezy version of her forceful rejection of his ardent passion. Harriette was so in love with Lord Ponsonby, he joked, that she had eyes for no one else. Harriette was therefore silenced and the first time she described the experience was in her *Memoirs*. But even here, in her harrowing account of Lamb's behaviour, she draws again on his stinginess, as though this fault were somehow comparable with his physical violence: 'I am sure Mr Frederic Lamb cannot assert that, on the day I believed he meant to have been my last, he had ever given me one single guinea, or the value of a guinea.'[33] For Harriette, Lamb's fault lay in breaking the rules, one of which was gentlemanlike behaviour and the other, more important, was respect for her professionalism. By not paying her, or by not paying her enough, he cheapened her. And Harriette was never in any doubt about her value and the privileged position of those on whom she bestowed her favours.

Out riding with Fanny in Hyde Park, they would find their carriage quickly surrounded by admirers. But because 'that adored, sly, beautiful face of Ponsonby's was fixed on me *à la distance*', Harriette encouraged all the 'trotting beaux' to Fanny's side. Once, walking in the park with her brother George, they happened across Ponsonby riding with his sister Lady Howick, who commented on the handsome pair. 'Ponsonby always described this as one of the very happiest moments of his life, nor could all his dread of notoriety, his constitutional reserve, and his sense of what was due, both to his wife and sister, prevent his acknowledging . . . that we had loved each other for more than a year.'[34] 'Good-natured' Lady Howick tut-tutted and then suggested that young George might like to go to sea as a midshipman, which thrilled the boy but devastated his mother. However much Ponsonby persevered with the idea, George stayed at home in Queen Street.[35]

One evening, about three years into their relationship, Harriette accompanied Ponsonby to the House of Lords and waited in the carriage until daylight for his return. When he appeared he seemed careworn and distressed. 'You are much fatigued, dear Ponsonby, said I, – I only wish to heaven I might stay with you, and take care of you for ever.' But it was not to be: Ponsonby produced from his pocket a letter that Harriette rightly guessed was to secure her the lifetime's 'provision' of which he had often spoken. He offered her £200 a year, which sum Harriette refused, knowing he could ill afford it. 'He will provide his purse with me, thought I. While he lives and loves me, – and I will never look forward, nor provide for one hour after Ponsonby shall be lost to me.' Harriette tore the letter into pieces and threw it out of the window.[36] The generosity of her gesture would be hard for her to forget. 'It is very hard upon us', Ponsonby then said, 'that we may not pass the whole of our lives together; but then be assured of this truth; and I hope that it may afford you consolation, happen what will, my affection for you, to whom I certainly owe some of the happiest hours I have ever known, will last while I exist.' As the carriage reached his door, he gave Harriette one last kiss, 'as long and as ardent as our first'. Harriette, unable to speak, 'kissed his hand eagerly and fervently, as he was hurrying out of the coach'. She never saw Ponsonby again.[37]

Ponsonby left her, Harriette told Byron, 'because *Mrs Fanny* would have it so',[38] but soon afterwards he began an involvement with Harriette's younger sister, Sophia, aged fourteen and just launched as a courtesan. Harriette is silent on this liaison in her *Memoirs*, perhaps because she found it too humiliating an incident to reveal to a readership she was bent on amusing. Ponsonby was not acting with unusual indifference; the traffic of lovers between the sisters and Julia seems to have been fairly constant. Like Lorne, who had traded Harriette for Amy, and like other lovers of the Dubouchet girls, Ponsonby saw them as interchangeable. Sir Henry Mildmay, currently Julia's protector, left her for an affair with Harriette; James Napier, a rich landowner who first pursued Fanny, was donated by her to Julia, who needed the money. But Ponsonby's relationship with Sophia made Harriette ill with grief and jealousy. 'Lord,' she wrote to Byron in 1823, 'if you could only suffer for one single day the agony of mind *I* endured for more than two years after Ponsonby left me . . . you would bless your stars and your good fortune, *blind, deaf* and *lame* at eighty-two, so that you could sleep an hour in forgetfulness or eat a little bit of *batter pudding*. Heavens! How I have prayed for *death*, nights and days and months together, merely as a *rest* from suffering . . .'[39] In the sentimental version of her illness, Harriette turned to charitable works, visiting Lord Craven's old housekeeper, imprisoned for debt in Newgate. ' "I wish I could pay your debt," said I, panting for breath, as usual, and speaking with pain and difficulty." '[40] She took home with her a sick girl she found sitting outside Ponsonby's house in the rain; Harriette then took to sitting outside his house in the rain herself. In the rendition of her collapse she related in the letter to Ponsonby of 1832, Harriette was more philosophical:

My indignation expressed in many letters is quite real and quite natural – were I to swear to you that I considered your conduct (in cutting me to attach a young *stupid* sister not half as handsome) with my feeling short of strong resentment and disgust you would not (if you know anything of human nature) behave thus – during three months of severe painful *illness* – I had time for reflection – and with a good deal of benevolence in my motive I could not but wish to think of you with less bitterness and dislike. It mattered not to you my opinion – but to myself hate was feverish and a *bore*. The result of calm candid inward reasoning on the subject brought me to this conclusion . . .[41]

Her *Memoirs* 'quote' the following letter, written to Ponsonby from Harriette's sickbed when she was strong enough to wield a pen once more:

Scarcely a month has elapsed since I possessed, or believed I possessed, with health, reputed beauty, and such natural spirits 'as were wont to set the table in a roar', all my highest flights of imagination had ever conceived or dreamed of perfect happiness on earth . . . Alas! I had not considered how unreal and fleeting must ever be the glories of this life, and I was, as a child, unprepared for the heavy affliction which has fallen on my heart like a thunder-bolt, withering all healthful verdue, and crushing its hopes for ever.

In encouraging so deep an attachment for a married man, I have indeed been very hardened; but, till now, I call my God to witness, I have never, in my life, reflected seriously on any subject . . .

Oh! I have known such moments of deep anguish, as I could never describe to you, Ponsonby, my dear Ponsonby! I throw myself on my knees before you; I raise the eyes you have so often professed to love and admire, now disfigured and half closed by constant weeping, towards heaven . . .[42]

Whatever Harriette wrote, Ponsonby remained unmoved. He asked her to return all his letters, and she duly complied. He had also given her letters he had received from his previous lover Lady Conyngham, and this act of blind trust would later result in a governmental crisis.

What are we to make of 'all this love and stuff'? How can we interpret the unnerving shift of gear in Harriette's *Memoirs* from comedy to tragedy, from mocking her lovers to abject adoration of them? She lards her woeful tale in order to satisfy the demands of her publisher, but this does not totally account for what is going on here. It is interesting that in a long career of feigning devotion, the only man Harriette was genuinely to fall for was already married. She recognized from the start the hopelessness of her feelings but nurtured them none the less. Because Ponsonby was unavailable, Harriette, who loathed being trapped, could afford to open the floodgates. But is this how she experienced love, as a sentimental fiction? Whenever she writes of her love for Ponsonby, the untutored natural style that characterizes the voice of her *Memoirs* becomes self-consciously 'literary', artificial, clichéd, and Harriette employs the stock images of the novels she claimed to despise. Not being able to write well about love, on the other hand, is hardly new; many an original voice has resorted to the mimicry of popular fiction in order to dramatize his or her most violent and vulnerable feelings. To see one's life in terms of a story we are writing, or in terms of stories we have read, is just one way of organizing chaotic experience and need not detract from the reality of the feelings involved. Harriette Wilson was always drawn to stories and she used them for various purposes; in this instance, adopting the language of a melodrama enabled her to describe an experience for which she might otherwise not have been able to find words: she had no natural voice for weakness and despair.

Harriette was twenty-three when Ponsonby deserted her. 'Never in the pathetics for long' and hating to be thought a maudlin figure, she was hurt, humiliated and defeated. 'My mind was now a complete blank. My imagination was exhausted, my castle had fallen to the ground, and I never expected to rebuild it, for even my cool judgement told me that Ponsonbys were not often to be met with.'[43] This was the first time that she had made the error of mistaking a business arrangement for a love affair. She would never again refuse money from a protector or allow her feelings to get the better of her, but she would continue to make the mistake of believing that she was appreciated beyond her sexual celebrity, that those she was closest to valued her as a friend as well as a courtesan.

Just as Harriette was at her lowest ebb, the Mary Anne Clarke scandal broke.

CHAPTER 11

The Mary Anne Clarke Affair

Mary Anne Thompson was born in 1776 in the tenement slums of Ball and Pin Alley, Chancery Lane. She eloped aged fifteen with Joseph Clarke, the son of a wealthy builder living in Angel Court, Snow Hill, and she married him at seventeen, after the birth of her first two children. When her infatuation wore off, Mary Anne saw that Joseph Clarke was a slothful drunk, incapable of providing for a family that now included a third child. After years of hardship she left him and, weighing up her options, Mary Anne decided on the life of a kept woman. Pretty, witty and gay, she moved through various well-heeled lovers until she caught the eye of the Duke of York, the King's second – and favourite – son, and Commander-in-Chief of the army. In 1803, the Duke installed Mary Anne and her children in a grand four-storey house at 18 Gloucester Place, between Portman Square and Baker Street. She had arrived: only Mrs Fitzherbert was superior to Mrs Clarke.

Mary Anne Clarke immediately set about the business of furnishing and decorating the house, making it fit for a prince. The Duke, whose loveless marriage had not produced children, wanted a family home, comfortable and relaxed, with the sound of infants playing and the smell of good food rising up from the kitchen. Having no idea what it cost to maintain his lifestyle, he gave Mary Anne £500 as a house-warming gift,

George Cruikshank, *The Duke of York*

to be spent on 'some little necessary things in plate and linen'.[1] The plate had to be of the best quality, and Mrs Clarke bought the silver service which had once belonged to the Duc de Berri. A tea service was also needed, as was a breakfast service and cutlery, crystal to drink from and an epergne to grace the centre of the table. Mary Anne needed dresses and jewels to complement her new position; her children and mother were also expected to be elegantly attired. The house wanted chandeliers, looking glasses, carpets, sofas, beds, chairs, paintings, writing desks. Staff had to be employed and dressed in livery, and Mrs Clarke took on a retinue of twenty servants; her new butler had been ten years with Lord Chesterfield, her coachman seven years with Mrs Fitzherbert. A cellar had to be stocked – the Duke drank heavily – and because he was very particular, the kitchen needed to be filled with his favourite food. 'There was always very elegant dinners went up,' said the housekeeper of the meals provided by the cooks at Gloucester Place; 'and what they could not do came from the pastry cooks . . . If there was any dinner found fault with by His Royal Highness she [Mrs Clarke] would have another.'[2] The carriage the Duke gave his mistress to use on her shopping trips was soon supplemented by a second one which could take her at weekends to her cottage in the country, so that she could be near him when he returned to his marital home at Oatlands. This required more horses, grooms, footmen, drivers. The Duke's housewarming present had been swallowed up long ago, and Mrs Clarke found that her allowance of £1,000 a year to run the royal establishment fell well short of what was required to keep her out of debt. The money the Duke provided only just paid for the servants' wages and liveries: Mary Anne Clarke needed three times that amount. Because of her position, tradesmen were more than willing to give her credit and so it was credit that she lived on. Credit, and what she earned through accepting bribes for influencing the Commander-in-Chief to obtain army commissions.

It was this enterprising scheme that brought Mary Anne Clarke to public attention. By the time of the House of Commons inquiry, the Duke had abandoned her for another woman and rescinded his promise to pay £400 a year towards her future living costs. Mrs Clarke wanted revenge, and her avenging angel came in the form of Colonel Gwyllym Lloyd Wardle, a forty-six-year-old Welshman and Radical member for Oakhampton,

Devon. Wardle, who was close to the Duke of Kent, the brother and bitter enemy of the Duke of York, befriended Mrs Clarke, promising to furnish her house if she went along with his plan to reveal to the Commons her involvement in the army commissions and promotions scheme. Colonel Wardle was after glory – nothing would give him more credit with the populace than to appear as the exposer of vice in high society – and Mary Anne had nothing to lose; she 'gayly admitted' to every angle of her professional life. It was the Duke of York's reputation that was at stake, and the inquiry that followed attempted to establish his complicity in the bribery by which his mistress administered army appointments in order to pay the bills.

Mrs Clarke was called to appear before six hundred MPs in the Palace of Westminster on 1 February 1809. She was unfazed by such an audience; in fact it was more shocking to the Members to see a woman in the House of Commons than it was to the courtesan to stand before such an august committee. 'When summoned to the bar,' an eyewitness wrote, 'she trips with light and airy steps and smirking countenance, as if she was going into a ballroom.' She dressed for the occasion with typical intelligence, wearing 'a long, powder-blue silk pelisse of classical simplicity, with high waist, and décolleté neck-line edged with lace. On her arm she carried a white swan's down muff.' Perched on her head was a lilac-coloured velvet hat with a veil, 'which', one journalist observed, 'at no time is let down over her face to hide it'.[3] 'Mrs Clarke,' William Wilberforce wrote that night in his diary, 'elegantly dressed, consumately impudent, and very clever. After two hours of cross examination in the Old Bailey way she had clearly got the better of the struggle.'[4] Sir Francis Burdett, the Radical who had seconded Colonel Wardle's motion for an investigation into the Duke, described Mary Anne Clarke as standing at the bar of the House 'like a potent witch, and no sooner did the sable band encounter her, than their faculties seemed to be withered, as it were, by wand of an enchantress'.[5] Mrs Clarke delighted the House: her smart, witty answers to the stodgy questions she received at the hands of Spencer Perceval had her audience in fits. It was easy to see why the Duke had been so infatuated by this woman: she was saucy, clever, beautiful and sharp as a blade. Other women paled by comparison. The public adored her, and Mary Anne Clarke became for the month of February 1809 almost a national heroine. She was a courageous mother abused by a royal prince; she was prepared to expose corruption in high places and to lay her reputation and the privacy of her children on the line in order to see justice done: 'All other business is at a stand,' complained Sir Arthur Wellesley, 'and nobody talks or thinks of anything but Mrs Clarke.'[6]

For Spencer Perceval, Chancellor of the Exchequer, father of twelve and staunch Old Testament Tory, the impudent, ungrateful Cyprian was too much to take.

Her sarcastic insolence, [he thundered,] her playful pleasantry, as if there were nothing in her evidence that weighed heavily upon herself, her general cleverness and versatility, the art and wit she displayed in answering those questions which she thought proper to answer, the most unblushing effrontery with which she disclosed things which would have abashed the boldest witness, the mode in which she was continually evading the questions which she wished to avoid, presenting new topics to the examiner, misleading him, turning him beside his object, and at last, when pressed and driven to extremity, sheltering herself in a total forgetfulness . . . The house cannot forget it . . . Perhaps . . . they might wish to forget but they cannot but remember how indulgently they tolerated her jokes, how they seemed to forget her vice in her wit, and be almost reconciled to her infamy by her manner of displaying it.[7]

No one can have been more relieved than Perceval when the inquiry ended on 23 February (Harriette's twenty-third birthday), after three intensive weeks. The next night the theatre in Drury Lane caught fire and the blaze illumined the whole of London. 'I think that even the dreadful calamity of the burning of Drury Lane will not be without its advantages,' wrote Fanny Williams Wynn of the Mary Anne Clarke scandal, 'if it makes people think and talk of something else.'[8]

Harriette does not say whether she ever met Mrs Clarke. They were not friends but it seems likely that the two women would have seen one another in the theatre and passed one another as they rode in the park. Many of Harriette's circle attended the inquiry about the Duke and would have given her first-hand descriptions of the woman who made a fool of Spencer Perceval. Here was a courtesan who had practically brought the Establishment to a standstill while executing the most magnificent revenge on her lover. The Duke was utterly humiliated; his love letters – written at the most senselessly infatuated stage of his relationship with Mary Anne –

had been read out to the Commons and were mercilessly lampooned by versifiers and cartoonists; the trivial details of his domestic life had been exposed to the amusement of all. He was left shorn of dignity; children sang songs about him in the streets and when throwing a coin, instead of 'Heads or tails?', people called, 'Duke or Darling?', referring to the term His Highness used to address Mrs Clarke. Although the House found him innocent – or rather ignorant – of involvement in his mistress's business affairs, the Duke still tendered his resignation as Commander-in-Chief. It was Mary Anne Clarke who had won the day.

The story of Mary Anne Clarke, like that of Harriette Wilson and any woman who becomes a media favourite, is a tangle of fact and fiction, but she emerges from the medley of contemporary accounts as an intelligent, reckless gambler who glowed when she was gazed upon. The similarities between herself and Mrs Clarke cannot have been missed by Harriette, and no doubt she took careful note of the next major incident in Mary Anne Clarke's adventures, every detail of which was published by a salacious press.

Mrs Clarke had written her memoirs. Eighteen thousand copies had been printed although they had not yet appeared in the shops. There was nothing new in this: women had used kiss-and-tell to avenge themselves on faithless lovers throughout the eighteenth century, and many courtesans had sold their stories for a healthy sum. What was striking about Mary Anne Clarke's promise of a full revelation of her life was the timing: there was no better climate in which to have her memoirs appear than during the anti-monarchical fervour that followed the Commons inquiry. Before the investigation took place, Mary Anne had threatened that if the Duke did not pay her annuity she would publish 'every circumstance [he] ever communicated to me'. Given her popularity and the soiled image of the royal family, her annuity was quickly reinstated, plus a promise of £200 a year for her two daughters following her death. In addition, on 1 April, Mrs Clarke agreed to receive £7,000 (she later raised the sum to £10,000) for suppressing her story. Mary Anne Clarke's memoirs were duly burned, and the printer received £1,500 for his trouble. The only copy left was kept by the Joint Paymaster General, Lord Chichester, who had negotiated the purchase. Her moment of glory was over: when the public heard that Mrs Clarke had willingly allowed herself to be bought out of exposing the fallibility of the House of Hanover she found herself ostracized. Harriette's respect for her would not have diminished one jot by her action; what would have struck Harriette is that money could just as easily be made by what you don't publish as by what you do.

Mary Anne Clarke's star was falling. She fell out with Wardle over the payment for her furniture (which promise he now revoked), and took him to court, where she won her case. Then she left London to live in a cottage in Fulham where she prepared another book, *The Rival Princes*. This second book, besides exposing the machinations between the rival parties of the Dukes of York and Kent and the hyprocritical behaviour of Wardle, used the occasion to make it absolutely clear that she had not 'incurred the exposure of myself, children, and family together with abuse, anxiety of mind, and fatigue of person, during my examination in Parliament from a pure PATRIOTIC ZEAL TO SERVE THE PUBLIC'.[9] She had done it for money, just as she did everything: Mary Anne Clarke was a professional. When it appeared in 1810, *The Rival Princes* sold well and Mrs Clarke was once more proclaimed a heroine.

While the Mary Anne Clarke scandal was taking over the country, thoughts of money and revenge were beginning to occupy Harriette's mind as well. She had no reason to complain about lack of income while she was under Ponsonby's protection. But she had refused his continuing support, and while she had enough to live on comfortably – even offering to pay her nephew's, George Woodcock's, school fees – her lifestyle was extravagant. Her memoirs describe Harriette as lying low for a while following Ponsonby's departure, unable to fall in love again and uninterested in the men who pursued her. No specific protectors are mentioned, and her narrative drifts off during this period into anecdotes about the lives of her sisters and other characters about town. If she really was refusing male attention while she was in mourning, it would have been hard for Harriette to keep up her profile as the most fashionable courtesan in London; it seems most likely that any silence in her life at this point was due to men being cut out of her *Memoirs* rather than excluded at the time from her bed. Harriette always needed attention and always needed money, and Mrs Clarke had provided a blueprint for the future.

CHAPTER 12

Sophia

In the year following the Mary Anne Clarke scandal, the Marquis of Lorne, who had come into his title of Sixth Duke of Argyll, married Lady Caroline Paget, the divorced wife of the Marquis of Anglesey. Amy had born the Duke a son, whom she called Campbell and who she hoped would be recognized, by Scottish Law, as the legitimate heir to the dukedom. Argyll provided Amy with a handsome annuity but remained uninterested in any future greatness she felt was owing to the child. Amy retaliated by ensnaring the Honourable Berkeley Paget, Lord Anglesey's brother, who left his wife and children in order to live openly with her, and was thus cut by such luminaries as the Duke of York. 'For beyond a doubt,' Harriette commented wryly, 'a man ought to be of royal blood before he presumes to commit adultery.'[1] Julia professed to be pregnant by Sir Henry Mildmay, a leading dandy, and Colonel Cotton was back on the scene. Sophia, now fifteen, moved on from Ponsonby to Viscount Deerhurst, who lived in Half Moon Street, across the road from the family home. Harriette narrates this episode as though Deerhurst had been Sophia's first lover.

The eldest son of the Earl of Coventry, Lord Deerhurst was first cousin to the Duke of Argyll and ten years older than Sophia. Harriette describes him, as she was to describe anything involving Sophia, as contemptible,

Sheraton Washing Comode, *The Book of Decorative Furniture*

but other reports of Deerhurst suggest he was an attractive man, 'distinguished for his good looks and manly bearing', the 'life and soul of the party', the 'cock of the walk'.[2] Deerhust had an ailing wife, Emma, daughter of the first Earl of Beauchamp, who died in 1810 after four years of loveless marriage. He was famous for 'hastening down Piccadilly after some pretty girl or other'[3] and his interest in Sophia seems to have preceded and immediately succeeded his bereavement. Sophia had the same dark, glossy hair as her sisters and clear white skin, with brown eyes framed by heavy lids and strong brows. Her mouth, however, was characterless, thin and weak. It was her weakness that men seemed to like; Sophia didn't have the bite of Amy or Harriette and was easily pliable in a way that her sisters were not. She combined unquestioning obedience with sexual looseness, seeming to be at the same time both dutiful wife and transgressive whore. It was an appealing mix, and for the four years during which Sophia sold herself she attracted a good deal of attention.

Harriette's dislike of Sophia was no doubt fired by jealousy over the Ponsonby episode, and in order to distance herself from her younger sister she describes Sophia as being the very opposite of herself. Harriette gives us a portrait of someone weak, dull, humourless and naive; someone for whom Ponsonby, who liked strong, interesting, witty and sophisticated women such as Harriette, would have only scant interest. One of the many mocking stories Harriette tells about Sophia is that before Deerhurst succeeded with her, he once encountered her walking down South Audley Street bringing Amy a black pudding wrapped in newspaper for her supper. Mortified on being discovered holding so undignified an object, Sophia panicked and folded it up in her new dress. But when Deerhurst held out his hand, she had no choice but to let the pudding surreptitiously fall to the ground so that she could greet him. '"Miss! Miss!" bawled out an Irish labourer picking the article up and wiping it clean with the sleeve of his filthy jacket, "How comed you let go o' this and never miss it?"' Sophia coloured and ran off too fast for Deerhurst, who was greatly amused, to catch up with her.[4]

But catch up with her he soon did, and 'having forcibly obtained all he wished', Deerhurst then returned the 'dreadfully frightened' girl to her family, feigning dismay at the distress he had caused her parents and sisters, and claiming to have spent the night with her in conversation alone – which, according to Harriette's portrait of Sophia, seems more impossible than unlikely. Never bright, Sophia was also feeble; hers seems to have been the type of character to go along with whatever was asked of her. Nor did she have many ideas or discernible opinions of her own, which meant that Sophia tended to agree with her converser on all points and echo him on every issue. 'All she was blameable for', wrote Harriette, 'was that obstinate innocent face of hers, in keeping up a sly intercourse with a man like Lord Deerhurst, and throwing herself under his protection at an age when girls less shy-looking had been afraid to have listened or spoken to any man, unsanctioned by the presence of their mother or sister.'[5] The jewels Deerhurst had given Sophia were paste, Harriette informed her; the man was not only profligate but parsimonious. He also had poor standards of personal hygiene; even Sophia complained that he was sparing of soap and water and thought that running a dirty wet brush over his hair had the same effect as washing it.

Still, once Sophia Dubouchet had been returned by Deerhurst, she chose his protection over that of her parents and meekly agreed to become his mistress. The viscount took her to an address where she could not be found. John and Amelia Dubouchet applied to Deerhurst for 'a provision' for their daughter, 'with a threat of law-proceedings in case of refusal. The only legal plea for obtaining a provision for a girl thus unfortunately situated was that of the parents having lost her domestic services. Deerhurst, after some months, at last said that if Sophia remained with him he would settle three-hundred pounds a year on her, as long as no proof of inconstancy to him should be established against her; but, on such an event taking place, the annuity was to be reduced to an allowance of one hundred a-year.'[6] John and Amelia Dubouchet were happy to concede.

Harriette presents Deerhurst as a social embarrassment. One night, when she was entertaining to supper her new lover, the young Duke of Leinster, his cousin, Henry de Roos, and Sophia, Deerhurst was announced.

'Dear me, how tiresome,' said Sophia.

'Do not send him here, pray,' said Leinster and De Roos in the same breath. I went down to ask him what he wanted, and informed him of my dinner-party, with whom I knew he was unacquainted.

'Oh, I wish much to know the Duke of Leinster, so pray do introduce me,' said Deerhurst.

'No,' I answered, 'I shall do no such thing. That's frank and flat. If you don't like Sophia to dine here, you may, with my consent, take her away with you, but I will never present you to any friend of mine. Sophia told you, this morning, that she was to meet the Duke of Leinster and his cousin.'[7]

Harriette continued to refuse Deerhurst entry; he continued to insist and at last succeeded in intruding himself on the company. Leinster took an immediate dislike to him and did little to disguise it; Henry de Roos ignored the uninvited guest. Deerhurst, not to be discouraged by the ill manners of two mere boys, placed himself next to Sophia.

'Well, Soph, my love, are you glad to see me?'

'Yes, I am very glad indeed,' replied Sophia.

'I'll tell you something, Lord Deerhurst,' said I. 'I do not like quarrelling with people, especially in my own house; but, seriously, I must tell you that these gentlemen expected to meet Sophia and me only, and your intrusion is really a little cool.'

Sophia said I was quite right, it was really very cool indeed, and she had heard His Grace request that we would fix on a day when nobody else was coming.[8]

Harriette suggested that Sophia show the assorted company the jewels Deerhurst had given her. When Sophia proudly displayed them, 'every body laughed heartily, but the loudest laughter of our party was Viscount Deerhurst'.

'And then,' said Deerhurst, trying to recover himself, 'and then, having won the lady by dint of these valuable jewels, Robinson, the attorney of Bolton Street, first draws up an agreement to secure to her an annuity of three hundred a year, and the next day tells you his agreement is not worth sixpence!!'

There was only one of our society who carried politeness so far as to seem amused at such disgusting profligacy . . . Leinster and De Roos, considering themselves too young to set an example, or reform the age, fixed their eyes steadily on the carpet, while De Roos's fair cheek was tinged with a deep blush. Sophia alone joined Lord Deerhurst in his laugh; declaring that it was very funny to be sure.

'Lord Deerhurst,' said I, 'Sophia is my sister, and if she chooses to submit to insult and ill usage from you, it shall not be in my house, where you were not invited.'

Sophia immediately worked herself up into a passion of tears, declaring that she did not want to be insulted, and would much rather not return to Lord Deerhurst, who, she was sure, was a very nasty man indeed, and hardly ever washed his head.[9]

Deerhurst took Sophia home, the rest of the party went on to Amy's. Amy wore a 'yellow satin dress fastened round the waist with a gold band. Her profuse raven locks were entirely unadorned, and her neck, arms, and fingers were covered with glittering jewels of every colour.' Fanny was dressed in a pale pink crêpe dress with her dimpled arms uncovered to display her bracelets of plaited hair clasped with a large ruby; Harriette wore her usual 'rich figured white French gauze, over white satin' with her hair unadorned and long diamond, ruby and turquoise earrings. Julia was also present, in a white silvered lama, on gauze, and a Turkish turban of bright blue, fringed with gold.[10] Harriette met for the first time Fanny's new protector, Colonel Parker, an officer in the Artillery who seemed seriously in love with Fanny. 'She shall bear my name', he said, 'and I will show her all the respect a wife can require, and she shall always find me a gentleman.' I could not, however, help thinking that Fanny, with her strictly honest principles, her modest, amiable character, and her beauty, ought to have been Parker's wife instead of his mistress, and therefore I did not advise her to live with him.'[11]

After several months, Lord Deerhurst moved Sophia into 'two dark small parlours near Grosvenor Place', and here the usual coterie of fashionables whiled away the afternoons in search of entertainment. But, as Sophia 'never opened her lips . . . beyond a mere yes or no',[12] what entertainment took place in her premises had to be provided by the guests themselves. On one occasion when Harriette was visiting, she found Sophia sitting mute in the company of Colonel Berkeley, a young man of twenty-two with a reputation of attacking 'both old and young, virtuous and wicked, handsome and ugly, maid, wife and widow' and was now clearly attempting to pounce on Sophia.[13] The tired afternoon was passing pleasantly enough between the three of them when suddenly Deerhurst burst into the room 'in an agony of tears . . . blubbering and wiping his eyes with a very dirty, little old red pocket handkerchief' and declared, 'Oh Sophie, I never thought you would have used me in this way.'[14] The scene continued, with Deerhurst 'rushing out . . . like the strolling representative of a tragic king in a barn, and seating himself on the stairs near the street door to sob and blubber more at his ease'. Sophia, ever vague, was nonplussed and Harriette insisted on her sister's innocence, before surmising that Deerhurst had cooked up the drama in order to get out of paying Sophia her full annuity. Colonel Berkeley had been planted – not unwillingly – by the Viscount in order to get his mistress off his hands. Deerhurst was not only concerned to save money; he was also about to remarry. In 1811 he wed Lady Mary Beauclerk, daughter of the Duke of St Albans.

It seems as if another of Harriette's sisters became involved with a member of the Coventry clan at around 1812. A letter in *Bell's Life in London* from someone who knew the Dubouchet family well suggests that Julia Dubouchet, three years younger than Sophia and 'an affectionate child', was involved with Deerhurst's younger brother, Thomas-Henry, and bore him several children. Julia, the correspondent writes, 'clung to the House of Coventry through poor Tom's days of adversity, and died early, leaving some unprotected orphans'.[15] This is all that is known of Julia Dubouchet's career as a courtesan; Harriette never mentions her.

Colonel Berkeley, otherwise known as William, Lord Fitzhardinge, was first cousin to Lord Craven. His brother, Augustus, was at some point a lover of Harriette's. They were the illegitimate sons of Mary Cole, daughter of a tradesman, and the Fifth Earl of Berkeley, owner of the ancient Berkeley Castle in Gloucestershire and of great estates in Mayfair. He had, his youngest brother Grantley recalled, 'very considerable mental powers' which he 'marred' by his 'inherent dislike to the best society. I have often heard him say that he hated fine ladies and gentlemen, and in their company was terribly bored.' As a youth he had been in the circle of the Prince of Wales, but as he grew older he dropped his old friends and began to mix with actresses and other 'second-class women', usually having one, but sometimes two, of them under his protection.[16]

One afternoon Harriette and Sophia agreed to accompany Colonel Berkeley and 'that young savage', Augustus Berkeley, on a trip to Richmond. Harriette's account of the conversation that took place during the excursion reveals much about Sophia's naivity and also about the complex etiquette between courtesan and protector:

Sophia said it was a charming day.

'The atmosphere', I observed, 'is heavy I think, and unhealthy.'

'Oh, quite shocking,' Sophia immediately replied, 'I am absolutely ill with it already.' . . .

'How delicious this is,' said the Colonel [referring to a boat trip].

'I never saw anything so beautiful,' echoed Sophia.

I remarked that I was a little giddy.

'So am I,' said Sophia, 'very giddy indeed.'

In less than an hour, I mentioned that the air of the river had given me an appetite, and Sophia, of course, had never been so hungry in all her life!

[The day continued into night.] . . . I, by this time, considered that I had talked quite enough for one evening. I therefore endeavoured, with all my might, to call Sophia out, and draw her into some kind of conversation.

Berkeley was beginning to consider himself a little trifled with, and, being naturally abrupt in such cases, he told her flatly that, if she meant to refuse him after all, she ought not to have admitted him so often.

Sophia continued to hint, with proper delicacy and due modest blushes, that her living with him or not must depend on what his intentions were: in other words, she gently intimated that, as yet, she was ignorant what settlement he meant to make on her. The gay handsome Colonel Berkeley's vanity being now so deeply wounded, he in sudden rage, entirely lost sight of what was due to the soft sex, at least that part of it which had been so hard on him.

'Do you fancy me then so humble and so void of taste, as to buy with my money the reluctant embraces of any woman breathing? Do you think I cannot find friends who have proved their affection, by the sacrifices they have made for me, that I should give my money to buy the cold-blooded being who calculates, at fifteen years of age, what the prostitution of her person ought to sell for?'

. . . We all returned home together in silence, and Colonel Berkeley never afterwards sought Sophia's society.[17]

Soon after losing both Deerhurst and Berkeley, Sophia caught the eye of another peer.

'"I've some news for you," said Fanny. "Sophia has made a new conquest of an elderly gentleman, in a curricle, with a coronet on it. He does nothing on earth, from morning till night, but drive up and down before Julia's door."'[18] Sophia's admirer was Viscount Berwick, described by Harriette as 'a nervous, selfish old man . . . afraid to drive his own horses'.[19] Berwick – forty-one years old, the same age as Ponsonby – had seen Sophia about town and decided that she was the woman for him. The news that Sophia had been under the protection of Deerhurst and now lived in a house with the fallen Julia Johnstone did nothing to deter him, and Lord Berwick asked Lord William Somerset to introduce him to the girl. Sophia thought her suitor a 'very dowdy dry-looking man' and on his first visit she 'would not hear of such a very nasty, poking, old . . . Man . . . but the second day, she was induced to drive out in his barouche. On the third she declared His Lordship's equipage the easiest she ever rode in; but then he wore such a large hat! In short, she could not endure him, even to shake hands with him.'[20] Sophia had never evinced so much character before; she positively loathed the Lord and refused to be alone in his company, which meant that Harriette reluctantly accompanied the courting couple in their various excursions in and around London. Berwick, in desperation, urged Harriette and Julia to talk Sophia into accepting his offer of a settlement of £500 a year and to place herself under his protection, the thought of which made Sophia 'sob and cry, as if she were threatened with sudden death'.[21] Still, Sophia continued to accept Berwick's gifts and his dinners, claiming that she had no reason to object to these aspects of the courtship. Berwick's ardour increased along with Sophia's indifference, but eventually all misery came to an end when Sophia's desire for a grand house overcame her revulsion for its owner, and she allowed Berwick to accommodate her in a mansion in Montague Square, provided that she should at least initially sleep there alone. Julia Johnstone, who negotiated the settlement, received from Berwick a commission of several hundred pounds.

Berwick explained to Harriette that Sophia appealed to him because she seemed honest and faithful. Certainly, Sophia had expressed her loathing for Berwick candidly which persuaded him that she was not generally attracted to men and so, it seemed reasonable to assume, would be faithful to him. 'His Lordship was horn mad,' Harriette said.[22] What little conversation Berwick had consisted of cuckolds and cuckolders. He wondered over supper one night 'how many men had been cuckolded that season, in London, without knowing it?'[23]

Sophia eventually agreed to marry Berwick and to give up Montague Square to join him in his magnificent family home in Grosvenor Square, around the corner from her first grubby quarters under Lord Deerhurst. When not in London, Lord and Lady Berwick would retreat to their country seat, Attingham Hall in Salop (now Shropshire). Sophia's delighted suitor approached John Dubouchet to ask for his daughter's hand, which Dubouchet was equally delighted to give. On this day at least, Dubouchet's reign of terror over his household was abated. 'My little sisters have since informed me that, when one of them, having had the misfortune to upset a box full of playthings, which made a violent noise in the room where he was, as usual, puzzling over a problem, just as they were expecting little short of broken heads, and were all running into the most remote corners of the room . . . he surprised them . . . by saying, *"N'importe, petites imbeciles, venez m'embrasser!"* '[24] Sophia, aged seventeen, became Lady Berwick on 8 February 1812 at Marylebone. After the ceremony, which only her father attended, Sophia 'ate a hearty dinner . . . which was what usually happened to that interesting young lady, every day of her life, at about six o'clock'.[25]

Sophia had joined the select group of courtesans who married their aristocratic protectors, and she found herself in the company of Mrs Armistead, Fanny Murray, Nancy Parsons, and Harriet Powell. As Lady Berwick, Sophia 'had the command of more guineas than she ever expected to have had pence' and she enjoyed her role as Lady Bountiful, clothing a beggar's family and building a little island on a pond.[26] She sent her mother the £2,000 she received from Berwick for the sale of the Montague Square property, as well as cartloads of crockery and saucepans. She also proposed that she furnish Amelia a house.

After their marriage, Lord and Lady Berwick adopted Harriette's younger sister Charlotte, who was born in the year that Harriette ran away with Lord Craven and was now eleven years old. They hoped, Harriette wrote, that in doing so they might save her from a career as a dancer. Dancing 'was not the profession my mother would have preferred . . . but Charlotte promised to do wonders in it, and with her striking beauty, there could have been little doubt of her marrying well from the stage; and a mother who has fifteen children to care for cannot do as she pleases'.[27] Amelia was overjoyed to have her child brought up in a refined atmosphere where she would receive an education in taste and be introduced to eligible suitors.

Dubouchet meanwhile enjoyed boasting to his neighbours, particularly those who derided him for his profligate daughters, of Sophia's new status. It was his belief that she had not married above herself but had found her natural level: both he and Amelia were from good families, and it was right that his daughters should work to preserve the Dubouchet dignity. Berwick, however, thought otherwise, and he soon asked that Sophia cut her less virtuous sisters, neither writing to them nor hearing from them.

'Very well then; I will give them up altogether,' said Sophia, with much placidity; and yet we had never been, in the slightest degree, deficient in sisterly affection towards her; and Lord Berwick expected to inspire, with affection, this heartless thing, who, for mere title, conferred on her by a stranger she disliked, could at once forget the ties of nature, and forsake forever, without an effort of a tear, her earliest friends and nearest relations; and not because she was more virtuous than they were since, on the contrary, she had begun her career before other girls even dream of such things. She had intruded herself on the cobbler at thirteen, thrown herself into the arms of the most disgusting profligate in England at fourteen, with her eyes open, knowing what he was; then offered herself for sale, at a price, to Colonel Berkeley, and when her terms were refused with scorn and contempt by the handsome and the young, she throws herself into the arms of age and ugliness for a yearly stipend, and at length, by good luck, without one atom of virtue, became a wife.[28]

Charlotte, who was beginning to attract more attention at the opera than Sophia, was sent off, Harriette says, to a country school to teach English and French grammar; in Harriette's terms, a fate worse than death. 'And there poor Charlotte has been forced to bloom unseen, wasting her sweetness on the desert air . . .'[29]

Letters sent to contemporary newpapers by those who knew the Dubouchets tell a different story. Lady Berwick, several correspondents agreed, used her position to the benefit of her family. She brought up and educated Charlotte, who was lame and unlikely therefore to be an aspiring dancer, and, following the death of her mother, Sophia took in her other siblings. The Berwicks intended both Charlotte and Rose for the Church, but a letter sent to *Bell's Life in London* confirmed that Charlotte was living with Jane in Church Street, Paddington, where Sophia continued to visit them and take care of their needs. Far from cutting her, as Harriette insists, Sophia visited her mother regularly in the three years between her marriage and Amelia's death. When one of her brothers was dying, Sophia nursed him to the end and paid his apothecary's bills. Sophia, it seems, was a dutiful daughter to the end.

When in years to come the bejewelled Lady Berwick attended the opera, Lord Deerhurst would hire the box next door in order to ogle her and offend her husband. Harriette would look down from her own box and spit on her sister's head.

CHAPTER 13

The Marquis of Worcester

Mourning Ponsonby, Harriette began looking for an equivalent Apollo to 'fill the void in my heart'. Lord Granville Leveson-Gower, she heard, was the most admired man in London. She thus sent a note suggesting that they meet, which event took place in Regent's Park at eleven o'clock on a baking hot Sunday morning. She walked him up to the top of Primrose Hill, then towards Hampstead and back to Great Portland Street; Granville declared that if he did not sit down he would die. Harriette hoped that 'such fatal consequences would not follow our little rural bit of pleasure', but informed him that he was 'not, in the least, the sort of person' she wanted.[1]

Lord Granville's nephew was Henry Somerset, Marquis of Worcester. Immensely tall, thin and pale (not in the least handsome, Harriette thought) with a long nose and a high brow, Worcester was nineteen years old and still a minor when he became infatuated with Harriette. He was an Oxford undergraduate and heir to the Dukedom of Beaufort and the Badminton estate in Gloucestershire. The Somerset family were staunch Tories whose male line descended from John of Gaunt; the mother of the First Beaufort, Katherine Swynford, was Chaucer's sister-in-law. Badminton, a hundred miles west of London, with its 117 rooms and the two hundred staff it took to maintain them, was built in the Restoration,

Kensington Gardens, *Views of London*

on the site of a much older house. Worcester's father, the Sixth Duke, was a soldier and a plain countryman. His mother, another cousin of Julia Johnstone, was a devout Christian.

Worcester was a spendthrift and a member of the elite coterie of dandies that included Brummell, Lords Alvanley and Argyll, Sir Henry Mildmay and Henry de Roos. Harriette was back on home ground. Since the departure of Ponsonby she had become the darling of a more carefree generation of aristocrats, young enough to be the sons of the men who had previously courted her. She put her attractiveness to this class and age group down to fashion, but there was more to Harriette's allure than this. To teenage boys fresh from public schools and universities, whose only previous female contact had been with relations or servants and who expected to marry someone approved by their parents, Harriette Wilson represented an opportunity of genuine intimacy: she was a Wendy to a party of Peter Pans. Harriette was someone with whom it was possible to be friends and this, quite as much as the promise of a sexual education or the glamour of her fame, was her appeal. She was in many cases the first woman in whom most of her young lovers had ever confided.

Lord Worcester craved emotional closeness. 'It is . . . to be lamented', one of his Somerset uncles wrote to the Duke of Beaufort, 'that Worcester is so easily led away by any woman for whom he happens to form an attachment . . . it is to be hoped that as he grows older he will grow wiser.'[2] His previous sexual relationships had been with Oxford prostitutes, one of whom gave him an infection, which his mother saw as a punishment from God. With Harriette he sought comfort and security; his relationship with her was more that of a dutiful son than an ardent lover – he preferred to make her toast and lace her stays than to escort her to parties and parade her on his arm. When she was ill, he 'ran up and down, from the kitchen to the drawing room, twenty times, and poured out my water gruel, and my tea, as though this had been his natural vocation'.[3] He had servants chase after her with coats and boots in case it rained while she was out, and when Harriette had her back double tooth pulled out, Worcester wore it around his neck.

It was Deerhurst, then involved with Sophia, who introduced Worcester to Harriette one night in 1811, as she held court in her box at the opera. Harriette had made it generally known that her days of love were over, and she was drifting through a series of lightweight relationships with flatterers. When she met Worcester she living with a friend and contemporary of his, the Third Duke of Leinster, whom she thought 'only about three degrees and a half above a good-tempered Newfoundland dog'.[4] Leinster was the 'bog-trotting' nephew to Charles James Fox, the Whig Minister, and Edward Fitzgerald, the Irish Nationalist. Harriette seems to have been fond of him but disengaged from the relationship: 'I am not going to sit down all my life to love this fool. I must have something for the mind to feed on.'[5] For both Leinster and Worcester, the charms of Harriette Wilson had been legendary for most of their adult lives.

Harriette was only vaguely amused to meet Worcester: 'having taken one good look at my conquest and thus convinced myself that I should never love him, I conversed indifferently, on common subjects, as people do who happen to meet in a stage coach, where time present is all they have to care about. Deerhurst was lively and pleasant; the Marquis scarcely spoke: but the little he did find courage to utter was certainly said with good taste, and in a gentlemanly manner.'[6] She let the nervous boy touch her hair and tease her glossy curls, observing, 'I never saw a boy, or a man, more madly, wildly, and romantically in love with any daughter of Eve, in my whole life.' Leinster, wounded by Harriette's thus encouraging his friend's affections, accused her of being cold-hearted. 'I was in love enough once, God knows,' she rejoined, 'and what good did it do me?'

It wasn't until several months later, when Worcester had left Oxford, that he and Harriette became acquainted again. Worcester and Leinster made it clear that neither could tolerate the other's presence, and Leinster, in order to avoid her inevitable affair with his rival, told Harriette that he was going to fight alongside Wellington in Spain, his only request being that they could spend his final six weeks alone together. Harriette was touched by his pain and agreed not to see Worcester until Leinster had gone, after which time, she told Worcester, 'You are welcome to try to make me in love with you. If you fail,' she warned, 'so much the worse for us both; since I hold anything which is not love to be mere dull intervals in life.'[7] Harriette managed to balance both lovers until Leinster's ship set sail from Portsmouth, thus belying her insistence on her own monogamy. In a brief moment of concern for him, Harriette went down to join Leinster while he waited for a fair wind; an added attraction of Portsmouth being that Fanny was there also, bidding fairwell to Colonel Parker, whose child she was expecting. Harriette noted that Leinster departed without enquiring after her finances, which does not seem unreasonable in the circumstances.

Having bidden Leinster farewell, Harriette agreed to place herself under Worcester's protection. Lord Berwick, Sophia, Worcester and Harriette, along with Worcester's uncle and Berwick's friend, Lord William Somerset, together attended the theatres and took day trips out of London, and Worcester took the part of Berwick – whom he called 'Tweed' – in his battle to persuade Sophia to marry, or at least to live with, her swain. In August 1811, Worcester joined the Prince Regent's regiment, the 10th Hussars, and went to Brighton where they were stationed. As he would not hear of going without Harriette, and Sophia would not hear of being in Berwick's company alone, Harriette, Berwick, Sophia and Julia Johnstone followed Worcester down, Berwick travelling 'in a magnificent equipage, drawn by four milk-white horses, or four of raven black, I forget which . . . followed by the more humble vehicles containing his cook, his plate, his frying pans and other utensils'.[8]

Worcester went on ahead of Harriette to find a house for them both, settling for one in Rock Gardens, west of the Pavilion, not far from where Harriette had lived with Lord Craven ten years before. When she arrived she found a groom, 'in the Beaufort livery . . . waiting for his Lordship's horse, which he handed over by the bridle to the undergroom, and the undergroom sent a soldier with it to the stable. What a bore it will be to have all these lazy porter-drinking men in one's house, thought I, with very unmarchionesslike humility; but then I never set up for anything at all like a woman of rank.'[9] Harriette's refrain throughout the several hundred pages she reserves in her *Memoirs* to her relationship with Worcester and its aftermath is that he adored her, she loved him like a brother, he wanted to marry her, and she had no intention of accepting him: 'Good heavens! What can he expect, from one who has loved as I have loved, and gone through what I have gone through!'[10] She insists that apart from being unable to love again after Ponsonby, she valued her liberty above all else.

What Harriette says about Worcester's impetuous passion is corroborated by family letters written at the time and also by his subsequent behaviour: Worcester seems to have been barely controllable when he fell in love, and love was a state into and out of which he fell with frequency. The Duke and Duchess of Beaufort behaved towards Harriette with contempt but also fear: 'This absurd attachment of yours for this vile profligate woman does but prove the total subjection of your personality,' Harriette reported the Duchess writing to her son. The Beauforts assumed that it was Harriette who seduced and then pursued Worcester with the sole intention of becoming the next mistress of Badminton. Harriette was determined to set the record straight: 'I, who might [have], as everybody told me and were incessantly reminding me,' she indignantly recalled, '. . . smuggled myself into the Beaufort family, by merely declaring to Lord Worcester, with my finger pointed towards the North – that way leads to Harriette Wilson's bedchamber; yet so perverse was my conscience, so hardened by what Fred Bentinck calls my perseverance in loose morality, that I scorned the idea of taking such an advantage of the passion I had inspired, in what I believed to be a generous breast, as might, hereafter, cause unhappiness to himself, while it would embitter the peace of his parents.'[11]

Did Harriette want to marry the Marquis of Worcester? She over-eggs the pudding in passages such as the above. One of the principal objects of her *Memoirs* is to show how shabbily the Beauforts behaved towards her. It seemed inconceivable to them that a whore might not want to be a duchess and Harriette must have enjoyed for a while the prospect of such a pro-motion. It would be a smart revenge on Ponsonby while enraging Amy and trumping Sophia, who had just married Lord Berwick. Harriette's behaviour during the Worcester affair was ambivalent: she was clearly restless and lacking in direction during these years and evidently not in love, but she kept her options open. She enjoyed the game she was playing with the Beauforts over control of their son. Whatever grand fantasies she might have flirted with, Harriette was a realist with no delusions about her-self: there was nothing in her character to suggest she could have borne for one moment the life of an aristocratic wife, stuck out in the sticks listening to clocks ticking and servants sweeping, acting Lady Bountiful while being sneered at by the locals. She would never be received in high society; nor would she belong any longer to her own world. Marrying Worcester would mean more than instant demotion: she would be without identity, position or power. From being top of the pile she would go straight to the bottom. Worst of all, she would be bored.

1 Harriette Wilson

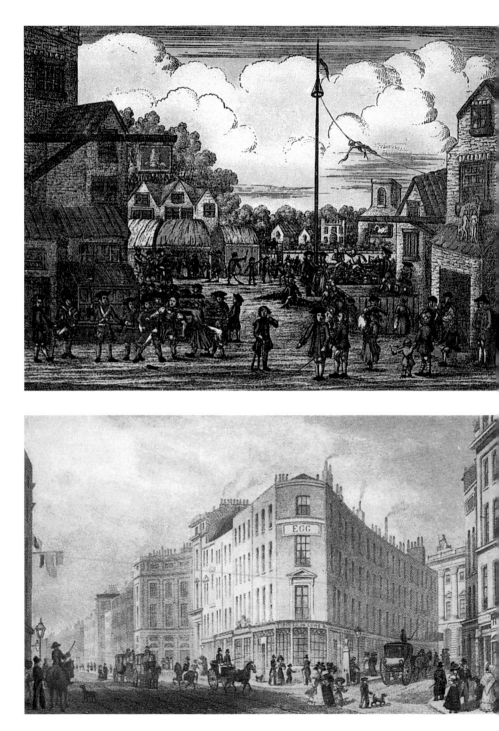

2 The May fair, 1716
3 Piccadilly from Coventry Street

4 Amy Dubouchet
6 Julia Johnstone

5 Sophia Dubouchet

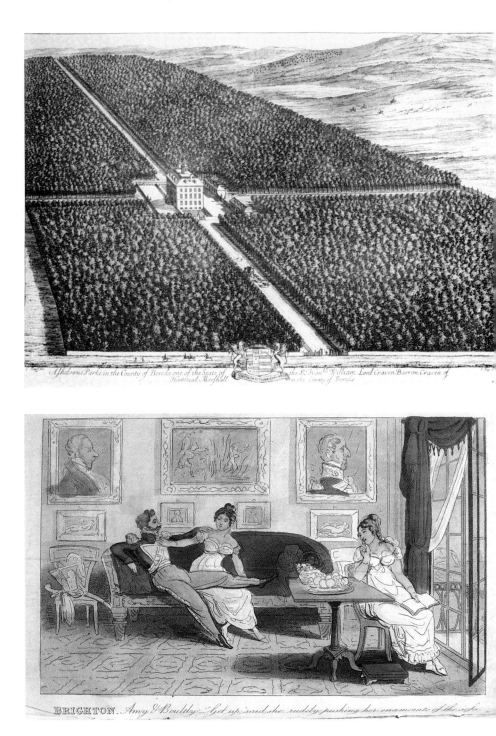

7 Ashdown House, engraved by Kip from a drawing by Knyff, *c.*1716
8 'Brighton, Amy & Bouldry – "Get up," said she, rudely pushing her enamorato of the sofa.'

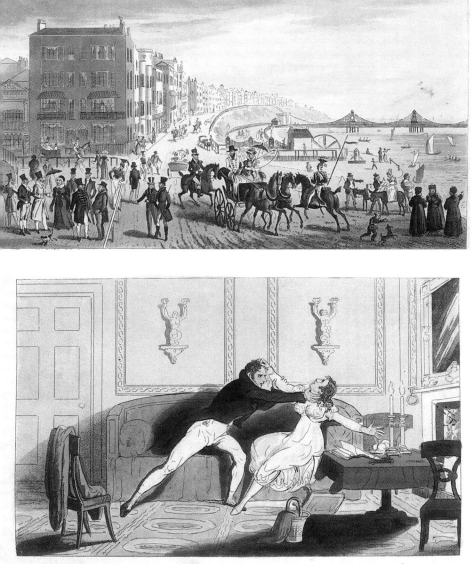

HARRIETTE'S APARTMENT — *Frederick Lambe rather too loving.*

9 Characters on the Steyne, Brighton, by Robert Cruikshank, 1826
10 'Harriette's Apartment, Frederick Lambe rather too loving.'

11 The Marquis of Lorne, from a
drawing by Henry Edridge, 1801

12 Harriette Wilson, 1825

Patience! The Duke of Argyle, whistling & sitting on a gate

13 'Patience! The Duke of Argyle, whistling & sitting on a gate'
14 Amy Dubouchet, date and artist unknown

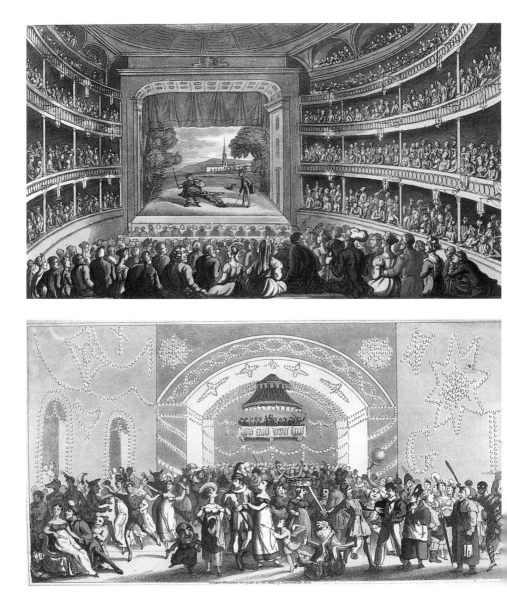

15 Covent Garden Theatre, by Thomas Rowlandson, from *The Tour of Dr Syntax*, 1812
16 'A Masquerade at the King's Theatre Opera House', by Robert Cruikshank,
from *Don Juan*, 1822

Another reason that she would not have liked marriage to Worcester is that Harriette combined practicality with a love of romance. Like Worcester, she needed to be constantly and newly in love. No sooner was Worcester safely in the Peninsula than she moved on to another admirer. How could she live without being continually on the crest of a driving emotion? Constancy and convention in relationships were anathemas to her: Harriette had about as much genuine interest in the life the Beauforts accused her of wanting to steal from under the nose of some better qualified woman as she would have in pig-farming. But she enjoyed taking them for a ride.

Lord Worcester had left his footman, Will Haught, at Rock Gardens 'to get all square' while he met Harriette on the Brighton road and journeyed back to the house with her. Haught was a 'stiff, grave, steady person of about forty. He always wore the Beaufort livery, which was as stiff as himself, and used to take his hat off, and sit in the hall, on a Sunday, with a clean pocket-handkerchief tied about his head, reading the Bible, offering thus, to the reflecting mind, these two excellent maxims: Respect God, but do not catch cold.'[12] He also respected Harriette and treated her as a prospective marchioness rather than the 'profligate woman' Worcester's mother described her as being.

Living with Worcester was all comfort. Knowing Harriette preferred to be surprised by her meals, Worcester organized the menus himself; hearing that she had consulted a doctor about a minor ailment, Worcester sent him a fifty-pound note in gratitude; hating the thought of Harriette's being alone while he dined with the regiment, he spurned invitations in order to spend the evenings at home. When he was invited to dine with the Prince of Wales, who had recently become Regent, Worcester was thrown into a frenzy of anxiety, greeting Harriette at the end of his evening at the Pavilion with all the enthusiasm of one returned from the Crusades. Having no idea how to run a house, Worcester was accumulating expenses that far exceeded his income and he started to borrow from a money-lender at an exorbitant interest rate. Discovering the loan and interest being charged, immune to the fact that his son had willingly made a contract with this man, the Duke 'threatened the lender with prosecution for fraud on a minor, if he did not sign a receipt in full for the bare sum lent'.[13]

Harriette enjoyed Brighton life and involved herself in the business of the regiment, taking great interest in the officers and the local scandals.

The 10th Dragoons was the most elite and fashionable regiment, composed of the sons of the grandest families in the country. Harriette observed that one new officer, 'a fine young man who had joined only a month previous' was ignored by the entire mess because while he had money, he had 'no family' and 'they denominate those who cannot boast recorded ancient blood in their veins'.[14] It was the regiment to which Beau Brummell had belonged until he heard they were to go to Manchester, the thought of which he could not countenance. Josiah Cotton had been Colonel in the 10th when he impregnated Julia Storer. Cotton sold his colonelcy on to George Leigh, the husband of Lord Byron's sister Augusta. In the year that Worcester joined, Leigh was forced to retire, being succeeded in the command by the unpopular George Quentin. The 10th counted among its officers several men whose paths had crossed with Harriette's. Lord Robert Manners had been one of her lovers, Lord Arthur Hill was a relation of Lord Berwick and friend of Worcester, and John Cotton, a lieutenant who was killed in 1813 in Spain, was a legitimate son of Josiah Cotton. Of the two colonels, Quentin and Palmer, Palmer was a 'former acquaintance' of Harriette. Worcester was so jealous of him that Harriette had to invite him to the house in order to assuage her lover's anxiety: 'Down came Colonel Palmer, trotting on a little ugly pony, his laced jacket covered with an old, short, brown, great coat, and a shabby round hat, while the rain was dripping down his face. "My dear fellow," said the Colonel, "I would not, for worlds, spoil your comfort. I have loved myself, and know what jealousy is."'[15] Colonel Quentin she claims never to have met, although Harriette could impersonate his accent and was brought to his attention when Worcester either failed to appear at parade in the mornings or appeared alongside his mistress, who was dressed 'like a young recruit . . . in a blue riding habit, and an embroidered jacket or spencer worn over it, trimmed and finished after the fashion of our uniform, and a little grey fur-stable cap, with a gold band'.[16] From the barrack room, Harriette would watch Sergeant Whitaker teaching the sword exercise: 'Tik nuttis!! The wurd dror is oney a carshun. At t'wurd suards, ye drors um hout, tekin a farm un possitif grip o'th'hilt! Sem time, throwing th' shith smartly backords thus! Dror!!'[17]

Worcester's infatuation with Harriette did not prevent his having a flirtation with the paymaster's wife, Mrs Archdeacon, while Harriette was in

London visiting her sisters. Worcester denied to Harriette that there had been an affair, but what took place generated enough concern for his Somerset uncles, his parents, and even Wellington and the Prime Minister, Lord Liverpool, to hear about it. Worcester's uncles also kept the Duke of Beaufort informed of Worcester's relations with Harriette, and Worcester received from his parents letters 'insisting on his immediately leaving [Harriette], unprovided for, and without the smallest ceremony'.[18] Needless to say, these only excited in both a spirit of defiance.

When the regiment was posted to Portsmouth to the not very glamorous duty of looking after prisoners of war, Quentin offered Worcester the chance of changing his troop. Worcester replied that so long as Harriette did not mind joining him in a 'wretched little village' he would be prepared to go. Harriette, refusing the use of the carriage and four horses appointed for her, travelled in a line with the 10th Hussars, 'dressed in my regimental cap and habit, like a little recruit'.[19] She lodged together with Worcester, the Duc de Guiche and Lord Arthur Hill in 'the same deplorable pothouse. Our bedroom served us for parlour, kitchen, and hall, and we dined together in the only spare room there was, in this apology for an inn, furnished exactly in the usual style of such places; to wit, twelve immense, high-backed, black leather chairs, too heavy for anyone . . . to move; and the wainscot adorned with such pictures as – a fox chase, and then the Virgin Mary, and cheek by jowl with that holy woman, Bellingham, the murderer of Perceval; next, a print of King George the third in his parliamentary robes – a county map – the holy apostles sitting at the last supper, and a poll parrot, done in what is, I believe, usually called clothwork; plenty of sand on the floor, and plenty of wine glasses, tooth-picks and cruets on the sideboard.'[20] It rained for two weeks and Worcester lay with his head on the table proclaiming his love to his 'adored, delicious, divine, lovely Harriette' who was 'about to make a very tender, warm and suitable reply, but at that critical moment, the woman brought in a large platter of ill-dressed veal cutlets and bacon'.[21] The party ventured out one night to the theatre, where they were pelted with oranges by the sailors in the gallery who thought that the Hussars were either Germans or French. Harriette and her party agreed afterwards not to leave their quarters again, and stayed put for the next two months.

After Sophia and Berwick married, the new Lady Berwick moved into 15 Grosvenor Square, a few doors away from the Beauforts, who lived at number 5. The Duke and Duchess were increasingly anxious that Worcester – if he had not done so already – would follow Berwick's suit and marry his whore. Harriette had made it known that she had in her possession dozens of letters in which Worcester proposed marriage, addressing her as his wife and signing himself her husband. In March, Harriette was approached by the Duke's attorney, Mr Robinson of Bolton Street, 'a notorious swindler . . . Who . . . had long been in the habit of doing dirty jobs for noblemen' and 'who has since been confined in chains for forgery'.[22] Robinson declared that Harriette had it in her 'power considerably to relieve the anxiety and distress of mind to which I had reduced the Beaufort family, by returning all [the Marquis's] letters in my possession'. If she could make an oath that she had handed the documents over, she could 'make her own terms with his Grace'.[23] Harriette asked for a week to consider this proposal, and contacted Thomas Treslove, a lawyer at Lincoln's Inn who had long been known to the Dubouchets. Treslove read the letters and advised Harriette that as she had been 'prevented,' due to her consideration for the Beauforts, from establishing herself in comfort as the Marchioness of Worcester, she should receive 'at least' twenty thousand pounds in damages. Harriette repeated to Robinson what she had been told, and he retorted that 'the Duke expected all this, and indeed he thought I [Harriette] might make better terms, without exposing the secrets of a noble family in a public Court of Justice.'[24] Harriette weighed up her options, seeing that she could either sell the letters to the Duke, which would make her look mercenary, use them to blackmail him, which would make him an enemy, or give them up willingly, thus increasing her chances of winning their approval if she ever did decide to marry the Marquis. She settled on the last option and sent the Duke a bundle of Worcester's letters, telling him that she would never sell his son's proof of love and declaring that she was ready to take any oath he required of her. She asked in return to be treated by the Duke and Duchess with less 'ill will'.

In the spring of 1812, when all fashionable London could talk about was a new poem called *Childe Harold's Pilgrimage, a Romaunt* by a young poet called Lord Byron, Harriette 'received a letter from Worcester so blotted over, from one end to the other, that it was scarcely legible, and some parts appeared actually to have been defaced by tears . . . It was all over wives and angels, and eternal constancy, and eternal despair! ! with miseries and tortures without end . . . All I could make out of this scrawl, as certain, was that Lord Wellington, at the request of Worcester's father, who had made it without his son's knowledge, had appointed him his aide-de-camp, and that go he must; for there was no remedy, or it would be called cowardice, if he hesitated.'[25] The Duke had been busy arranging to get Worcester out of the country as quickly as possible and Beaufort's brother, Lord Edward Somerset, who was in the Peninsula, wrote confirming that the Marquis could join Wellington in Portugal. Having heard about Worcester's infatuation, Wellington, whose own infatuation with Harriette he kept quiet, agreed that 'the best thing you can do is to send' the boy 'to him'. So long as he could be got to army headquarters and kept away from Lisbon – 'where he before had a connection of which you are aware', refer- ring to the paymaster's wife, Mrs Archdeacon, now a resident there – Wellington guaranteed that Worcester would be on safe ground. So as to avoid loitering in Lisbon, Wellington and Lord Edward came up with a plan to 'request Lord Liverpool to give [Worcester] dispatches and order him to deliver them himself to Lord Wellington'.[26] 'I am happy to hear that Worcester is coming out to this country on Lord Wellington's staff,' Lord Edward Somerset wrote to the Duke on 6 May, 'and it is very gratifying that the latter should have proposed it in so obliging a manner – I hope it will be the means of breaking off that abominable connection, which I am not surprised to hear has made you so uneasy. I should think the sooner Worcester leaves England the better.'[27]

According to Harriette, she was so shocked by the prospect of Worcester being sent to war that she paid a personal visit to his father: 'It now struck me very forcibly that Worcester had deserved all my devoted attachment, and that I had not been half grateful enough to him. That he would lose his life in Spain, I felt convinced, and that since his regiment remained in England, I should have his blood on my head. What was to be done? My crimson velvet pelisse, trimmed with white fur, and also my white beaver hat, with the charming plume of feathers, were spread out in my dressing room, ready for Hyde Park, and conquests!! and poor Worcester, perhaps, might soon be numbered with the dead! Food for worms!'[28] On went the crimson pelisse and the white beaver hat, and 'in less than half an hour behold me standing at the Duke of Beaufort's street door, awaiting an answer to my humble single rap'. The porter who let her in eyed Harriette suspiciously, 'as though it had struck him as just possible that I might have come . . . for the purpose of swearing a child against his noble master'. Harriette was kept waiting in the hall while the Duke dressed, during which time she wept. Hearing a voice, 'I raised my head, and, seeing a handsome-looking man, in a court dress, who appeared to be a very little older than Worcester, I grew brave, as I always do from desperation.' Harriette told the Duke that 'I felt so very shocked at the idea of being the sole cause of His Lordship sent into danger . . . that really, I found it impossible to resist making any effort to prevent it, by proposing to His Grace to do all in my power to induce Lord Worcester to consent to our separation; and even if I failed, rather to agree to go abroad myself, and keep my residence a secret from his son.' Harriette stressed again that she had no intention of marrying Worcester; he stressed again that he did not believe her. They parted on good terms, she says, having shaken hands.[29]

The object of the story is to illustrate Harriette's virtue and the Duke's villainy: he was decent and co-operative in her company, so why did he need to send his henchmen to her, or otherwise treat her with contempt? He was also a hypocrite, she implies, and in order to avenge herself on him she tells a story, barely believable, about a bashful visit he made her before Worcester had even sailed. '"Who makes your shoes?" he asked, "to say nothing of the feet and ankles."' The Duke, Harriette reported, shuffled away, having 'made no single proposal, nor said one single word, which could in any way assist my guess, as to why he did the honour to call on me'.[30]

Far from being distressed, Worcester was, his mother reported, 'really delighted' that he was joining Wellington's staff, as indeed was she. 'I have according to your desires', Lord Edward wrote to the Duchess from Portugal, 'communicated to Lord Wellington your feelings of gratitude at his assisting you . . . in this hour of your distress. You may depend upon it that care has been taken to prevent his having an opportunity of loitering at Lisbon, and I hope the campaign will be sufficiently active to prevent his pining at his loss.'[31] Worcester entreated Harriette to go with him, an offer she rejected: 'The army was not expected to to be stationary. If I remained at Lisbon, I should see no more of him than by remaining in London. The misery, expense, and privations, perhaps insults, I must endure in my attempt to follow the army would scarcely be surmounted; and Worcester could not deny that I should make a coward of him; that fight he could not, supposing I might be suffering under sickness or difficulty.'[32] It was decided that the couple would have a year's separation. 'In twelve months from the day I leave you, supposing I am not on my road to join you in England, remember you are to come to me,' Worcester begged, and he told Harriette that when the year was up he would declare to his father that they were to 'part no more'.[33] It was agreed in the presence of Robinson that Harriette would receive regular quarterly payments from the Duke: Worcester would not leave the country until this was certain. Robinson told Harriette that anything Worcester himself signed would be 'good for nothing' but he passed on the Duke's word that 'the allowance Worcester requires for you shall be paid to you in regular quarterly payments, after all your house debts etc have been discharged'.[34]

The Marquis was dragged from Harriette's arms by his uncle, Lord William Somerset, and placed with Will Haught in the Falmouth coach, minutes before it started. 'I almost believe he would have preferred love to glory,' Harriette wrote, 'and given Wellington the slip.'[35] He arrived in Portugal in mid June, reportedly 'in perfect health, [and] in the highest spirits'[36] and fought in the battle of Salamanca on 22 July. America had declared war on Britain three days earlier.

CHAPTER 14

Meyler

The Marquis of Worcester had been at Christ Church with an Etonian called Richard Meyler, the last in a line of Bristol merchants trading in the West Indies. Meyler was an only child; his mother died during childbirth and his father died on his way home from Jamaica, where he had considerable sugar plantations in Westmorland. Aged fourteen, Meyler was heir to £30,000 and an estate at Crawley Manor Court near Winchester. When Harriette met him, Meyler was twenty-two with a plaintive beauty exacerbated by what Fanny recognized as the 'churchyard skin' of a consumptive. He was known to the men of fashion and a member of all the right clubs; Gronow includes Meyler in his list of dandies,[1] but his money was too new to make him part of their inner circle ('that damned sugar-baker', Alvanley called him, 'that damned methodistical grocer'). He was a 'hard drinker, and a very hard rider, and a good tennis and cricket player'.[2] He liked the Duchess of Beaufort and disliked Harriette Wilson. 'It would be impossible for any man in his right senses', Harriette has Meyler say to the Duchess, 'to be in love with that woman called Harriette Wilson; she may have been better once; but she is now in ill health, spoiled by flattery, and altogether the most disgusting type of woman I know.' 'There is novelty', Harriette told Fanny, 'in being an object of disgust to any man, just when Worcester has cloyed me with so many sweets!'[3] Meyler knew

Lyme Regis, from a contemporary print

many women of Harriette's type; his affections were at the moment divided between 'a Mrs Bang, a Mrs Pattern, and a Mrs Pancrass', all of whom were 'ladies of Covent Garden notoriety'.[4]

Harriette's box at the opera that season – paid for by Worcester, shortly before he left – faced the Beauforts' own box, from which direction an icy chill would descend on her as she appeared in her finery, flanked by Fanny and Julia and followed by her minions. Harriette's friends were pleased to be able to enjoy her company again and her prospective lovers crowded about her, 'believing, of course, in the absence of my jealous Lord, it would be no difficult matter to obtain favour in my sight, and, whether I was the style of woman they liked, or just the reverse, still it was always worth cutting a man who had been so proverbially in love as Worcester'.[5]

Richard Meyler was often in the Beauforts' theatre party, and he observed from his vantage point Worcester's grass widow, whose public appearances commenced even before her beloved had set sail into what Harriette fancied would be certain death. 'Well,' she reasoned, 'since Worcester cannot well be shot by the enemy previous to his reaching head-quarters, I may as well take the opportunity of seeing two or three more ballets; for, as to indulging in gaities while a parcel of shots are flying about his head or across his brain, is not in my nature.'[6] This was not the same woman who had watched Ponsonby's empty house for months, venerating his very door knocker, while he was visiting his estates in Ireland.

When Meyler sent a message to Harriette's box saying that he wished to be introduced, she assumed that he was acting as a spy on behalf of the Duchess of Beaufort and that his motive was to 'acquaint Worcester with what a loose woman I am'. Predisposed to dislike him, Harriette instead found Meyler 'a beautiful creature . . . unaffected and gentlemanlike'. He was slight and feline, with soft feminine features and small hands and feet: exactly what she liked in a man. Meyler thought her 'cheap' and 'anything but desirable' and to test his theory he tried to kiss her. She refused him 'rather coquettishly, on purpose that he might be induced to renew the attack at some future day, with a little ceremony'.[7]

Enquiring about Meyler, Harriette heard that 'No woman can do anything with [him] in the way of love, for Meyler really don't know what sentiment means . . . [He] is a mere animal, a very handsome one, it is true, and there is much natural shrewdness about him, besides he is one of the most gentlemanlike young men I know . . . His countenance . . . is beautiful, and so peculiarly voluptuous that, when he looks at women, after dinner, although his manner is perfectly respectful, they are often observed to blush deeply, and hang down their heads, they really cannot tell why or wherefore.'[8]

Edward Somerset sent regular reports to Badminton on his nephew's progress, reassuring the Duke on 14 July that he did not 'apprehend' that Worcester 'feels his absence from a certain person sufficiently to endanger his health' but confiding to the Duchess in September that, 'I feel your apprehensions regarding the continuance of Worcester's correspondence with the Person to whom he is so unfortunately attached are not groundless, indeed I know he receives letters from her constantly, and I am aware that he sometimes writes to her in the terms which she boasts of . . . "My dearest little wife" . . . Altogether I console myself by thinking that if he remains here long enough he will get the better of this attachment . . .'[9] Wellington was also kept informed of the contents of Worcester's mail and confirmed that he would keep the Marquis in his service as long as was necessary, although he was 'of the opinion that his return to England with the intelligence of victory would have no bad effect, provided he was obliged to come back to the army immediately'.[10]

Harriette claimed that during the period following Worcester's departure she could have secured at least a dozen annuities were she not determined to stay loyal to her Marquis, and yet it was Meyler to whom she was drawn like a bee to pollen. He was shady, distrustful and unsteady, 'abominably cool and impertinent', and he operated at the heart of the Beaufort camp. Nothing could excite Harriette more or better whet her appetite for drama and conflict. And nothing could give the Duke and Duchess more pleasure. If Harriette acted the whore with Meyler, her annuity could be dropped and their son would be free. Harriette was caught between the twin challenges of wanting to prove wrong the Beauforts' judgement of her as a faithless gold-digger and keeping her flirtation with Meyler on the boil. She decided to leave London's temptations and settle in a village, 'where I was to pass one of the most brilliant years of my life in perfect solitude'.[11] The difficulty was finding somewhere: 'Where is there a village?' she asked Luttrell. He told her that he knew of one called Charmouth in Dorset. '"That will do," said I, sick of the dry, dull subject',[12] and she booked a place for herself and her maid on the Exeter mail coach. Charmouth – not a village but a small, polite town – was either not chosen so randomly or was a happy choice: it was on Worcester's road back from Spain, and Harriette's plan was that, should they survive the separation, it was in Charmouth that the reconciliation would take place.

Before she left London, Meyler's pursuit of Harriette gathered apace. He walked home with her one night after the opera and she arranged to meet him the next day at Julia's, as it would hurt Worcester – to whom she told everything – if Meyler were to court her in her own home. She then withdrew the invitation, anxious that Julia was being unhelpfully encouraging of the affair. 'All this is infinitely amiable of me,' Harriette reflected as she wrote to Meyler excusing herself, 'for I was very dull by myself, and Meyler, as to externals, was much to my taste.'[13] Nevertheless, Julia was soon drawn in once more as Harriette's chaperone and the three of them 'wandered about the fields' by moonlight, while 'Meyler sighed, and talked downright sentimentally about leading a chaste life for my sake, and sending away all his women'.[14] He offered to give Harriette any settlement she wished if she were to leave Worcester.

Fanny and her baby daughter were now living with Julia in Camden Town, a district north of Somerstown whose 'rural lanes, hedgeside roads and lovely fields made [it] the constant resort of those who . . . sought its quietude and fresh air to reinvigorate their spirits'.[15] In a few years' time, the arrival of the canal and railway would irreparably change the idyllic spot where Fanny waited for Colonel Parker to return from the Peninsula and where, after Worcester left England, Harriette moved to within a few doors of her sister and friend.

Julia had lost to Amy the 'cold hearted, beautiful, profligate' Sir Henry Mildmay,[16] Member of Parliament for Winchester. From Amy, Mildmay soon moved on to Harriette. But Meyler retained his hold on her, and Mildmay continued to wreak havoc elsewhere. In 1809, he had married Charlotte Bouverie, who died a year later having produced the heir to the baronetcy. Four years afterwards, he fell in love with his dead wife's younger sister, a mother of four who was married to the Earl of Rosebery.[17] While Mildmay was shuffling between these various sets of sisters, Julia had transferred her dependence, but not her adoration, to a

Gloucestershire landowner called James Lenox Naper or Napier, who had been at Eton and Christ Church with Meyler. Born in the same year as Meyler, Napier was worth £20,000 a year and so had been handed on to Julia by Fanny, anxious that Julia's debts were out of control. Harriette thought Napier looked more like Julia's son than lover and Julia thought him a repellent 'long backed odious creature'.[18] If it were not for the fact that he provided for her children, she claimed she would drown herself in the Serpentine rather than declare herself to him. Julia's children, and the child she bore him, seemed to be all that Napier provided for: Julia herself continued to be distressed – in debt to the sum of a thousand pounds – and she had her house and furniture seized while her protector was hunting with Meyler at Melton Mowbray in Leicestershire. When she travelled to Melton to inform him of the disaster, Napier gave Julia just enough money, so Fanny wrote to Harriette, to replace his own 'little elegant necessaries . . . for the rest, her drawing-room is covered with a piece of green baize, and, in lieu of all her beautiful little knick-knacks and elegant furniture, she has two chairs, an old second hand sofa, and a scanty, yellow cotton curtain'.[19]

Charmouth is 142 miles from London and a mile along the coast from the popular watering place of Lyme Regis, described by Harriette as 'a sort of Brighton in the miniature'. Lyme, a guide book of 1810 reported,

is built on a declivity of a craggy hill, at the head of an inlet of the sea, and contains many respectable looking houses; but the streets are steep, rugged, and unpleasant. In the lower part the houses are mean, and the streets so intricate that a stranger, it has been wittily remarked, will sometimes find himself bewildered, as if he were entangled in a forest or the labyrinth of a fox den. Here the lower order of the inhabitants in general reside, having that position which nature and fortune assigned to them. To be a person of consideration at Lyme, it is necessary to toil up hill, and to fix one's abode where it is in danger of being assailed by every wind that blows.[20]

Jane Austen, who loved Lyme and Charmouth, described the area eight years later in *Persuasion*. It is one of her few excursions into landscape and out of irony:

As there is nothing to admire in the buildings themselves, the remarkable situation of the town, the principal street almost hurrying into the water, the walk to the

Cobb, skirting round the pleasant little bay, which, in the season, is animated with bathing machines and company; the Cobb itself, its old wonders and new improvements, with the very beautiful line of cliffs stretching out to the east of the town, are what the stranger's eye will seek; and a very strange stranger it must be, who does not see charms in the immediate environs of Lyme, to make him wish to know it better. The scenes in its neighbourhood, Charmouth, with its high grounds and extensive sweeps of country, and still more, its sweet, retired bay, backed by dark cliffs, where fragments of low rock among the sands make it the happiest spot for watching the flow of the tide, for sitting in unwearied contempla- tion . . . these places must be visited and visited again, to make the worth of Lyme understood.[21]

Harriette, one of Austen's strange strangers, loathed Lyme: 'solitude or the best society', she wrote, 'but I abhore little sixpenny assembly places',[22] and she never suggested visiting the Dorset coast again. She was here doing time, and not only were Lyme and Charmouth out of London but out of season.

Harriette claimed that she lived in Charmouth for a year, but it seems more likely that she stayed only for the winter and spring of 1812–13, when the London season was over and her circle had retreated to their country estates. A letter from Lady Bessborough to Lord Granville Leveson-Gower, written in September 1812, says that 'Harriette Wilson is living at Ryde [on the Isle of Wight] in great retirement, saying she passes for the most Virtuous Woman in the Island; and that she is waiting for Ld W's coming of age, when he is return and marry her. She shew'd some of his letters all ending with yr. Affectionate Husband.'[23] Harriette must then have been in Lyme during the same chill, empty autumn months as Jane Austen herself and *Persuasion*'s heroine, Anne Elliot, when the sixpenny assembly rooms were 'deserted and melancholy'[24] and the sea was a steely grey. It is hard to imagine Harriette spending longer than a few months in this backwater with only her maid for company, but she generated there enough bustle to keep herself entertained.

Charmouth was 'a very genteel village, inhabited by people of small fortunes', and Harriette's account of finding, against all odds, a lodging with a widow called Mrs Edmund is reminiscent of her tale of meeting Julia Johnstone: 'We had twice walked through the village, and round about it, and were bending our steps towards our little pot house, in mute despair, when my attention was arrested by the striking loveliness of a young lady who was watering some flowers at one of the windows of a house I had before admired for its peculiar neatness. She smiled so very graciously that I was encouraged in my wish to address her. The moment she saw me make towards the little street door, she ran and opened it herself.'[25] Mrs Edmund was the lady's mother, a virtuous widow who devoted her life to her daughter's happiness. The presence of Harriette in the house would give the saintly Miss Eliza a taste of good society, and Mrs Edmund begged that Harriette and her maid might reside with them. 'Eliza', Harriette wrote of her new companion, 'lived and breathed but to serve, oblige, and benefit others.'[26]

Here the Edmunds observed Harriette waiting by the window each night to receive a constant stream of letters from Worcester and Meyler, delivered by the postwoman who made her way down the hill to Charmouth with a lantern and the mailbag. Harriette attended church on Sundays, wearing a straw bonnet and offering her arm to the curate's ancient father; she paid visits to the sick and delivered wine, solace and medicine to the poor. Her payments from the Duke, however, were not so constant or so charitable and, being unable to pay for her bed and board, Harriette took the advice of a general she knew from London and approached a local lawyer called Hugh Evans Fisher, who was described to her as 'the lady-killer of these parts . . . the beauty of Devonshire. Such black eyes! And six feet high!' 'He is a most particularly sharp fellow,' the general assured Harriette, 'and being a lawyer, who knows who you are, and all about you, he is the very man to consult.'[27] Eliza Edmunds trembled and warned Harriette that Fisher was 'a very shocking man' who 'made love' to several women at once. Harriette promptly wrote to him.

'Madam,' Fisher is said to have replied, 'Since secrecy is an object with you, I request you will come to my chambers just after it is dark, on Thursday next, that being the only hour I can command, as free from the interruption of clients; it being my constant habit to refuse admittance to strangers after daylight . . .' 'Sir,' Harriette answered, 'Whether I am, or am not, Lord Worcester's wife, be assured that he has too much respect for me, to permit a country attorney to insult me by his invitations to meet him in the dark. You may, of course, do as you please, with regard to the secrecy I mentioned; but it is my and Lord Worcester's pleasure that you never presume to insult me again with your odious and very humiliating proposals.'²⁸ Meeting the general once more the next day, Harriette discovered that Fisher found her 'anything but desirable'. 'What in the name of the devil can Lord Worcester see to admire in that ugly piece of goods?' the general had heard him exclaim. 'Why, I vow to God, I would not have her if she were to fall on her knees to me. She has not a good point about her.'²⁹ Harriette, who enjoyed being thought an object of disgust, says she was greatly amused by her mistake. Fisher was less amused when, thirteen years later, he saw her account of him printed in her *Memoirs*.

In the summer of 1812 Harriette wrote to introduce herself to Lord Byron, currently the rage of London. This and subsequent letters to the poet reveal that she yearned for some of her old celebrity as opposed to her recently acquired notoriety, and to be the lover of someone more challenging than Worcester or Meyler.

As nobody is to be found to introduce your Lordship, have you any objection to introduce yourself to a very impertinent young woman, who feels anxious to be allowed the honour of speaking to you? – I feel I am doing a very cool thing, but it was never in my way to think of *forms* much. At the same time, I shall be miserable if I have disgusted by my want of ceremony the very person I am most disposed to admire; but really I thought it a pity to defer what *can do* no harm and *may perhaps* be productive of pleasure to *both* of us – I mean in a *simple, honest sense*. If you think it is to make anything like *love* to you, don't come; but if you think you would like to see me (and I tell you I am melancholy and not worth it) write me word when you will call, that I may be alone. If not, pray don't tell anyone that I wrote to you . . .³⁰

Harriette's introductory letters tended to have a high score rate, but Byron, who received a dozen such letters each week, replied starchly that he did not think himself suited to be her lover. Harriette's second letter, in which she describes herself as 'ill and melancholy' and without 'talent or beauty' suggests that she romanticized what she saw as Byron's own melancholy and was caught between wanting to nurture him and to identify herself with him. 'And though you are a stranger to me, I can never cease to regret that *you* are not happy, and still more that you can think it *happy* not to wish to be beloved.'³¹ Although Harriette said that she would not make herself '*de trop*', she clearly did and Byron tried to cut her with 'an *affected, prosing, stupid scrawl*', instigating an angry response. 'If I presumed for a moment to imagine that your Lordship's condescension and good nature would be found to equal the talents that had made such a strong impression on my mind, I *humbly* implore your pardon for having done you so much injustice.' He wrote a sarcastic note reminding Harriette of her 'humble situation and of [his] own rank and talents'.[32]

Harriette had written to Byron as an equal, as one overnight success to another, and his rejection of her offer of acquaintance was a sign that he was on his way up and she was on her way down. Her heyday was over, the Beaufort affair had harmed her image; Harriette was now regarded by those in the *grande-monde* who had heard about her from the Beauforts as being difficult and a menace, not qualities likely to attract a self-conscious fashionable to a courtesan. And there is nothing celebrity dislikes so much as an intimation of its own mortality. Harriette, who had been famous since Byron was a schoolboy, had about her a desperation to remain in the public eye that he must have found unsettling. For the moment their correspondence ended here, picking up again several years later. Harriette was not used to failure and she bore her rejection with characteristic dignity.

By September, she was having difficulty getting her quarterly payments out of the Duke, despite the letters in which she informed him of her 'destitution'. 'The Duke, perhaps, hoped to starve me into putting up with the first man I could find; at all events, it was clear I might have starved, or begged, or thrown myself into the streets, before he would have offered me the least assistance while he could possibly have avoided it.'[33] The Badminton archive contains a letter from Robinson that admits that Beaufort had asked him to remain 'quiet with the lady', which order Robinson obeyed, 'until yesterday when I received a message from the sister requesting to see me "on business of a very urgent nature".'[34] This sister we can assume was loyal Fanny, whose own protector, Colonel Parker, was also in the Peninsula, and with whom both Harriette and Worcester were constantly in touch.

On his way to Fanny's house, Robinson 'revolved over and over again in my mind what could be the object of this interview and nothing struck me as so probable as that the Lady had upon reflection found that love and a cottage was not so agreeable as a house in town with its etceteras'. Fanny asked if Robinson 'had not made a proposition to pay the debts of the lady and to make a settlement on her beyond it', to which he replied, 'I certainly had done so but only to pay debts contracted during the connection which I understood to be about £200 and as to the settlement no sum was specified nor was I authorised to make any as there were conditions to be preferred on the part of the lady before any sum could be stated.' Robinson continued to tell the Duke, 'But to save her and myself much time and trouble I begged to acquaint her that in consequence of a letter I had received after such propositions had been made and which was laid before the parties interested, that it was determined that lady should follow the bent of her inclinations as no further trouble would be taken, of course I was not now authorised to act.' Robinson may have been referring to a letter proving that Harriette had been unfaithful to Worcester. Fanny was alarmed at the threat, said she would contact Harriette immediately, and begged that Robinson should communicate to the Duke her sister's 'sentiments, which she was convinced could not have been so long withheld but from some misunderstanding'.[35] The Badminton archives contain a receipt dated 7 December 1812, signed Harriette Wilson, confirming that she 'received of Mr Robinson the sum of two hundred and fifty pounds being the amount due 10 October'.[36]

Despite the continuation of letters passing between England and Portugal, eight months of separation was having its effect on Worcester.[37] In late January 1813, Lord Edward wrote to Beaufort, 'Absence, as you observe, is the best thing for both parties, for I flatter myself if he stays abroad some time longer, there is a chance of the Lady's patience being exhausted and of her forming another connection. If anything of that sort could be proved I shall answer for his giving her up directly. When I spoke to him on the subject I mentioned to assure him that I had no doubt you would willingly settle a reasonable annuity upon her, and I am happy to find that in so doing I entered into your wishes.'[38] The 10th Hussars were due to arrive at any time; the appearance of his regiment would be an impetus to Worcester's staying in Portugal. There was, however, another attraction keeping Worcester abroad: Mrs Archdeacon had turned up in Lisbon. Lord Edward reported in February that Worcester's 'passion' for Harriette was 'diminishing considerably, and will, he thinks, be brought to a happy termination if he passes another campaign in the Peninsula'.[39] Mrs Archdeacon, whose 'character and conduct previous to her connection with Worcester were, I am told, notorious', had left her husband to 'go up the army' with the Marquis, but Lord Edward reported to the Duke that he had 'great hopes that Worcester's last business at Lisbon will not prove of such serious consequence as there was at first reason to apprehend. He has left Lisbon some time and is, I believe, at present with the 10th.' He ended with what was becoming the lietmotif of the Somerset correspondence about Worcester: 'It is to be hoped that the operations of the campaign will divert his mind from this new object.'[40]

As her year of waiting was coming to an end and Worcester's majority had now been reached, Harriette took the matter of her allowance into her own hands and wrote to the Duke of Beaufort.

Lord Worcester agreed to go abroad, on condition that I was taken care of, and I promised to remain in England for one year, during which time you pledged yourself to send me a quarterly allowance, or rather your man of business pledged himself, in your name, in the presence of your son. I conceive a conditional arrangement to be null and void, when the conditions are not fulfilled. I therefore propose immediately joining Lord Worcester in Spain, in case I do not receive a due remittance from your Grace by return of post. I cannot help adding, that I should be very sorry to act with such want of feeling, towards my greatest enemy, as you have invariably shown yourself to me, who have from first to last, made every sacrifice in my power for your peace and happiness.[41]

Unaware that Worcester had absconded with Mrs Archdeacon, in March 1813 Harriette set off on the Falmouth mail in order to sail for Lisbon. ('Poor Meyler,' Harriette thought, 'and I will tell my readers a secret, I would much rather have gone to London.'[42]) This information created a frenzy in the Somerset camp. 'I immediately wrote to Fitzroy,' Lord Edward told the Duke,

to beg he would send Worcester a peremptory order from Lord Wellington to join without delay at Frenada, and I likewise commissioned a friend of mine at Lisbon who I can depend upon, to ascertain if the lady is actually there, and to communicate any particular on the subject that may come to his knowledge . . . You may be assured no exertions on my part shall be wanting to break off this . . . connection, and if I think it necessary, I will myself travel to Lisbon. After what passed between Worcester and me when I last saw him at Frenada, I cannot bring myself to think that he can have the most distant idea of marriage, nor can I absolutely believe, without more certain information, that it was his desire that she set out for Lisbon.

It is not improbable that she made that excuse for her journey, but still her influence over him seems so great that it is extremely desirable to separate them as soon as possible.[43]

Harriette travelled for two days and a night across Dartmoor and through Cornwall to the port town, taking as a companion Eliza's Aunt Martha. 'I am old enough, and thank God I am no beauty,' Aunt Martha declared, 'and I may do what I please with my little fortune. I have never been ten miles from my native place, and I want to see the world.'[44] Mrs Edmund and Eliza helped to modernize Aunt Martha's twenty-five-year-old riding habit into something 'smart and fashionable', and off the two of them went, on a fine clear morning. They arrived, the game courtesan and the retiring spinster, to find Falmouth teeming with prospective travellers, held back from sailing for the past three weeks due to poor winds. The hotels and inns were full, but they found a 'comfortless-looking' room which had just been vacated by a Londoner who had lost patience with the weather, and this they shared for the duration of their stay, initially leaving it only to find food as Aunt Martha thought Falmouth such a 'wicked' place. The Consul, whose presence at their inn was the cause of there being nothing left for anyone to eat, recognized Harriette and invited her and her fair companion to dinner and the theatre. Aunt Martha was thrilled and 'while she admitted that [Harriette] must have been the principal attraction', wished that she had packed her purple silk dress. Aunt Martha began to mourn her wasted years: 'How I regret not having seen something of life a little sooner . . .'[45] At last released from delivering broth to the village elderly, the two women settled into enjoying themselves as they waited for Harriette's day of departure. 'My health was scarcely ever so good as during the time I spent at Falmouth, nor do I recollect ever to have been thrown into society where there was so much vivacity and wit, and no trouble in dressing for it.'[46]

When Harriette received the news, which came from an officer who had just sailed in from headquarters, that Worcester had run away with Mrs Archdeacon, it was 'without, I confess, much agitation'. She also heard that if she arrived in Lisbon she might be deported to America. To the great relief of the Somerset family, she packed her bags and bid Aunt Martha farewell. 'Life is short, and I have been quite patient enough. I don't care one straw about money; but I must have something like enjoyment of some sort before I die.'[47] The captain of her ship refunded Harriette half of the twenty-five guineas she had paid him in advance, and she took her place on the mail coach, bound for Camden Town to see Julia and Fanny. 'It was a tremendously long journey; but I was tired of the country, tired of suspense, disgusted with the whole set of the Beauforts, and dying to be refreshed once more by the sight of Meyler's bright, expressive countenance.'[48]

Back in London, Harriette renegotiated her terms with the Duke, saying that she was ready to put herself under the protection of Richard Meyler as soon as she was provided for, 'according to his first proposal of giving me 500 pounds a year'. Beaufort replied offering an annuity of £300. Shortly afterwards, Worcester wrote to Harriette reiterating his love for her and saying that he had not in fact run away with Mrs Archdeacon even though she had 'followed him up to the army'. Harriette readjusted herself and informed the Duke that the situation with Meyler was changed and she was now returning to Worcester; he must not get the annuity made out under the wrong impression. The rumour about Worcester and Mrs Archdeacon then reached the Duke's ears and thinking that Worcester had forgotten Harriette, the Duke told her that there would be no money forthcoming 'and that I might starve if I did not like to live under another man'. Harriette, severely provoked, replied that she had several more letters now from Worcester promising marriage, and the Duke retorted that he would give her a small sum – and only a small sum – for their retrieval. Harriette's response was that 'if the annuity is not made out directly, I will publish the promise of marriage, and put an execution into your house for an annuity'.[49] A reduced annuity of £200 was eventually made out in late July, under the condition that Harriette never write to nor have contact with Worcester again, and that she give up all his letters. Worcester, hearing from his father what had happened, wrote telling Fanny how miserable he was at being left by her in this way.

Worcester's loyalty to Harriette had apparently been spent. 'I cannot tell you how sorry I am that HW still pesters you,' he wrote to his father on 22 July, the day after the battle of Vitoria, 'or how much I feel all your goodness in regard to her. I had a letter from her of the 13 June taking leave of me stating that it was the last she should ever write to me as she was to sign a bond in three or four days to that effect, but as you mention that you had not made up your mind on the subject she must have been mistaken. However, I trust and hope that you will not give her the £200 per annum on those terms as I do not think she will publish those letters and even if she does it will be better not to be bullied into it.'[50] Making mischief, Worcester wrote to his father again after the battle of the Pyrenees in August, thanking him again for 'all your kindness to me about HW' and owning that he thought 'it a pity that you have given her this sum after all her behaviour to you; as she certainly did not deserve it and I still fear from a hint she dropped in her letters to me of the beginning of July (the 10th or 12th I think) that one or two of the letters may still be kept back. However, if she herself says she has given them all up and has promised herself never to write any more I have then no fear as she will not do anything dishonest.' Writing to the Duke on 20 September 1813, Worcester confirmed that 'all correspondence and communication between us is at an end forever'.[51]

According to Harriette it was Worcester who broke the bond, writing a pitiful letter directly to her to which she took the risk of replying. 'It was, so I said to Fanny having read his letter, very mercenary, cruel and unnatural . . . were he to be killed abroad, I should never enjoy another hour's rest, and in spite of all they could say or do to prevent me, I wrote to tell Worcester that I trusted to God and to his good heart for seeing that I was somehow provided for; but that nothing should again induce me to cut him, while I believed him still fond of me, and unhappy for my sake.'[52] Harriette sent the letter and faced the consequences. Another version of what happened, which, given Harriette's previous experiences with Amy and Sophia, is rather more believable, can be found in *The English Spy*. Here it was reported by someone who knew the family well that Harriette's seeing Worcester flirt with one of her sisters sent her into a jealous rage, 'and in a moment of irritation, she in a most unequivocal manner publicly asserted her right to his person: the gallant yielded, the bond was null and void, the promise burnt, his grace relieved from the payment . . .'[53] In January 1814, Beaufort sent his attorney to Harriette to retrieve the second payment of £100 she had received on 9 January. Her annuity was lost.[54]

During his return to England in November 1813, Worcester joined Meyler and Julia's lover, Napier, in Melton Mowbray for some foxhunting.

Also there was Wellington's niece, Georgina Fitzroy. Worcester wrote home on 2 2 November that he was about to join Berkeley Craven, Napier and Meyler, who had now left Melton, to be the guest of Lord Craven at his estate of Coombe in Berkshire.[55] There was only one member of the ensuing Coombe party who had not been involved with Harriette, and he was Julia's protector: Harriette had been fodder for them all. While she describes each of these men as being possessive of her, sharing her body would seem to have consolidated rather than challenged the camaraderie between them. Having enjoyed the same woman, they were on an equal footing; their manhood had been approved by the person who knew best. Having had a taste of Harriette created between her lovers a sort of homo-erotic fellowship, as with Wellington's support of and protection over Worcester, and their circle closed a little more tightly.

The year 1 8 1 4 began in darkness. The fog at the dawn of the new year was so dense that carriages overturned and horses had to be led by lamp-light. The Thames froze over for Harriette's twenty-eighth birthday and Londoners enjoyed the first frost fair since 1 7 8 8, the year of her birth. A mall running down the river from Blackfriars Bridge was so busy that it was named the 'City Road'. Stalls were set up on the river selling ginger-bread, ale, bread and sweetmeats, and oxen were roasted on burning spits. Mary Anne Clarke reappeared, this time being tried for the libel of William Fitzgerald in *The Rival Princes*. She was defended by Henry Brougham. Harriette took note.

The frost was followed by six weeks of snow, and on Easter Sunday the war with France was declared over: Napoleon had abdicated and retreated to exile on the island of Elba; the Bourbon King was reinstated. London lit up in celebration; fireworks exploded into the night skies and a round of dazzling parties began. Pagodas, bridges and oriental temples were erected in the London parks surrounding Mayfair; Charles Lamb wrote to Wordsworth that 'all that was countryfy'd in the Parks is all but obliterated. The very colour of green is vanished, the whole surface of Hyde Park is dry crumbling sand (Arabia, Arenosa), not a vestige or hint of grass ever having grown there, booths and drinking places all around it for a mile and a half I am quite confident . . . the stench of liquors, *bad* tobacco, dirty people and provisions, conquers the air and we are stifled and suffocated in Hyde Park'.[56] 'I remember well', Harriette wrote, 'that

London had never been so brilliantly gay in my time before.' The French King paid a visit – 'Louis the Gouty is wheeling in triumph into Piccadilly,' Byron told Tom Moore – and following his swollen form came the triumphant allies, the Prussian sovereign and the Russian Tsar. Harriette recalled that 'the Opera House was perhaps never so crowded, in the memory of any person now living, as on the night that these two crowned heads, accompanied by our beloved sovereign . . . appeared at this theatre. Thirty guineas were, I know, refused for a box on the upper tier. Amy, with her usual selfishness, forced herself into my box, which was already crowded beyond endurance, because it exactly faced the royal one.'[57] Central London was so overcrowded that the cows were frightened out of Green Park by the noise, which resulted in a shortage of milk, and washer-women were scarce because they were busy scrubbing the costumes of the royal visitors.

Wellington returned to England in June and took his seat in the House of Lords as Viscount, Earl, Marquis and Duke. On 21 July, the Regent gave a fête in his honour at Carlton House, for which occasion Nash built a special hall. That night Worcester announced his engagement to Miss Georgina Fitzroy, the woman who had accompanied him to Melton. 'I hope that it will turn out well,' Lady Frances Shelley wrote in her diary, 'but I have my doubts! Lord Worcester is only twenty-one and very wild.'[58] The wedding took place four days later; the Duke of Wellington gave away the bride. Harriette says that she was past caring about the Beauforts by this point, but the blow to her pride – and to her reputation – was severe; rejection is contagious. Harriette had taken a well-publicized year out of social circulation in order to wait for her lord to return and claim her. Worcester had eventually found her charms resistible. He had made her look ridiculous by marrying another within a year of declaring his undying love to Harriette. She took consolation from the rumour that Miss Fitzroy's features 'very closely resembled' her own, but Julia John-stone remarked that she never saw two women less alike, 'the one all paint and perfume, with a hair-dresser's window dangling round her head; the other breathing pure nature'.[59]

CHAPTER 15

Paris

The end of the conflict with France had removed London's artificial atmosphere, the protective coating that had hardened and intensified city life since 1793. Many of Harriette's friends had gone to war as contented debauchees to return as heroes; even Worcester came home from the Peninsula a respected figure with a reputation to uphold.[1] There was an air of supremacy, of absolute triumphalism about England's victory over Napoleon, but twenty years of conflict had left the economy in the doldrums. John Dubouchet announced that, now the Channel was reopened, he was leaving his family to return to his native Switzerland. He persuaded a reluctant Amelia and those of their children still living at home to leave as well and settle in Paris, where the English were flocking in their thousands. Lord Berwick, keen to see the back of his in-laws, strongly supported the idea of their moving, and Harriette, having nothing much to keep her in London, considered joining her mother. Their departure would have been sooner had not Colonel Parker returned home with the news that he was to be married. Fanny fell ill and lay for two days in the darkened sitting room of the house she shared with Julia. She never spoke of Parker again and changed, Harriette said, from being 'gay to serious'. She eventually 'forced herself to go back into society . . . but her lips now assumed a blueish tint, whenever she made the slightest exertion, or hurried upstairs,

Corinthian Tom, Pierce Egan's *Life in London*

or walked fast, and she would put her hand on her left side and say, "There is something very wrong, and odd, about my heart, of that I am certain . . ."'[2]

Harriette got back in touch with Meyler. He was 'unusually romantic' on hearing from her, but she passes swiftly over his endearments: 'It is not my intention to dwell on Meyler's love, or Meyler's raptures, since such subjects, in prose, are very prosy.'[3] He rented for them the same house on Lisson Grove, off the New Road and near Regent's Park, in which she had lived for a while with Worcester. Initially Harriette enjoyed the novelty of Meyler's company. 'But alas! In rather less than three weeks,' she wrote, 'I discovered that Meyler, the lively Meyler, was one of the worst tempered men in all England! This was very hard upon one who, like myself, had been spoiled and indulged by a man who was a slave to my slightest caprices! I cannot describe Meyler's temper, for I never met with anything in the way of temper to be compared to his. It was a sort of periodical temper; and when he had passed a whole day in sweet soft conversation, I was perfectly sure that a storm was at hand for the next day, and vice versa.'[4] Harriette had ended up in the same position as her mother: living with a domineering and temperamental man.

Harriette's relationship with Meyler was dictated by emotional rather than financial need. She stayed with him because there was no one else to whom she could move on; her reputation had been besmirched by the Beaufort affair and Harriette was seen now as troublesome, money-grabbing and hankering for marriage. She and Meyler loathed one another, Harriette said, but could not let each other go; they were 'eternally at variance when together, yet . . . were ever miserable and jealous while separate'.[5] Harriette had never before stayed in a situation in which she was not happy: boredom with Craven and poverty with Lamb had not been tolerated by her, and she remedied both by moving on to someone better. This was not the case with Meyler. Since the Beaufort debacle, Harriette was less sure of herself, more readily undermined and in need of approbation. She was in her late twenties and no longer had the pick of London's finest men. All the same, she knew that Meyler was 'not up to me, either in hand or heart'.[6] He had no title, he was 'new' money, his behaviour was beneath her dignity and he brought her down to his level. Harriette frequently said that after losing Ponsonby her only interest was in living 'free as the air' but with Meyler she was trapped. He would become angry, she would kick him out of bed and 'cut' him for a few days. He would return to his house in Grosvenor Square and then skulk back to Lisson Grove, after which the couple would reunite. This was the pattern of their affair. 'We had,' Harriette recalled, 'in one month, mutually agreed to part at least twenty times over, and then made matters up again. The deuce was in us both.'[7]

Even their periods of separation made Harriette miserable. 'To conceal my real feelings, I dressed gaily, I went blazing to the opera, and to every other place of resort where I might expect to meet Meyler's friends . . . He shall see me merry, and surrounded with handsome admirers, if I am to die the next hour. The little, provokingly handsome sugar-baker must not know that I still remember him, and am dying for his kiss.'[8] He had only to hold his 'beautiful, white, *petite* hand' towards hers for Harriette to find herself 'seated in his carriage, on our way home'.[9] And so the cycle would continue: Meyler attended the parties and balls of the *grande-monde*, to which Harriette was not invited, while Harriette ruled over her sphere of the *demi-monde*. He became jealous when she attracted attention; she became jealous when he went out alone. When they were together in public, each nervously eyed the other across the room, checking who they were speaking to, guessing what was being said, eventually intercepting and taking their lover away.

Living with Meyler, Harriette began to take on his characteristics and to lose her usually bright temperament: 'I must confess', she said, 'I was sometimes a very tyrant towards Meyler; and yet I know my temper is naturally good; but my feelings towards Meyler were all made up of passion. I neither esteemed nor trusted him; and yet I was never so jealous of any other man.'[10] His jealousy was, Harriette said, 'downright selfishness, for he would be jealous of my pianoforte, if that instrument amused me. He was, in fact, always jealous, unless I was counting the minutes of his absence. If I procured a private box, to witness a play . . . with my sister Fanny, he would send a note, by his coachman, to this effect: "Dearest Harriette, I send a carriage to convey you to the play, to prove my wish to put no restraint on your wishes; but if, for my sake, you would stay at home, I should feel both grateful and happy, and will return to you as soon as possible."' Harriette, for her part, once sent in the box-keeper when

Meyler was accompanying the Duchess of Beaufort to the opera, to request that he come out and speak to her in the passage. 'Meyler,' she said, 'if you return, even for an instant, to the Duchess of Beaufort's box, we part this night and forever. I cannot endure it.'[11] Meyler, gratified, went home with Harriette.

Meyler's relationship with the Beauforts continued to be as intimate as before and he regularly went to Badminton as their guest, which event, Harriette wrote, 'never failed to render me completely wretched. "My God," said Meyler one day, striking his head violently with his hand, "what am I to do? I would rather blow my brains out than be thus the slave of any woman. Mine is not the passion of a day, or a year. I shall never cease to love you; but I must enjoy a little liberty."' Meyler was so rich, Harriette reasoned, and 'so very very beautiful, and it would be so shocking to lose him altogether. I will therefore put up with him in his own way, as long as I have reason to believe him constant to me. I ought to be grateful, since I know that half the women in London would fain tempt him to forget me.'[12] In an attempt to disguise her sadness at Meyler's departing the next morning, Harriette kept up high spirits; Meyler accused her of not loving him if she could be so happy to see him go. Harriette retorted that she was happy because she trusted him and, besides, jealous women were unattractive; Meyler answered that if she were not jealous of his spending time with the Duchess of Beaufort then she couldn't feel anything for him at all and so, in order to punish her, he declared he would not now be going to Badminton. Harriette, delighted, admitted that she had only 'acted with indifference from dread of disgusting you; but now, since you will stay, I am so very, very happy', at which point Meyler, 'satisfied that it would make me miserable, set off for Badminton the next morning'.[13]

On another occasion, Meyler was invited to a ball at the Duke of Devonshire's. He dressed himself in regimental uniform in which 'he looked so handsome, and his red coat reflected such a fine glowing tint on his transparent pale cheeks, that I was selfish and wicked enough to determine against his exhibiting himself at His Grace of Devonshire's'. Harriette became once more wretched at the thought of being alone while Meyler attended a party to which 'all the world' had been invited, and she begged him to stay: 'Meyler . . . I have given way at all times to your caprice and jealousy. This once, humour mine, and I shall feel most grateful. My health and spirits are low tonight. Pray cut the Duke and return with me. This is the first time I ever interfered with your amusements, therefore do not refuse me.'[14] If he left her alone, Harriette threatened, she would call on Lord Ebrington and 'make love to him'. Meyler duly went home with Harriette.

On 1 July 1814, a masquerade ball was held by the members of the notorious Wattier's Club at Burlington House in celebration of the English victory over Napoleon. Coaches blocked Piccadilly from five in the afternoon until ten at night. John Cam Hobhouse, who attended with Byron, described the seated supper for the 1,700 guests as 'the most magnificent thing of the kind ever seen',[15] and Harriette agreed that 'it was the most brilliant assemblage I had ever witnessed'. She, Amy and Fanny got tickets and Julia, unable to obtain a lady's ticket, had to attend as a boy. So off Harriette and Julia went to Mr Stultze in Clifford Street, to choose their costumes. Harriette gives more attention to their dress that night than she does on any other occasion; in tribute, perhaps, to the elegiac nature of the event. This was to be the last appearance of the Three Graces together and Harriette's last glorious party.

Julia wore 'black satin small clothes, plaited very full round the waist . . . fastened tight at the knee, with a smart bow, fine, black transparent silk stockings, black satin shoes, cut very short in the quarters, and tied with a large red rossette, a French cambric shirt, with beautifully small plaited sleeves, a bright blue, rich silk jacket without sleeves, trimmed, very thick, with curiously wrought silver bell-buttons, and a plain round black hat with a red silk band and bow'. Harriette, as Julia's companion, came in 'a bright red, thick, silk petticoat, with a black satin jacket, the form of which was very peculiar and most advantageous to the shape. The sleeves were tight, and it came rather high upon the breast. It was very full trimmed, with a double row of the same buttons Julia wore. My shoes were black satin, turned over with red morocco; my stockings were of fine blue silk, with small red clocks; my hat was small, round and almost flat, the crown being merely the height of a full puffing of rich pea-green satin ribbon. The hat was covered with satin of the same colour, and placed on one side at the back of the head. The hair was to fall over the neck and face in a profusion of careless ringlets, and, inside my vest, an Indian amber-coloured handkerchief'.[16] Fanny went as a country housemaid and Amy as a nun. The Dukes of Devonshire and Leinster, dressed in light-blue dominoes, received them at the door; as members of Wattier's, they did not have to be masked or in character. The best characters were, Harriette thought, Douglas Kinnaird 'as a Yorkshireman in search of a place', and Colonel Armstrong as an 'old stiff maiden-lady' in the reign of Queen Anne.

Meyler spent the evening in a state of high anxiety, searching behind the masks for Harriette. Julia's gender was a point of discussion for everyone; 'the leg is a boy's, the finest I ever saw . . . but then that foot, where shall we find a boy with such delicate feet and hands?'[17] Harriette was kissed by a mysterious stranger 'in a rich white satin Spanish dress, and a very magnificent plume of white ostrich-feathers in his hat'. 'Had I known you before my marriage,' he said, 'my dearest and most generous of all human beings, you should never have been exposed to the cold-blooded unfeeling wretches who have always taken such an unfair advantage of you.' He told her that he once had loved her and Harriette hoped the mask hid Lord Ponsonby.[18]

The masquerade was Harriette Wilson's ideal environment. 'I love a masquerade,' she said, 'because a female can never enjoy the same liberty anywhere else. It is delightful to be able to wander about in a crowd, making my observations, and conversing with whomsoever I please without being liable to be stared at or remarked upon, and to speak to whom I please, and run away from them the moment I have discovered their stupidity.'[19] No one was who they appeared to be, the rules were to be deceptive, flirtatious and mysterious – arts Harriette had been practising all her adult life. She always liked to keep people guessing at the truth of who she was and what she said, and in her *Memoirs* she would show to perfection how she had learned to speak behind a persona. The account she gives of Wattier's masquerade is fantastical and melancholy. She turns herself into a mythical figure and the ball into a dream sequence in which 'Harriette Wilson', the Regency's most sought after courtesan, meets Lord Byron, the Regency's most celebrated poet. Byron, dressed as a monk, stands gazing before him at some object Harriette cannot discover, in a room filled with pale-green silk ottomans fringed with silver, and exotic flowers whose odours bleed into the warm night air. Harriette, disguised as the peasant girl, watches him, motionless, unseen. Music and voices dip and rise around them but where they stand it is as still and silent as the moon. His brown robes fall in ample folds to the ground and his hood frames a face of almost unearthly beauty – a noble forehead, olive complexion, bright, intense eyes and full, curvacious mouth. When she at last approaches him, on the tips of her toes, he starts and reddens, his reverie broken. She seizes his hand and speaks in French. He had seemed like something supernatural, she says, pressing his arm to be sure it is indeed flesh and blood. She would leave him in peace for the rest of the night, she pleads, if he would gratify her curiosity now. It is not his heart she wants, she would never risk that; it is his mind she wishes to engage. The stranger sighs, evidently relieved, and tells her how weary he is of women's love and worldly things. Together they speak of his genius, his despair and his ennui. 'You', the peasant girl says, 'must be Lord Byron.' 'And you', he replies, 'are Harriette Wilson.'[20]

They discuss Lady Caroline Lamb and her scandalous novel *Glenarvon*, in which Byron appears as a child-murdering Irish Revolutionary. No matter that the book will not be published for another two years; Harriette never knew Byron anyway. 'We will never meet, and never *have* met,' she later wrote to him.[21] Byron attended the masquerade and Harriette certainly saw him there, but that is as far as their physical intimacy was to go; he responded to the letters she wrote him, but her tales of Byron's hungrily seeking her out for philosophical conversation were pure fantasy. He married six months after Wattier's masquerade and went into exile the following year, when the marriage disastrously collapsed. Eight years after that he was no longer alive to contradict the account of him Harriette gave in her *Memoirs*. Byron, like her, had become in his lifetime a fictional figure: no one would know if Harriette's story about their encounter was true, and no one would care.

The accounts Harriette gave to Byron himself of their 'encounter' at Wattier's are as romantic as the version of events she printed in her *Memoirs*. 'I knew I could never inspire affection in your breast . . .' she wrote to him years afterwards, 'and all I ever thought of was to look at and touch the hand of the author whose lines had so taken hold of my imagination. *This* I accomplished without your knowledge. I shook hands with you, felt your breath and lips upon my hand and admired you "as one would a particular star" . . . It was at *Wattier's* masquerade for the *Emperor Alexander* in the

Burlington that I shook hands with you and you admired my feet and hands." [22] Again in a nostalgic mood, when both were living abroad, she told him that 'I looked at you for half an hour together one night and while studying your *very* beautiful countenance I could fancy a new sensation produced by the warm pressure of your lips to mine, beyond what *my* nature could endure – wild and eager as your poetry – terrifying by its power to *wither* and destroy me . . . Are you as dark as at the masquerade or were you painted?' [23]

Soon after Wattier's masquerade, Harriette left for Paris accompanied by her maid and Fanny's young son, George Woodcock. Fanny, who was ill, stayed in London with Julia, who couldn't bear to leave Napier – 'Ladies on the wrong side of forty become so very tender!' Harriette observed [24] – and Amelia was packing up the London house in preparation to join Harriette. Knowing that she was no more able to separate from Meyler than Julia was from Napier, Harriette suggested altering the terms of their relationship: 'I hold myself no longer', she told him, 'under your protection . . . I don't mean to say that I will be unfaithful to you: but from this hour I am my own mistress, and you, when we meet any visitors, are to be turned out, the first moment you treat me with want of politeness.' [25] Under this new arrangement, their quarrels ceased and Meyler agreed to meet Harriette in France after a week.

Her good friend and sometime lover, Lord Frederick Bentinck, drove Harriette's party the first two stages of the way to Dover, 'and then after a world of good advice and many questions as to where I expected to go after I was dead, he took his leave'. [26]

There was no better place for the jaded and disillusioned than Paris in 1815. The streets, which for the last seventeen years had been the site of slaughter and bloodshed, were now perpetual fairs. 'When the good Lord is bored in heaven,' so one proverb went, 'he opens the window and watches the boulevards of Paris.' The chief contrast between Paris and London were the open spaces: the Parisians lived outside and the city was designed around this. The Tuileries, the Palais Royal, the parks and cafés; life was lived in public where the *grande-* and the *demi-mondes* mingled in a relaxed, conversational manner unknown in London. Along the tree-lined boulevards were shops of every description, coffee-houses, milliners, clothes-menders, rope-dancers, musicians, small theatres, booksellers, one-man shows. 'You can suppose nothing more brilliant in the way of general out-of-door display', one contemporary wrote,

than the show of the boulevards of an evening, after the lamps are lighted. The road is constantly traversed by carriages, and the borders of the causeway are occupied by lines, two or three deep, of chairs, filled by persons of both sexes. From the very young to the tolerably old, their appearance sprinkled with a considerable portion of the fancifulness of fashion, and all of them in the most satisfied and communicative humour possible. Talking – making love – laughing – amusing themselves with trifling purchases from the baskets of the surrounding vendors of fruit or flowers – with the refreshments of the contiguous coffee houses – sitting to see and be seen, or listening to the voices and performances of erratic minstrels, who successively appear and disappear among the crowd. These form the pleasing occupations of the Parisians every fine evening through the summer . . . and as almost every evening here is fine, they become very seldom subject to inter-ruption.[27]

Paris was again the first city in Europe, a babylon of pleasures, 'the most interesting place on earth'. It was estimated that a third of the House of Lords crossed the channel that summer; Harriette's whole world had reconvened there. 'It is raining English here,' Prince Metternich wrote to his wife, 'five to six hundred a day . . .' In 1816 there were twenty-nine thousand English living in Paris; 'Where are all the French?' one dismayed Englishman asked. 'Nowhere, all is English.' They made the fifty-hour journey not only to see the sights – 'The beauty and magnificence of it sur-passed anything I could form an idea of,' Wellington's niece, Lady Burghersh, wrote. 'All the Arcs de Triomphe, pillars etc which Buonaparte has erected are perfect'[28] – but to shop, eat and drink. There were three thousand restaurants and more cafés; a four-course meal could be had for a fraction of the price one might pay in London. Everything was finer here and cheaper too, including dress material. Harriette could enjoy a better quality of life in a city where wit and conversation held priority over rank. The Parisians were less formal than the London fashionables; dinner parties, the lifeblood of English high society, gave way to after-dinner salons, where guests might wander in and out of the hostess's drawing room at their leisure, wearing what they chose.

Harriette rented elegant rooms in 35 rue de la Paix where for her first two days she slept off the exhaustion of the journey, before joining the throngs who had taken over the city. She admired the Parisian women, visited the Place Vendôme, the parks, and the Louvre. Here she saw the Apollo Belvedere, looted by Napoleon from its native Rome, and was struck 'not for its beauty, but for the appearance of life, fire and animation, which never can be described, nor imagined, by anybody who has not seen it'.[29]

The Duke of Wellington arrived that August to begin his term as British Ambassador to the court of the Tuileries. His duties were 'to hunt amicably with the royal family while hammering away at King Louis to abolish the Slave Trade in his colonies'.[30] Now a hero, Wellington brought with him to Paris boatloads of admirers, including Lady Caroline Lamb, who clung to celebrity like a vine to a wall.[31] He purchased for himself the beautiful Hôtel de Charost, formally in the possession of Napoleon's sister, Pauline Borghese. The new embassy was at the heart of Paris's *quartier brillant*. Ever keen to humiliate the Duke, Harriette tells of a farcical story of his galloping past her carriage in the Bois de Boulogne one morning and asking to pay her a visit. 'You are a little fool,' she has him murmur, decked 'all over [in] orders and ribbons of different colours, bows and stars' as he tries, publicly and forcibly, to kiss her.[32]

When Meyler arrived, he informed Harriette that he had never before had an 'intrigue' with a Frenchwoman and 'must try them, merely for fun, and to have something to talk about'.[33] To hide her indignation, Harriette acted indifferently, which fired Meyler's passion and increased his own insecurity. Harriette, hoping to beat Meyler at his own game, set out to seduce the young Frenchmen who she expected 'would be tumbling over each other in their great zeal to show me their national politeness'. But she discovered that they were 'as indifferent as even Brummell himself to every woman turned of twenty'.[34] Meyler's hotel was opposite Harriette's, and each would spy on the coming and going of the other's cabriolet and the arrival and departure of their guests until they were demented with jealousy. Meyler, Harriette realized, sought the company of as many Parisian women as he could find, and she bore the insult with pride. 'I wanted to convince him of my perfect contempt and indifference. I should have preferred being pointed at by the whole world, as one of the most profligate women breathing, rather than that anyone should imagine me capable of wearing the willow for a mere sugar baker, who could forsake me and openly seek the society of the lowest women in preference to mine.'[35] All was not lost, however, because Viscount Ebrington was also in Paris.

It is revealing of the state of Harriette's confidence that the only man she considered leaving Meyler for was someone with whom she had already, in the days before she knew Ponsonby, had a brief affair. She had separated from Ebrington then because they were 'too alike in temper to agree'; how could she be sure that they would suit one another now?[36] Lord Ebrington contrasted well with Meyler: he was widely read while Meyler had read nothing; he gave 'lively, pleasant conversation' while Meyler 'seldom spoke at all'.[37] Ebrington was a connoisseur of the arts and an avid admirer of Bonaparte; Meyler was interested in whores and horses. Meyler was an 'animal' whom Harriette loved for his beauty; with Ebrington 'I began to grow in love with his mind.'[38] He was three years her senior and the son of the Earl of Fortescue and Hester Grenville, whose brother was the first Marquis of Buckingham. He was therefore another relation of Julia Johnstone. His family was ancient and prestigious, he was 'shy, proud and reserved', reminding Harriette, as did so many men, of Ponsonby.[39] Harriette, as was her wont, first asked Meyler what he thought of Ebrington, and Meyler, confident, in Harriette's account, that this was one man she could not seduce, confirmed that he was 'the handsomest, most sensible, and distinguished looking young nobleman in Europe', concluding that, 'I am not such a vain fool as to believe any woman breathing would have me, or remain an hour with me, if she could be tolerated by Lord Ebrington'.[40] She did not attack Ebrington's heart with her usual quickfire offensive; Harriette was cautious about making advances. 'In the first place, though Meyler was a torment to me, my jealousy prevented me from throwing him upon the world; in the second, I could not deceive any man; in the third, I said to myself, why should Lord Ebrington like me now, when my health and freshness are gone, though he did not care for me in the days of my earliest youth and beauty!'[41] None the less, determined not to stay unhappy, Harriette sat down and wrote to the viscount in her buoyant style, suggesting that they renew their acquaintance. 'If you were tired of me long ago, when I was quite a different sort of person, you may like me now; while, at the same time, I may be less afraid of you than I was formerly.'[42]

Ebrington was flattered by the letter and the pair immediately met up, able to 'converse more freely' now than before. Since their previous separation, he told her over cups of chocolate the next morning, he had heard of 'nothing but Harriette Wilson wherever I went. I could not help wondering what Ponsonby or Worcester had discovered in you that was so very charming, and yet could have entirely escaped my observation.' Ebrington claimed that she had once been 'too shy for my taste' but was now exactly what he wanted: he 'dearly' loved his 'dear Harry'. 'Ebrington and I were excellent companions,' Harriette recalled. 'We both knew the world well, and well we both knew how to laugh at it.'[43] But she also found his satirical arrogance 'odious' and disliked the way the blood froze in his veins when he grew angry with her.

Meyler wept when Harriette broke him the news of her success, and begged to have her back; she refused on the principle that she did not humiliate herself with men who had betrayed her. Harriette's two lovers then decided to 'sit one another out', much as Leinster and Worcester had done, and the trio spent many an hour trying to 'hit upon subjects for conversation. We had gone over that lame one, the weather, at least three times, and the dirty streets of Paris, the French cookery etc. Ebrington now tried Bonaparte, then pictures, next statues: but Meyler knew no more about them all than the man in the moon.' Needless to say, it was Meyler who won; his pleading and frailty as ever drawing Harriette back for another miserable term, following which she left him once more and wrote telling Ebrington that the coast was now clear if he still loved her. Ebrington was reinstated, Meyler wept; Meyler was reinstated, Ebrington discharged; Meyler retreated, Ebrington was summoned; Ebrington went to Italy; Harriette 'regretted him for a whole day and night'. Meyler returned, followed by Ebrington.

While this eternal merry-go-round was keeping Harriette entertained, Amelia and her children arrived and settled in a house outside Paris. They were followed by Amy, with the inseparable wits Luttrell and Nugent in tow. Amy's black-pudding soirées became a significant social event, and Harriette gave her sister a seat in her opera box. Amy, tired of Berkeley Paget, had sent him back to his wife and was now enjoying the attentions of Mr Grefule, 'the most absurd, affected, mean, contemptible blockhead I had ever met with'.[44]

News reached Paris in March that Napoleon had escaped from Elba and was now marching towards the capital with an army. Peace was over, Louis XVIII fled the city and the English hastily gathered together their belongings in the rush to cross back over the Channel. Before Napoleon entered the Tuileries for his final hundred days of rule, Harriette and her family had arrived back in England. The celebrations of 1814 had, it seemed, been premature; the old regime seemed doomed after all. But in June 1815, Wellington and the allies defeated Napoleon at Waterloo. Their victory was total.

That same summer, Fanny Parker died aged thirty-three. She was buried in the churchyard of St Mary Abbots in Kensington but her grave has long since disappeared, razed to the ground in the middle of the nineteenth century, when the old church was rebuilt. Fanny's final protector was the Earl of Bective, son of the Marquis of Headfort who, Harriette said, 'had long been our family's friend, equally at hand to congratulate us on our marriages, our simple fornications, our birthdays, or our expected deaths'.45 Lord Bective was not there for Fanny's expected death. She was attended by Sir William Knighton, physician to the Regent and later confidant to the King. It was not Bective but Lord Yarmouth, Fanny's sometime protector whose devotion to her had never waned, who arranged for her to have such superior care. It was also Yarmouth who moved her to rooms in Queen's Buildings, on the Brompton Road near Knightsbridge, where the air was better, and he had straw laid outside her door to soften the noise of the horses. When there was little more that could be done for her, Yarmouth rode into London to buy eau de Cologne for Fanny's fevered temples. Amy returned from France to nurse her sister during the day, Harriette watched her by night. Sophia too sat at her sister's bedside.

Fanny's death left Harriette stricken with grief. Fanny, she said, had been her only friend, and a brief glance at the motley players left strutting about her stage suggests that she was not exaggerating the enormity of her loss. Harriette had no other confidant or ally. There was no one else with whom she was so intimate; her mother was the only other woman for whom she felt equal respect. Fanny was the one person with whom Harriette can be said to have enjoyed a committed long-term relationship and she always presented herself and her sister as a traditional couple; she was masculine while Fanny was feminine. Lovers came and went, Julia and Amy were more usually out of favour than in. Harriette's point of stability was Fanny.

Amelia's health 'visibly declined' following Fanny's death and she died three months later, on 13 September, aged fifty-three. Harriette's mother lived for the last year of her life in a newly built house in a handsome row at 10 Stafford Street, a road running parallel to Lisson Grove, now at the foot of where London's Westway flyover now stands. John Dubouchet was back in the Canton de Berne and Amelia is recorded as the sole ratepayer. It is likely that Sophia paid for her mother's home; Lady Berwick was a regular visitor, arriving every day in her carriage to take the family out for rides. The only children who remained in Amelia's care were Henry, aged eleven, and Rose, aged sixteen; fourteen-year-old Charlotte was living with Lord and Lady Berwick. When their mother died, Henry and Rose joined their aristocratic sister.

Those Harriette had loved most deeply, Ponsonby, Fanny and Amelia, were each now gone, and from 'this hour', she said, her 'habits and character became more serious'.[46] The deaths of Fanny and Amelia were a turning point in Harriette's life, as Ponsonby's leaving her had been. She also saw their deaths as the end point: it is here that the 1825 edition of her *Memoirs* close. She has nothing left to say. It is hard to imagine, had Amelia and Fanny lived, that Harriette would have continued as she did.

Harriette revered goodness and this is what those she loved best symbolized for her. Ponsonby was perfection itself, and Fanny and Amelia represented in Harriette's eyes all the virtues: beauty, modesty, sacrifice, generosity, frailty, kindness, honour and dignity. These were qualities she would never aspire to; in the years following Ponsonby she was happy to see herself as a fun-loving, broken-hearted, hard-living whore. What Harriette loved in other people was difference; she idealized it, eroticized it, invented it when she needed to. Fanny she saw as her negative, her mother was a martyr to home and husband. Harriette was the war-like protector of each, viciously on guard against anyone who might hurt or attack her idols.

She describes her mother and sister as having been killed by the unbearable pain of loss: Fanny's of Parker and Amelia's of Fanny. Fanny, at least, was consumptive. 'She screamed to live,' Julia (who was not present) wrote, 'and had no hopes of a blessed hereafter. I fear it may prove a family death-bed.'[47] Harriette does not say from what Amelia died. Julia said it was '"two pints of brandy and a great chair *per diem*". A strange disorder but a true one; and almost a natural death for all the de Bouchets.'[48] Harriette projected the feelings she found most unbearable on to those she was closest to; whatever pain Fanny and Amelia may have felt, it was Harriette herself who was struggling with the deteriorating effects of grief; Harriette who had to remould herself around the losses she endured, who felt herself becoming a graveyard of dead souls. She dealt with mourning by empathizing with vulnerability; she accepted her losses bitterly, but she never let go of the object of her love. With Ponsonby, she finally acknowledged that he would not return and could not be replaced, but she never relinquished his idealized image and still howled in pain thirty years later. The same is true of her mother and sister. As ever, in grief Harriette combined realism with romance.

Depressed, Harriette took to her bed in the autumn of 1815 and was tended by Dr Nevinson of St George's Hospital, who 'would daily pass hours by my bedside, month after month in succession, while I was only in low nervous health and required no medical aid'.[49] At the point when her 'spirits and health were at their very worst', Harriette was informed that Julia Johnstone was also dying and had asked to see her old friend. Poor Julia's 'features bore the fixed rigidity of death when I entered the room. Her complaint . . . was a disease of the heart and there was no remedy.'[50] Harriette wrote to Napier, who was hunting in Melton, and he returned to kneel by his lover's bedside and 'read the service of the dead'. When Julia had breathed her last, Napier pulled out his hair, called her name and threw the sofa cushions around the room. He paid off half of what Julia still owed to Mr Smith, the hosier and haberdasher of Oxford Street, and Mr Peacock, the shoemaker of Titchfield Street. He ensured that her children were distributed around relatives and friends (giving one of her sons to Lord Folkstone) and, 'after her body had been shown to the neighbours residing about Chapel Street, Grosvenor Place, where she died', he had her buried in the family vault.[51]

CHAPTER 16

Henry Brougham

Following the deaths of her mother and her sister, Harriette returned to Paris. It was 1817 and also in Paris, having run away with and then from Mrs George Lamb, was Henry Brougham. Brougham had gone with his mistress to Geneva where the monotony of the landscape – '*Ennui* comes on the third hour, and suicide attacks you before night'[1] – cooled his ardour. When Mrs Lamb returned home to her husband, Brougham became acquainted with the Lambs' old friend, Harriette Wilson. The relationship was to be one of the most enduring and significant of her life.

Brougham's visit to Geneva coincided with the arrival there of Lord Byron, who had run away from England after his wife, Annabella Milbanke, a cousin of the Lambs, ran away from him. The poet would never return home, and while London salons mourned their most dazzling star they flocked to booksellers to buy *Glenarvon*, the fantastical novel about herself and Byron written by the wife of William Lamb, Lady Caroline.

During the time of the Byron scandal in 1816, Meyler, or 'Dick the Dandy-Killer' as he became known,[2] finally broke with Harriette and began the ruin of high society's other favourite, Beau Brummell. The Beau's fate, like that of Byron, was all too inevitable; his sun, as Harriette put it, had long been setting. 'Empires had risen and fallen while he experimented with the crease of a neck-cloth,' Virginia Woolf wrote in her

Houses of Parliament, *Views of London*

elegant essay on Brummell, 'and criticized the cut of a coat. Now the battle of Waterloo had been fought and peace had come. And it was peace that undid him.'[3] The armies disbanded, pouring soldiers into London's gaming houses; Brummell's game got higher, he lost his lucky coin, he spent his last guinea, he borrowed money and won, he played again and lost. He made an enemy of the Regent, a sure sign that his days were numbered.

Together with his closest friends, Robert and Charles Manners, Brummell had set up various schemes to get capital, and in 1816 he joined Lords Alvanley and Worcester to raise a loan of £30,000 on their joint securities. 'The weight of the debt', Harriette recalled, 'was expected to fall on the Duke of Beaufort, who, after strict enquiry, ascertained that Brummell was deeply involved and without even the most remote prospect of ever possessing a single guinea.' Meyler, who had lent Brummell £7,000, went in a hot-headed rage to White's 'for the sole purpose of saying to every man who entered that Mr Brummell's late conduct both towards the Marquis of Worcester and himself had been such as rendered him a disgrace to society and most unfit to remain a member of that club'. Panicked, Brummell sent a note to Meyler, 'begging to be informed if such had really and truly been the expressions made use of'. Meyler, immune to the implied threat, replied that 'not only had he used the expressions but that he further proposed returning to the club on the following day for the sole purpose of repeating them between the hours of two and four, to anybody who might be present, and if anybody had anything to say to him in return, he would be sure to find him at White's during that hour'.[4]

The next day, 16 May, Brummell dined on cold fowl and red wine, paid a last visit to the opera, bid farewell to 'about a dozen of his former acquaintances'. 'I now throw myself on your compassion,' he said in Harriette's dramatization of the scene, 'being in a wretched plight.' When these 'half and half sort of gentry' asked what Brummell could offer in exchange for being given large sums of money by them at this precarious stage in his life, the Beau replied, 'Why, have I not called you Dick, Tom and John, you rogues? And was not that worth all the money to you? But for this, do you fancy or flatter yourselves that you would ever have been seen picking your teeth in Lady Foley's box, or the Duchess of Rutland's?' He slipped out of London, arriving in Dover before dawn. He sailed to Calais where he lived for the rest of his life and was, Harriette said, visited by 'half the world . . . as though he had been a lion'.[5] In a 'pair of much-mended trousers' and 'a tattered cloak',[6] Brummell continued to entertain and was visited by all the old crowd on their way to and from Paris. Harriette, out of curiosity rather than concern, called and found him, plump and bewigged, at his second *toilette* of the day, in a room stuffed with watches, snuffboxes, seals and chains, all presents from English ladies of rank. '"Play", he said, "had been the ruin of them all." '[7]

Two years after Brummell fled the country, Meyler, aged twenty-six, fell from his horse during a hunt at Melton Mowbray and broke his neck. His body was laid out in great pomp and state at the Three Crows, Leicester, and he was buried in Crawley on 12 March 1818. Richard Meyler was the last of his family line and his will was unfinished; nine years later the administration of his considerable estate was still being fought over by disparate relations.[8] Harriette mentions Meyler's death only in passing and does not say how it affected her.

The party was over. Those of Harriette's friends who were still standing were sobering up. In June 1817, Lord Ebrington married the daughter of the Countess of Harrowby, whose sister was the Duchess of Beaufort. The wild figures of the Regency were not only disappearing but closing ranks. In their stead emerged heroes of a different kind: grand patriarchs and orators; those who became the great Victorians were the new gods. No poet would again be so desired by his readers as Byron, and no one since Brummell has been again been lionized for the tie of his cravat. In Henry Brougham, Harriette met a man of the next age, someone of a different cut from the playboys she had attracted. Brougham 'plunged with the energy of a Titan into a thousand projects'.[9] Eight years Harriette's senior, he was one of the most remarkable figures of the nineteenth century; a polymath of extraordinary ability, an intellectual, a social and educational reformer, a debauchee. He published, aged seventeen, a paper in the *Transactions of the Royal Society* on experiments and observations on light. Fascinated by mathematics and physics, he studied humanity and philosophy at Edinburgh University for four years and then trained as a lawyer before becoming a member of parliament. He gave his name to the light one-horse carriage he designed, and he was also the greatest legal mind of his time. 'This morning,' Samuel Rogers said of him, 'Solon, Lycurgus, Demosthenes, Archimedes, Sir Isaac Newton, Lord Chesterfield, and a great many more went away in one post-chaise.'[10] Greville described Brougham in 1828 as 'certainly one of the most remarkable men I have ever met; to say nothing of what he is in the world, his almost childish gaiety and animal spirits, his humour mixed with sarcasm, but not ill-natured, his wonderful information, and the facility with which he handles every subject, from the most grave and severe to the most trifling, displaying a mind full of varied and extensive information and a memory which has suffered nothing to escape it, I never saw any man whose conversation impressed me with such an idea of his superiority over all others'.[11]

In 1802 Brougham helped to found the *Edinburgh Review*, which quickly became the authoritative literary periodical of the next century; Thomas Carlyle described it as 'a kind of Delphic oracle'. Brougham's reviews, by which he supported himself, were seering and merciless; his savage denunciation of Byron's juvenile *Hours of Idleness* – he counselled him to 'forthwith abandon poetry'[12] – was typical and his future relations with Byron reveal a great deal about Brougham. The poet was only nineteen and still unknown while Brougham was a thirty-year-old lawyer: to attack with such energy so easy a target suggests an insecurity in Brougham, a need to impose himself; he made no concessions to Byron's youth or fragility and showed no compassion when his blows had been dealt. Nor was he able in later years to laugh off his lack of judgement. Brougham's animosity towards Byron had 'almost an obsessive quality',[13] one commentator has noted, and he waited until Byron's fame had turned to infamy in order to continue his attack. Byron put Brougham's hatred of him down to something he might have said about Mrs George Lamb when she was Brougham's mistress, but the lawyer's animosity was older than that, and deeper. It was the envy of ugliness faced with beauty – Brougham tastelessly attacked Byron for his club foot – of a politician towards a poet, of a self-conscious and self-promoting commoner towards an arrogant, posing milord.

Brougham was a peculiar-looking man, a gangly figure with a nose like a snout. 'A more complete antidote to the tender passion never walked upon two legs (Broom-sticks I mean) than Henry Brougham' – the description is Julia Johnstone's – 'his features apparently stamped on a toad stool, and his eyes like marbles floating in mortar; his chin and nose like the toes of Grimaldi's slipper, when dressed for Whang-fong.'[14] Meeting him as a young man in 1798, Francis Horner wrote to the Reverend Hewlett, 'Have you had any conversation with Brougham? He is an uncommon genius of a composite order, if you allow me to use the expression; he unites the greatest ardour for general information in every branch of knowledge, and, what is more remarkable, activity in the business, and interest in the pleasures of the world, with all the powers of a mathematical intellect. Did you notice his physiognomy? I am curious to know your observation on it.'[15]

Henry Brougham was complex and calculating, born to be a politician. Hugely ambitious, he was strong and able to thrive in an environment where other men were dropping like flies. He lived as hard and fast as the Regency bucks but he kept to the front of the race. His life was so voluminous and tangled that it makes the lives of his contemporaries look like footnotes. While he was Lord Chancellor he was caught in a drunken orgy in a public house, and he once lost the Great Seal in a game of blind man's bluff at a country weekend; there was an arrogance to Brougham's carelessness. One of the most revealing things about Brougham is that, while Harriette's other lovers burned her correspondence, he kept all her letters. This was typical of the man: he thought like a lawyer but lived like a gambler and he held on to the very evidence that could bring him down. The relationship that he kept secret during his lifetime he left to posterity to judge.

The grandson of a principal of Edinburgh University, Brougham was outside the closed circle of titles, Oxbridge and the army. Having no pedigree, it was his sociability, wit and ambition that earned him a central place in London's Whiggish circles, and when he was elected MP for Winchelsea in July 1815, the Whigs found their most brilliant speaker. Brougham restored energy to the beleaguered party; he was the new hope.

Brougham would also restore hope to another beleaguered party, the hapless Queen Caroline, who had lived abroad since 1814. The Regent was anxious to procure a divorce and when he became King George IV in January 1820 it became a matter of urgency that the Queen did not attend the Coronation as his wife. He brought the matter before Parliament and hoped to gather enough evidence to prove that Caroline had been unfaithful. Brougham, acting as the Queen's legal adviser since 1815, suggested that she be bought off with an enormous annuity – £50,000 – as an inducement to stay in Italy and he put it to the government that if he were rewarded with the silk gown of King's Counsel he would do his best to ensure that Queen Caroline lived abroad. Brougham hoped at this stage that he might become prime minister in a new government. The Regent detested Lord Liverpool, the present premier, and getting rid of His Highness's wife, Brougham reasoned, would do his career no harm at all. Liverpool told Brougham to put the offer to the Queen, which Brougham did in his own time before advising her to reject it. Brougham played a double hand throughout the sordid affair, and was always one step ahead.

While he was not pleased when she returned to England in the summer of 1820 to face 'trial', Brougham conducted a brilliant defence. His opening speech, which lasted two days, was 'one of the most powerful orations that ever proceeded from human lips', his fellow defendant Denman declared;[16] it had Lord Erskine, the former Lord Chancellor, rushing from the chamber in tears. His closing speech, Charles Grenville wrote, was 'the most magnificent display of argument and oratory that has been heard for years, and they say that the impression it made upon the House was immense; even his most violent opponents were struck with admiration and astonishment'.[17] 'Brougham has just finishing his opening,' Thomas Creevey wrote to his daughter of the same speech, which had so far lasted for twelve hours, '. . . and I never heard anything like the perfection he has displayed in all ways . . . In short, if he can prove what he has stated in his speech, I for one believe she is innocent, and the whole case a conspiracy . . .'[18]

Anyone would think Brougham himself believed the Queen innocent and the whole case a conspiracy. But he began his defence unconvinced by her proclamations and at best, he later admitted, 'he had never been very much for the Queen'.[19] Brougham defended her not because he felt, along with the rest of the country, that she was an injured wife and a victim of the corruption of the State, but because it suited his interests to do so. He wasted his time on nothing that did not further his career; he was without fixed principles. An eyewitness account of a meeting between the Princess, as she then was, and Brougham in 1813 catches precisely the nature of their relationship: 'His manner does not please her: they look at each other in a way that is very amusing to a bystander. The one thinks, "she *may* be useful to me;" and the other, "*He* is useful to me at present." It does not require a conjuror to read their thoughts; but they are both too cunning for the other.'[20]

Brougham was a genius at manipulating public opinion and 'doing all the world's business as well as his own', as Thomas Love Peacock wrote in *Crotchet Castle*, where Brougham is lampooned as the 'learned friend'. Brougham's efforts at what we know now as spin-doctoring paid off. It is largely thanks to him that the national propaganda around the Queen's case reached the peak of intensity it did. 'It is impossible to describe the universal, and strong, even violent feelings of the people,' Brougham himself wrote of the atmosphere during the time of the trial, 'not only in London but all over the country, upon the subject of the Queen . . . The crowd collected wherever they knew her to be, and called her to appear at the windows of whatever house she was in. The noise and cheers were excessive and exposed her to great annoyance and fatigue . . .'[21] It was he who organized public meetings and lobbied Whig and Radical MPs to circulate petitions and bombard newspapers with letters about the case. Brougham played magnificently on the public's sense of the Queen's dis-honour being linked to their own disenfranchisement and the case brought him fame, which he relished. The Queen eventually accepted the offer of an annuity of £50,000 and a house in exchange for the dissolution of her marriage. There was only one real winner to emerge from the Queen Caroline affair, however, and it was neither of the royal couple. 'The only person who is cheerful and pleased with himself', Princess Lieven drily commented at the termination of the trial, 'is the King of Parliament: Brougham.'[22]

He was not the type of man to attract Harriette, but it was legal advice and not love that she sought from Brougham. She was still bothered by the loss of her annuity from the Duke of Beaufort, and Brougham was sym-pathetic. Harriette might well have seen him as the champion of wronged women. He had previously defended Mary Anne Clarke, and in the year before he first became acquainted with Harriette he was appointed one of Lady Byron's team of legal advisers, following her separation from Lord Byron. Brougham used this position to spread malicious gossip and to make impossible any attempt at the couple's reconciliation. The reason for the separation was, Brougham whispered abroad, 'too horrid to mention',[23] and his spite against Byron was one of the main causes for the poet's ostracism by the very people who had idolized him. John Cam Hobhouse, Byron's friend, realized that some of the worst rumours about Byron *were traceable to Lady Byron's legal advisors themselves*[24] and among them was the story started by Brougham that Byron had cheated his landlady, the Duchess of Devonshire, of £500. Information Brougham received about Byron through the channel of George Lamb's wife, who had heard it from Caroline Lamb, he spun with artful dexterity. It was Brougham who was responsible for the offensive publication of Byron's 'Separation' poems in the journal the *Champion*, which resulting scandal besmirched what little was left of the poet's reputation.[25] Far from representing Lady Byron's interests, Brougham surreptiously added whenever he could to her distress.

His relationship with Harriette was, like his relationships with everyone and hers with many people, dependent on mutual usefulness. He gave her advice; she gave him sex. He took her to the theatre, introduced her to gentlemen, and invited her to dinners. 'One day,' she wrote, Harriette 'took the liberty of consulting him on the subject of my annuity from the Duke of Beaufort . . . Brougham said boldly, and at a public dinner table, that it was a mean, paltry transaction, the object of the Duke being fully obtained by my final separation from his son, to seize hold of such a pretext for depriving me of a bare existence.'[26] He advised Harriette to bring the matter to trial and told her she had every chance of winning, as Worcester would never be able to face the shame of bringing the offending letter to court. His offer to defend Harriette was payment for enjoying her body.

The day of the trial arrived, the Duke and Brougham waited in court but there was no sign of Worcester. The Marquis, it seemed, was either defying his parent out of respect for Harriette or had too much pride to reveal to the world his correspondence with a courtesan. The Duke, in a fluster and having no other witness, proposed an out-of-court settlement: he would pay Harriette a lump sum of £1,200, which bond Brougham had just signed when a carriage rattled up and Worcester stepped out, holding Harriette's letter in his hand.

Harriette accompanied Brougham to Westminster Hall to make an oath that she had 'set forth a full and true list of all the letters, papers, and writings in her possession, or power, written by the Marquis of Worcester . . . and that she hath not retained or delivered to any person, any copies, or extracts of them . . .'[27] Harriette then claimed her money; a paltry amount considering that she had hoped for a lifetime's annuity. It was Beaufort who won the day. She never spoke to any member of the family again, but while she lived in Paris she continued to see Lord Worcester walking in the park with his wife, looking for all the world 'as if he did not even know me by sight, while I often forget, until he has passed me, where or when I have seen that man before, the face being familiar, and perhaps the name forgotten'.[28]

By the next year the money from the Duke had disappeared. The extravagance of Harriette's lifestyle, her rents, debts, cellar, servants, jewels, dresses, dinners, the fact that her entire life was lived in public, in opera boxes and carriages, and that it was expected of her to sparkle with luxury, to outshine every other woman, meant that money never lasted long. She was reduced to writing begging letters to her old friends, including Lord Byron, who always sent her money when she asked him. This she did without losing a jot of dignity; in fact her brilliant letters are worth what he paid for them. She was now thirty-two and more level-headed than before, amused at herself and her life, taking nothing too seriously. She lied about – or simply forgot – her age and lived in the past but seemed relaxed about the future, having no interest, other than financial, in what it might hold for her. She wrote to Byron as one great figure from a lost world to another, and continued to remain unfazed by the curtness of his replies. She is seeped in nostalgia but her freshness and flirtatious appeal are if anything greater now than before:

Pray, dear Lord Byron, think of me a little now and then (I don't mean as a woman, for I shall never be a woman to you) merely as a *good little Fellow* who feels a warmer interest in all that happens to you and all that annoys you than anybody else in the world. Forget me when you are *happy*; but in gloomy moments, chilly miserable weather, bad razors and cold water, perhaps you'll recollect and write to me . . .[29]

CHAPTER 17

Retirement

From now on Harriette Wilson gets harder to see; only through her letters to Byron does she come back into sharp relief. Between 1817 and 1825 she was living between Paris and London. She had never lived anywhere for long and so the unsettled nature of her life was nothing new, but she had lost her way. She never again had a long-term protector or a professional relationship she could consider what she called 'romantic'. Instead she embarked on a series of brief and passionless encounters, one of which was with Henry John Temple, Third Viscount Palmerston.

Palmerston was familiar with Brougham and the ubiquitous Lamb family: Brougham was his great political antagonist and Lady Emily Cowper, the sister of Frederic Lamb, was his great love. Emily Cowper was Palmerston's mistress for nearly thirty years before becoming his wife for nearly another thirty. When her mother, the formidable Lady Melbourne, lay on her deathbed in April 1818 she is said to have urged her daughter to be faithful, not to her dull husband but to Palmerston. Emily, who was, according to Creevey, 'one of the most notorious and profligate women in London', was rarely faithful to anyone and she began in that year an involvement with a mysterious 'count' called Giuliano. Tortured with jealousy at Lady Cowper's infidelities, Palmerston retaliated by having an affair with Harriette Wilson.[1]

Chippendale Sofa, *The Book of Decorative Furniture*

Palmerston's diaries, which recorded in code, as his father's diaries had done, his sexual triumphs and failures ('visit', 'fine day', 'fine night', indicate assignation and success, 'failed' records the opposite, and the number '2' marks occasions on which he excelled himself), say nothing about Harriette. He was always to keep her a secret. In fact, their affair was kept so quiet that biographers have wondered how it could have happened that Harriette, who had slept with all of his friends, could have missed out on Palmerston, who had slept with everybody. 'He is scarcely mentioned in the *Memoirs* of Harriette Wilson', F. E. Baily writes of Palmerston, 'and at that period it was something of a distinction for a man of fashion to have loved neither Harriette nor one of her beautiful sisters.'[2]

Before becoming one of the eminent Victorian prime ministers, Lord Palmerston was an undistinguished Regency buck known as 'Lord Cupid'. He was a Tory politician who mixed in Whig society, and his career seemed to have come to a standstill. When he met Harriette he had been Secretary at War for nine years and would continue in that minor office for a further nine; the war having been over since 1815 made his work less important than it might otherwise have been.

Their brief affair occupied the summer of 1818, when Harriette was visiting London. In July of that year, Palmerston wrote to her under his pseudonym enclosing a present: 'Mr Ellis sends his best love to la belle et aimable Harriette, and is much flattered by her note, and all the cruel things which she has been pleased to say of him . . .'[3] It is doubtful whether Harriette got much pleasure from their encounter: politicians bored her anyway, and being made love to as revenge by a minor statesman obsessed with another woman was not her style. Lord Francis Conyngham, however, was. A beauty without two ideas in his head, Conyngham took after his mother, who was once paid the compliment of having 'no damned brains about her'. Conyngham met Harriette in 1818 and it was he, Harriette told Brougham, who along with George Lamb encouraged her to write. Conyngham liked older women (he later found himself under the spell of Lady Emily Cowper) and was better suited to Harriette than Palmerston had been: doting and less sexually experienced, he was in need of what Harriette could do for him. Twenty-one years to Harriette's thirty-two, Conyngham had been four when Harriette ran away with Craven and eight when she became famous. As did her other youthful conquests, he saw Harriette Wilson more as a legend than a person, an illusion Harriette aimed to destroy. 'I *hate* boys,' she wrote to Byron of her 'new conquest', 'so I have been setting him to hunt and pull out all my *grey hairs* to destroy his *illusions*. He found *ten* and I did not know I had one.'[4]

Lord Francis Conyngham was the second son of the Regent's mistress, Lady Conyngham. He disliked his mother's relationship with the Prince, but it earned his father promotions to Viscount Slane, Earl of Mount-charles and Marquis Conyngham. When the Regent was crowned King George IV in 1821, Marquis Conyngham became Lord Steward of the royal household. The influence Lady Conyngham had over her lover was famous. Once, while at Brighton, she ordered the Pavilion to be lighted up, to which the King is said to have replied, 'Thank you, thank you, my dear, you always do what is right; you cannot please me so much as by doing everything you please, everything to show you are mistress here.' When in town, Lady Conyngham had her dinners sent up to her house in Hamilton Place from the kitchens at St James's Palace, and the use of the royal carriages was at her disposal. Her servants were paid for by the Prince and, liking diamonds, he lavished them upon her. Lady Conyngham's credit with the Regent did little to rub away the smear of being *nouveau riche*. Preferring money to politics – she came from banking stock – she was considered vulgar, not the type of society, Madame de Lieven sneered, one has to dinner. In her youth both Lady Conyngham and Madame de Lieven had been lovers of Lord Ponsonby, and Ponsonby had given Harriette letters written to him by the Marchioness.

'I did not fall in love with him,' Harriette said of Francis Conyngham, 'partly because he had the tremendous bad taste not to fall in love with me'.[5] While she found him 'rather cold' he was 'amiable and truly unaffected'.[6] Conyngham called her '*ma chere mama*' in his letters to Harriette and this mother–son fantasy, which other young men, such as Lord Bath, indulged in with her as well, seems to have provided the erotic basis of their relationship.[7] 'His ill health and his cough induced me to encourage somewhat of the tenderness of a mama towards him,' Harriette wrote, 'and I used to dream about his eyes, they were so very blue and beautiful.'[8] He was calling Harriette 'mama' even after his marriage in 1824.

In the winter of 1818 Harriette rented a cottage near the coast at Brighton where she lived alone, receiving no one and going nowhere. It was a mild winter but Brighton was deserted; Harriette spent her time walking on the cliffs and reading. During one of her walks she found herself being followed by a stranger.

I hastened onwards, till I was quite out of breath, to avoid him. He increased his pace, and still kept close behind me. I turned back, so did he. I struck a new path, my persecutor did the same. My patience at last completely forsook me, and in the irritation occasioned, perhaps, by ill health, I turned suddenly round and asked him, in an angry tone, what he saw in my appearance to imagine he had a right to follow me about, in that conspicuous manner? The stranger seemed thunder-struck at the asperity and suddenness of my address, and stammered out some very unintelligible apology. By this time I had arrived at my own door, which . . . I banged . . . with violence in the very face of the stranger as he was rudely pressing forward and reiterating his incoherent apologies . . . On the next morning I again met my tormentor and this time he addressed me with some firmness entreating, humbly, to apologise again for the liberty he had taken with me the day before. I made him no answer . . .[9]

The next morning, walking on the Steyne, Harriette met a general with whom she was slightly acquainted through Fanny. He was accompanied by a 'middle-aged' man whom Harriette did not know but who, when he joined in their conversation, she recognized as the man who had previously followed her home. He was introduced to her as Lord Charles Stewart, half-brother of Lord Castlereagh, the Marquis of Londonderry. Stewart, a widower, was eight years Harriette's senior; his wife had died a decade before while he was returning from the Peninsula having earned an impressive war record. His 'reputation for debauchery was a by-word'.[10] Stewart had been Ambassador to Vienna but since 1815 had settled for the life of a libertine in Paris, where he cohabited openly with the Duchesse de Saga, a previous mistress of Frederic Lamb. He and Harriette quickly became intimate: 'As an acquaintance he was far from unpleasant: but he was a most jealous and whimsical lover.'[11]

When Harriette returned to London early in 1819, Stewart sought her out. He wrote to her regularly in a style she called 'impassioned' and urged her to meet with him. They met and argued; he proposed to another woman 'in the most brilliant situation of life'.[12] Hurt and angry at having been rejected for someone more 'brilliant' than herself, Harriette cut Lord Stewart. He was indignant and told her the engagement to his heiress,

Lady Emily Vane Tempest, was off; Harriette and Stewart were reunited. She wrote to him and her letter was answered by a Mr Brown who said that Lord Stewart was unable to respond to her correspondence. The match was back on again, and Harriette, once more rejected, was out for money. She had more 'impassioned' letters from Stewart in which he expressed his indifference to his fiancée, and Harriette threatened to expose them if he did not pay her £100. Stewart, wanting to avoid paying the money while keeping Harriette quiet, claimed that he would be her friend and champion for life – that he would never give her up – if she would just keep quiet until his nuptials were over. Harriette, unimpressed and more desirous of exposing Lord Stewart than of earning his friendship, reminded his henchman, Mr Brown, that 'I can put a stop to his match; but let the gentleman thrive! I have no desire for him provided he makes me proper amends for having trifled with me.'[13] She received the payment only when she threatened to send a copy of the letter she had written to Mrs Angelo Taylor, Lady Emily's guardian, on to Lord Castlereagh. Harriette, having him over a barrel, then told Lord Stewart that 'a hundred pounds won't do now. Had you sent half that sum in the way of kindness I should have thanked you . . . and been satisfied; but since the brave and mighty Stewart is only to be worked upon by his fears of a threat, to use a very vulgar phrase, I must work him . . . I want a lot of money and I must have it. *Arrangez vous là dessus* or I'll place your effusions in the hands of your nightmare, Mrs Angelo Taylor who, as her husband says, is impenetrable!'[14]

Harriette now asked for £1,000, which Lord Stewart refused. She wrote him a furious letter which he said he received on the night that his sister died in his arms. He thought the timing of Harriette's letter deliberate; Harriette was mortified that he could believe her so pitiless. She wrote regretting his loss; they agreed that she would receive the £1,000 in batches over the next two months. She gave up his letters, he married Lady Emily Vane Tempest that spring, and the payments, which presumably came out of his bride's dowry, began. In 1821, the newlyweds bought Seaham Hall in Durham, the house in which the doomed nuptials between Byron and Annabella Milbanke had taken place. The following year, Stewart's brother, Lord Castlereagh, afraid that his homosexuality would be exposed, slit his throat; Lord Stewart became the Third Marquis of Londonderry.

This was Harriette's first taste of blackmail, and it was to her liking. The power she had felt slipping from her was reinforced. She could get the money she believed she was owed, and Stewart could be treated with the contempt he deserved.

During the period immediately following her affair with Lord Stewart, Harriette took up once more her correspondence with Byron, who was living in Ravenna. As ever, she confided in him, asked him for money, and spoke of him as a friend:

You would not let me *love* you some time ago, when I was in the humour; you held me too cheap. Will you let me respect you and think of you always with *gratitude warm* and sincere as my nature is capable of feeling toward *a very superior* person? I have no more right to ask you for money than reason for being angry if you refuse it me, but they tell me you have *feelings* not merely *poetical* but compassionately disposed towards any unhappy person and therefore I presume to tell you that I have wretched *health* and *am poor*, too eager an imagination destroyed my health and too much generosity has spoiled my fortune . . .[15]

The version of this letter reproduced by Harriette in her *Memoirs*, which was probably a first draft, has less vulnerability. 'I hate to ask you for money,' she says in her book, 'because you ought not to pay anybody: not even turnpike men, postmen nor tax-gathering men: for we are all paid tenfold by your delicious verses, even if we had claims on you and I had none.'[16] There is no doubt that Byron sent her money, but the flattering reply quoted by Harriette, in which he tells her that 'I had no wish to hurt your self-love',[17] is likely to have been embellished. Harriette's response to the letter Byron actually sent, stored in the Murray archive, chides him for signing himself 'your *most obedient humble servant*', begs him not to 'despise me without knowing me, nothing Lord Ponsonby has dearly loved can be *vile* or destitute' and insists that he '*must* bestow (with your very kind donation) a *little* friendship on me'.[18] While the *Memoirs* fictionalized Harriette's relationship with Byron, writing that the poet whom she never met visited her often and was fascinated by her conversation, he did always reply to her and, judging by her letters in the Murray archive, at least one of the replies Harriette quotes, sent by Byron on 15 May 1818, is genuine. Enclosing a bill of a thousand francs for her, Byron complains that 'the Italian pens, ink and paper are . . . two centuries behind the like articles in other countries'.[19]

While Byron kept his letters to her brief and to the point, Harriette's letters to him exhibit the offbeat, eccentric charm that made her company so entertaining, even now that she was increasingly bitter and suffering 'wretched health'. They also reveal how easily she struck up intimacy with people; she wrote to Byron as if he were the only person in the world (other than Ponsonby, she was keen to stress) who held any interest for her, and Harriette was able to flatter Byron's ego without losing her own poise. In fact, her compliments to him increase her stature while diminishing his – 'it was too bad to cut me off with a shabby short letter and such an *excuse* just to chose the very moment when the horse was waiting and the divorce going on'[20] – making her seem open-hearted and honest while he comes across as cool and snobbish. Harriette presents herself as protective of the poet in the same way that she had been protective of her mother and Fanny. Loving people suited Harriette; it brought out the best in her. And despite being given no encouragement from her correspondent, she insisted on flirting with him and was able to apply her easy wit and irony to the most inconsequential event:

Apropos, there was a man; I met him somewhere in the road leading from Italy; he had not *one bit* of skin on his *nose*, the sun had burned it off while enjoying the charm of your society under the '*delicious Italian sky*'. Lord keep me from such a nose, however poetically bestowed upon me, but the poor man's *nose* is nothing to the purpose – noses are not of such consequence or so *expressive* as people imagine; he told me many amiable things of you and from all I heard I *really* think you must be in a fair way to become a *good sort of man* by the time you are forty –[21]

Amy, meanwhile, had given up her opera box, cold-chicken suppers and queue of admirers and, on a mild day in late December 1818, travelled by coach to St George's, Hanover Square, to marry her sister Sophia's harp teacher, Nicholas Robert Charles Bochsa. Amy was thirty-seven, Bochsa twenty-nine. She was Bochsa's second wife; his first, the daughter of the Marquis Ducrest, was still living and nor were the couple divorced.

Excepting the inconvenience of his being already married, Bochsa was highly eligible and Amy must have seen him as something of a catch. Born in Bohemia but raised in France, he was a celebrated musician who had performed his first public piano concerto aged seven, written his first flute duet and symphony aged nine and his first overtures for the ballet aged twelve. There was no instrument he could not play to perfection but it was the harp whose range he transformed. At twenty-four he became court harpist to the Emperor Napoleon and gave lessons to the Empress Josephine, and after 1814 he gained the patronage of the Bourbons and was adopted by the court of Louis XVIII. He wrote several operas, ballets, and over a hundred and fifty works for the harp. He was also handsome, elegant and very fashionable; as such he lived beyond his means. To clear his debts, Bochsa began a counter-career of forging bonds, signing them with the names of, among others, Sir Charles Stuart, Ambassador to Paris, and the Duke of Wellington. When he was discovered in 1817, he fled to England, being sentenced in his absence to twelve years of forced labour if he returned to France. He was greeted rapturously by London society, becoming 'nearly a second Brummell'.[22] His skills as a harp tutor were greatly in demand – his pupils included not only Lady Sophia Berwick but the Duchess of Wellington – and he continued to publish an annual average of eighteen pieces for the harp. Two years after his marriage to Amy he accompanied King George IV on a trip to Ireland, acting as court minstrel. He was later invited to become musical manager at the King's Theatre and, after 1822, professor of the harp at the Royal Academy of Music. Every year he gave a grand benefit concert for which he composed the music, the receipts of which could each fetch up to £2,000.

In 1826 a musical journal called the *Harmonican* exposed the double life of Bochsa. The newspapers were quick to reprint the charges against him – calling him 'a forger, bigamist, runaway, and galley-slave' and 'Beelzebub, the prince of devils'. Bochsa retaliated with libel actions, which went in his favour. The publicity, however, was damaging and he was forced to resign his post at the Royal Academy. The couple were still together in 1828, but the 'Signior composer . . . never found a more difficult task [than] to preserve the *equilibrium* of *domestic harmony*'.[23] After this, Amy vanishes from the records.

Harriette wrote again to Byron after the publication of *Don Juan*, begging him – without irony – not to 'make such a coarse old libertine of yourself' while proposing that she produce a 'new stile [*sic*] of French blank versification' for his poem. She sent him a stanza of *Don Juan* in French as an example. Wanting to be taken seriously as an author, she had sent a farce to her friend Robert Elliston, manager of Drury Lane Theatre.

Harriette had admired Elliston since, aged thirteen, she had been taken by her mother to see him in *The Honeymoon*, after which she 'did not recover [her]self for more than a fortnight'.[24] When she was famous she was introduced to the great actor and found him out to be a drunk and 'one of the most mercenary, selfish creatures I ever met with'.[25] He did not encourage Harriette's thesbian leanings, and while she had no great pride in her drama, Harriette did not expect to be treated with the disdain Elliston then showed her. After his wife died in 1821, Elliston asked Harriette to marry him, but he was a bankrupt alcoholic with gout and epilepsy and Harriette, although interested in the idea of marriage, aspired to something more in her future husband. She wanted at least to equal her elder sister and win a man with the merits of Nicholas Bochsa.

Shelley's 'old, mad, blind, despised, and dying King' expired in 1820 after sixty years on the throne, and the Regent at last succeeded him. The openly dissolute age of the Regency was starting to give way to the forces of reform and Harriette's friends were crossing back to the sunny side of the sword. Her old lover Frederick Bentinck married in September 1820, after which he dropped her. Harriette was losing money as well as friends; the two came together. Her anger with those who had used and discarded her strengthened.

After years of steady perseverance in such good faith, [Harriette reflected,] I have discovered the heartlessness of the whole set. I except not one of those at whose expense I have amused the public. I certainly do not feel disposed to strive for the glory of keeping the secrets of those who never did anything with the view, nor with the intention of contributing to my future comfort. Even Lord Frederick Bentinck, although I have said no harm of him, beyond a little gentle ridicule . . . only sought me for his gratification, cut my acquaintance, suddenly, without the slightest hesitation and has never once, since the period of his marriage, sent to enquire after *la petite santé d'une belle amie*, although he had been, for years, professing warmest friendship towards me.[26]

Worcester's wife died in the following year and the Marquis began his immediate pursuit of Lady Jane Paget, whose mother had eloped with the Duke of Argyll while Amy was in labour with the Duke's son. Worcester, who signed his letters to Lady Jane 'your most affectionate and dear husband', recovered his senses as readily as he had done with

Harriette and the next year he married the half-sister of his dead wife, creating another scandal. Two years later the jilted Lady Jane married Lord Francis Conyngham.

Early in the year, Harriette once more left Paris and once more leased a cottage in Lisson Grove. It was 'prettily fitted up; but having had the bad luck to fall into the hands of a set of heartless, fashionable men, who had ever been ready to take advantage of my extreme generosity, I found myself unprovided for'. Here she lived 'a retired sort of life; my health having required me to give up the opera, as well as every evening party'.[27] Her face, she said, had considerably changed since the deaths of her mother and sister 'broke her spirits'. She had not been seen out of her house after daylight for over a year when one night she 'was seized with a sudden desire to take a peep at [a] masquerade'. Dressed as a Normandy peasant girl, she found herself in the supper room next to 'a thin youth, with straight hair, and no calves to his legs, dressed in silk stockings, to show where such things ought to have grown . . . He was not handsome, but he appeared intelligent, and gentlemanlike'. He took not the slightest notice of her, and being ravenous Harriette's only concern was with watching a hungry shopkeeper seize the last chicken wing. Her neighbour, seeing her frustration, ordered the waiter to bring the lady tongue, burgundy, chicken and salad. The ice broken, the young man then offered to take her arm if she would remove her fool's cap. 'I never heard anything half so benevolent!' Harriette retorted. 'But listen to me child! You shall not only walk about with me cap and all, but you shall love me, mask and all!'[28] Harriette then asked the name of her companion, and he whispered in her ear that he was Ulick John de Burgh, Fourteenth Earl of Clanricarde. Aged nineteen, he had run up to the masquerade from Oxford, consulting neither proctor nor doctor. When they parted, Clanricarde agreed to correspond with Harriette, still without having seen her face.

Clanricarde was, Lady Grenville wrote, 'immensely rich, quite good-looking enough, clever and very gentleman-like'; his only fault was his preference for 'low-life'. Lady Cowper, on the other hand, thought 'the youth hardly presentable'; he lacked manners and looked like an Irish chairman. Harriette liked him well enough; she found him warm, forgiving, humorous; he had 'the true, genuine, Irish character'.[29] 'He is', she wrote, 'a shrewd, clever young man, possessing a good memory and much gentleness, but he was in the habit of showing my letters to everybody he met.'[30] They wrote to one another while he remained at Oxford, and when he came up to London the two settled into an 'excellent friendship' which lasted for a year or so. Harriette and Clanricarde regularly quarrelled, he accused her of not loving him, and she accused him of not being sufficiently 'romantic'. 'These quarrels were rather amusing than otherwise,' she recalled, 'for we loved to sharpen our wits against each other.'[31]

In a letter to Byron in 1822, Harriette wrote teasingly that 'I venture to love you *myself* and think of you as a *man*, brilliant, *capricious*, voluptuous, ill-tempered and delicious, for a moment a poet, the next a *devil*, the next a God!! But I have not thought of you at all lately, for I have been in love! And nothing you have imagined in the shape of youth and beauty was like him, Vive les dames de mon âge pour aimer et adorer!! For the last *eight months* I have prayed with all my *soul* to die at the very instant *he* ceased to think of me. I was the first, the only human being he had ever loved, and it was love as pure as an Angel's, only much more *sanguine* (les *anges* ne sont pas faits pour le *coup*).'[32] However, Harriette concluded, it was she who tired of Clanricarde first, leaving him to pay a visit to her father in Switzerland.

Harriette described herself during the time of her affair with Clanricarde as 'always ill and past [her] bloom'.[33] Occasional visits by noblemen cheered her, but she missed the colour, drama and adoration of the past and badly needed an income. Clanricarde was young and eligible; soon he would marry. He said that he would make a settlement on her if he and Harriette were still on good terms after he came of age, but many of Harriette's friends promised to continue supporting her after their relationship had run its course and she was never able to secure payments.

In her *Memoirs*, she writes that 'no person had ever made a firmer determination to quit her evil ways and lead a sober righteous life than I had',[34] but those can be found whose determination has been firmer. In her attempt to raise money for an annuity, Harriette said that she 'wrote to such as who were rich and well able to provide for me, and they laughed at the story of my being out of health and out of bread. I wanted only one poor hundred pounds a year, between Fred Lamb, Argyll, and others, who were infinitely richer. They had been my earliest friends, had made themselves happy, for months and years, in my society, and yet I might have begged and tramped, bare-footed, those streets, which in their society had resounded to the triumphant neighings of my horses, rattle of my carriage-wheels, and stentorian voices of my footmen, ere these noble souls of true nobility, would put forth a scanty pittance to rescue me from such appalling prospects!'[35] Harriette's asking for money was not unusual; money circulated around her set as if they all shared one bank account. Mrs Robinson, who had been the Prince of Wales's mistress when he was a young man, thought to finance her retirement by asking the fashionable world each to buy a subscription for a book of her poems. The *ton* were endlessly bailing one another out; Byron handed banknotes to his friends as readily as he might pass round cigars. Her lovers' refusals to support her were motivated by spite, she felt; Harriette was not 'one of them', her usefulness was over. It was now that she determined to avenge herself on the lot of them. 'I never attempted to expose them,' she insisted, 'till all my civil, humble, and abject prayers and protestations had failed to wring from their impenetrable hearts (not excluding my brother-in-law, Lord Viscount Berwick and my sister, his Viscountess), one, single, paltry hundred a year.'[36]

Harriette sent out copies of some 'light sketches' she had written containing, in disguise, various characters in her past life ('my Lord *Red Head* for the Marquess of H—d, Lord *Pensiveham*, for P—m, and so on . . .'[37]), and threatened publication unless she was paid off. None of her victims felt it was worth their while buying her silence. 'Have I solicited, over and over again, of Fred Lamb, Argyll, or Wellington?' she later protested, '– but, as they flattered themselves that my heart being soft and tender, my head must be soft, they likewise turned a deaf ear to my requests and entreaties. She'll not publish anything, not even truths, which do not redound to our honour and glory, no doubt the Honourable Fred Lamb said to himself, so let her starve or beg.'[38]

She took her *Sketches in the Round Room at the Opera House*, as she called her book, an embryonic form of her *Memoirs*, to John Murray, Byron's publisher. Her choice reveals a naivety in Harriette: Murray was one of the leading publishers of the day, an Establishment figure with large contracts from the government. Harriette clearly saw herself as a mainstream writer; at this point she had little idea not only of the operations of the publishing world but of the explosive quality of her story. 'I told Murray', she recalled, 'that I had so little confidence in myself that I really could not be induced to go on with my work till I had obtained his verdict on the few pages I ventured to offer for his inspection. Murray looked at me with such contempt as though Ass had been written on my countenance.' He told her to leave the manuscript and send for it the following evening, when he returned it unread. Harriette was 'beginning to feel as much contempt for her manuscript as the vicar of Wakefield did for his horse', and submitted it to another publisher, Allman of Prince's Street, Hanover Square, as 'the first attempt of a friend of mine'.[39] Messrs Allman liked the work, did not consider it libellous, and said they would share with the author all expenses and profits. Encouraged, Harriette let the idea wait. The revenge she was planning was worth waiting for.

Then one night, while Clanricarde was paying an extended visit to France, a tall, dark stranger appeared from out of the London smog. Harriette's nemesis had arrived.

CHAPTER 18

The Moustache

April 1822 was a stormy month; for four days it hailed, after which the evenings were ominous and overcast. Irritated by Robert Elliston's failure either to return her drama or to pay her for it, Harriette took a night walk. 'I felt that my health required that I should leave the house and breathe a little fresh air, yet I wanted courage to make the attempt. Suddenly a certain, odd presentiment came over me that if I went out something desirable in the shape of a novel adventure would occur to enliven me. I had more than once been seized with the like superstitious sensations and they had not deceived me.'[1] She wrapped herself in her pelisse and walked down to Baker Street, where she stopped to do some shopping, and then turned into Oxford Street, heading towards Orchard Street where, on the Bond Street side of the road, her novel adventure appeared in the form of a man sporting a 'superlative wig'[2] and an enormous black moustache. 'His air was decidedly foreign, independently of his moustaches, and his age might be six and twenty. His dress was black, without any relief or variation: so very black, indeed, that I fancied he must have worn a black shirt too. The sleeves and body of his coat were made very tight, in order, no doubt, to set off to the best advantage and render more striking, the fine symmetry of his manly person. His bust was so high, and so strikingly beautiful, that one could scarcely avoid noticing it . . . his carriage was

Bergami, *The Trial of Queen Caroline*

lofty and soldier-like, which made one fancy him at least six feet high, although in fact he was only five feet nine or ten.'[3]

The night was pitch black, unillumined by moon or stars, and Orchard Street was deserted. The 'terrible looking fellow' stopped to examine Harriette. She hurried on ahead, afraid that he might have caught her examination of him, and then she heard the menacing sound of footsteps on the pavement behind her. 'I had been blue-deviled for the last week, and now I was frightened out of my wits. My breath was almost exhausted by over-haste, yet I made a last desperate effort to increase my pace without turning my head round to ascertain what or who my tormentor was.'[4] Harriette gathered the courage to turn round and confront the mustachioed stranger – for it was he – who was alarmed at her fear. She realized by his accent that he was not foreign at all and she expressed her surprise; he offered to accompany her home in order to avert her night fears. Harriette accepted. 'In our progress we chatted on various subjects. My companion's manner was graceful, and the tones of his voice acted, like a charm, against earlier prejudices, till my reserve gradually vanished. There was a careless, successful air about him, it seemed to be the natural result of that beauty, which might easily be supposed to have caused our sex many heart-aches . . .'[5]

The Moustache told Harriette that he was penniless and that women disgusted him; as he spoke the moon appeared from behind the heavy clouds and illuminated his 'brilliant, ivory-like teeth'. His tone reminded Harriette of Tom Sheridan, whom she had not seen now in nearly twenty years, and while she was in awe of the stranger's beauty – 'such as we seldom meet with' – she thought his character 'odious'.[6] The idea 'flitted across' her mind, however, that this odiousness might lessen with a kiss, and while a kiss would satisfy her curiosity about his evident appeal to women, it need not be an altogether unpleasant experience in itself, 'since the man was in the habit of cleaning his beautiful teeth', and anyway, she did not expect to ever see him again.[7]

The couple arrived at Harriette's cottage at Regent's Park where she decided that rather than retire they might take advantage of the moonlight and continue walking. This they did until the watchman called out one in the morning and Harriette, growing alarmed, 'thought a little hypocrisy was quite necessary in order to rid [her]self at once of her beau'. She told him she needed rest but would be happy to see him on another occasion. The Moustache then left her, but not until the kiss had been tried and tested. While it was 'a very good kiss . . . all a kiss ought to be . . . sweet, and ardent, and thrilling', it was still 'wanting in magic to me'.[8] Harriette then told her maid that a gentleman with a tremendous moustache would call the next day and he was on no account to be let in.

Various gentlemen did call the next day – Harriette was also being courted by Lord Boringdon, Lord Clonbrock and the Marquis of Graham – but there was no sign of the Moustache. Nor did he appear the next day, or the next. It was three weeks until Harriette saw him again and by then he had been forgotten by her. She was lying on the sofa with a cough on the night that he called, and had been bled by leeches, which left her exhausted. It was ten o'clock and Harriette did not know her visitor in the darkness, thinking that this black-faced man must be either a dustman or delivering coal. Only when the moonlight fell on his moustache did she recognize her stranger. She was faint and ill; he was melancholic and mysterious. He did not return the next day, nor the next. Another three weeks passed until she heard from the Moustache again, and this time he sent her a note apologizing for his elusiveness, but before he had time to receive Harriette's proud and offhand reply, telling him to contact her no more, he was knocking on the door of her cottage. He told her that night that he was Colonel William Henry Rochfort and that he was imprisoned for debt in the Fleet Prison; every time he came to see her he went beyond the boundary known as the Prison Rules. He had 'fought a duel with a noble lord, got a certain lawyer's daughter with child while he was pleading at the Old Bailey, slept with the said lord's wife, by previous appointment, on the very night after her marriage . . . and lastly, in a fit of despair, proposed marriage to an old woman, backing his proposal with a copy of pathetic verses on her eye-brows'. Harriette thought he was 'one of the most manly, interesting, and lovable beings I had ever met with in my life'.[9] The Moustache was the nearest thing to gentlemanlike perfection Harriette had met with since Lord Ponsonby.

The Fleet Prison, medieval in its age and administration, stood on Farrington Street in the City of London. There were 660 inmates in 1821, 113 of them, Rochfort included, living within the 'Rules'.[10] The 'Rules', whose original purpose had been to allow debtors – the majority of its prisoners – to leave the prison confines and conduct their affairs with creditors, now simply allowed the prisoner, for a price, freedom to roam abroad at specific times. Along with his liberty to wander, certain 'rulers', like Rochfort, were allowed to rent their own lodgings within a limited area around the prison. The Rules went as far as Ludgate Hill on the south, Cock Alley to the east and Fleet Lane to the Old Bailey in the north. In 1824, the year after Rochfort was released, they were extended to include Chatham Place, St Paul's and Shoe Lane, but the Moustache ignored his restrictions anyway and went out when and where he chose. He enjoyed privileges, but he also incurred expenses. All debtors were required to support themselves as well as pay the warden for their keep and provide a security, but as a 'ruler' Rochfort had to pay more for his lodgings – which, due to the competition to get good rooms in a rough area, were not cheap – than he would do for his room as a prison inmate. He also had to finance his daily freedom. If ever he was caught in the city at large without express permission, he would be fined. Given that he was imprisoned for debt and would not be released until his debts had been settled, these additional fees were onerous and his financial situation was not improving.

During his midnight excursions, Rochfort and Harriette became lovers. He occasionally declared that he wanted her to give up Clanricarde and her other admirers and be his alone, but Harriette remained cautious, still knowing nothing about the stranger, even where he lived (she addressed all her letters to him to the coffee-house in Ludgate Hill), and refusing to believe in the constancy of any man so handsome. 'As to your thoughtless plan', she wrote to him, 'of our living together forever, it is downright nonsense; for all men grow tired and were I young and dearly loved by you but steadily, for a year, I should die a slow perhaps, but miserable death when you left me. Once I suffered what now would surely destroy me. Since that time, it has been my prayer, the object of my life, to avoid all steady attachment.'[11]

She was faced with a dilemma. 'If Clanricarde and I meet again as lovers,' Harriette realized, 'I lose this proud, fine looking creature for ever . . . It is true Lord Clanricarde is rich, independent, and appears to be, just now, waxing tender and inclined to be loving!'[12] She was honest with Clanricarde about her new beau, and he teased her about her infatuation. 'I am obliged for Rochfort's verses; like them very much,' he wrote to her, '– only don't mix quite so much prose about him. In your two letters there were three sheets of nothing else besides the verses, and you are too clever to throw so much of a letter away on a subject. To you, I perceive, it is a very, very interesting one, more than I wish . . .'[13] Should she give up her young beaux for the Moustache? Harriette measured all the fine and noble dandies she knew next to Rochfort. 'Having weighed thus in my mind the merits of all the gay Lotharios of my acquaintance in the fashionable world, I decided that poverty with the Moustache would be more to my taste than a good annuity with Lord Clanricarde, or any other of the set.'[14]

Her decision made, Harriette examined her wardrobe, putting aside all the finery that would be unbecoming to a 'a poor but faithful wife' who was about to go and live within the Prison Rules.[15] She ordered two neat coloured gowns which looked both modest and seductive. She then received a letter from the Moustache urging her not to exchange Clanricarde's money for his poverty. She replied that she would not be a mere instrument of pleasure to Clanricarde. Rochfort seemed more interested in keeping up Harriette's income and prestige than in claiming her for himself. His vacillations made Harriette ill; still knowing nothing about the Moustache, she rose from her sickbed on a rainy night and went with her maid in a hackney cab to the Rules, determined to find out where he lived and who he was, 'in short, all and everything about him'.[16]

It was a Saturday night and the shops were open. The territorial confines of the Rules meant that the area around the Fleet became part of the prison community. It was stinking and seedy, the filthy streets populated by slaughter and gaming houses, taverns and innumerable brothels teeming with prostitutes. Guards stood on the street corners to prevent prisoners escaping; what they could not prevent was the number of debtors who found their way in, so as to escape their creditors. Harriette sat in a pastry cook's shop in Newgate Street while she waited in trepidation for her maid to make enquiries about the Moustache in the local coffee-houses and taverns. 'Never, in my earliest youth, having been thought vain, though always very proud, and of a fearless independent spirit, I was now, more than ever, disposed to think meanly of my personal attractions and as I stood shivering and watching the drops of rain, enveloped in my old furred cloak, a sort of stubborn pride took strong possession of my mind, arising out of the very excess of my humility . . . I have had my day, and am but a poor shadow, weak and unequal to him in every pleasing quality.'[17]

Harriette's maid returned with the information that the Moustache – whom everyone knew by sight – lived above an undertaker's at 1 Fleet Street, but she did not discover whether he 'slept single or double'. Convinced that another woman was the cause of his elusiveness and opacity, Harriette posed as a dressmaker to whom the Moustache's mistress owed money and in this guise she made enquiries of the local apothecary and greengrocer as to where the lady might be found. The greengrocer knew Rochfort's mistress well; she passed as his wife and often ordered vegetables to be delivered to their lodgings. Harriette and her maid made their way to 1 Fleet Street, and Harriette waited in the doorway while her maid went upstairs and knocked; Rochfort's servant told her that his master and mistress were in bed.

Harriette determined to forget Rochfort and wrote to introduce herself to Lord Ashley, the son of the Earl of Shaftesbury and an undergraduate at Christ Church – as Meyler, Worcester and Clanricarde had been – who was 'well made, clever, proud, cold, gentlemanly, and ugly'. 'For heaven's sake, since you are the first youth in the land,' she wrote, 'let me see you directly to cure my attachment for a most unworthy object who treats me ill. For the good of the nation, come and cure me!'[18] Ashley replied that he would call on Harriette next time he was in London, hoping that her skin would be less yellow than her writing paper.

The affair with Ashley came to nought and Harriette continued to be in contact with the Moustache. She discovered from his greengrocer that he had lived with the woman for two years or thereabouts, which she found easier to forgive than his having formed another attachment since meeting her. She confronted Rochfort with her discovery and he wrote begging Harriette to stay loyal to him until he became free, which would not be long; Harriette replied that she would always love him. She sent him a lock of her hair, curled, perfumed and tied in a blue ribbon; he wrote telling her that he would keep it for ever. That same day there was a knock on the door and a messenger delivered a letter for Harriette which contained the same lock, dirty, dishevelled, ingrained with sand. 'The insult was so coarse and unmanly that I felt my blood freeze in my veins. My heart sickened as I thought on the time I had lost and the tender friendships I had thrown away on this heartless coxcomb . . . Enough of folly and the Moustache, said I to myself, rising with a certain dignity and walking towards my little library for the purpose of selecting some sensible and amusing book.'[19]

The lock, Harriette later discovered, had been soiled and returned by the Moustache's mistress. Harriette remained in ignorance about the identity of her rival, and was still in the dark about the Moustache. 'You shall learn all and everything about me when you are decided to become mine,' he told her ominously.[20] It is at this point that Harriette's narrative about Rochfort comes to an end. The reader is left with the impression of a cloak-and-dagger pantomine villain; it was Harriette's habit to describe her most significant moments and complicated emotions as tuppenny melodramas. Her considerable narrative abilities were cut short by the challenge of seriousness and self-reflection.

The Rochforts were descended from the De Rochforts of Poitou; by the marriage of one of their clan to a daughter of King Aedred of England, they also claimed descent from Alfred the Great. The family settled in Ireland in the twelfth century and gained extensive properties and land in Westmeath, which county they reigned over for generations in the two hundred years before William Henry Rochfort's birth. Rochfort's grandfather, George Rochfort, sired a tempestuous brood. In 1736, his eldest son, Robert, who later became the First Earl of Belvedere, fell in love with and married Mary, the sixteen-year-old daughter of the Third Viscount Molesworth, which made Rochfort a cousin of Ponsonby whose own mother, Louisa, was Mary Molesworth's half-sister. Seven years after the marriage, Robert Rochfort locked his wife up, believing she had been adulterous with his younger brother. She was confined for thirty years in Gaulston Park, a gloomy fourteenth-century mansion, allowed neither to leave the grounds nor to receive visitors. Even her four children were eventually banned from seeing their mother. The 'guilty' brother, Arthur Rochfort, fled to England with his devoted family, where the Earl followed him with a gun.

Lord Belvedere was a handsome, tasteful, occasionally charming man, a distinguished soldier much admired by George II, but prone in his private life to jealousy and vindictiveness on a grand scale. When Arthur

Rochfort eventually returned to Ireland sixteen years later, Belvedere sued him for adultery and won £20,000. While he was converting his old house into a prison for his wife, Lord Belvedere built himself a new seat, five miles away, above Lough Ennell near Mullingar. Another of the Earl's brothers, George, built his own house next door, which he called Rochfort. When the Earl eventually quarrelled with George as well, he built in his garden a magnificent sham ruin to obstruct the view.

Belvedere inevitably also fell out with his youngest brother, William, against whom he brought a lawsuit – later decided against him – by which he severely lessened his sibling's fortune. The third of William Rochfort's sons was also called William and two months after Harriette Wilson was baptized there, the young William, who had grown up with the injustice incurred on his father by the behaviour of his uncle, married in St George's, Hanover Square, the daughter of Henry Sperling, of Dynes Hall, Halstead, Essex. On 11 September 1795, after seven years of marriage, the couple were blessed with their only child, and he too was called William. William Henry Rochfort – 'the Moustache' – was born into a family branded by the violence and greed of the the First Earl of Belvedere, and the boy inherited from his father and grandfather his sense of deprivation. But this seems not to have been his only legacy. It is from his uncle, the wicked Earl himself, that Rochfort inherited his ability to hold a grudge and his grasp of melodrama.

The Second Earl of Belvedere was childless, as were his brothers. The title, which William Henry Rochfort believed he should now inherit, died with the Earl in 1814. The estates in Kilbrenan, Midan, Tyrrell's Pass, Templeoran, Garryduffe, Leghegare and Bloomfield and his house in Dublin were divided between the Earl's sister, the Countess of Lanesborough, and his second wife. The only other male in that generation of the Rochfort family to have had children was Rochfort's bachelor uncle Henry, and it was on his good will – in both senses – that Rochfort depended.

When Rochfort's father died in 1798, he left his own considerable estates to his widow, under the trusteeship of his brother; only after her death would they revert to William Henry. Rochfort, who lived in poverty while his mother basked in wealth, consequently hated her with a passion worthy of the nephew of the First Earl of Belvedere, and the terms of his father's will resulted in legal complexities and family feuds sustainable only by those of the Rochfort clan. Believing that his mother swindled him out of his inheritance 'by a system of fraud and concealment almost unprecedented in the annals of maternal turpitude',[21] Rochfort saw himself as a long-suffering victim, an aristocrat deprived of his natural station, the offspring of an unnatural parent, an outsider. Due to the past negligence of assignees, he claimed to have 'lost an entire estate, value £20 to £25,000 and for which there is no adequate remedy as the law stands at law or at equity . . .'[22] Another of his potential estates was also 'fraudulently concealed from my knowledge by my own mother to favour the offspring of [her] pauper second husband . . .'[23] Rochfort never stopped hoping that he would wake up the next day a landowner, someone to whom other men touched their hats. As a poor man only by default and only for the moment, he lived as a rich one, borrowing extensively against the estates he expected one day to inherit, and falling into deeper and deeper debt.

The Rochfort family was distinguished by its production of good soldiers and profitable marriages. William Henry had failed in both areas. Following military college in Sandhurst, he had a brief and unremarkable career in the artillery corps in India under the commands of Major General Thomas Gage Montresor and the Honourable Colonel Lincoln Stanhope. Rochfort's own claim to be a colonel was at this point completely unfounded, and nor had his charms managed to attract an heiress. He had been pursued by a Miss Scarlett who was due to inherit £1,700 a year on the death of her mother, but Rochfort broke off the engagement on discovering that this annuity was *all* he was to expect – there being no other estate besides – and there was a long enough wait for that.

William Henry Rochfort's achievements by the time he became Harriette's lover were to have attracted in the space of a few years two of the most notorious figures of his day. In 1818, when he was twenty-three, he went to South America as aide-de-camp to General Gregor MacGregor, who a few years later established himself as a fraudster of some brilliance. MacGregor was born in the same year as Harriette, and came from an ancient Highland family; he was descended from Rob Roy, his grandfather was 'Gregor the Beautiful' of the Black Watch and Laird of Inverardine. He served briefly in the British Army until 1811 when Simon Bolivar, the Venezuelan liberator, came to London looking for

British protection against the Spanish presence in the Americas. Bolivar was considered a hero (Byron named his boat after him); his dream was an English form of constitution for 'Greater Colombia', a federation of the modern neighbouring countries of Venezuela, Colombia and Ecuador. The British took a sympathetic interest in South America's struggle for independence and recruits to join the revolutionary cause were never hard to find. MacGregor duly offered his services and was put under the command of the ageing General Miranda. He distinguished himself as a soldier and, together with Bolivar, MacGregor inflicted a series of masterly defeats on the Spanish, among which was the independence of Venezuela and Colombia. Bolivar acknowledged MacGregor's heroism by offering him the hand of his niece.

Rochfort probably first became involved with MacGregor when the General was recruiting a task force to liberate Portobello, on the isthmus of Panama. The expedition would have appealed to Rochfort's spirit of adventure and to his greed: 'glory and gold' are what a soldier was presumed to bring home from South America. The attack on Portobello turned into a massacre; the troops who survived suffered atrociously. And there was no gold to be found.[24] Following Portobello, Rochfort returned home, having become a good friend of MacGregor.

After 1820, Bolivar and MacGregor followed different paths. Bolivar's next plan was an invasion of Ecuador, MacGregor's was no less extreme. He took a boat, landed at the Mosquito Shore on the Atlantic coast of Nicaragua, and persuaded the chief of the Poyais Indians who had settled there to grant him a concession to the land. By the time MacGregor returned to London later in the year he had reinvented himself as Prince Gregor of Poyais. While being supportive of South American struggles, the British knew nothing about the place. The scam MacGregor pulled was dependent on this ignorance. The bleak and empty Mosquito Shore which he claimed was his kingdom became the mythical paradise of 'Poyais', a heaven on earth. Its grand boulevards, lined with banks, government buildings, churches and opera houses, were surrounded by mountains which abounded with mahogany and cedar trees and rocks veined with gold. The land was fertile, the cattle were fat, the fantastical country produced everything from cotton to coffee. Prince Gregor invited all he met to emigrate to this nirvana and experience wealth and happiness beyond their wildest dreams. George IV, Gregor's 'brother sovereign', gave him a knighthood and welcomed Sir Gregor's 'Chargé d'Affaires' – a scoundrel called William John Richardson – to St James's Palace. Never thinking to doubt the credibility of anyone received by the King (or perhaps knowing when he was on to a good thing), a City banker and one time Mayor of London, Sir John Perring, floated a loan of £200,000 'for the purpose of consolidating the State of Poyais'.[25] Shares were printed and sold. Poyais immigration offices were set up in London and Edinburgh and land on the Mosquito Shore was purchased by the prospective émigrés. The first boat-loads set sail into their new life in September 1822, arriving four months later to find a deserted wasteland without a building or human being in sight. A hurricane then swept away their ships and the homeless settlers were left to the mercies of malaria and yellow fever. One man killed himself when he realized the extent of his losses. It was not until the autumn of 1824 that the prospective settlers returned to British shores and revealed the truth about Poyais, by which point MacGregor, now rich, had disappeared to Paris, where he began to sell the same story to any Frenchman who would listen.

At the time that MacGregor was selling his shares for Poyais, Rochfort had landed himself in the Fleet and was taking his nocturnal excursions along Orchard Street. He was still on the lookout for gold and adventure.

What is apparent in Harriette's attraction to and subsequent relation-ship with Rochfort is not that he was the mysterious 'other' to her she describes, but that she had, for the first time, fallen for her double. Rochfort was like her: alluring, unfaithful, a player of masquerades, venge-ful, energetic and a spinner of yarns. He should have inherited the earth but he languished instead in a debtor's prison. He was someone who would have greatly enjoyed wealth; an extravagant fantasist, he loved clothes and adventure and courted the company of fashionable people. He was obsessed, as, increasingly, was Harriette, with justice and revenge, and they recognized in one another themselves. Rochfort was a familiar figure in other ways too. Harriette described him as another Ponsonby but rather he resembled her father, who had also been a charming, disreputable fallen gentleman, a wanderer, social climber and magnificent failure.

Rochfort cuts an unusual and engaging figure. He had great imagina-tion and ability and his money-making schemes were invariably inventive.

He was endlessly optimistic, never becoming jaded or losing enthusiasm for any of his ventures despite repeated pitfalls, setbacks and disappointments. In his own writing, he comes across as neat, methodical and diligent (his letters look as though they were typed in italics), boyish and somewhat hair-brained, keen to please and comically ill-fated. People liked Rochfort; his looks were attractive to women while men admired his virility and energy; it was hard not to respect his determination. He was a chancer and a thorn in the side of those he pestered, but wanted to be neither. Rochfort longed to belong, and his attraction to Harriette was his sense that she 'belonged' to the world from which he was excluded. Her catalogue of powerful lovers he must have found vertiginous and while he identified with her anger at the way in which she had been treated, his future communications with men such as Palmerston, Wellington and Brougham suggest that he saw Harriette not as a conduit for his bitterness but as a bridge into a better world. Harriette actually regarded Rochfort as more of a hopeless child than a dashing hero and she mothered him in much the same way as she did Lord Conyngham.

When Harriette met Rochfort she came full circle and returned home. Rochfort was her friend, they were equals, they could do better together than apart. They admired and protected one another. In 1823 they announced that they had married; she was thirty-five, he was twenty-eight. Much as her *Memoirs* fictionalize their relationship, if Harriette had indeed married – and no evidence exists either way – she was acting realistically. Her decision to become a wife, or to represent herself as such, was the result of considered thought. It is clear that she was attracted to and thought highly of Rochfort, but it was not because of love alone, or at all, that she would have married him. It was usual for courtesans to marry as a sign that they had retired and Harriette was no more likely to become a traditional wife now than at any other time; nor would she have married Rochfort had that been the deal. Harriette had decided in the wake of Ponsonby that the object of her life was 'to avoid all steady attachment', and her relationship with Rochfort met these terms. They were an unconventional couple, rarely living in the same country, let alone the same house. Their marriage resembled the aristocratic arrangements of which Harriette had seen so many. Neither party had bourgeois illusions about the other, or about domesticity and fidelity; being married suited their legal and financial needs. Harriette's old friends and the power she potentially had over them could get Rochfort support in high places, while being married offered her vital protection. As a wife, she had to surrender her property rights to her husband, and this must have been a major factor in Harriette's decision to become known as Mrs Rochfort. Having no money of her own, she could be neither sued nor declared bankrupt; were she to obtain any, she had an agreement with Rochfort whereby she could keep it.

Harriette settled enough of Rochfort's debts to get him out of prison. They then lived for the summer of 1824 in lodgings at Warwick Court, Holborn, where an acquaintance of Harriette's reported being spied by the couple from the window and called up to their rooms.

'Times are a little changed,' said [Harriette], 'Mr Crony, since we last met': 'True madam,' I responded; and then to cheer the *belle* a little, I added, 'but *not persons, I perceive*, for you are looking as young and attractive as ever.' The compliment did not seem to please the *Colonel in the wig*, who turned round, looked frowningly, and then twirled the dexter side of his *lip wing* into a perfect circle. It is not possible that this THING can affect jealously of *such* as woman as Harriette? thought I: so proceeded with our conversation; and he shortly resumed his polite amusement of spitting upon the children who were playing marbles beneath his window. 'I really am married to that monster, yonder,' said she, in an undertone: 'How do you like my choice?'[26]

Harriette continued to tell Mr Crony that she had been writing some sketches of her life and to ask if he could recommend a publisher. He suggested that she try Henry Colburn, which she duly did. She had embarked on the first stage of her plan to storm London once more and hold the British aristocracy to ransom.

CHAPTER 19

Stockdale

Henry Colburn, publisher of many successful books including Caroline Lamb's *Glenarvon*, refused to touch Harriette's *Sketches*. He was, Harriette told Brougham, 'afraid of making *ill will* by publishing' such material.[1] She had also been rejected by John Murray and had decided against Allman as a publisher. It is not known how or when Harriette first came across John Joseph Stockdale, but it is clear that theirs was strictly a business partnership. She either introduced herself to him in the spring or early summer of 1824, or Stockdale, having heard about Harriette's *Sketches*, was quick to introduce himself to her. Harriette was exactly what Stockdale needed; after eighteen years of graft in the business, he had never secured a bestseller. As Sir James Scarlett remarked, 'It is impossible to conceive of a book more calculated to advance the fortune of a bookseller . . . In the present day, the appetite for scandal is so great, the curiosity to pry into the details of individual life so active and restless, that he who would give, or pretend to give, a history of the secret vices of mankind, is sure of speedily realizing immense gains . . .'[2]

Stockdale was a libertarian Tory, a God-fearing pornographer, a moral campaigner, militant Protestant, monarchist and political opportunist. He would later see himself as a martyr, a lone voice crying out for truth and justice in the face of the oppressive powers of the law. Like his father, John

Haymarket Theatre, *Views of London*

Stockdale, he was also a publisher and bookseller. In 1806, when John Joseph was thirty, he set up his own business at 41 Pall Mall.

He was an ambitious and hard-working man, who liked to feel he had his finger on the pulse of the current climate and was always on the look-out for events he could exploit. He invested great belief in the authority of the press to shape opinion and saw his role as that of a public educator. He published nothing he would not have written himself or at least of which he highly approved; much of what he produced he did write himself. Typical of his style was the manner in which he approached Sir Arthur Wellesley on his return to England after the Cintra Convention in 1809. 'On his arrival,' Robert Lowe wrote to Lord Lonsdale, '[Wellesley] was sent to by that pushing fellow Stockdale who, with great professions of admiration, hoped to be honoured by publishing anything he might like to draw up in his defence – to which Sir Arthur replied that he meant to publish nothing whatever, knowing no doubt that the people of England would very soon do him justice.'[3] Wellesley soon realized that Stockdale's instinct about the people of England was right, and in 1809 Stockdale published *The Interesting Proceeding on the Enquiry into the Armistice and Convention of Cintra* and *A Narrative of the Campaign which Proceeded the Convention of Cintra*.

The Mary Anne Clarke scandal followed soon afterwards and Stockdale, who professed to be a great friend of the Duke of York, joined in the publishing frenzy the inquiry initiated by circulating a pamphlet attacking Gwyllym Lloyd Wardle, the Whig MP who had brought to the Commons' notice the illicit sale of promotions going on in the Duke's love-nest. Wardle was seen by the nation as a hero; to Stockdale he was a menacing anti-Royalist whose credibility was over-rated, and he wrote an anonymous pamphlet, *The Claims of Mr Wardle to the Thanks of the Country*. Here Stockdale, who would later also make use of a popular courtesan in order to promote himself, described Mrs Clarke as 'a person of abandoned character and depraved habits'.[4]

If Stockdale was not able to muscle in on events, he liked to suggest that he had played a formative role in their history. The subsequent destruction of Mary Anne Clarke's *Memoirs*, 18,000 copies of which were burned in exchange for an annuity for the author and a down payment of £10,000, also caught Stockdale's imagination. The book's printer, T. C. Gillet of Salisbury Square, was used by the Stockdales as well, but John

Joseph's involvement in the affair of Mrs Clarke's *Memoirs* went, he claimed, further than this. 'By my suggestion,' Stockdale wrote, '. . . one PRINTED BOOK, with such other documents as were obtained by Mrs Clarke, were sealed up and deposited in the hands of Messrs. Drummonds, the bankers, of Charing Cross, where they yet remain! The object of preserving these documents was that the Duke, having purchased them, they became his copyright and, in the event of their surreptitious publication, his Royal Highness could suppress them by injunction, and punish the publisher for the invasion of His Royal Highness's property . . . At length the Duke of York, regardless of cost, wisely adopted my advice, and terminated all further disclosures and intercourse with Mrs Clarke . . .'5 Whatever fantasy Stockdale entertained about his relationship with the Duke, there is no doubt about his interest in the bargaining power available to courtesans and their publishers, and he was not to forget the panic unleashed by the possible appearance of Mrs Clarke's book.

In 1810 Stockdale was approached by a young poet called Percy Bysshe Shelley, who wanted to get published his first collection, *Original Poetry by Victor and Cazire*, written by himself and his sister. The poems, Stockdale realized, were not so original; as part of her contribution, Elizabeth Shelley had plagiarized some lines by M. G. Lewis. The book was withdrawn. Stockdale's relationship with Shelley continued to go downhill, and after publishing the anonymous novel *St Irvyen, or the Rosicrucian* in 1811, Stockdale began to suspect his author of atheism and wrote to inform Shelley's father, Sir Timothy. 'Booksellers possess more power than we are aware of, in impeding the sale of any book whose opinions are displeasing to them,' Shelley wrote to his friend, Jefferson Hogg. 'No other bookseller would have violated the confidence reposed in him.'6 Shelley was right about the power of booksellers, and it was typical of Stockdale to put his prejudices and opinions before the talent of an author. After Shelley's death, Stockdale grew to regret his decision and milked as much as he was able their early connection. He even considered writing a memoir of the poet's life organized around the brief and professional correspondence that took place between the two men. His project was discouraged. 'What degradation and self-abasement might have been spared', Stockdale later bemoaned, 'to the widowed wife and fatherless orphans who perhaps, at last, may be indebted to my brief *Memoirs* for the only ray of respect and hope which may illumine their recollections of a father when they have attained an age for reflection, and shed a gleam of ghastly light athwart the palpable obscurity of his tomb.'[7] Eventually he settled on selling Shelley's letters to the highest bidder.

When he met Harriette, Stockdale's business had moved to 24 Opera Colonnade, one of the shops on what is now called Charles II Street, which then ran beneath the Haymarket Opera House and into St James's Square. He had expanded his range of publications and under the pseudonym 'Thomas Little', borrowed from Byron's friend, the Irish poet Thomas Moore, moved into the realm of pornography and scandal. Stockdale's recent publications, of which he was also author, included *The Ton: anecdotes, chit-chat, hints . . . dedicated to all the gossips, Life High and Low, Secret Memoirs and Love Letters of G. H. Ames, Esq., Banker, and Mrs Penfold; comprising Naughty Occurrences in numerous families,* and *Beauty and Marriage in all nations, Little's New Art of Love, Confessions of an Oxonian.* He later published *Private Memoirs of a Devonshire Baronet* and *Love-Letters addressed to one of His Grace's Mistresses, by the Duke of Marlborough.*

It is unlikely that the courtesan and the pornographer liked one another; all Harriette and Stockdale had in common was a disregard for opinion and a need for money. She must have found him humourless and egotistical and in her former life Harriette would have had nothing to say to Stockdale. He was a methodistical family man devoted to his wife Sophie, a former justice's clerk's assistant, and the six children who survived her twenty-two pregnancies. He could be pompous, pious and self-pitying, identifying his sufferings with those of Caleb Williams, the Merchant of Venice and Othello. But he was also vastly resourceful, courageous and energetic, and he emerges from his liaison with Harriette as one of the great characters of nineteenth-century publishing.

Possessing only a modest quantity of principle or scruple, Stockdale shamelessly exploited Harriette's celebrity in order to advance his own. He increasingly hijacked her narrative, regarding the story of the sufferings he had undergone as her publisher as more significant. In many ways Stockdale was an ideal man to publish Harriette's *Memoirs*, as he would stop at nothing to promote himself.

Stockdale saw that Harriette could be made into a heroine along the lines of Mary Anne Clarke and Queen Caroline. Despite the Queen's death in 1821, the affair was still fresh in the popular imagination. It had confirmed that there was no end to the public appetite for tales of wronged women and hypocrisy in high life, and pamphleteers and publishers had exploited the scandal for all it was worth. In fact, many helped to create the public support for the Queen.[8] The estranged wife of King George IV was regarded as not only a wronged woman, but 'the heroine of a gothic-romantic fantasy'.[9] Many of the numerous sentimental, mythological and semi-pornographic fictions circulating about Caroline in chapbooks, ballad sheets, 'memoirs', poems and pamphlets turned into melodrama aspects of her plight such as the mother's enforced separation from the beloved daughter, a potent image whose power was intensified by the early death of Princess Charlotte. If the public liked Mary Anne Clarke and Queen Caroline, they would love Harriette Wilson; she had been abused not by one man but by the entire Establishment.

Harriette's story fitted Stockdale's bill completely: persecution was his favourite subject, and he represented Harriette not as a person of 'abandoned character and depraved habits', as he described Mary Anne Clarke, but as a moral pioneer, a divine figure fighting alone for justice. This is also how he presented himself, and his hallowed regard for Harriette's bravery was really self-congratulation: 'Who has, hitherto, ever had the courage to beard the lion in his den,' Stockdale wrote, 'to drag forth the monster from his secret recesses, from his most impregnable fastnesses, in the castles of earthly power, strip him of the armour with which he had been, as not he only, but almost every one, supposed, invincibly clad, but the very giants of rank and fortune, and exhibit him shorn, at once, of all those glorious beams, whose dazzling glare blinded even the strongest sighted spectators, deprived of all his means to do mischief and harmless and submissive as the veriest pet-lamb.'[10] Harriette's book – the book he was brave enough to publish – was, Stockdale said, 'the most important work, for its truth, for its moral effects on society, which, always excepting such as are of divine origin, has ever appeared, in any country since the world began, and which, I feel no hesitation in declaring, will be an imperishable monument of the society and manners of the present day, so long as time and literature shall endure'.[11]

Stockdale had a genius for publicity. It was his brilliant idea to serialize the *Memoirs,* thus heightening the suspense and speculation with which they would undoubtedly be received. As 'seditious' publications were not protected by copyright laws, they could be reproduced by other publishers at competitive prices; the gradual and, as it was, unpredictable appearance of the *Memoirs* at least gave Stockdale a head start. Serialization had other benefits too, the relatively low price of each number increasing circulation, and for those who were embarrassed by their interest in Harriette Wilson's story, a thin paper-covered book could be easily secreted away. Serialization was a method of publication later employed by Harriet Martineau in her *Illustrations of Political Economy* in 1832, and in 1836 by Charles Dickens with his *Pickwick Papers,* but Stockdale had few precursors. Rogue publishers had reissued Byron's *Don Juan* in instalments throughout 1821–22, and at the same time Pierce Egan's popular adventures of Jerry Hawthorne and Corinthian Tom, *Life in London,* were published in twelve monthly numbers. The serialization of the Bible, to the horror of the Church, had enjoyed a huge market since the late eighteenth century. Stockdale's originality lay in creating a climate of tension, an added layer of real-life drama, around the appearance of each number of the *Memoirs*. In his hands serialization became not just a method of selling the story but a vital component of the story's very construction, enjoyment and suspense. Purchasers knew, because Stockdale advertised the fact on the cover of every part, that for each name that appeared in print negotiations had taken place. Whether the full advertised cast list appeared in subsequent instalments or obvious omissions had taken place was a matter of great interest and amusement to the general reader, who was kept informed of the tremendous dramas going on backstage. 'Various rumours are afloat,' *Bell's Life in London* reported on the appearance of the *Memoirs,* 'and among others, that large sums have been given for the suppression of the names of certain persons who were known admirers of Harriette and her sisters.'[12] 'It has been currently stated', the same paper wrote in the following month, 'that the delay in the publication of the fourth number . . . has arisen from the policy of omitting an exposure of a certain distinguished family, with whom Harriette had been placed, at one period in her life, in a most interesting situation.'[13] The family alluded to was, of course, the Beauforts.

Under Stockdale's supervision, Harriette discarded her original *Sketches* and began her book again, replacing – this Stockdale insisted on – her fictitious figures with real names. Stockdale and Harriette struck a deal whereby he agreed to shoulder all responsibility for libel, to pay all expenses, and to give Harriette half the profits should she complete the agreed four volumes. Harriette signed a contract stating that Stockdale was to be the joint proprieter of any '*Memoirs* she has written or *shall write*'. Stockdale risked everything to ensure that her book was a success. It might be regarded as so scandalous that it would be prosecuted under the criminal law, although this was unlikely. It might also be the subject of action for libel under the civil law by any individual who felt aggrieved, although this would help the publicity. But, from the commercial point of view, the biggest risk Stockdale faced was that the *Memoirs* would be denied copyright protection. The whole book industry was well aware of the series of court judgments involving Byron's *Don Juan* in 1822 that confirmed that an immoral book could be not accorded intellectual property rights. If the *Memoirs* were regarded by the law in the same light, then the way would be open to any printer to pirate the text, bring down the price, and take on a large part of the profits.

Harriette stayed with Stockdale and his family in Acton while she worked. With her publisher hovering around her desk, she wrote using 'a sort of shorthand' in order to speed up the process. The words poured out; her strong, slanting hand sweeping over page after page. 'I shall not say why and how', she began, in what must be one of the most alluring openings to any piece of autobiography, 'I became, at the age of fifteen the mistress of the Earl of Craven. Whether it was love, or the severity of my father, the depravity of my own heart, or the winning arts of the noble Lord, which induced me to leave my paternal roof and place myself under his protection, does not now much signify: or if it does, I am not in the humour to gratify curiosity in this manner.' Harriette's *Memoirs* made a radical break with convention by presenting her introduction to the life of the *demi-mondaine* in such a bold and unapologetic fashion. The memoirs and biographies of other courtesans situate as their defining moment a 'deflowering' which nowhere occurs here. The biography of the eighteenth-century Cyprian George Anne Bellamy is typical in the story it tells: 'While yet a girl in her teens, she suffered herself to be seduced by one of those fashionable ruffians, who, in the shape of young noblemen of honour, spend the prime of life in committing depridations on the innocent.'[14]

Harriette makes it clear at the outset that she had no innocence to violate and has no reputation to uphold. Not only was it she who approached Craven, but it was she who left him when he failed to live up to her expectations of a lover. Whether this was the case or not is irrelevant; it was Harriette's version of events. She does not even give Craven the credit of having taken her virginity; at no point does she state that he was her first lover and she typically elides the incidental detail of her virtue, which may have been lost to his brother Berkeley or to Tom Sheridan on the journey to Ketridge House. Or perhaps, as Julia Johnstone tells us, Harriette lost her maidenhead to a red-headed boat-boy, the son of a washerwoman, on the Thames at Hammersmith. There might at least have been some cut and dash in Lord Craven's going down in history as a rascal. As it was, he is preserved for posterity as a cuckold and a bore.

Despite the 'authenticity' of her narrative voice, Harriette Wilson succeeds in revealing precisely nothing of herself. She never corrected her prose, and Stockdale encouraged the conversational naturalness of her style. Harriette completed the first volume in six days. 'I wanted to look over all that dirty paper, but Stockdale called on me every morning and tucked my foolscap MS *à mesure* under his arm, so that when I saw it in print I was really agreeably astonished and puzzled to guess why it was not worse still.'[15] She leaves us a comic picture of writer and publisher working together:

I have often sate at the same table with him of an evening, while he was looking over my MSS. Observing that he could neither make head nor tail of it,

What's the matter, Mr Stockdale, enquired I, laying my book aside. No imperfections in the style or language, I confidently hope?

Why really, said Stockdale, with a suppressed laugh, followed by a sigh, as he turned over leaf after leaf of my blotted, and highly disfigured sheets of fools cap really, all these sentences run into one another so oddly that in three long pages I am striving in vain to put in a single full stop. I, who doat on short sentences!

Lord, what is to be done, Mr Stockdale, in this extreme case?

Heaven best knows, said the despairing editor with a groan . . . for if I meddle with this light, pleasant rattle to mend it, by rule it will read heavy and dull.

And is this rendering a work heavy and dull what you call mending it? Do pray, Mr Stockdale, let it alone. I would rather see fifty grammatical errors than the word queer in my book. There are certain words which make me sick, however grammatical, and I cannot help it. They operate like antipathies.[16]

Harriette had completed three of the four planned volumes when she left England to join Rochfort, who had been living in central Paris, at 111 rue de Faubourg St Honoré. At this point in his life, Rochfort was no longer acknowledged in society. A rare account of him is given to her daughter by Mrs Brereton, the mother of Byron's friend Trelawny. Mrs Brereton describes cutting Rochfort in a Paris drawing room in late 1824, despite being related to him. 'His Sister had told me when in London that her Mother had now determined that his conduct continued so bad, that she could not countenance him . . . His conduct, embezzling the money which was to pay the soldiers, in fact his swindling tricks and debts in London, made me shrink from such a man.' If she had acknowledged him, Mrs Brereton continued, 'he is so forward and pushing that he would soon have found an entrance into all the English Houses, & I could not answer for his conduct.' Insulted by his treatment, Rochfort wrote Mrs Brereton a letter reminding her of 'some services rendered my Son in the Navy, which ought to make me grateful'. Rochfort had, Mrs Brereton noted, 'no modesty, and would soon push forward if I allowed him a loop-hole'.[17] She would later pay the penalty for snubbing Harriette's husband.

In her 'easy chair' at the rue du Faubourg St Honoré, Harriette completed the final volume of her *Memoirs* and started on a vast number of black-mail letters, inviting all those she had included in the book to buy themselves out for an annuity of between £20 to £40 or for a lump sum of £200.[18] She and Stockdale had agreed on this as well, although it is not known if he was to take a cut of what hush money she received. The chances are that he was – given that he wrote many of the blackmail letters himself.

The autumn of 1824 must have been a good time for Harriette. There is nothing like the pleasure of plotting revenge and the final mockery was dispatching her letters and the freshly penned chapters to London in the diplomatic bag through the auspices of the British Ambassador, Sir Charles Stuart, a former lover of hers who preferred that his name was kept out of her book. Harriette was once again living dangerously: she was married to a handsome young man, she had secured a publisher for her *Memoirs* who would support her all the way, she was anticipating great sums of money, and she had found her medium as a writer. As Sir James Scarlett later said, being only a 'common prostitute', Harriette had 'nothing to risk, nothing to lose. She might invade the [. . .] peace [of her victims], destroy the harmony of their families, and inflict on them the most exquisite torture which the spirit could infer, and yet remain impervious, because she could sink no lower.'[19]

Revenge writing is a female genre.[20] Men who have been left by women or made cuckolds by rivals either lick their wounds in humiliated silence or start the Trojan Wars. Having no other power or public voice, the betrayed woman reaches for her pen. When she was abandoned by Byron, Lady Caroline Lamb translated her grief and fury into *Glenarvon*, the *roman-à-clef* in which she published the poet's final letter to her and tried to stain his image. Women want a sympathetic audience by whom they can be enveloped; they spread their stories abroad, turning the personal into the archetypal and joining the annals of those abandoned and unloved female figures who populate literature, myth and legend. Revenge writers want their tales to seep, like poison, into the lives of those they expose. Through portraying themselves as victims they hope to become the victors, but their trust in the reader has always been abused. In revenge tales the woman's role as an emotional casualty is consolidated; it is a suicidal move. No woman who ever wrote for revenge has emerged from the experience unscathed, and no one whose behaviour was ever exposed in a book has not had his or her reputation enhanced as a result. In *Glenarvon*, Caroline Lamb inadvertently created the first Byronic hero, and it was her own reputation she destroyed. She bestowed on Byron the dignity that she herself lost.

Although Rochfort was fully behind the *Memoirs* and added fuel to his wife's rage at the way in which she had been mistreated, it was Stockdale and not he who acted as Harriette's evil genius.[21] Harriette regarded Rochfort more as a wild and impetuous child than a fount of wisdom, and Rochfort tended to follow her lead. There is no sign in the *Memoirs* of Rochfort's influence, emotional or otherwise, over Harriette; for the most part she writes as if she had never met him. While many new lovers review their versions of a disappointing past in the light of the improvements of the present, Harriette's view of her history seems not to have been affected in any way by her feelings for Rochfort. Ponsonby is still her great love and it is still Meyler who drives her to jealous despair, never to be repeated. It is only in the tired, additional chapters that appeared in Stockdale's 1831 edition that Rochfort enters the story at all and in which any bitterness at her treatment makes an appearance, with the consequence that Harriette's felicitous prose loses its poise. Otherwise her style is nostalgic, humorous, and frequently loving; there is no sign of the indignation that she says fired her on. In fact, the *Memoirs* are remarkable for the genuine enjoyment they take in retrieving old emotions and experiences; pages pour out on her sisters and old friends, she recalls anecdotes and spins yarns, she re-creates a time during which she had been happy. Rochfort was interested only in the money to be gained; Harriette's investment was more complex than this. Money provided her with a conscious motive for writing the book, but the task afforded her other, deeper, pleasures. Her writing is far more than an opportunity to blackmail her lovers and secure her future; it is also a chance to relive, rewrite and re-create her past.

Harriette discovered that she could write, and she was thrilled by the fact. 'Now, we are the two greatest people in Europe! Scott in his way, I in mine!' she declared. 'Everything which comes after us will be but base copies.'[22] Beneath the hyperbole was a genuine sense of pride: 'I always said to my sister Paragon, whom, at that period, I was in the habit of visiting, that the first twenty pounds I should be able to earn by honest labour would make me more happy, and do me more good, than the finest equipage with as many thousands, which should be given me by a lover as the price of my dishonour.'[23] The dramas she had previously composed were weak and the novels she would later produce were without plot, but *Memoirs* she could do. Harriette's writing tells us all we need to know about her appeal. Her impact is immediate; she is impossible to resist. She addresses her reader (assumed to be male and aristocratic) as a potential lover, in a voice that is rich, vital, amused and charming. Her tone is impudent, conspiratorial, seemingly artless in an artificial age. She is funny, clever, sexy, ironic. She whets the appetite and gives nothing away, she raises questions she has no intention of answering, drawing her helpless reader into her confidence with astonishing dexterity while all the time refusing to gratify the curiosity she has aroused. With the cool assurance of an accomplished coquette, she controls her writing as if she were conducting a dinner-party flirtation; she plays with her prose as she might tease a fan, letting it alternately mask and reveal her features. Writing, Harriette was in her element; she created a timeless world in which she was the dazzling sun and all the great men she had known were mere stars. She turned up the volume so that her voice drowned out all others. She organized chaotic experiences and events into a manageable form; she wrote people out of her life, whether or not they had paid her to do so, she killed people off, she shifted the dates, she puffed herself up as a heroine of the age. She became once more 'angelick Harriette', the darling of the dandies.

Harriette sold her story in a spectacular way, but she was not the first courtesan to kiss and tell. Plenty of memoirs and confessions by, or purporting to be by, courtesans preceded the appearance of her own. The eighteenth century had been 'a melting point for the interplay and divergence between fiction and "true story"' and many memoirs 'by' courtesans and actresses served to 'highlight both the cross-dressing and the rivalry between the genres of the novel and the memoir'. The memoirists were able to '"mix and match" the garb of other genres, drawing on features of two popular figures in erotic literature: "the sentimental courtesan" and the "libertine whore".'[24] Thomas de Quincey claimed in his own *Confessions* that most English confessions proceeded from the pens of 'demi-reps, adventurers, or swindlers'. He identified autobiography with the prostitute, but sex sold well in other genres as well. Moll Flanders and Fanny Hill were the happy-go-lucky, nymphomaniacal heroines of some of the century's most popular novels, and both books were written in the style of the memoir.

Following the Mary Anne Clarke scandal, the *chronique scandaleuse* became a political instrument and radical publishers began to use the courtesan's confessions as a means of exposing and condemning the behaviour of the upper classes. These publications tended to be semi-pornographic. Lady Conyngham and her husband were favourite targets: *The Memoirs of the Celebrated Lady C—* appeared in the same year as Harriette's *Memoirs*, and three years earlier the Marquis of Conyngham featured in *An interesting narrative of the Poll house*.

Nor was Harriette Wilson the first fallen woman to blackmail her lovers. The eighteenth-century courtesan, Constantia Phillips, had blackmailed her patrons prior to penning her *Memoirs*, as did the wit and poet Laetitia Pilkington. Blackmail, moreover, was a thriving activity in the literary underworld. Harriette's *Memoirs* were striking not because of the originality of the form adopted by her narrative or the originality of her voice. They were striking because she made no claim to tell the truth. Readers knew, from the list of names on the back of each part, that they were getting an edited version of events, that these memoirs bore very little relation to memory and that Harriette Wilson herself had no control over the direction her story would take, over who would buy themselves out and thus leave a gap to be filled in the plot. Her *Memoirs* were, for Harriette's readers, both a documentary-in-the-making and a highly edited fiction, and this was their great appeal. Those Harriette wrote about saw her behaviour as a violation of every social code, but the *Memoirs* never 'descend' into pornography, Harriette avoided scenes of sexual intimacy and never mocked the prowess of her lovers; she might send them up for their personal hygiene or the dullness of their conversation but never for their performance. Throughout, Harriette retained the courtesy required of the courtesan. Despite the contemporary outrage at the supposed licentiousness of her book, many readers must have found it disappointing.

Writing, Harriette found, was regarded as more transgressive than the sale of her body had been. It was unusual for a woman's name to be attached to a book; novels by lady novelists tended to be anonymous and names attached to scandal tended to be asterixed out after the initial letter. For Harriette's name to be part of her title, to be emblazoned across her cover in such an immodest way, was scandal enough in itself. But it was not so much what she wrote or the manner in which she wrote it that made Harriette outrageous: it was the mere fact of writing at all. Women who write have long been distrusted, and it is the combination of writing and female sexuality that has baffled readers and critics. It is only recently that Jane Austen or Emily Brontë have begun to be discussed without a reference being made to their virginity, as if by way of explaining their talent. To write well, the assumption is, a woman must sacrifice her sexuality. The better she writes, the less of a real woman she is thought to be. Harriette discovered that as soon as she exchanged the roles of lover for writer, she was stripped of her famous appeal; she had traded her femininity for monstrosity.

The first instalment of the *Memoirs* appeared in February 1825, and the violence of Harriette's reception was a tribute to the power of her book.

CHAPTER 20

The *Memoirs* and the *Confessions*

'Few publications in modern times have excited such curiosity, or produced such extraordinary sensations in fashionable life,' observed *Bell's Life in London* of Harriette Wilson's *Memoirs*. 'It finds its way into all circles, and the grave and the gay – the starched puritan and the professed libertine, are equally sedulous in perusing its pages.'[1] 'Perhaps you may find time to read this trash,' wrote Poodle Byng, who featured in its pages, to Lord Granville, who featured in them also; 'not my letter but HW's *Memoirs*,' he added, '– Heard of it you must – it has caused sensation here and is almost as much talked of as the Mining Shares . . . Like most other people I suppose you like to see what is said of your relations . . .' Lord Montagu told Sir Walter Scott that the entire Cabinet was reading them because of the mention of one of their members. 'I am impatient', Scott replied, 'to see Harriot Wilsons [*sic*] biography and have sent an order for it accordingly.'[2] The *Memoirs* were mentioned in Parliament by Dr Stephen Lushington, who complained that the University Club had rejected a request to purchase a Bible for its library while at the same time ordering a copy of Harriette Wilson's book. A member of the Club replied the following day that although requests for the purchase of the *Memoirs* had been legion, it had not in fact been bought. Ministers and opposition joined forces to hold emergency meetings at White's, Brooks's and the

Sheraton writing desk, *The Book of Decorative Furniture*

United Service Club, 'to extinguish this burning shame', Stockdale imagined, 'which threatened an extent of desolation which, it was said, would make England not worth living in'.[3] 'But', Poodle Byng reported to Lord Granville of the crisis in the gentlemen's clubs, 'it was determined that nothing in the way of opposition could be done.'[4]

A notice had appeared in the papers on 6 January announcing the publication the next day of part one of *Memoirs*, the contents of which were to include 'The King – Dukes Wellington, Devonshire, Argyll – Marquess of Hertford – Marchionesses of Conyngham, Londonderry – Lords Craven, Melbourne, F. Bentinck, Byron, Proby, Burghersh, Alvanley, Dudley, Palmerston, Lowther, Ponsonby – Ladies Fanny Ponsonby, Berwick, Jersey – Counts Woronzow, Beckendorff, Orloff, Palmella – Honourables F. Lamb, General Walpole, Miss Storer – Sirs John Shelley, James Graham – Generals Mackenzie, Maddan and Lady – Colonels Cotton and Lady, Trench and Lady, Sydenham and Lady – Dr Nevinson – Messrs Sheridan, Beckford, Woodcock and Lady Luttrell, Nugent, Brummell, Mitchell, Ponsonby, Freeling, Graham, Kemble, Young, Eliot, Street, Croker, Murray, Mrs Porter'.[5] 'A pretty list indeed,' said Brougham on seeing the advertisement. 'Almost every one of my particular friends is among them!' Several more of Brougham's friends were sufficiently threatened by Stockdale's warning to ensure that this was the last time their names were linked in print with that of Harriette Wilson. Lady Berwick, whose humiliation was immense, tried and failed to prevent further circulation of her sister's story. It seems, from Harriette's representation of Sophia, that no money was exchanged, but publication was delayed due to behind-the-scenes negotiations and the first number of Harriette Wilson's *Memoirs* did not appear until the following month when the small shop in the Opera Colonnade was teeming with prospective purchasers.

The crowds in and around Stockdale's premises were so great that he erected a bar outside his door, which was removed only when the final number of Harriette's book was sold that autumn. Between February and May the *Memoirs* appeared in nine paper-covered successive parts. The last three instalments appeared in late August bound together in one volume. Publication might have been postponed due to the libel case Stockdale was fighting in July. The instalments included a preface in which Stockdale laid out his own defence: '[As] a weekly exposé will guard public morals, spare them not, from the coronet to the counting-house, from the dashing men of fashion, to the sober citizen, from the young and flippant to the sage, sentimental, and hoary sinner', and continued his attack, 'It will be seen that this work does not assume to be a complete confession. How much further it may be carried, will probably depend on the reception of what is herein submitted to the public.'

Each instalment sold at 2s 6d, making it cheaper than the serialized editions of Pierce Egan's *Life in London*, which had cost three shillings per number four years earlier, but it was still a high price to pay. The cost restricted Harriette's readership to Byron's 'twice two thousand, for whom earth was made', and it was only later when the price came down that the *Memoirs* would have been available to a wider market. On the back cover Stockdale listed, in order of rank, the names of those Harriette had included in her story and those who would appear in the future if they did nothing now to prevent it: '*Dukes*. Argyll, Beaufort (and Duchess), de Guiche, Leinster, Wellington. *Marquesses*. Anglesey, Bath, Headfort, Sligo, Worcester.' The front cover announced the day and hour on which the next part would be available, but publication was increasingly delayed due to negotiations with significant parties.

Lord Craven, who refused to pay, lived just long enough to see his name emblazoned across Harriette's opening line. He died, more famous than he might have been, in the summer of 1825. One month after the first instalment appeared, Clanricarde, who also refused to pay, married the only daughter of the Foreign Secretary, George Canning, and began his career as a Canningite Tory. Canning, who had himself been a lover of Harriette's, had bought her silence.

An illustration by a new artist, Henry Heath, intended as a frontispiece to the *Memoirs*, was published on 21 February by the radical S. W. Fores of Piccadilly (plate 28). Titled *La, Coterie, Debouché*, it shows Harriette, fresh and youthful with a crown of red roses in her hair, poised, quill in hand, at a round, cloth-covered table on which sits a large packet of letters, labelled *For Future Observation*. Twelve admiring swains crowd together before her, each trying to get her attention. Ponsonby is holding a dog; Wellington, in uniform, doffs his cocked hat; Worcester, Yarmouth, George Lamb, Argyll and Canning all rush in to compliment the author; 'an elegant figure'; 'what brilliant wit'; 'the soul of sentiment'; 'what an expressive countenance'; 'such smart repartee'.[6]

Harriette's *Memoirs* went through thirty-five editions in the first year alone. While many of these 'editions' are not reprintings but unsold sheets bound together with a new title page, there is no doubt that the book sold. Successful translations simultaneously appeared in France, Brussels and Germany. *The Age Reviewed* reported in 1828 that 50,000 copies of the *Memoirs* had been sold, but the quantity of piracies produced make the full circulation impossible to calculate.[7] Stockdale used at least two printers, and James Barnard, the son of one of them, recalled his father printing off 7,000 copies of the *Memoirs*; Pollett, another of the printers, was contracted to print 1,000 sheets a week but found that 17,000 sheets were called for.

Stockdale was fighting hard to keep up with the demand for Harriette's story. 'Some of its numbers are out of print,' *Bell's Life* wrote, 'but we understand the publisher is making gigantic efforts to gratify the taste of his customers.'[8] The fourth number, *Bell's Life* reported on 6 March, appeared only after a 'long and mysterious delay'. Rumours were afloat that publication was withheld until the Duke of Beaufort and Stockdale had come to an agreement about certain passages. 'A negotiation was opened,' thought *Bell's Life*, 'and we understand the offensive matter was withdrawn, and something else substituted upon the trifling consideration of restoring Harriette to the full enjoyment of her bond. We give this as the *on dit* of the day – it is the topic of general conversation among the lovers of scandal, and may or may not have foundation. It is evident that the present number is by no means so interesting as those which preceded it, and from that fact alone, added to the delay which has taken place, greater confidence is attached to what we have related. Should any more of those little suppressions meet our ear, we shall not fail to include them in our columns.'[9] When the fifth number appeared on 9 March, again 'after considerable delay', 'the moment the specified time for delivery arrived, Stockdale's shop was almost taken by storm. It is rumoured that negotiations have been going on for various suppressions: but to this Stockdale pleads "Not Guilty". We would rather apprehend, however, that there is good ground for such a belief, and hope to be able to get a peep behind the curtain . . .'[10]

As the regular instalments accumulated, Stockdale brought them out in volumes selling at 7s 6d. The first edition contained twenty-eight coloured plates, which he also sold separately at two shillings, eighteen of which were scenes from the *Memoirs*. Illustrated books showing real people were extremely rare, so the *Memoirs* appeared unique. Lorne sits whistling on a gate as he waits for Harriette to appear from her house in Somerstown (plate 13); Frederic Lamb attacks Harriette by the throat (plate 10); Wellington stands in the rain as Argyll, disguised as a duenna, speaks to him from Harriette's bedroom window (plate 19); Worcester laces Harriette's stays as he makes toast over the fire for her breakfast (plate 24). The illustrations are comic caricatures, picking up on the satirical humour of the *Memoirs*. Ten of the plates were reduced copies by George Cruikshank of Richard Dighton's *Characters, at the West End of Town*, which illustrated the present state of the gay lotharios whose youths had been immortalized by Harriette. Argyll appeared as stout, bewhiskered and patrician, in a top hat, Worcester as an ageing dandy walking his poodle, and a bloated Lord Alvanley was depicting staggering, as usual, to White's.

Stockdale's profit would have been greater had not the populist publishers of the day, such as Onwhyn, Duncombe, Dugdale and Benbow instantly seized on the fact that copyright laws could not protect publications such as Harriette's. Stockdale's fears were realized when the first pirated editions – 5,000 copies – were sold at a bargain four shillings. On 11 January 1826, he appeared with Brougham at the King's Bench to prosecute the publisher, Mr Onwhyn, of Catherine Street in the Strand. This was the only time Stockdale sued for infringement of copyright, and he was hoist by his own petard. Onwhyn's defence was that, given their 'licentious, libellous' nature, the *Memoirs* could not be defended at all, and he was therefore exempt from prosecution. Stockdale, in a move that does not reflect well on him, had employed this same line in *Poplett* v. *Stockdale* on 1 December 1825, when he was taken to court for non-payment of one of his printing bills. 'No one who has assisted in putting forth such a work to the public,' the Lord Chief Justice then ruled, 'can recover for the labour he has employed upon it . . . He who leant himself to the violation of the laws in his country in this gross and shameful manner, shall not be allowed to claim payment for what he has done in execution of such a criminal purpose.'[11] The verdict in both cases was Non Suit, on the grounds that 'the law cannot recognize as property the history of the low amours of a notorious courtesan'.[12] After this judgment, the pirates were safe from all fear of interruption from the law.

Pirated editions were advertised everywhere in the press. *Bell's Life* carried an advertisement on 27 March for Duncombe's 'verbatim' '*Memoirs* of Harriette Wilson, the cheapest edition, price 2s. 6d . . . including her amatory adventures with most of the Nobility of the present day'. 'Thomas's edition' was advertised on 10 April, at eight shillings for the first two volumes. Different styles of illustration appeared in the different editions. In the *Memoirs* published by Douglas in 1825, Harriette is the heroine of a sentimental novel. In one scene she sits with Ponsonby, the two of them gazing into one another's eyes, he looks amorous, she looks anxious, he clutches her left hand, her right hand sits demurely on her lap (see illustration to Chapter 10). In another scene, Harriette, in white silk, waits patiently in an elegant room in Brighton while, through the open window, Lord Craven is sailing his boat (see illustration to Chapter 5). There is no sign of the boredom Harriette describes having suffered during this period. Some editions contained semi-pornographic images: Amy, breasts exposed and hair tumbling down, sits on a bed in a state of surprise while William Ponsonby pokes his head through the curtains. Favourite scenes for illustration in all editions were Wellington's being refused admittance by Argyll to Harriette's house, Sophia's dropping her black pudding when she encountered Deerhurst in the street, and Harriette's being waited on in Brighton by an abject Worcester. In an illustration by Henry Heath for one edition, Harriette sits up in bed while Worcester, in nightcap and nightshirt, makes toast on the fire. 'Oh Worcester, what a *tender* and *affectionate* Husband you will make!!!' she exclaims. 'My dearest dear Harriette,' he answers, 'this menially waiting upon you is ecstasy in comparison with the Regent's Music.' Harriette's narrative could fit into the comic, pornographic or sentimental, and the type of illustration chosen suited the type of reader being targeted.

Bell's Life itself reproduced the *Memoirs* as the instalments appeared and serialized them on its front page between 13 February and 2 October 1825, making no bones about the desire to hurt Stockdale's sales. Chapbooks of edited highlights appeared and the magistrate of Bow Street gave orders to his officers to 'apprehend any of those hawkers who should be found vending "The Adventures of Harriette Wilson"'. On 15 March, a penniless apprentice shoemaker was found holding a placard on which was Robert Cruikshank's caricature of Harriette riding backwards on a black lamb.

> Here I am like a W— as I am
> Riding on my black LAMB
> Who for my frincum crancum
> Have lost my bincum bancum
> And for my tail's game
> Have come to this Worldly shame
> Which makes the DUKE a public game
> And Harlotte Wilson is my name.[13]

The 'poor lad,' an apprentice to an impoverished shoemaker, had been sent out to sell pamphlets called *The Whole and Amorous letters from Harriette Wilson to the King, the Duke of Wellington and other noblemen* in order to make an 'honest penny'.[14] The magistrate conceded that there was nothing obviously libellous about the placard and agreed that it would be difficult to prosecute 'this young retailer of a strumpet biographer' when every bookseller's shop in London was selling her *Memoirs*. A letter appeared in *The Times* and other papers sending up the rich variety of *Memoirs* on the market: 'We are delighted to be able to inform our readers on the most undoubted authority, that an edition of the moral and instructive *Memoirs of Harriette Wilson*, adapted for families and young persons, by the omission of all objectionable passages, which cannot with propriety be read aloud, by the Rev. Thomas Bowdler, FRS, etc, author of the family Shakespeare, is in the press, and the true friends of undefiled morality and our holy religion may shortly expect this previous addition to their libraries.'

Stockdale despaired over the piracies and Harriette wrote to Brougham on 14 July for advice on copyright law. The pirates and the costly libel case Stockdale had lost on 1 July eventually threatened to put a stop to the *Memoirs*. 'Respecting the rest of my history,' Harriette asked Brougham, 'is it not a crying shame that this great national loss is to be permitted? Six more parts, in manuscript, lie in Stockdale's desk, a dead loss to him and to the public. Who is to blame? Pirates, shabby lawyers, judge and jury. Oh pray do continue these dear *Memoirs*, says everybody I meet, saving and excepting the immediate figurantes. We are all so delighted with them, says a formal lady, the wife of a principal character in the book: these vile men, our husbands, have at last got what they deserve. Pray don't let people buy themselves out and thus destroy the interest of your book. You are such a sweet writer . . .'[15]

Stockdale's reason for bringing out the final three instalments in August as one volume was correctly assumed by *Bell's Life* 'to ensure a few days further delay from piracy, while the publisher can get off a profitable stock'. However, 'we shall', *Bell's Life* concluded, 'in two or three of our numbers, dispose of everything really worth notice in this seven and sixpence book'.[16]

But there was someone else who was also determined to dispose of everything really worth notice in Harriette's book, and six weeks after the appearance of the first instalments of Harriette's *Memoirs*, Julia Johnstone rose from the grave.

Harriette, it seems, had fancifully killed her friend off in the way that one does when a character in the plot becomes *de trop*. According to Harriette, Julia had been in the family vault for the last ten years, but the instalments in which her death was described had not yet been published and so Harriette's readers did not yet know what cruel blow fate was to deal her unhappy rival. Julia, who was alive and well and living in Hampstead, had heard rumours of her death at Harriette's hands, 'for Harriette has industriously circulated through her Pall Mall agents and retailers of her infamy, "that I *died in a workhouse and she knows both my executors*".'[17] What offended her was not the fact that she was presumed dead but the suggestion that she might have died in such a lowly state. This was not what Julia had planned; if Harriette had indeed believed Julia to be dead, it was because Julia herself put it about that she was.

Julia had cut herself off from Harriette in the aftermath of the Worcester scandal in order to attempt a reconciliation with her family. One of the principal things they insisted on, Julia wrote, 'was that I should give up all the acquaintance made in my degraded state, before they would extend protection to me or my children; so of course [Harriette] was the first whose society I abandoned. In truth, those who knew me, and the reasons I had for total seclusion from the world, took some pains to convince [Harriette] that I had died in Scotland . . .'[18] Harriette therefore had reason to believe in Julia's death; it seems that her only embellishment had been her place at Julia's bedside when she breathed her last. 'The first number of [Harriette's] *Memoirs*, and probably the second, were written by her at the time when she was ignorant that such a one as myself lived to refute her lies. *But* I had taken care she should now know whether I was dead or alive, and no doubt she actually wished I had long ago vanished from the world's surface . . .'[19]

By the time her *Memoirs* appeared, Harriette knew that Julia was alive and breathing fire and approached her through an attorney, Charles Hemley, who proposed that she give up all Harriette's letters and 'abstain from exposing her' in exchange for £400. Julia rejected the offer, claiming that she valued her 'good name more than money'. Julia was actually planning on using her knowledge of Harriette as a means of clearing her own bad name, while making more than £400 in the process; she was badly in need of money. On 25 March, there appeared the first part of Julia Johnstone's *Confessions: In Contradiction to the Fables of Harriette Wilson*, published by William Benbow.

Julia started to dictate her *Confessions* to Benbow shortly after the first instalments of Harriette's *Memoirs* had appeared. Having seen only the first three instalments, she had no idea what Harriette was going to say next and therefore what it was that she, Julia, was therefore going to have to confess: this explains the random-fire nature of her 'narrative'. Contradict everything, just to be on the safe side. Harriette did nothing to edit the account of Julia's death from the *Memoirs*. She kept it in to amuse her readers, to avenge herself on the ex-friend, and to discredit what Julia had said in her *Confessions*.

Just as Harriette's *Memoirs* are in part a letter to the Duke of Beaufort, Julia's *Confessions* are addressed to the Earl of Carysfort. The reason Julia set out to contradict Harriette's tale was to redeem herself in the eyes of her uncle. 'But for these *Confessions*,' Julia wrote, her family 'would have forsaken me as the *guilty thing* Harriette Wilson made me appear in her *Memoirs*'.[20] Julia means to tell a story of good versus evil and congratulates herself at the close of her book on having been able 'to acquit my conscience of a heavy debt, on the score of religion and morality. I say with St Paul, "I have fought the good fight – and have finished my course."'[21] Lord Carysfort would also expect Julia to estrange herself from Cotton, with whom, it appears, she had reunited. Cotton had long ago separated from his wife and Julia insists in her *Confessions* that she had broken with him completely: 'I have long ago parted, no more to engage with the Colonel; so that I am advocating his cause from no interested motives – nay, probably I am foolishly doing a friendly act to one who laid the foundation of all my misfortunes, and has since treated me with an indifference bordering on inhumanity.'[22] It is possible, however, that Julia cut off from the world after 1815 not because she was whitewashing herself but because she did not want it known that she was in fact living with Cotton once more.

If Julia's domestic situation became known to him, Lord Carysfort would discontinue her allowance, and Julia and Cotton could not afford to lose his money. Poverty had dogged their relationship; Cotton had got into financial trouble back in 1797 through a substantial loan of £8,000 he had made to a bankrupt uncle which had not been repaid.[23] It was his subsequent embarrassment that led him to sell his colonelcy in the 10th Dragoons in 1799, and to leave Julia without support during the following years. It was his failure to provide for her in Primrose Cottage that led to Julia leaving Cotton to live with Harriette in Bloomsbury. But Josiah Cotton never stopped loving Julia Storer; Harriette says that he never disappeared from Julia's life, continuing as her loyal 'swain' throughout her years with the three graces. It was not Cotton who tired of her, as Julia would have us believe: she, rather, grew tired of Cotton and was encouraged by Harriette to earn her own keep in the *demi-monde*. It is this fact of which Julia seems most ashamed in her *Confessions*, and which she makes most effort to deny.

Julia had another reason to keep her relationship with Cotton a secret from her family: she may have once again given birth. Baptism records of the Old Church at St Pancras, near where she lived, show that in 1823 a child called Julia Storer Johnstone was born to Josiah Johnstone ('Gentleman') and Eliza Catherine. The coincidence of names is so striking that it is possible the scribe confused mother with daughter, and that Julia Storer and Josiah Cotton, alias Johnstone, therefore had another child, Eliza Catherine. Julia was forty-six, and had been with Cotton now for thirty years.[24]

Julia's *Confessions* are a bilious attack on Harriette's supposed dishonesty, with the stated aim of lessening her rival's sales: 'My simple explanations have already materially injured the sale of her lying work, the last number not having come up to any of the former in quantity sold, by some thousands: and if my health permitted, and I could write faster, so as to publish a book at once, I would soon drive her totally out of the market.'[25] And so the fortnightly appearance of Harriette's *Memoirs* was promptly followed by a contradictory instalment from Julia. Every detail of Harriette's story is challenged. Harriette was never, Julia claims, 'connected with Lord Ponsonby and never spoke to him above twenty times in her whole life'.[26] While waiting for Worcester in Charmouth, Harriette had a child by a soldier; Amy, on the other hand, never had a child by Argyll and nor did Worcester ever propose to Harriette; Fanny was a drunk; Amelia Dubouchet was a 'shocking vulgar woman, very forward and coarse in her language';[27] the family lived in Hammersmith with Dubouchet maintaining them all on a captain's commission. The list of Harriette's supposed fabrications is endless. Throughout the *Confessions* Julia argues that she was a key player in all the major events in Harriette's life – that she was listening behind the door when Harriette first met Sir Arthur Wellesley, that she was the confidante of Ponsonby and Worcester, that she accompanied Harriette to Charmouth. It is a further mark of Julia's confused motivation that in the attempt to dissociate herself from Harriette she writes herself further into her former friend's life. Ever on the side of the powerful, Julia says that it was she who informed Beaufort of Harriette's infidelity and that is why he subsequently stopped the annuity and her own relationship with Harriette came to an end. It is, most significantly, Julia who tells us that Harriette sent Wellington a letter asking for '£300, threatening in the case of non-compliance to write anathemas against his moral reputation' and that the Duke returned 'her letter with "write and be d—d" written in red ink on the back of it'.[28] The fact that Julia Johnstone originated the phrase that has gone down in history as 'publish and be damned' is evidence enough of her influence on the public. Wellington's apparent retort being now more or less all that is known about Harriette Wilson suggests that Julia's *Confessions* were read by many and assumed to tell the true story. She succeeded in reducing her rival to a catchphrase that confers dignity on Wellington and damns Harriette.

Julia's *Confessions* are still treated as the rational corrective to Harriette's fictions.[29] What becomes increasingly apparent, however, about the

Memoirs is how accurate much of what Harriette says actually is. She uses dramatic licence to entertain her readers and amuse herself (as in her anecdotes about Byron), dates are chaotic and confused, and important episodes of her life are erased and embellished according to what payments she has received by those who were involved. But, in general, the version of events as Harriette tells them can be borne out by what secondary documentation exists. This is particularly apparent in the Worcester episode. Julia's story, with the occasional exception, is written so wilfully 'in contradiction' to Harriette's, and offers so little other than contradiction, that it might almost be the work of John Mitford, the prolific Regency pornographer, or even of Julia's own publisher.

There is of course a chance that Julia had indeed died and that William Benbow, wanting to cash in on the success of Harriette's *Memoirs*, rushed out an equally scandalous book under Julia Johnstone's name.[30] The case would not be unusual; many courtesans' memoirs of the time were written by hacks. There are, however, strong arguments against this theory. Firstly, Julia challenges her readers to write to Benbow for her address if in doubt as to her continued existence.[31] And among other signs of Julia's continued existence is a report from the *Morning Herald* in 1824 that she was found drunk and disorderly on King Street, clad in her 'silks and satins'.[32] Secondly, there is something authentic about the troubled voice of Julia's *Confessions*; rather than trying to trump the sauciness of Harriette's *Memoirs*, the *Confessions* are the work of a confused, jealous, disappointed woman. The courtesan, Julia says, 'breathes pestilence and walks in corruption – her course is that of a crazy and rotten barque, gliding rapidly along a turbulent and impure stream, among rocks and quicksands, where it is prematurely wrecked, or after many weary struggles, is lost in the dark ocean of oblivion'.[33] The narrative tone lacks the blandness of most ghost-written revelations. The narrator's unhappiness is so extreme that she might be thought a one-dimensional creation were it not for variations in her character too subtle for any speed-writing hack to imagine. She is a fallen angel trying to clamber home, she is unconfident, foolish enough not to know that she is dull, too dull to know the difference between her *Confessions* and Harriette's *Memoirs*. She has no understanding of Harriette's appeal and what she says to lessen her rival's attractions serves only to enhance them while lessening her own: 'There are many who read this, will recollect

[Harriette's] riding like a mad woman through the Parks, on a stout cream-coloured charger, with her hair streaming loose in the wind, and her beaver half off, with a servant on a cart horse, in brown livery, toiling after her – she was then upon the wane, like a shop that has ceased to attract customers . . .'34 Julia gives us a picture of Harriette Wilson aged thirty-eight in which the writer's competitive malice is tempered by genuine pathos and what begins as mockery ends in elegy.

Imagine to yourself a little woman in a black beaver hat, and long grey cloak . . . No *tightening* at the waist to show the *figure* of the wearer, nor any ornament to be seen what-ever. Her figure, at a short distance, might not inaptly be compared to a milestone with a carter's hat resting on its summit. Her once little feet, now covered with *list shoes* to defend them from attacks of a desultory gout which she has suffered long in both extremities. Her *face*, at the time I allude to, was swollen with this disorder to distortion. She has no colour – *le couleur de rose a disparu* [*sic*] – and in its place appears a kind of dingy lilac, which spreads all over her once light countenance, and appears burnt into her lips. The *crow's feet* are wide-spreading beneath her eyes, which, though sunken, still gleam with faded lustre through her long dark eyelashes. She bears the remains of what was once superlatively lovely – the wreck of the angel's visage is yet to be seen; it looks interesting in decay – not the decay brought by age and infirmity, but beauty hurried away prematurely, from the practices of a licentious and dissolute life; such is the once celebrated Miss Dubochet, alias Wilson.35

Newspaper reports confirm the dramatic change in Harriette's appearance, but only Julia Johnstone could write like this. She is at the same time furious and profoundly embarrassed by Harriette's *Memoirs*: 'I scarcely can show myself abroad.'36 She is doubly humiliated: not only has she been exposed as a courtesan but as a second-rate one at that. Julia's *Confessions* attempt the contradictory task of proving that she was never Harriette's rival because she never sunk so low – 'I have been no rival demirep of Harriette's, but attended her as the fabled pilot star does the comet, until it "curbs its red yoke and mingles with the sun"'37 – while being the only courtesan who rose high enough to be able to rival Harriette: 'The ironical manner in which Miss Wilson speaks of me throughout her *Memoirs* tells a plain truth, that I was her most successful rival, or [as] she once phrased it, the decoy duck that carried away all her sportsmen.'38 What Julia inadvertently ends up doing is competing over who was the better courtesan. Harriette was, 'Lord Ponsonby once flatteringly observed to me, "the *meteor* that dazzled from its borrowed lustre for a time, and then faded away; but . . . I was the *steady planet*, a source of never fading attraction, whose vivifying heat was by all acknowledged and felt by all"'.[39]

William Benbow could not have produced something so psychologically complex. Nor would he have ever written as Julia did about royalty and the aristocracy. The writer of the *Confessions* is preoccupied above all else with reclaiming her rightful place in the hierarchy; abjection and snobbery dominate the text. Julia sets out to defend the libelled King – 'the most exalted character in the nation' – and the other names whose greatness Harriette has attempted to diminish: 'My book may restore peace into the bosom of many families, from whence it has been driven by the Demon of Discord.'[40] It is Julia's preoccupation with the virtues of the ruling class as against the sins of the *demi-monde* that presents the strongest argument for its having been her, rather than her publisher, who wrote the *Confessions*.

Benbow was forty-one, a trained shoemaker, and an active member of the Radical movement, although his politics were far to the left of the Radicals: he belonged to the political underworld; he wanted armed revolution to create a new order. He began his literary career as William Cobbett's publisher and then moved on to pamphleteering, writing, printing, editing and bookselling. In 1821 he published a series of pamphlets, *Crimes of Clergy*, attacking the Church of England, which landed him in prison for the second time in his career. He approved of Byron and Shelley and pirated much of their poetry; he railed against Southey, who renounced the radicalism of his youth; he produced editions of Thomas Moore's works, M. G. Lewis's *The Monk*, Henry Brougham's critique of Byron, and a series of letters from an American Indian in London to his friends back home. Six months before Julia approached him with her *Confessions*, he had been in the bankruptcy court.[41] Benbow had the political vision that Stockdale lacked, which included exposing the sexual hypocrisy of the aristocracy. He was working towards political change while Stockdale was tapping into the Zeitgeist.

Benbow was what Stockdale never managed to be: a man of the people. His publications in 1820–21 captured the public feeling about Queen Caroline, the estranged wife of George IV, and he ended up back in prison for his lampoons of the King. Benbow could not have written, even in jest, the following account of the young Prince of Wales at a ball attended by Julia: 'His affability, cheering smiles, and restless anxiety to make the party happy, were perfectly captivating. He had something to say to all, and wandered about the ball-room like a fond father among his doating [*sic*] children. Those who have seen our gracious Prince at such moments when he casts off Majesty and descends to the state of a private gentleman, can never forget the impression he makes on the finer feelings of our nature.'[42]

It seems at first ironic that it should be Benbow – who challenged the Establishment to which Julia wanted to be reinstated – who published her *Confessions*. He seems more suitable as the publisher of Harriette's *Memoirs,* while Stockdale's politics have more affinity with Julia's. While Benbow clearly missed the point of Julia Johnstone, he saw something else in what she had written. Her tale represented the ultimate in the hypocrisy of the aristocracy; Julia was properly displaced, belonging neither to her own family nor to Colonel Cotton's, neither to the *demi-monde* nor to the *grande-monde*. She was the ideal class victim, but this would not have been her only appeal. Benbow approved of courtesans whom he saw as representing physical pleasure, and women's bodies he thought of as the great class leveller. The fact that the pleasures of Julia's body were restricted to the aristocracy alone was a fault of the system of limited ownership, and not of the traffic in women. Courtesans should belong to the many and not to the few.

After the publication of her *Confessions*, there are no further records of Julia Storer. It is not known when, how or where she died, who grieved for her or what became of her children. Even the Proby family tree, complete in all its details, omits Julia's name and dates, acknowledging only that Elizabeth Storer, née Proby, had a 'daughter'. Cotton kept his rooms in Hampton Court until his death in 1848. It is unlikely that Julia would have lived there with him, more likely that she died in poverty, her uncle having disowned her once more after the appearance of the *Memoirs* and *Confessions*.

When the *Memoirs* were published, both Harriette and Stockdale received a torrent of abusive and anonymous mail; Harriette eventually made it known that she would open nothing that did not contain the sender's name and seal on the envelope. Beau Brummell, whom she visited in Calais, 'declared . . . that my book was infamous, abominable, shocking! And at the last exclamation, he turned up his eyes . . . What has that truly amiable woman, the Duchess of Beaufort, done, pray? . . . Abused me most shockingly to begin with, in letters addressed to her son – I replied . . . The Honourable Berkeley Craven . . . was equally abusive at being left out of the *Memoirs*, as was Mr Brummell for having figured in their background. Of course, I mean what I say; nothing more nor less than that Brummell's very low birth placed him at the bottom of the list of fashionables.'[43]

But not all of the fashionables were against Harriette Wilson. Mountcharles, previously Lord Francis Conyngham, supposedly enjoyed Harriette's malice and as long as he was not a part of it he was happy to see anyone else's behaviour, especially his mother's, laid bare. Harriette told Brougham that she had been 'persuaded and encouraged to write the *Memoirs* by Lord Mountcharles', and she quoted a letter he had written to her on 1 March 1825 saying how that he hoped 'that 5 part will soon appear' and that she was 'quite mistaken about the *Memoirs* – my book-seller knowing my eagerness for them sends them me almost before I know they are published – I wish you could get Stockdale to send me one of the contact copies of no. 6'.[44]

'Ayes for the *Memoirs*,' Harriette noted, 'His Royal Highness the Duke of York, and I hope, the King, whom I am afraid to begin the page with.' King George in fact lay on his deathbed two years later cursing her, but the Marquesses of Graham and Hertford (formally Yarmouth), whom she both cited as supporting her, seem more credible candidates, the former having bought himself out and the latter being unashamedly debauched. 'Of its merits as a literary companion,' the press reported, 'men of the first taste have spoken in the most favourable terms; and among others, an eloquent minister of State, in whose library it occupies a conspicuous place.'[45] The Foreign Minister, George Canning, who purchased Harriette's silence, thought them clever. 'It is impossible but that the work must be delicious scandal,' Walter Scott wrote, 'and I will bet on Canning's side without having seen a letter of it.'[46] 'Even Berkeley Craven and Brummell', said Harriette, 'in the midst of their fury, declared to me the *Memoirs* were excellent, and that they had never heard two opinions on that subject. In short, the ayes are innumerable.'[47] Frederick and Charles Bentinck neither bought themselves out nor protested their inclusion. According to Harriette, Charles Bentinck shrugged the whole thing off. 'We are all in for it . . . my brother Frederick and I are in the book up to our necks; but we shall only make bad worse by contending against it; for it is not only true, every word of it, but it is excellently written and very amusing.'[48] Scott disagreed on these points, arguing that 'though the attempt at wit is very poor, that at pathos [is] sickening'. What he liked was Harriette's skill at mimicry. 'There is some good retailing of conversations, in which the style of the speakers, so far as is known to me, is exactly imitated, and some things told, as said by individuals of each other, which will sound unpleasantly in each other's ears. I admire the address of Lord A[lvanley], himself very sorrily handled from time to time. Someone asked him if HW had been pretty correct on the whole. "Why, faith," he replied, "I believe so" – when, raising his eyes, he saw Q[uentin] D[ick], whom the little jilt had treated atrociously – "what concerns the present company always excepted, you know," added Lord A[lvanely], with infinite presence of mind . . . After all, HW beats Con Phillips, Anne Bellamy, and all former demireps out and out.'[49] 'Among other confirmations of the genuineness of the pictures', wrote *Bell's Life,* '. . . is that of his Grace the Duke of Wellington, who in a conversation with the Duke of York and the Marquis of Hertford a few days back, candidly admitted that some of the stories representing himself were true.'[50]

When Harriette Wilson became once more the talk of London it was a very different place to the sleepless city of which she had been crepuscular queen, and this difference was a vital component in the book's reception. The mood was changing; men who had been proud to be seen with Harriette twenty, or even ten, years before, were ashamed of the connection now. The Radical tailor Francis Place remembered that in the 1780s tradesmen did not care if their daughters became kept mistresses, but in the 1820s it was considered scandalous. 'A tradesman's daughter who should misconduct herself', he wrote, '. . . would be abandoned by her companions, and probably by her parents.'[51] By 1825 it was generally accepted that the duty of the husband was to provide for his wife and children, the duty of wives and daughters was to be chaste, and the bonds of matrimony should be not only respected but revered. Middle-class criticism of the domestic lives of the upper classes was reaching its height, and sexual reputation was the focal point of the burgeoning evangelical campaign. The Puritanism that had been increasingly practised by the middle classes was fast spreading upwards. 'It is a singular satisfaction to me', wrote the pioneering moralist Hannah More, 'that I have lived to see such an increase of genuine religion among the higher classes of society.' Worcester's mother, the Duchess of Beaufort, was among those who caught the evangelical fever and she withdrew herself and her eight daughters from society.

The shifting mood of the nation was evidenced not only in the public's support for Queen Charlotte and the pilloring of the loathed King, but in the response to Byron's death in the spring of 1824. Initially mourned as a national hero, Byron was fast becoming the scapegoat for all that was considered decadent and debauched in the Regency, and approving of him was tantamount to devil worship. 'Many make the sign of the cross at the mention of his mere name,' wrote the German rake and traveller, Prince Pückler-Muskau.[52] After ten years away, Pückler-Muskau returned to the city in 1826 to find it now a 'seat of Government . . . and not an immeasurable metropolis of "shop keepers".' But he thought this one of the only improvements. 'London is now so utterly dead as to elegance and fashion, that one hardly meets an equipage; and nothing remains of the "beau monde" but a few ambassadors.'[53] The 'sublime Exclusives' of this new age were 'nothing more than . . . bad, flat, dull impression[s] of a "roué" of the Regency'.[54]

Newspaper editors were in general united in vilifying Harriette and her publisher, regardless of how much they exploited the pair in order to sell more papers. Stockdale wrote of 'a conspiracy, formed at the beck of an unmasked aristocracy, and disgracefully, servilely, embraced, by even the boasted, independent press of the self-constituted, moral metropolis, of this moral United Kingdom in this Bible-age of sanctity, to put down the humble publisher who has dared to strip vice of its fascinating mask and exhibit the monster in all its native deformity, even though it had taken refuge in the highest places!'[55] 'The whole weight of the press,' he further argued, 'being thown into the scale of the pirates, may be accounted for on the score of interest, as if I had succeeded against Onwhyn [the publisher who first pirated the *Memoirs*], I must also have succeeded against the proprietors of the newspapers, every one of which had pirated the *Memoirs*, however they might abuse them, and me.'[56]

At the forefront of the campaign against Stockdale was the *British Lion*, a Sunday paper that ran for only a few months in 1825, almost for the purpose, Stockdale believed, of ruining him. 'Let all the individuals who are libelled,' the paper's editor wrote, 'and whose purses can bear the outlay, put him to the expense of law proceedings . . . really, some combined effort on the part of those who are in a situation to make it, is due to themselves and the public – to the great cause of National Morals and Domestic Peace . . . We . . . implore those who have the power, to come forward and crush this female pest, and thereby read a lesson to hireling publishers, which, to the permanent advantage of society, they will never forget.'[57] This battle cry worked. 'One sapient resolution', Stockdale wrote of the paper's attempts to curb circulation of the book, 'was that they should not buy these *Memoirs*; but the private curiosity of each to see what figure his companions cut, rendered that resolve nugatory in a moment. Another resolution was to withdraw all custom from the publisher, and discountenance and annoy him in every possible way, especially by actions of law against him.'[58] 'The whole and sole conduct of the editors', Stockdale reflected later in the year, 'may be defined in one word, selfishness. Their private pecuniary interest, and that alone, influenced their proceedings. They, one and all, expected to derive pecuniary advantage from the conduct they adopted in regard to these *Memoirs*, and, while many of them were abusing her, for having endeavoured to get money by her work, their single object was the very same . . .'[59]

Harriette Wilson continued to be frequently discussed in the press. The editor of *The Times*, 'in a paragraph of, at least, a foot long, with true, genuine, manly dignity loads me, a female, who never injured him, nor meant him harm, with the coarsest abuse, bestowing on me the most gentleman-like epithets! . . . I am sorry', she continued, 'he has worked himself up into such a desperately vengeful fit against me because really, when I, in the first volume, mentioned Sophie's porkman having wrapped her black-pudding with a piece of dirty *Times* newspaper, I never thought of calling its editor a dirty fellow . . .' The editor's outrage increased her circulation rather than putting a stop to it, Harriette reasoned. 'There were, no doubt, thousands of young ladies who had neither read [my book] nor dreamt of reading it, when this paragraph of the kind and judicious editor, like the apple upon Eve, so worked upon their imagination and excited their curiosity.' He was a coward, she said, for 'loading with abuse a female like me, whose only proprietor resides on the continent' and for never applying 'those same epithets to Lady Caroline Lamb, nor, in short to any lady whose husband happened to be at hand . . . what can be more immoral than Lady Caroline Lamb, a wife and mother, publishing her own desperate love letters to Lord Byron, written under her husband's own roof?'[60]

On the morning of Tuesday, 15 March 1825 the following letter appeared in the *Morning Chronicle*:

MR EDITOR – In this age of *Memoirs*, Recollections, and Reminiscences, it is not to be wondered at that Old Harriette Wilson has been as successful as her neighbours . . . in gulling the public. From all she or her Ambrosial Friend has written for her one might be led to believe her, when she states such broad facts, in spite of her omitting dates, but with any of our wits about us, we can never forget that people not contemporary could not hold converse; – you must see I allude to bringing the Marquess of Lorne and the Duke of Wellington together, though there were eight years difference between those titles. Poor Tom Sheridan's account of his father must be equally untrue as it is malicious, from the known fact of the father and son being both taken from us within a few weeks of each other. If this Lady's *Memoirs* had been complete, she perhaps might have recollected a little dirty girl, whose name was Du Bouchet, who was five and twenty years ago a regular *tramp* in St James's Street, and the courts adjoining, being picked up by a nobleman and converted into a *lady*; after growing too old for any success in begging from those persons of high rank, whose names she could collect from the *Court Guide* (her constant practice), she liberated a prisoner from the Fleet, and set him sailing after his pretensions to an Irish Peerage; if she should see this, she will know who wrote it, and perhaps I may receive a round sum not to say any more. She formerly got her living by mending and cleaning silk stockings, at which she was very expert – she was never handsome, though she had good eyes, but was hog backed, narrow chested, and had an awkward shuffling gait, and was not at all like the handsome portrait which is published as that of Harriette Wilson; but this can be of no consequence now, as she must be next summer in her 42d year. But what am I who can recollect such things? Why,

AN OLD RAKE
South Moulton Street, Grosvenor Square.[61]

This 'Old Rake' knew more about Harriette's past life than most of the scandalmongers of the last ten years who claimed to be authorities, but his suggestion that the *Memoirs* were written by her 'Ambrosial Friend' was based on nothing more than current gossip. The next day, a letter appeared in the paper from an S. Bertie Ambrose, who identified himself as the ghost-writer alluded to, denying that he had anything to do with the authorship of Harriette's book.

Captain Ambrose had known Rochfort from his days in India when they were in the same regiment. He had since spread the word, Harriette said, that he had been one of her lovers. 'The fact is', Ambrose supposedly told her, 'that knowing you is such a feather in a man's cap that I could not resist saying I had the honour.' In a letter to Sophie Stockdale, following an attack on him in the press by Ambrose, Stockdale reminded her, 'It was Ambrose you know who first gave out that he was the author of Harriette Wilson's *Memoirs*, and when they were threatened with prosecution, inserted a letter in the newspapers denying them and afterwards, being asked by Rochfort which lie he would now chose to abide by, confessed that he had nothing to do with them; but treated the whole as a good joke!'[62] The rumour that Ambrose was the author of Harriette's book continued to be treated as a fact for several years.[63]

Popular prints were only occasionally more sympathetic to Harriette than the newspapers. One caricature, titled *Cupid conducting the Three Graces to the Temple of Love*, published by King in March 1825, shows Wellington, Sir Frederic Beauclerk and the Duke of Argyll arm in arm, dramatically striding to Harriette's house. She calls out of the window, 'One at a time please gentlemen and I am not afraid of twice as many.' Wellington, as always in full regalia, says, 'She is a fine girl I assure you and I declare she has run more in my mind than Spaniards Russians or French, if this *guide* leads us into an ambush I'll have him hanged.' Argyll, in Highland costume, says, 'Eh Lord Sirs there she is and as bonny a lassy as there's in a-Britain including *Argyleshire*, I am thinking you twa had better stay where you are till I come back again, as I am an unco judge of the premises.' Beauclerk, in his parson's apparel, says, 'I hope I have too much *good manners* to refuse seeing a pretty girl and though I belong to the church I don't think she will find much cant about me.' A print by Robert Cruikshank called *The Flat Catcher and the Rat Catcher*, published by

Fairburn in February 1825, showed Harriette looking elegant and triumphant in an evening gown standing with Wellington, who looks ridiculous in uniform, in a room surrounded with portraits of figures from her *Memoirs*. 'I understand', Harriette tells her guest, 'they are going to *hang you*, who would suppose such a *thing* could beat Napoleon! I declare you look exactly like a *ratcatcher.*' 'Eh? – What? – I never heard a word of it before,' Wellington replies. He is dripping with rats (there is a rat in the place of the sheep on his Order of the Golden Fleece, another on his ribbon and one on his tail coat). The Portraits behind them are arranged alphabetically. Duke of A[rgyll], Marquis B, Earl of C[raven], Viscount D[eerhurst], Lord E[brington], Sir – F. Lambskin Pinxit [Fred Lamb], Honourable Mr G[eorge Lamb] and so on. Harriette is the dignified figure in this case, and her lovers look like cowards.

In April, Fairburn published the print of a coloured engraving called *The Ducking Stool – A Punishment for Fornication. Or – the Dukes and the Dons shewing up Harriette Wilson.* Harriette is tied to a chair which is suspended by a pole above a pond. Holding the pole are Frederic Beauclerk, Wellington, Argyll and Lamb, who each exclaim against her. 'Go home and mind *your wives* and don't *persecute me* you set of Nincumpoops!' Harriette calls. 'I'll expose ye all in *the next volume* – I appeal to John Bull to protect me from your violence.' John Bull, pictured as an affable chap in smock and gaiters, turns to the four persecutors and says, 'Ye ought to be ashamed of yourselves! First to seduce the poor wretch, and then to ill use her, I think if you had what you deserve it would be the ducking pond instead of her! By Goles if I hant half a mind to give you all a good wapping!!' The men standing around John Bull cheer him on.

Harriette remained in Paris during the furore generated by her revelations. She was busy all summer writing further instalments and their attendant letters, while Stockdale, who had the manuscript with him in London, scored through those passages of her book which had been bought out.

CHAPTER 21

The Blackmail Campaign

Few of us would care to be remembered by our love letters, less because they are embarrassing than because they do not sound like us. However original the experience feels, lovers' voices blur into one. Although an accomplished seductress whose charms distinguished her from her peers, Harriette was as limited as most by the language of love; to describe her feelings for Ponsonby she adopted the vocabulary and plot of the romantic novel and the identity of its heroine. When we hate we are more original; hate allows us to redefine and sharpen our edges. The difference between the voice Harriette employs in the more sentimental moments of her *Memoirs* and that used in her blackmail letters is remarkable; when she was venomous she crackled and shone like foil. The rage, indignation and complexity that are otherwise absent from her accounts of relationships are poured into her extortion letters, and it is these which give us some measure of the nervous excitement she felt about the path she was pursuing.

Harriette had always taken a specific pleasure in feuds; she was more stimulated by her rivalry with Amy than by her adoration of Fanny, she had enjoyed winding up the Duke of Beaufort, and she clearly relished the anxiety the appearance of her *Memoirs* was causing her old friends. Feuds animated her; she was as excited by the pursuit of a new enemy as she

George Cruikshank, 'L – Longed for it'

was by the forging of a friendship. She liked and needed the competition involved in battle, it made her feel alive.

She saw her blackmail campaign as a long-term venture, extending beyond the appearance of the *Memoirs* themselves. It lasted for the rest of the decade – in some ways, for the rest of her life. Her plan was to write a sequel to the *Memoirs* that would be more scandalous than its predecessor. Her blackmail victims therefore fell into two categories: those she threatened to include in the first book – and because it appeared in instalments over nine months, there were continual negotiations going on until the eleventh hour – and those she threatened to include in the second book. Some were included in both camps. Those appearing in the second collection of *Memoirs* would be, unless they stopped her, the King, Lady Conyngham, the Countess of Clare, Ponsonby, the Duke of Richmond, the Marquises of Londonderry, Westmeath, Exeter, Hertford and Headfort, the Marchionesses of Londonderry, Salisbury and Bath, Lord Maryborough ('Grand Master of the Mint, and of the Art of Love'), Mr Arthur Chichester, and the Earl of Clanricarde.

Various of her lovers, such as Lord Stewart (now Londonderry), Frederic Lamb, Wellington and the Duke of Argyll, had been threatened by Harriette before she met Stockdale, but she began intimidating in earnest, or professionally, during the summer of 1824. On 15 July of that year, she wrote to Brougham ensuring that she could rely on his legal advice:

I hope this once you'll assist me. My *Sketches of Character in High Life* which I began a long while ago I cut because Colburn was afraid of making *ill will* by publishing then – a publisher in London now offers to take the blame on himself there being *no direct libel*, pay all expenses and give me half the profit if I finish them. All *admit* them excellent well drawn, short and not vulgarly severe only just right to make you *feel them* – not *you* unless you'll let me – at all events there's nothing I can say but good of you and of course for Rochfort's sake I can't talk of you as a lover. However if you say '*No*' I won't mention you – but as to Leinster and Graham I'll make them as much laughed at as I can.

God bless you – if on Tuesdays or Fridays before 5 o'clock you would at any time write to me under cover to his Excellency Sir C. Stuart and send your letter to the Foreign Office I should get it cheap safe and pleasant.[1]

'I am sure these old friends of yours would provide for you, if applied to civilly,' Brougham is supposed to have suggested to Harriette.[2] If the

Whigs were to win the next election, Brougham would get the high office
he coveted; being named by Harriette Wilson might scupper his chances
of becoming prime minister (he did not then realize that two future prime
ministers were also paying her off while another one would defy her to
publish). Harriette knew she could play Brougham like a puppet. Many of
her other old friends, including Lord Francis Conyngham, the Marquis
of Graham, George Lamb, Charles Manners, Earl Spencer, Lord Stair,
Lord Rivers, Sir Robert Wilson, Lord Palmerston, Sir Charles Stuart, Lord
Tankerville, George Canning and a Mr Fermor, settled with her between
the summer of 1824 and January 1825. Stockdale was put out that he
received no credit for suppressing anecdotes about the Archbishop of
Canterbury and the Bishop of London, 'but I shall not promise that they
shall continue so, any more than the Right Hon. Charles Manners Sutton,
the Speaker'.[3]

Her finished book, Harriette claimed, would have been 'much more
witty and amusing had not the best of the wit been bought out, at so much
a line, by certain dukes, lords, commoners, and ladies to keep their fair
fames afloat'.[4] Escapades were duly erased from the manuscript, often in
ways that made it obvious to all that Harriette's discretion had been won
at a cost. Lords Spencer, Rivers, Palmerston and Henry Brougham are
damned by her praise:

I cannot omit to acknowledge the generous condescension of Earl Spencer.
Though I have not the honour to be in the least acquainted with him, he has, very
repeatedly assisted me. In short, his Lordship has promptly complied with every
request for money I ever made to him, merely as a matter of benevolence.

Lord Rivers, with whom I have only a bowing acquaintance, has not only often
permitted me to apply to him for money, but once, when I named a certain sum to
him, he liberally doubled it, because as he kindly stated in his letter, he was so
truly sorry to think that one who possessed such a generous heart as mine should
not be in affluent circumstances. Lord Palmerston also, one fine day, did me a
pecuniary service, without my having applied to him for it. Nor can I express half
the gratitude I feel and shall entertain, to the end of my life, for the steady, active
friendship Mr Brougham has invariably evinced towards me, actuated as he is
solely by a spirit of philanthropy. When I see a man of such brilliant talents,
pleading the cause of almost all those persons, whose characters I have sketched in
these pages, with such honest warmth and benevolence of feeling, as Brougham

did yesterday, to say I look up to him, and love him, is but a cold description of the sentiments he inspires in my heart.[5]

Earl Spencer offered to buy Harriette's original manuscript, with all the names crossed out, for £1,000. Stockdale refused.

Harriette received £400 from her share of the sale of the *Memoirs*. Stockdale lost a lot of money in libels, but whether his share of the profits exceeded these payments cannot be estimated. Any money Harriette was going to live on in the long term was to come from blackmail. Her eventual income when the lump sums were received and the annuities drawn up is unknowable – a good number of her victims would have settled on less than she asked for – but she wrote over two hundred letters and so may have received several thousand pounds. A week's lodging, cooking and fires for a working man in London cost one shilling and sixpence; a man of fashion paid four guineas per week for the same. After she marries, Elinor Dashwood in *Sense and Sensibility* plans to live in the country on an annual income of £850. Mary Berry, the society bluestocking, estimated at the end of the eighteenth century that in order to have 'every comfort necessary to a small establishment in London' would cost £2,000 a year.[6] Living in Paris was cheaper than living in London, and the exchange rate was in Harriette's favour. She could have lived comfortably on £200 a year. Harriette was not the prudent type and money seems to have disappeared in her hands; after 1829 she was on the bread line. Where did it all go? It seems most likely that much of it never arrived. Despite promises being made and documentation being drawn up, many of the annuities due to her were never paid. Harriette was not the first woman to have been mistreated in this way. Craven's father had rescinded on his payments to a popular courtesan and the actress Mary Robinson ('Perdita') was pledged by the young Prince of Wales £20,000 which never materialized. She died in poverty.

Some of those who had been threatened by Harriette and her publisher threatened legal action themselves. 'Another hero in a passion!' Harriette wrote. 'Another lover threatens prosecution!'[7] Frederic Lamb, now an ambassador, had stormed into Stockdale's shop on receipt of his letter and threatened 'prosecution, death and destruction if his conduct towards [Harriette] in times auld lang syne was printed and published in any part of my *Memoirs*'. But if Lamb had 'only opened his heart, or even purse',

Harriette reflected, 'to have given me but a few hundreds, there would have been no book, to the infinite loss of all persons of good taste and genuine morality, and who are judges of real merit'.[8]

On 16 December 1824, Stockdale wrote to Wellington:

In Harriette Wilson's *Memoirs*, which I am about to publish, are various anecdotes of your Grace which it would be most desirable to withhold, at least such is my opinion. I have stopped the Press for the moment; but as the publication will take place next week, little delay can necessarily take place.[9]

Wellington's reply no longer exists, but he had been sent a similar letter from Harriette as well and it was on the envelope of this that Julia Johnstone reported that he wrote, in flaming red letters, 'write and be damned'. Wellington felt sufficiently invulnerable to threaten Stockdale with court. Three days after Christmas, Wellington heard again from 24 Opera Colonnade:

Mr Stockdale has obtained one half of the property of Harriette Wilson's *Memoirs*; his chief motive in which was to protect, as well as he could, any friend who might be disagreeably implicated in them. Instead of exulting, he was grieved and pained, far, very far beyond what he shall attempt to describe, in the discovery of the prominent figure which the Duke of Wellington & the Marquis of Wellesley cut in those pages from which S[tockdale] was anxious to obliterate them, though it would diminish the interest of the work, and its consequent produce, perhaps, not less than 5000 pounds. Indeed, as a friend of that illustrious house, S. does not hesitate to say that twice that sum would be a cheap purchase of the destruction of those details, which, a few hours will place beyond the possibility of redemption . . . If a jury can now be worked upon, to declare the facts stated in these *Memoirs*, libels, the work does not contain one page which would not be sufficient to overwhelm, in its consequences any publisher whatever . . . Mere Justice, however, compels Mr S. to say that there is scarcely a line which does not carry . . . the fullest conviction of its veracity, & the unequalled number of fashionables, implicated in it all named at full length without reserve, combined with the dramatic air which the author flings over the whole, cannot fail to give it an interest & circulation exceeding all which was anticipated of the suppressed *Memoirs* of Mary Ann Clarke.[10]

Harriette's response to the Duke's threats was to present him in her book as a fool and to regale her readers with memories of 'my own Wellington, who has sighed over me and groaned over me by the hour, talked of my wonderful beauty, ran after me, bribed Mrs Porter over and over again, after I refused to listen to her overtures, only for a single smile from his beautiful Harriette! Did he not kneel? And was I not the object of his first, most ardent wishes, on his arrival from Spain?'

Harriette spent the Christmas of 1824 back in her lodgings at Warwick Court. From here she wrote a second letter to Brougham, her first having instigated no reply. Her style has none of the cool, acidic, hand-rubbing glee that characterizes Stockdale's letter to Wellington; she is typically impassioned, determined and uncertain of herself; at times frightened, at times apologetic. She never planned her letters beforehand nor read them through afterwards; as with all her writing, Harriette fired pages off when she was overtaken by a certain mood:

I must make myself independent now or never. It won't do to be eternally dunning the few friends I *do possess*. I have been very ill used. This then is a desperate effort to live by my *wits* since I cannot make up my mind to make an unfaithful wife. If my book does not procure me an annuity it is my last chance save hanging – and after all expenses are paid (at least 450 pounds) I only devide [*sic*] the rest with my publisher – and old Wellington is writing to us threatening letters about prosecution hanging etc which we laugh at. Two noble Lords have preferred buying themselves out quietly, or rather a Lord and a Duke. Now your flaming love letters etc would certainly add to the value and interest of the book, so would anecdotes of three more who have been kind to me viz – Marquis Graham, Ld F. Conyngham & Ld R. Manners. I begin by not putting anything in my book about them or you which can possibly teaze – if anything [at all] and then I leave it to them to *dedommanger* me with whatever they can spare – towards making me independent once and for all that I may have no excuse for troubling any body again since I live with the most careful economy in France. If I only get 100 pounds a year no friend of mine shall ever be troubled with me again and of this I hope I have every chance – if not of more. I leave it to your generosity as to what you will contribute. F. Conyngham, Graham etc have openly sent me quite as much as they could reasonably afford towards purchasing a small annuity. If you cannot afford £50 perhaps you can send £25. In short I have really suffered so much lately that I throw myself on your good heart, confident that you will contribute your might towards my permanent relief and you shall have the satisfaction of seeing that I have made good use of your kindness. Rochfort is truly anxious that what I may get should be settled entirely on myself and out of even his power to touch it or mine beyond the yearly allowance.[11]

Brougham, who was also receiving threatening letters from Stockdale, gave Harriette enough money to hold her pen, but only for the moment. He was to be independently pursued by Harriette, Rochfort and Stockdale for the rest of their lives. It is a sign of her mettle that Harriette persisted in persecuting a man as influential as Brougham. She had used the most brilliant forensic legal mind in the country to support her *gratis* in the Beaufort case, she relied on Brougham again to advise her on potential libels in her *Memoirs*, and she continued to blackmail him when he was England's Lord Chancellor. Harriette saw Brougham's power as something that should work for and not against her, and she had no qualms about measuring her danger against his.

Few of Harriette's blackmail letters survive, but they seem to have been written to formula. They were presumably all sealed with one of Harriette's own devices, a cupid whispering 'Hush!' or the ironic '*Andeante Felice*' ('Go in Happiness'). On 12 March 1825, the wealthy MP Edward 'Bear' Ellice, sent to the *Globe and Traveller* the missive he had just received. The letter, called by Harriette her 'circular', was reproduced the next day in *The Times*, prefaced with the following: 'We think Mr Ellice does but justice to the public in permitting us to publish the following letter. It displays at once the objects and motives of the authoress and editor of the detestable publication now circulating under the above title. He has desired us to leave blank the names of the other parties alluded to . . .'

People are buying themselves so fast out of my book, *Memoirs* of H. Wilson, that I have no time to attend to them should be sorry not to give each a *chance*, if they *chuse to be out*. You are quizzed most *unmercifully* – Two noble Dukes have lately taken my word, and I have never named them. I am sure — [dash in the original] would say you might trust me never to publish, or *cause* to be published, aught about you, if you like to forward 200*l* directly to me, else it will be too late, as the last volume, in which you *shine*, will be the property of the Edetor [*sic*], and in his hands. Lord — [dash] says he will answer for aught I agree to so will my husband. Do *just as you like* – consult only yourself. I get as much by a small *book* as you will give me for taking you out, or more. I attack no poor men because they cannot help themselves.

Adieu. Mind I have no time to write again as what with writing books, and then altering them for those who *buy out*, I am done for – frappé* en mort.

What do you think of my French?

Yours,

Harriette Rochfort, late Wilson

Don't trust to bag with your answer.

*We adhere to the lady's grammar, which, like her morality, is not closely bound to vulgar rules.[12]

Later that month, Fairburn published a caricature by Robert Cruikshank called *Harriette Wilson's last letter – or a new method of raising the wind!!* The print has Harriette penning her blackmail letter to Ellice while Rochfort, dressed as a dandy with devilish horns appearing through his curls, stands deviously behind her. Ellice is then shown reading the letter outside his London house and proclaiming 'Oho! A letter from Harriette Wilson – very good, now I shall send this letter to the Newspapers and expose her – I shall not be such a fool as others – and if she was in this Country I should know what to do with her – £200 indeed what would my wife say?' His wife leans out of the window asking, 'What can he know about Harriette Wilson?' Out of the postman's pocket drop other letters from Harriette, addressed to the Lord Mayor, the Duke of York, the Bishop of London, the Duke of Devonshire and the quack, Dr Eady. The suggestion is that Harriette blackmailed at random.[13]

Six months later, when she was confirming the contents for her second collection of *Memoirs*, an article appeared in the *Bath Herald* claiming that

We have this week received a letter from the well-known Harriette Wilson, in which we are requested to obtain for her 'some funny anecdotes' relating to a most respectable gentleman of this neighbourhood, with whom she acknowledges herself to be unacquainted, for the purpose (to use her own words) of obliging him 'to buy out of her book'. Feeling such an application as an insult to ourselves, we have thought it right thus publicly to notice it; and to add, that the letter to which we allude, will, if necessary, be always at the service of the friends of that gentleman.[14]

Another 'highly respectable gentleman',[15] Rowland Mitchell, followed Ellice's example and sent to *The Times* and *Morning Chronicle* the letter he received from Harriette in November 1826:

I don't much think you are worth the trouble of again addressing, but I *will* not send your part of my *Memoirs* to the *press* without once more offering to sell you the MS relative to your *low* intrigues, love of the slave trade, &c.; because, though strict truth is only related, I know it will make you *very unpopular*. If I receive a letter from you *directly,* promising to pay me, for old acquaintance sake, 20*l* a year as long as your name is not mentioned in any present or future publication; and in case this mode may please you better than buying the manuscript *at once* for 200*l*, I shall be pleased if you pay always 20*l* as a year's annuity, *in advance*. If this *does not please* you, your silence will settle the business. You are *very welcome* to publish this letter, if it so pleases you. No one will dispute your love of flogging black women, and flashing about with all the lowest white ones.[16]

Following his exposure of her letter, Harriette wrote to Rowland Mitchell again and published her reply. 'Can anybody in England prove', she said, 'that Rowland Mitchell, the slave merchant of 58 Wimpole Street, ever does any one thing worth mentioning during the four and twenty hours? . . . And will Rowland attempt to say, he did not, in former times when I have met him at my sister's, who was kind enough to admit him to her parties, *endeavour* to be eloquent in his zeal to persuade me to prevail upon Meyler, Fred Bentinck and other MPs of my acquaintance, to vote for the Slave Trade?'[17]

Shortly after the appearance in the press of Harriette's letter to Edward Ellice, she received at her address in Paris a letter signed simply 'P', which read:

A letter has appeared, in most of our London public journals, purporting to be a correct copy of one from you to Edward Ellice with the view to exhort from him two hundred pounds. Now, although many years have elapsed since we met, I cannot believe you are guilty of such conduct as now to commence betraying principles which were honourable to yourself merely to obtain the reputation of being a mercenary and cold-blooded creature, for undoubtedly no other name can be attached to one who can be guilty of such conduct. Remember, I write as a friend, and as I firmly and honestly believe the production of the letter to Ellice to be written by a person with no other view than to prejudice the world against your *Memoirs*, I beg, as an old friend, you will write in reply to this as early as possible to the direction given . . .[18]

Harriette replied along the lines that she 'was too poor to keep every thick-headed ass's secrets for nothing'.[19] She believed that Ponsonby was the author of the letter – she would have liked to think, or to have her readers think, that he still cared enough to scold her – but it seems unlikely that he would have written to Harriette, or in such a way.

In March 1825, Ponsonby returned from an extended stay in the Ionian Islands to find himself immortalized in Harriette's *Memoirs*. He was in a considerable state about his sudden celebrity. 'Indeed I have read the Book,' Sir Robert Lawley, who married Lady Conyngham's sister, wrote in reply to a distressed letter he received from Ponsonby, 'and was as angry at it as you most justly are and on your account, as the effect such a publication must have had upon your first appearance in England was unfortunate.' Lawley advised him of the 'signs of the times' and the social changes that had taken place since Ponsonby had been away, specifically 'the reading of sentimental and voluptuous novels' which has 'prepared the female mind . . . especially in the middle ranks, for that degenerate profligacy which desolates English society . . . there is a shamefulness in it which accounts for the avidity with which such publications as those you allude to are read'. He assured his friend that 'by the time you have been in London for a week the Book will have been forgotten', and encouraged him to not 'mind' it and to 'laugh at all the hypocrites and false friends in the world'. But for all his support, Lawley could not disguise his enjoyment of the affair. 'Were you twenty years younger the book would be of interminable value to you,' he observed, no doubt correctly, 'as the lady talks of Irish knights and of their delight as soon as she had formed your acquaintance and in these . . . days of profligacy such a recommendation could be worth much. I own I could not help laughing when she caught you skulking behind the trees in the park.'[20]

Harriette had in her possession compromising letters from Lady Conyngham, sent to Ponsonby twenty-five years earlier. She also had a fund of anecdotes regarding Ponsonby's relationship with the Countess of Clare, and she had various schemes in mind about how best to employ this material, including writing a play about the royal mistress. In late August 1825, Ponsonby, staying with the Duke of Argyll, received the following letter reminding him of the annuity Harriette had turned down twenty years before:

You must be sensible that I have no reason to make you an *exception* if I show up *others* for you as *yet* have done me only *harm* – The pirates have spoiled our prospect of *Memoirs* so far I have sold the copyright of what is in Stockdale's hands namely 18 parts – the rest I publish on my own account – I am sure the stories you recalled to me of Lady Clare and Lady C[onyngham] were such as you do not wish to see published – neither do I wish to publish them – I never broke my word to you or any body – let me be grateful to you for something before I *die* that I may remember you with kindness – I am printing in Paris at my own expense – can you afford to send me two hundred pounds? If you assure me upon your *honour* that 200 is more than you can afford I will be satisfied with one. I leave all to your *good heart* if it is *good* and I hope you remember me with *good will* – I shall like *one* simple proof of it and all things considered I shall be *furious* if I do not get it.

Pray answer directly for your own sake – I shall be very *sorry if you don't* for it really is [word illegible] that you and I should be otherwise than *friends* . . . à la *distance*

Yours –

Harriette Rochfort

Pray don't put off money till the *last* part of *Memoirs* are in the press –

The story you told me of ravishing Lady Clare behind the door and breaking a blood vessel etc will be fine fun for *all* but the lady and son . . . I do not *wish* to hurt you but then you *ought* to *serve* me. I returned you a draft you *wrote* for me surely you may send me what *was* mine and tended to me by you – I had *not* returned it had I not *loved* you, n'est ce pas?[21]

Ponsonby neither replied to the letter nor threw it away. Instead, mindful of a potential prosecution, he wrote on the back of the envelope, 'This most infamous lying letter was taken no notice of by me,' and signed his initial.

Lord Ponsonby's ill-timed reappearance in London brought with it several other shocks. When Lady Conyngham, who had not seen her old lover since she became the King's mistress, met him accidentally in the drawing room at Lady Jersey's, she was quite overcome. The story, as Princess Lieven relates it, is that the King, hearing of his mistress's reaction, was overcome too, so much so that 'he sent for Canning, as being the only doctor capable of curing him of a very unpleasant disease. He asked him if he had no post as Minister abroad to give to Lord Ponsonby, who never in his life had thought of adopting a diplomatic career. Mr Canning tumbled to the solution; and at once sent for Lord Ponsonby and offered him a post in Brazil, inviting him to await his instructions abroad. Lord

Ponsonby, who hasn't a halfpenny, accepted.'[22] What this version of events – the unofficial explanation behind Canning's sudden turn in political fortune – elides is the role played by Harriette in the ambassadorial career of Ponsonby. Greville's *Memoirs* tell a more intriguing tale. According to Greville, Harriette threatened to publish Lady Conyngham's letters, 'if she was not paid a large sum of money. This produced dismay and panic amongst all the parties involved. The disappearance of Ponsonby became imperative, hence Canning came up with the idea of sending him as Ambassador to Buenos Aires.'[23] A different version still is told by Harriet Arbuthnot, the confidante of the Duke of Wellington. She confirms the rumour that Ponsonby had given Lady Conyngham's letters to Harriette, and then repeats what the Duke himself had told her, that Ponsonby was to be shipped abroad because *he* had threatened Lady Conyngham. 'It is pleasant to feel how perfectly unnecessary principles of honesty or honour are in the choice of a representative for England. I believe Lord Ponsonby is a clever man, but he is a ruined gambler, profligate and Lord Grey's brother-in-law – the last man one would think fit for such a situation.'[24] Creevey noted that on the eve of Ponsonby's departure, 'Lady C. throws herself back on the sofa and never speaks; and the opinion is (which I don't believe) that she *hates kingy.*'

Whatever the details, Harriette's fate mirrored that of many other female revengers. 'In my opinion,' wrote Stockdale, 'the influence of your traduced *Memoirs*, and that only, has been the electrical conductor of Lord Ponsonby to represent His Majesty in the South American republic . . . When all comes to be known, his lordship will be even a greater favourite of the Buenos Aires ladies than before . . .'[25] Rather than exposing Ponsonby as unfit for public office, she inadvertently succeeded in promoting him.

CHAPTER 22

Stockdale's Persecution

'Stockdale talks much of lawsuits and God knows what,' wrote Harriette in an address to the London Fashionables, 'but I don't believe any of you wish to go to law with me: and as to my *Memoirs*, of course, out of your regard to me you ought to have prevented their publication.'[1] For all the puffing and blowing that went on around the legal status of her book, not one of her lovers sued either Harriette herself or Stockdale. Married to Rochfort, Harriette was legally protected; everything she owned belonged to him. It was Stockdale who had to take the brunt of any legal action. 'Why do not the parties, said to have been libelled, prosecute?' Stockdale wrote to the *Morning Herald* in 1825. 'Simply because they know they have not been libelled.'[2] Much was made of the immorality of the *Memoirs*, but only two people challenged its essential truthfulness, and neither man was known or powerful. These two libel cases, however, managed temporarily to ruin Stockdale, and he referred to the events that took place between 1825 and 1827 as his 'persecution'.

On 18 April 1825, a writ was served on Stockdale by a solicitor called Robinson; six days later a letter appeared in the *British Lion* in which Robinson introduced himself to the nation as the representative of Mr Blore, whose name had been immortalized in Harriette's book. Commending the editor of the paper on his 'excellent suggestion' of 'pursuing by actions

George Cruikshank, *'Go draw your quills, and draw five bills'* the publisher of Harriette Wilson's *Memoirs*', Mr Robinson announced that litigation against Stockdale on behalf of his client had begun.

Robert Blore was a stonemason of Half Moon Street. Harriette claimed, in Part 6 of the serialization, that he had proposed to Fanny when she was first under the protection of Colonel Parker. At the time this proposal was said to have occurred, Blore was married with several children. It is unlikely that he would have sued Stockdale had he not been put up to the job as a front man for others; Blore's case was taken up by those men who were unwilling to take legal action themselves but were anxious to bring Stockdale down and to throw at least some doubt on Harriette's revelations. Stockdale believed, probably correctly, that the 'group chose Blore to represent them because Fanny was dead'.[3] Blore, Stockdale wrote, 'was encouraged, desperately to stand the cast of a die which might, haply, obtain him the countenance of those agonized great who dared not fight the battle, in their own persons, who had declared, in club, their mutual interest in stopping the further progress of such a publication, and overwhelming its proprietor, by length of combined purses'.[4]

Another figure encouraged to prosecute Stockdale, 'not only by private persons . . . but by attorneys . . . who offered to advance the law expenses'[5] was Harriette's Oxford Street haberdasher, Thomas Smith, whom she mocked as a lecherous fool, accepting favours instead of money for the hats she had bought from him and being bundled out of the house to make way for Ponsonby. Smith's business suffered as a result of the *Memoirs* and Stockdale publicly apologized for this, while reminding Smith of the 'advantages' he had previously enjoyed, 'in trade, from Harriette's numerous family and connections'. That Smith did not proceed against Stockdale was seen by the publisher as a mark of the shopkeeper's being 'too high minded' to do so and because Thomas Smith, unlike Blore, 'felt as a man!'[6]

On 1 July, Stockdale was called to the High Court accused of libel. He elected to defend himself. The claim against him was not only the suggestion that Blore proposed to Fanny, 'a woman of the town', but that Blore was ridiculed in the *Memoirs* as a 'person of low and vulgar mind, manners and conversation'.[7] The conversation between Fanny and Blore described by Harriette was contained in a letter she 'quoted' from Fanny. 'Look ye, here, my dear lady,' Fanny reports Blore as having said, 'these here officers cut a splash! And its all very fine being called Mrs Parker and the like a that; but then its nothing compared to a rale husband. Now I means onerable, remember that . . . Come I don't ax you, my dear, to make up your mind this morning. Marriage is a serious kind a thing, and I wants no woman for marry me till she has determined to make an industrious, good wife . . .'[8] Sir James Scarlett, who was prosecuting, informed the jury that his client sought redress for 'one of the most offensive and unprovoked libels which ever were framed to sink an individual in the moral estimation of his fellows . . . Far better that Mr Blore should have married his housemaid, than made a creature, so prostituted, his wife . . .'[9] Scarlett distinguished between Harriette, the author of the libel, 'actuated by passion, by resentment, by a sense of imagined wrong' and Stockdale, 'the base, cold-hearted, the calculating scoundrel, who plays on the passions of the irritated, only to put money in his purse . . . If the wretched being who is represented as the author of this work, in the depth of wretchedness to which her conduct naturally led, under the pressure of hunger and in the bitterness of poverty, wrote this book, I would deem, even her, less infamous than the bookseller who coolly shared the profits of her desperation.'[10]

Stockdale's complaint to the jury that he was labouring under a heavy cold and sore throat did not stop him from speaking at length about his own courage, not only in facing the rebuke he had suffered, 'the unceasing mental harrass, of the personal attacks of such a combination of wealth and power, as was never, until now, concentrated against one person',[11] but in acting as his own defence. While he had not gone to bed the previous night, 'for the purpose of throwing the ideas, which I propose addressing to your consideration, into some kind of order',[12] there was little coherence to his address, which was a combination of self-pity, Aesop's Fables and large doses of homespun wisdom. He barely mentioned the *Memoirs* and Blore himself was brought up only in the closing comments. Stockdale's point was that the case had nothing to do with Blore; that he, Stockdale, had been set up as a result of the campaign in the *British Lion* and that the entire court and judicial system was levelled against him. It was hard to believe, Stockdale argued, that Blore's business could have suffered much as a result of Harriette's representation of him. After all, people would always want gravestones, regardless of whether the man who cut them had pursued an attractive young prostitute. After twenty minutes' deliberation, the jury awarded the plaintiff damages of £300. Stockdale's move for a retrial was refused.

There was already something of a ritual about the way such trials were conducted, with the prosecutors waxing indignant about the harm such immoral books could do, and the defendants claiming that they were part of a long and honourable tradition of improving society by exposing its abuses.

Exposing the behaviour of the aristocracy was one thing but libelling a working man quite another, and it cost Stockdale the support of those who would otherwise have been behind him. A print by Cruikshank appeared shortly after the trial called *Scarlet Fever Versus Yellow Jaundice Or the Libel Publisher Cut Up. July 1, 1825* (plate 30). Stockdale is pictured as a grotesque green figure, falling from a writing table on which are papers inscribed *More Anecdotes* and *Harriette*. He is holding up a paper headed *Defence of Harriette's Memoirs* and says, 'I say this book is a very *good* book, and exposes the vices of the great. I am a poor worm of a publisher, & they want to *crush me*, but I'll be off to Van Deimans Land before I pay a farthing. Blow me!' Beside him are papers inscribed 'Portraits of'; 'Bought off 8000'; '50,000 Copies of the Memoires', and money bags inscribed '£4,000', '£8000', 'Ill Gotten Gold . . . oo'. Behind him is a picture of Harriette writing 'Sheer Slander'. Smoke circling around him inscribes 'Damages 8000', 'Damages 9,000', '700', '4000', '3000', '100', '200'. Sir James Scarlett, in whig and gown, stands in front of a statuary cutting an inscription on a tombstone reading '£3,oo. July 1. 1825'. Behind Scarlett angry faces shout, 'If I was a stone cutter I'd fit the fellow for an Opera House Singer'; 'I'll have satisfaction'; 'My damages shall be 20.000'; 'I'll have redress, damages'.[13]

On Monday, 14 July, at 8.30 in the morning, as Stockdale was journeying with his son from the family home in Acton, west of London, to his shop in Opera Colonnade, their carriage was stopped by a man he identified as Blore. An officer opened the door and 'thrust himself inside, desiring my son to make room for him, as he had taken me in execution . . . The officer told my coachman, as I learnt afterwards, he must no longer mind my orders, bur drive whither the officer directed.'[14] The officer told Stockdale that he wanted £379 and 8 shillings from him; unpaid libel damages. Once in London, the officer, whose name was Levy, kept Stockdale prisoner in his premises until the bookseller's son had brought the required money. Levy informed Stockdale that his harsh treatment was 'in revenge for the letter I had written to Robinson. I replied in amaze[ment that] I did not understand him, that I had never written to Robinson, not even, though I confessed my want of courtesy, in answer to his letter to me. He said that Blore told him I had written Robinson a letter, signed by my own hand, stating that he was a damned infernal scoundrel, and might get the money how he could! I returned that I now began to see through it. Robinson wanted an excuse for his own conduct, and had trumped up this letter, which I had now, for the first time, had any intimation of, direct or indirect; that Robinson knew that I was not capable of it, and he did not believe it was either written by me, or with my privity, and that, if Robinson knew that I was not capable of it . . .' and so on.[15] Stockdale conceived here 'a flagrant and violent abuse of power'. 'Is it not probable', he mused, not for the first time, 'that I have been made a martyr?'[16]

Harriette was also causing Stockdale problems that month. She wanted their partnership dissolved and to sell to someone else what remained of her *Memoirs*. In a barely legible letter to Brougham, sent from Paris on the day that her publisher was accosted by Blore and Levy, Harriette apologized for Stockdale's attempt to blackmail the politician and claimed that she 'had *no hand* in it'. She then went on to describe a recent conversation with the publisher of Thomas Moore, who had experienced problems with the pirating of Moore's songs. It is clear from her letter that she had become a perceptive business woman:

The law it seems is that a copyright must be the author's til he had properly made an assignment of it to another (this is the first question I wanted answered). Moore having made the assignment, his Editor got every other cause he tried 'because' said Lord Ellenborough 'if that work is immoral the pirates by underselling it add ten-fold to the circulation of immorality'.

My next question is this . . . I have given [Stockdale] the full 12 quires I proposed and written more which I can sell elsewhere, he having made up no regular accounts or paid me more than £400 in all for sale of work – and yet he says on the strength of the work in agreement thus '*what she has written or shall write*' – (my meaning being only up to what he has now got) Stockdale threatens to lay an injunction on any *future Memoirs* I may *publish*. Will you allow your

Attorney to write me a candid answer to this question. I don't know who he is and he need not sign any name – I should be very sorry if any body connected with you suffered from . . . politeness to me – but if Stockdale is the rogue they say he is, it is hard to be quite at his mercy and no friend to advise at all. All I want is to dissolve partnership and have done with him. Am I liable for his difficulties as partner in what does not regard my own work or actions upon it? I mean if I go to London. There had been no book if he had not *enduced* [*sic*] me to use names in full etc etc. Of course I know nothing of law and it serves them all right (as to the *Memoirs*). Blore did make love to Fanny I can swear – only as usual I mistook dates and it was when I was a child at home.

Moore's editor says he is sure Stockdale's present agreement of *partnership* is good for nothing to him . . . you must understand this sort of law perhaps yourself but your attorney will and I shall greatly thank you if you will ask him to read this letter and write his opinion . . .[17]

On 15 July 1825 Harriette wrote to Brougham again, apologizing for the previous day's 'hasty scrawl' and asking this time if his attorney could help Rochfort as well, who had an insolvency writ served on him in London (at the instigation of his mother) and was thus unable to return there in case of arrest. Rochfort's creditors had 'all his estate in their hands which must pay them all and more than all when sold, but still right or wrong, if Rochfort is put in prison again he will be half mad – he has had so much of it and my business suffering much because he is not in London'.[18] This was the first of dozens of letters Brougham would receive about Rochfort's financial mess and its relation to his Irish estates.

Harriette's relationship with Stockdale resolved itself quite smartly. She 'tenderly sympathize[d]', Stockdale wrote, 'with her unhappy publisher, who had not forgotten that most extraordinary verdict which had been given against him, in Blore's case'.[19] She continued to send him chapters of her *Memoirs*, and on 13 September he published her 'modern romance', *Paris Lions and London Tigers*. As the last instalments of the *Memoirs* had only just appeared, with further revelations promised, Stockdale hoped to cash in on the public's anticipation and rage for anything by Harriette Wilson.

Paris Lions and London Tigers was written, Harriette said, in eight days. It was a more conventional book than the *Memoirs* had been, much of it satirical in the manner of Dr Syntax or Pierce Egan's *Life in London*. It reads rather like her original *Sketches* must have done: harmless, teasing and forgettable. It tells the story of the visit to Paris of the Callam family whose money comes from boiling soap in Whitechapel. Harriette sends up the English in Paris, observes class structures, mocks dandies and courtship rituals, and while not being on a par with her *Memoirs* for wit and originality, it is well observed and often funny. She writes herself in as one of the local tourist attractions, having Peter Callam exclaim, 'I have seen that wicked creature, Harriette Wilson, who wrote those paw paw *Memoirs*, that made such a stir, and such a to-do, in London. She wasn't so flashy, as I expected, from the prints in the caricature shops; on the contrary, she looked rather serious than knowing or funny, as she passed us in her very pretty green calash. I have also seen a child, with two heads . . .'[20] Harriette was at her best when the subject was herself or those she knew, when she was not required to be 'literary' and could use her idiosyncratic conversational voice, and when she was transgressing. There is much of merit in the unaffected, farcical style of *Paris Lions*, not least her rare and 'lively picture of an utterly extinct state of society'.[21] Occasionally there is a touch of Jane Austen in her romantic irony. After Mary Callam has been wooed by her lover, Villers, with the proposal that she accompany him to India in order to 'smoke a real Persian filligreed hookah, and hear me call out, like a sultan, hookah burdar, whenever I want it lighted', she replies, ' "Why am I singled out, Mr Villers, to have my ears assailed with more nonsense than you bestow on any other lady in the room?" Mary asked this question with an effort to seem indignant, and yet, strange to say, life almost hung on the question, did he, or did he not, distinguish her from the rest? What would she not have given to be convinced that the former was the case?'[22] Of Hannah Pure, a methodistical maidservant (based on Hannah More, the leading patron and writer of the Religious Tract Society), Harriette writes that 'though there existed many women who might be judged uglier, it were difficult, perhaps impossible, to find one more calculated to calm and quiet the passions of the other sex'.[23]

The reviews of *Paris Lions* were poor. *Bell's Life* wrote:

. . . such tame, insipid and harmless trash never before issued from the catch-penny press. There was some point in the former works of this heroine – there was something like naivety in her ridicule of those who deserved to be ridiculed . . . but where she attempts to draw upon her own invention, she is, in the words of our poet, 'weary, stale, flat, and unprofitable . . .' Harriette, when in demand and accessible in London, had some stories to tell, and a little humour, often suggested by the subjects themselves, to make the narrative sometimes spirited – but when sunk into the colonel's wife in Paris, she is laid up and ordinary, she has no resources caught from the gay and licentious society of English bucks . . . her inventive facilities are feeble, and her powers of description, when not copied from real life, are far-fetched, monotonous, and dull.[24]

Stockdale was unlikely to take any great risks at the moment but nor did he want his opponents to think he had been silenced by the result of the Blore trial. *Paris Lions* has a faintly sinister edge to it, enough to invite good sales but not enough to land him in court. It begins with a key in which various of the figures who frequent Parisian society are listed alongside their fictional representatives, and ends with a vague threat: a number of fictitious names were still 'in want of an owner'. Sir Violet Sighaway is Sir Henry Mildmay and Lord Chatterbox the Earl of Clanricarde. Rochfort dashs through as the heartbreakingly beautiful Mr Bellfield, and Gregor MacGregor ('Prince MacGregor') is the ludicrous MacGruffin the First, who 'visited no one, not even ladies, it being contrary to the etiquette of kings . . . Bellfield was his highness's confidential friend, and prime minister.'[25] Lord Stair, who exempted himself from the *Memoirs*, got the harshest treatment of all. Appearing as the Spanish Duke of Lerma, he is described as 'odious', 'lustful', a 'monster', 'the greatest fool in nature', and as having 'inspired the strongest sensations of disgust I ever experienced towards a human being in my whole life'. His peccadilloes include being flogged.[26] Another of those sent up is Mrs Brereton, the relation who had cut Rochfort in Paris the previous November; an incident that Harriette repeats here more or less word for word. Renamed Mrs Brawney Be-at-em, she and her daughters are given an illustration of themselves and five pages in which they are described as 'much ridiculed' in Paris, where they have fled because they are unable to 'get into any tip-top society' in London. Mrs Brereton's attempts to get her daughters married off are mercilessly lampooned. 'I am told that one is not allowed to sit down, except when dressed in black, nor the other to stand up at any party; and the reason assigned is, fear of creasing the dress of the one, and that the other is so overpoweringly tall, that it is, absolutely, quite shocking, to see her stand in the midst of an assembly of ladies and

VENUS AND MARS! *He look'd very much like a Rat-catcher*

17 The Duke of Wellington by Juan Bauzit, 1812
18 'Venus and Mars! He look'd very much like a Rat-catcher'

19 'Disopintment! The Duke of Wxxxlxxxtxn, Alais, the <u>Rat</u> <u>catcher</u>
refused admittance to H. Wilson.'
20 'Harriette Wilson and Byron at Wattier's Masquerade'

21 Mrs Mary Anne Clarke, *c.*1809
22 'Harriette Wilson with Lord Ponsonby's farewell letter'
23 'Lord Ponsonby's house: Disappointment – despair – madness'

24 'Employment! the Marquis of W—r laceing H. Wilson's Stays,
& makeing toast for breakfast'

25 'The Sugar Baker's decent, from the Duchess to the Demirep'

LA COTERIE DEBOUCHÉ,—Intended as a Frontispiece to Harriette Wilson's Memoirs.

26   List of names on the back of the first instalment of the *Memoirs* (Stockdale, 1825)

27   Henry Brougham, by Lonsdale

28   'La, Coterie, Debouché, – Intended as a Frontispiece to Harriette Wilson's Memoirs'

29 Harriette Wilson, frontispiece to Harriette Wilson's *Memoirs*
30 'Scarlet Fever versus Yellow Jaundice, or the Libel Publisher Cut Up, July 1, 1825'
31 'The Cyprian's Ball at the Argyle Rooms', Robert Cruikshank, 1826,
Harriette shown dancing with Stockdale below the harpist.

32 The Fleet Prison
33 King George IV, by Lawrence
34 Elizabeth, Lady Conyngham, by J. Singry

35 Edward Bulwer Lytton

36 Brougham arranges Harriette's funeral:
'My dear Duke

Our old acquaintance Mme de Bochet
(Harriet Wilson) died ~~last~~ the week before
last and left a note says she hoped two or
three of her former acquaintance would give
the few pounds (fifteen) required to bury her
– she having had an estimate price in with all
the particulars . . .'

37 The Pavilion, Hans Place, Chelsea. From an engraving published in 1810

gentlemen. She makes the assembly look like the house, and she resembles its chimney.'[27]

'I was quite vexed and shocked,' Mrs Brereton wrote to her daughter on discovering her name in the key to Harriette's new book. Her surprise suggests that Harriette had not offered those she was including the chance to buy themselves out of *Paris Lions*. Revenge and malice rather than blackmail appear to have been the purpose of the book. Mrs Brereton was advised to 'prosecute for defamation, but I think very differently, for as ladies we must be quiet. You must consider if it would be a proper step for you to write Stockdale that we are not fit subjects for her pen.'[28]

On 12 November, Brougham appeared in court on behalf of Stockdale to move for the setting aside of Blore's award. 'Pray Mr Brougham,' the Lord Chief Justice asked, 'what was it that I ought to have done at the trial which I did not do?' Brougham, greatly embarrassed, was unable to answer the question. Blore's award remained intact.[29] Almost a year after the publication of the first instalment, Harriette's *Memoirs* were still keeping the titled classes on their toes: Sir Walter Scott recorded in his journal the next month, 'The gay world has been kept in hot water lately by the impudent publication of the celebrated Harriet Wilson – who, punk from earliest possibility, I suppose, has lived with half the gay world at hack and manger, and now obliges such as will not pay hush-money with a history of whatever she knows or can invent about them.'[30]

The success of the Blore trial was to stimulate the second libel action brought against Stockdale. Hugh Evans Fisher had been married for twenty-six years and had several children. Sent up by Harriette during her stay in Charmouth as the 'lady killer' of Lyme Regis whose amorous intentions she had misread, Fisher waited until 5 December 1825 to write to Stockdale.

For some time past I have been much annoyed by the animadversions of my friends on my being introduced into your '*Memoirs* of Harriette Wilson' in which I am represented as a very profligate character.

The whole narrative in which I am represented to have been consulted with regard to the Duke of Beaufort and the alleged correspondence is pure invention neither is my name 'Charles Frederick', the only transaction I had with Miss Wilson was the paying her a sum of money on behalf of a friend who had been unfortunate enough to form some connection with her, nor did I ever see her in my life; the money was enclosed in a note. I am at a loss to know what other redress I can obtain than through the medium of a Court of Justice and I am therefore to request that you will furnish me with the name of your attorney.[31]

On 31 December Fisher wrote to Stockdale again, repeating his 'request that you will furnish me with the name of your solicitor'. Stockdale replied that he acted as his own attorney and counsel.[32]

The trial of *Fisher* v. *Stockdale* took place in the spring of 1826, during which time Stockdale was also involved in a furious dispute with his land-lord over trespassing cows, wayward fowl and a potato field. The Lord Chief Justice railed against the 'abominable' book and its publisher. Stockdale, in the standard defence used by satirists, protested that the *Memoirs* raised the level of morality in the country. He also tried to argue that Fisher was not in fact who he claimed to be – Harriette had described a Charles Frederick while this one was a Hugh Evans. Mr Sergeant Spankie, for Stockdale, argued that Fisher was 'in fact represented as reject-ing what might be considered as the overtures from this vile woman. He himself should not think the worse of Mr Fisher for this silly statement, in this silly book, and he was quite sure no one else would.' During the trial, Stockdale quoted from what he claimed was a letter from Lord Byron ('One of Lord Byron's letters from Italy seems very apposite. I cannot tell how I came by it.'):

It has always appeared to me extraordinary . . . that you should value women, so highly, and yet love them, so little. The height of your gratification ceases with its accomplishment; you bow, and you sigh, you worship, and you ABANDON.

With a contempt for the race, I am ever attached to the individual, in spite of myself. I would not hand a woman, out of her carriage; but I would leap into a river after her. I grant you that, as they must walk oftener, out of chariot, than into the Thames, you gentlemen-servitors, cortejos, and cicisbei, have a better chance of being agreeable, and useful; you might, very probably, do both; but as you can't swim, and I can, I recommend you to invite me to your first water-party.[33]

Buried in Stockdale's long, tedious deposition which can have had almost no readers either at the time or since, the letter has escaped the notice of all editors of Byron's correspondence. There is, however, no reason to doubt that it is, in part at least, genuine, and the most likely reason for Stockdale's having written to Byron is that he was planning to publish a collection of love letters to distinguished persons and wondered if the poet had anything he might contribute. Byron is known to have received some publishing offer from Stockdale in 1821 and to have replied by letter.[34] But, whatever its status, and despite the absence of any information other than what can be gleaned from the letter itself, it is typical of Stockdale that he has tried to turn remarks that are of no relevance to his case, and that were evidently intended as some kind of snubbing brush-off, into evidence that his friend, the great exiled poet, was on his side.[35] The trial closed at the beginning of May, and the jury returned a verdict for the plaintiff: damages, £700; costs, £40.[36]

On leaving the court, Stockdale found that his horse and chaise were immediately seized; by the time he had made his way home to his wife, pregnant for the twenty-second time, an officer had arrived. The executions at Winter House were issued on the 31 May and shortly afterwards Sophie Stockdale miscarried. On 12 June, a sale of all Stockdale's possessions took place, and his family was left with three straw mattresses to share between them, and no bedclothes. His shop at Opera Colonnade was also possessed, and his books and pictures sold by auction. 'There cannot be a shadow of a doubt', Stockdale believed, that 'the main object of Fisher's interests' was the unpublished part of the *Memoirs* which remained in his hands, which were of greater potential value than any of his other possessions. 'What! The *Memoirs* which he had brought ruin upon me and mine for having published, he would promote the publication of? But what would he not do, for money?'[37] The net produce of Stockdale's effects after deductions of tax, expenses and rent came to only £226 11s. On top of the damages, he owed £105 10s in costs. On 4 September he was taken to the Fleet Prison.

Arriving at Rochfort's Alma Mater, Stockdale realized that while he was acquainted with only two other inmates, he was a well-known figure himself. Wanting privacy, he was given a single room for which he paid twelve shillings in advance every fortnight. He hired makeshift furniture for seven shillings; his meals, breakfast, a lunch of roast pork, potatoes and ale, and half-a-dozen oysters at bedtime, cost eleven pence per day. 'Our prison system', he wrote to Sophie after his first night, 'as far as I can collect, is scandalously conducted. Here am I, an insolvent, with a large family which I must subsist in some way. Before I quitted the lock-up house, I was called on to pay 3s 6d. for a room, in which were many other unfortunates . . . On entering the prison I was directed, by the warden himself, to pay 1 1 8s 8d. for a chum ticket. This morning Johnson and I were sent for by the turn-keys who explained that it was usual to give them a fee.'[38]

Not one for idling, the prisoner immediately set about planning for the future when he would issue those parts of Harriette's *Memoirs* which he had not yet published, write a weekly newspaper revealing the 'truth' about those running the country, and bring out his collection of love letters from distinguished people, whose 'sale, if the collection be to my wishes, will fully equal that of the *Memoirs*'.[39] Stockdale also used the rich network of Fleet prisoners to gather together disclosures about several 'maculate' figures, material that Sophie Stockdale, 'having made up her mind that her husband would be detained as illegally as he had been convicted', was preparing, along with her own recollections of the great and not-so-good, for publication. 'I was going to add', Stockdale wrote one night to his wife, 'a story of Lord Pomfret, but as it is rather maculate, it shall be yours in private, as Coriolanus said.'[40] These stories, along with scraps he had purchased from Harriette, were to provide the content of a serialization he proposed to call *Holly-Grove*.[41] And if Stockdale could gain more money by what he suppressed than what he sold, he was, as ever, happy to oblige.

The Stockdales exchanged daily letters. Sophie and her family did not seem to be suffering any particular financial hardship in Winter House. They employed new servants, ate well, and carried on much as usual. She sent her husband geese, chickens, plum puddings, fresh eggs, apples and cigars, and he sent home his washing. Their bulky prison correspondence, which contains in minutiae an account of his current life and moral and religious thought, Stockdale published in the 1831 edition of Harriette's *Memoirs*. 'I really must publish all our letters,' he told Sophie; 'they are fraught with so much interest. The natives will think that we have not been wholly unemployed during our separation, and they will pay us well, I am sure, to give them this opportunity to think.'[42] The letters are generally upbeat and affectionate; John Joseph was devoted to his wife and 'matchless children' and they worshipped him. Mrs Stockdale worried about Mr

Stockdale's bowels, which he told her had 'been a good deal out of order for the last eight and forty hours', and she reminded him – 'I have told you often and I tell you again' – that he must 'hold the *candle* and be *cozy*. It is the way to go through the world and be liked, instead of disliked.'[43] His family longed for him to return home. 'Nine o'clock,' Sophie wrote. 'We have had our suppers, and they are all wishing me to send their loves to you and a kiss, and last of all myself. I do not say much; but nobody can tell what *I feel*. My hope is in meeting again and being happy.'[44] Stockdale longed also for them. 'Some child has repeatedly, in the course of yesterday, and this morning, cried dah as it passed my door, in a voice very much like our darling's! I have not yet had resolution enough to take a look at it.'[45] In another letter he asks Sophie to 'Get a pudding for my birthday, on Sunday. I think I shall be forty-nine or fifty!!'[46]

The couple were defiant in their belief that John Joseph was innocent of all charges and they refer throughout their letters to the heroic and fearless 'publisher of HW's *Memoirs*'. God, they never doubted, was on their side, and Stockdale even believed that Fisher had seen the error of his ways.

Fisher told Humphreys [Stockdale's attorney], at my request, that I might go on publishing – He never cared for libel – he used to laugh at it, til he went to Bath, where some one put on a grave face and shook his head, and was very significant; but when he came to London, he found that, as he passed people, they nudged each other and said that is Beau Fisher – Harriette's Fisher, and this really annoyed him, and he determined to prosecute!! Humphreys said it was a pity that he had not sooner expressed such feeling, as he would have made a proposal to satisfy him, without going into court, but that Dangerfield [Fisher's attorney] carried himself so high, that Humphreys could not, without compromising the interests of his client, open his lips. I fear that there was a great deal of underplot: besides the fact is, that Blore had got his money and that Fisher had pretty accurately ascertained the feeling of all that is good and noble and amiable in this country, the judges themselves included previously to having taken his resolution.[47]

Fisher, meanwhile, flushed with the success of his legal action, had now sued the editor of *Bell's Life in London* for satirical verses in which he was mentioned. On 28 May following Fisher's triumph over Stockdale, *Bell's Life* published ST–CKD–LE *and* HARRIETTE W–LS–N, *A London Eclogue*, a witty piece of doggerel in which Fisher plays only the most minor part.

'Twas at the hour when most agree
To take a sober cup of tea
(A very economic meal,
As sundry folks in London feel,
Who are not able to afford
Each day to sit at dinner board).
St–ckd–le and Harriette W–ls–n met.
(The Colonel too, a little wet –
His custom of an afternoon),
With recent verdicts out of tune.
To Fisher, Blore, large sums were given:–
To one *three* hundred, to t'other, *seven*.
Much St–ckd–le feared lest such a sample
Make others follow his example.
The Colonel in his armchair sat,
And took no notice of their chat.
Indeed, he was not in a state
To enter much into debate!

The rhyme ends with Harriette's throwing her tea in Stockdale's face, his escape into the street and the arms of a bailiff. 'I like that,' Stockdale said on hearing that Fisher was suing for libel. 'Go it my lads! Fight dog! Fight bear! I hope he will have nous enough to attack the pirates too.'[48] Fisher again won his case, only to have the judgment reversed the next year, after *Bell's Life* insisted on a retrial on a writ of error. In July 1828, Fisher took *Bell's Life* to the King's Bench for the third time. 'As to the publication of Harriette Wilson's *Memoirs*,' Sir James Scarlett, defending, said of the editor of *Bell's Life*, 'there could be no one who detested it more than he did; but she [Harriette], a poor abandoned creature, could not have brought it before the world. It was Stockdale who published the scandalous *Memoirs* of that abandoned strumpet for the sake of horrid profits . . . The verses merely held Stockdale and Harriette up to ridicule.'[49] Brougham pointed out that the object of the verses was 'not to reassert the truth of the imputations against the plaintiff's character, but rather to expose and hold up to public odium the writer and publisher of the *Memoirs*.'[50] Hugh Evans Fisher lost his case.

After seven fruitful weeks in the Fleet, on 24 October Stockdale was released. Fisher had eventually agreed for his damages to be paid in instalments. Stockdale was bounding with energy and charged straight back into battle. His first act was to campaign for the freedom of another prisoner, for which he applied directly to 'Mr Secretary Stephen Rumbold Lushington': 'I am not aware that any of your family ever had communication with Harriette Wilson; but there are coteries within coteries as well as wheels within wheels, and this has been one of my gratuitous suppressions to which you little thought I alluded when you last called upon me at the Opera Colonnade.'[51]

Within days, he had set up shop in St James's Square, a stone's throw from his old premises, and begun work on the publications of the so far suppressed instalments of Harriette's *Memoirs* and his journal, titled (the irony was his own, taken from Lord Chief Justice Best's description of the exhibitors in Harriette's *Memoirs*), *Stockdale's Budget: Of 'All that is Good, Noble, and Amiable in the Country'*. Stockdale was now operating from the heart of the Establishment; he was based in one of London's most exclusive addresses, moments away from St James's Palace. 'The big wigs were already horrified, not to say stark, staring mad, at my affrontery in sitting myself down in St James's Square,' he wrote to Harriette, '. . . but, as we become better acquainted, I hope we shall also become the best of friends.' He hoisted outside his premises a 'flaming board, "Office of Stockdale's Budget", in letters of gold, on a ground of dark blue'. On the shop door outside of which queues would again form to buy the new parts of Harriette's *Memoirs*, was a coat of arms with lion trampling on a naked man. The motto was RESURGAM ('I shall rise again').[52]

Stockdale's Budget allowed its publisher to continue his single-handed attack on the country's power base and to run through once more his criticisms of the legal system. He also gave himself space to expound his views on the freedom of the press, to report and comment on the 'news', to discuss his particular line on morality, promote his early relationship with the young Percy Bysshe Shelley, and slander Whig politicians. Stockdale's energy was immense: apart from a few letters from Harriette, who had agreed to act as Paris correspondent, Stockdale wrote the entire newspaper himself. He never used one word when two dozen would do and he had voluminous opinions on most topics. His main interest, however, was his own story and the *Budget* was principally about J. J. Stockdale. He was reckless about what he wrote. 'Having not been trusted,

I can break no confidence' was his defence. Of Canning, for example, Stockdale revealed that the then Foreign Minister 'went to Paris disguised as his own man of business, to buy himself out of Harriette Wilson's *Memoirs*'.[53] Harriette's letters from Paris began in like spirit, with some libellous anecdotes about the slave-loving Rowland Mitchell, but her contributions stopped after three weeks.

The *Budget* also advertised the imminent appearance of Harriette's 'Unpublished *Memoirs*' and served as the vehicle to recommence Stockdale's own blackmail campaign. 'I shall no longer delay to publish the remainder of the *Memoirs*,' he informed the public, 'including those parts which I had suppressed without fee or reward. Should I now keep anything back, my readers may rest assured that I have been paid for my forebearance. If I can henceforth make more by suppressing than by publishing, I shall do so. I have purchased, at an enormous price, the copyright of the *Memoirs*, and whether like the merchant, I am paid to withhold my cargo from market, or remunerate myself by transporting it thither, can be of no consequence to anyone.' The first issue of the *Budget*, which appeared on 13 December 1826, listed, under the heading of 'Harriette Wilson's *Memoirs*, Exhibits in the Unpublished *Memoirs*', the names of 'The King and Queen and Duke of York, The Prince and Princess Esterhazy, Dukes of Wellington, Beaufort, Portland, Devonshire, Richmond and de Guiche', and so forth. Each week until the paper folded, more 'exhibits' were named, lord chancellors, lord chief justices, judges, counts, honourables, ladies, messieurs, doctors. Stockdale also issued a number of threats to individuals and tempted the public with salacious starters; the truth about 'Amy's maidenheads', of which she 'had as many as a cat has lives', would be revealed, while 'Mary Ann Clarke's friend', should he contact Stockdale's office, 'will be well received'.

'I long to hear that you are getting money,' Harriette wrote to Stockdale in December 1826.

When do you publish the other *Memoirs*? . . . As I am dreadfully abused in the newspapers, for proposing to publish my late friend's adventures, I ventured the other day to write a friendly, humble letter to one who, to get himself out of the book, had professed a lively interest in my welfare, and a very strong regard for me. No answer came. Again I wrote, merely for a five pound note to hasten back to Paris with; because while I was in London writs were taken against me, and officers surrounded my door, heaven knows why! Still I had no answer. What think you, said my third letter, of a brief but true sketch of your virtuous life . . . and since the naked truth could do you no harm, I beg permission to publish the truth, by your own written consent.

She received from her 'friend' ten pounds the next day.[54]

In January 1827, Stockdale's *Budget* reported that 'anxiety for the further publication of Harriette Wilson's *Memoirs*, has increased, is increasing, and can only be diminished by gratification'. It was not until 4 April that Stockdale's readers were informed that Part 13 of the *Memoirs* was now published. In June, the *Budget* was suppressed by the new Attorney General, Sir James Scarlett. The instalments of Harriette's *Memoirs*, however, continued to appear; an advertisement in the *Morning Post* on 27 November announced that the 'new volumes' were 'now ready', and another in *Bell's Life* on 10 Febuary 1828, heralded the imminent arrival of 'the new parts of Harriette Wilson . . . 19 and 20'. Stockdale also used *Bell's Life* to promote his latest project, 'Harriet the Second! . . . Price 3 pence. Among the many disclosures in the Duchess of St Albans' *Memoirs* are the secret history of Sir W. Beechey, and his celebrated picture of Miss Mellon, as Volante . . .'[55]

Parts 13 onwards of the *Memoirs*, about 650 pages, do not survive and we cannot be certain how many more parts there were. But they were published, in a slightly altered form, in Stockdale's extended 1831 edition of Harriette's book. The new instalments are largely without the merits of Parts 1–12. They consist of scraps of narrative and bits and pieces of unconnected anecdote written in an occasionally charming but generally garrulous, haphazard and chaotic style. 'I must now, in reality, think about concluding,' Harriette writes after several hundred pages of scattering names, 'as I am somewhat tired. I must first tell my readers that I have just recollected the name of that excellent good man who used to make love to me so methodically in Lisson Grove. It was Lord Clonbrock who used to call in new leather breeches and fell into such a furious passion with my maid when I was denied to him . . . By the bye, I should like to know how Lord Clanricarde relishes matrimony . . . To change the subject, which as I said before, is a very dry one, has anybody read a certain little book called the Confessions of Julia Johnstone? Stockdale has often mentioned it to me, but I never felt any curiosity about what of course I knew could only be a catch-penny effort of some poor soul or other, because I saw Julia . . . in her coffin long ago.'[56] Stockdale interrupts Harriette's chatter throughout with accounts of personal nobility in the face of persecution. These interludes he tries to pass off as coming from the pen of his author.

The most revelatory aspects of Parts 13 onwards are the details Harriette gives of her childhood, her parental heritage, and her introduction to Rochfort. These sections, which take up a bulk of the space, she can have written only for pleasure, blackmail playing no part in the stories. Among the dozens of new names to appear are the young Lord Weymouth, who addresses her in a letter as '*Ma chère, et belle maman*', Lords Stair, Londonderry (formally Lord Stewart), Boringdon, Clanricarde, Palmerston and Exeter ('a sort of pocket Apollo in form, calves, shoulders and all, neat, though small to match; one might be led to suppose a seven months production of his mamma'[57]), Frank Hall Standish, Sir Charles Style, Lady Emily Vane, Ladies Conyngham and Clare (about whom nothing is revealed beyond their past relationships with Ponsonby), Edward Ellice, Sir Henry Hardinge and George Canning.

And from what Stockdale says in his Introduction, by publishing this material he was exposing many of those whose silence Harriette had already guaranteed. 'I have been driven into a corner,' he told his readers. 'What I had intended to have suppressed, both of the *Memoirs*, and other matters, were known only to myself. I shall break no confidence which has ever been reposed in me; therefore the great numbers, who have made me their confidants, need be under no anxiety; but where I have not been trusted, I cannot betray . . . my family must and shall be provided for.'[58]

Stockdale was back in business but he felt that his own persecution was never over. He was in the dock once more in December 1826, for non-payment of rent. He again lost, his family were evicted from Winter House and came to live in his office in St James's Square.

Brougham's own trial had hardly begun.

CHAPTER 23

Panic at the Palace

'No eye', wrote Ponsonby on arrival at his first diplomatic post in December 1826, 'ever saw so odious a country as this Buenos Aires is . . . I really sigh when I think I may spend my days here . . . no horse, no road, no houses . . . no books, no theatre that can be endured . . . Nothing good but beef.' Even in this land of 'mud and putrid carcasses',[1] Ponsonby was plagued by Harriette. Not only did she continue to write to him but a letter received at the North and South American Coffee House declared that all 'appeared delighted with the noble presence of the English Lord (who happens to be Irish!), and we Englishmen felt not a little proud at the praises bestowed upon him. Besides, since the publication of Harriette Wilson's *Memoirs*, his lordship has become an object of great curiosity, even to us.'[2]

Harriette also continued to threaten the King, who had not shown his face in years for fear of public insult. How far the *Memoirs* actually reached into the nervous entrails of the Establishment can be seen in the scale reached by the Conyngham crisis instigated by Harriette, who had compromising letters from the Marchioness sent to Ponsonby thirty years before. Half of those government members involved in the tricky business of silencing her and protecting His Majesty had bought themselves out of her book. The other half appeared in it because they refused to be blackmailed. Lord Granville, formerly Granville Leveson-Gower, was

St James's Palace, *Views of London*

Worcester's uncle and Ambassador to Paris. Harriette's relationship with him went back to her days in Somerstown, when she had marched him up to Hampstead and back on a baking hot day. Lord Dudley and Ward, Foreign Secretary since 1827, had, as the Honourable John Ward, been a member of Harriette's coterie and was a great friend of Lord Ebrington. He had also been one of Fanny's lovers until she refused to 'submit to something . . . improper'.[3] Both men are mocked by Harriette: Dudley she describes as a vain, petulant, bad-tempered 'reptile' and Granville she turns into her 'fool'. George Canning, Foreign Secretary and from 1827 Prime Minister, had been Harriette's lover, as had his son-in-law, Lord Clanricarde; Sir William Knighton, the King's doctor and confidant, had ministered to Fanny on her deathbed and taken advantage of her there, for which he was also buying Harriette's silence. Brougham, as ever, was acting on Harriette's behalf in her negotiations with Lady Conyngham, and, as ever, used the opportunity to promote himself. 'I know as well as you know yourself', Harriette stormed in a letter to him written in 1833, 'that you could have inclined Lady C. to provide for me had you been as true to your client, as warm in *her* cause as you were in your own which mar'd it. But I want to forget all those things . . .'[4] Given that King George was only one of many names being blackmailed by her, the complexity of Harriette's campaign is quite astonishing.

The King, who had already paid her to suppress their own liaison of twenty-five years before, would do anything to suppress what Harriette had to reveal of Lady Conyngham now. Harriette was threatening to publish a comic play she had written, *Bought in and Bought out*, 'in which Dorset, Argyle, Lady Hertford, Conyngham, Alborough, Lord Bridgewater, Brighton, Beckford, Lord Mountcharles and many more figure as applying to me to buy themselves out of my book on certain stipulated terms which they have not achieved.'[5] Ponsonby vehemently refused to be intimidated. He held firm to the belief that to pay Harriette was 'not only wholly useless as a cure for the evil but . . . must encourage the woman's desire for plunder and shew her the certain means of gratifying it'.[6] Ponsonby's determination to prosecute rather than pay did nothing to calm the King or Lady Conyngham, who feared exposure in any form, whether in a court of justice, a comedy, or a best-selling memoir. Getting Ponsonby out of the country became even more imperative.

The following events, covering the years 1825–29 and reconstructed from the various letters that survive, remain fragmentary. But they leave no doubt that whatever Harriette had on Lady Conyngham made the King frantic with stress. These official and confidential letters tell the tale of the attempts made by the governments of England and France to suppress Harriette's secrets, along with all the intrigue, bribery, hysteria and threats such a suppression entailed. They give us a picture of the world beyond the nostalgic, egocentric bubble constructed by Harriette in her *Memoirs*, but they confirm her centrality, showing just how dangerous the courtesan was thought to be, operating at the heart of the political world, knowing its figures too well. These letters show us once again how Harriette was a social adhesive, how men were able to consolidate their power through the sharing of her body or the silencing of her voice.

But to the very people who had greedily passed her around she had now become the stuff of nightmares; she had violated the courtesan's code of honour on which they believed their relationship with her was founded. Without sympathy for her or concern, these men, Harriette said, would rather she starve than reveal to the world how they had once desired her.

When Lord Granville replaced Sir Charles Stuart as Ambassador to Paris at the end of 1824, he put a stop to Harriette's exploitation of the diplomatic bag. Through a contact, she continued to use this route to send her mail to London but her letters were intercepted, delayed and sometimes withheld. Stockdale held that even when their letters were sent through the General Post Office they were pilfered, right up until 1827. We have to assume that the government saw everything Harriette wrote, a situation that might have encouraged them to exaggerate both her threat and their ability to control the situation.

By historical accident there have survived two highly revealing Foreign Office documents that would normally not have been preserved in diplomatic records. These previously unseen manuscripts reveal for the first time quite how far Harriette Wilson was considered a threat. In the autumn of 1825, Granville had a confidential meeting with M. Tranchet of the French Foreign Office, his memorandum of which is among the Granville Papers in the Public Record Office. The subject was Harriette Wilson. 'I said that this woman had published *Memoirs* which were . . . atrocious libels against the most distinguished characters in England, both male and female' and that 'having established her residence in Paris, she boasts of the power of continuing her libels' through the 'French press' and continuing her methods of extortion.[7] Granville discovered from Tranchet that Harriette was well known to the French government who, until recently had her under surveillance. 'He was aware of her [method] of obtaining money from individuals and threatening to publish circumstances regarding them unless they bought her silence by paying a certain sum which she demanded – the Lord Stair had been attacked by her here in this manner.' Her publisher, Tranchet revealed, was called l'Huillier (l'Huillier had published the French edition of the *Memoirs* in 1825), and he had been 'convicted of selling libellous and seditious publications and in consequence deprived by the Government of his Brevet of Bookseller', but the only work of Harriette's currently in the press was a book called *Roman Historique à la Suisse* (which was never published). L'Huillier had been bribed by Tranchet to inform him of anything Harriette was about to publish. It was known that she lived entirely with Rochfort and associated with General MacGregor and his previous aides-de-camp. 'I am aware', Granville wrote, 'of the objection felt by the French Government to delivering up British Subjects who had offended against the laws of their own country, and my interview with M. Tranchet had not been asked with the view of obtaining the extradition of Harriette Wilson; but I was anxious to know whether M. Tranchet could allow her to continue practising in France these schemes of extortion which she was prevented from pursuing by the laws of her own country – her libels not only inflicted harmful wounds upon unoffending individuals of the purest character, but were an outrage to public morals.' Tranchet said that he believed Harriette was now in England – 'a record was sent for by which it appeared that she left Calais towards the end of May – but I told him that I had met her in the streets within the last ten days – he then said that he should be very glad to be relieved from the presence of such a person in France . . . the laws of France he observed were severe against [such behaviour and] I should find that there would be no difficulty in prosecuting her . . . for letters written to persons in England with the purpose of frightening them into giving her money.'

Tranchet said that if Granville made an application 'on the part of His Majesty's Govt he had no doubt it would be attended to – I said I had no [authority] from my Govt and would make no official application; my conversation with him was not official, but knowing how deeply Persons of the highest consideration were affected by the machinations of this woman . . . I had been anxious to learn from him what were his feelings and sentiments upon the subject – I asked him whether if she were about to publish, he had the means of knowing beforehand her intentions – he said a declaration of intention to publish must be made by the publisher and the police, but as that declaration might be made only twelve hours before the publication took place, the book might be in circulation before steps could be taken to [prevent] it.' Granville put it to Tranchet that 'other means . . . were at his disposal, by which he might know whether such publications were in the press'. Harriette could be put under surveillance once more.[8]

Also among the Granville papers is an undated draft of a letter to the King of France, in which the Ambassador struggles to find the right way to request a conversation 'in complete confidence, about a woman who lives in Paris and of whom you have no doubt heard'. Her 'immoral' books, Granville continued, contain 'the most infamous lies and atrocious libels against all those who are most distinguished in London society. Her aim in publishing these books is not only to make a profit, but also to use them as weapons to frighten people . . . English laws would bring these crimes to justice – were she living in England.' She can find 'no printers in London who dare publish her libels. Now she has established herself in France, however, she continues to threaten the system from outside . . .'

Granville's aim in going to the very top was Harriette's extradition – 'I know that the French Government is well disposed to agreeing to the extradition of criminals who had taken refuge in France . . .'[9] – but he was playing as well on the profound weariness of the French monarchy towards courtesans and their stories. In the years before the French Revolution the authority and dignity of the King had been slowly sapped by a flood of scandalous stories about the French court, many untrue, published abroad and smuggled into France. Neither the French nor British monarchies could risk a repetition. One of the pre-revolutionary bestsellers in France had been *Anecdotes sur Mme la comtesse du Barry*, a rattling collection of yarns about Louis XV and his last mistress, who was widely considered to be several notches beneath the empowering status symbols usually selected by kings to grace their beds. The *Anecdotes* demonstrated the feebleness and moral degeneration of the King, portrayed as drunken and lecherous while du Barry ran the country. Du Barry was portrayed as a sluttish spendthrift and confirmed as the most expensive mistress in French history, draining the coffers of 18 million livres.[10] Du Barry's reputation had done the monarchy nothing but harm and public appetite for the anonymous *Anecdotes* had been voracious. Harriette and her *Memoirs* were bound to touch a nerve in the recently restored Bourbons, and Harriette Wilson was portrayed to the French King by Granville as an English du Barry whose presence in Paris was a serious threat. As it is, there is nothing in Harriette's letters to suggest that she had any political motivation.

Harriette had control of the English King also. On 30 June 1826, George IV told Granville to expect a visit from Sir William Knighton. Knighton was initially the King's doctor but had proved his worth as a confidant when, nine years before, he retrieved from Sir John McMahon, Keeper of the Privy Purse (and procurer of virgins for the Prince's pleasure) numerous secret and damaging papers relating to the royal private life. George now depended on Knighton to deal with anything unsavoury and scandalous, and Knighton was duly sent to Paris 'for the purpose of communicating with Lord Granville on a subject upon which the King is most deeply anxious'.[11] Canning, who earlier in the year had travelled to Paris to buy himself out of Harriette's proposed book,[12] also wrote to the Ambassador on 30 June, confirming that 'the business is one which causes great disquietude in a quarter, in which I am sure it will be as much matter of inclination as of duty on your part, not only to lend yourself to any mode of removing uneasiness, but to devise means for that purpose if you can'.[13] After his arrival, Knighton told Granville that the Director of the Paris Police was to be asked to put 'the individuals under question' under police surveillance, and to let 'you confidentially know from time to time what their conduct and employments seem to be. If this could be done it would perhaps be a satisfactory auxillary [*sic*] to our own watchfulness! At any rate it would be a demonstration to those at home, who are so anxious on the subject.'[14]

While the object of Knighton's secret missions to the Continent on behalf of the King was kept an official secret, it is clear that they concerned the machinations of Mr and Mrs Rochfort and that Harriette was being bribed by Carlton House to hold her pen. It was rumoured that the money paid to her came from the Secret Service, the raiding of whose coffers was authorized by Canning. Not only was Harriette a threat and a nuisance, but Rochfort's close relationship with General MacGregor, presently in a Parisian gaol under suspicion of planning to aid an invasion on Cuba, made him a dangerous figure in his own right.[15] Rochfort involved himself passionately in MacGregor's plight, insisting on the General's innocence of all charges and taking the credit for his eventual release.[16] In September 1825, Rochfort had been accused of '*attentat contre la sûreté de l'état*' ('an attempt against the safety of the state') as if he were a terrorist – and interrogated by the Paris police 'under the authority of the Catholic King'. His home with Harriette on the grande rue de Chaillot was ransacked and articles were removed which Rochfort was assured would be returned to him '*quand le procès intenté contre le Général MacGregor serait terminé*' ('when the case against General MacGregor was closed').[17] Harriette's being acquainted with MacGregor was a source of concern to the British government, who had been made fools of by them both.[18] What trouble might ensue if the ex-courtesan and the South American liberator combined their forces?

Despite the renewal of her surveillance, Harriette's network continued to expand. In October 1826, the King wrote Knighton a frantic letter: 'There certainly seems as if there were some sort of fatality that inevitably attends upon your leaving London, be it only for a single day, for your back is no sooner turn'd than some disagreeable unexpected and unforeseen *something*, is *sure almost instantly* to *start up*.'[19] He was dispatching his page, he wrote, to tell Knighton in person what he knew about the 'villain' George Wharton, who had worked as a second clerk in the kitchen from 1824 to 1827. Wharton had the day before appeared in the Court of Justice and the page had been subpoenaed as a witness; the cause was withdrawn, much to the King's relief, but the business was by no means over. Wharton, who had been spreading gossip about the King and his mistress, had now struck gold:

. . . this young villain has to a great extent, acknowledged . . . his privacy to, & connection with Harriet Wilson, in particular, as well as others of her hellish gang.

This I consider as a matter of much too great importance, to leave you a single instant, in ignorance of. It is true the cause is withdrawn, but upon what plea, I know not, but, though it be withdrawn, yet, having been so nearly before the publick, & such a number of persons connected with it, & collected upon the spot to hear it . . . & learning . . . the rancorous & revengeful spirit & sheer villainy which alone actuates the proceedings & objects of this vile monster, I am sure you will see the absolute necessity there is, of some step, be it only of precaution, being immediately taken.[20]

King George, whose remaining grip on the public was crumbling, was terrified of Harriette's effect on his image. He was little enough respected already; the fact that eight years earlier he had remained singularly preoccupied by the problem of his wife while crowds in Manchester, including women and children, were mown down by troops during a peaceful meeting in St Peter's Fields was symptomatic of his alienation from the nation. He was a twenty-five-stone drug addict, so conscious of his girth, gout and age that hedges were erected in order for him to take his constitutionals unobserved; even his servants were forbidden from looking at him. His dislike of popular ridicule was his Achilles' heel, and the amount Carlton House spent on trying to buy off Radical caricatures – at least £2,600 between 1819 (the year of the Peterloo Massacre) and 1822 – reveals how greatly he feared the burgeoning industry of monarch-mocking. Whatever material Harriette had to reveal was more demeaning to his sense of majesty than anything the lampoonists might say about the size of his waistcoats.

Rochfort suffered another disappointment when the will of his unmarried uncle Henry revealed that his vast wealth had been left not to his nephew but to his illegitimate son, Cowper Beeby. Brougham's authority was instantly called on. 'Late Mr Rochfort being single,' Harriette stormed, 'his property ought to belong to his heir . . . I hope you will not lose us comfortable income by inattention to the subject. The young man who now enjoys his property is a selfish miser who refused to lend his cousin 10 pounds in a moment of distress although he puts by 600 pounds yearly out of seven.'[21]

In the autumn of 1826, Rochfort moved to Tournai de St Remay, near Chimay on Belgium's French border, where his latest doomed scheme was to lease premises belonging to the Prince of Chimay and re-establish a blast coal furnace for smelting iron. This was a plan he had been hatching since summer 1825 and it seems that his money-raising tactics involved a mixture of preying on government ministers and exploiting his bad name and connections.[22] Between November 1826 and June 1827, he lived in Chimay alone while Harriette was in Paris managing her own affairs. Rochfort's mother remarried in 1827, and her third husband, General Brown, was more disposed to Rochfort than her second had been, thus doing something to repair family relations. Rochfort's hopes of future wealth increased. Harriette's health, she said, was 'miserable' and Paris, out of season, was deadly dull. As well as conducting her extortion campaign, she was writing letters for *Stockdale's Budget*. The new instalments of her *Memoirs* started appearing in April 1827 and, in July, Harriette joined her husband in Chimay. On the last day of the month she wrote to Brougham in a fury. Rochfort had repeatedly asked him for help and repeatedly been ignored. Canning had opposed Rochfort's appointment to the Foreign Consulate, which a beleaguered Lord Mountcharles (formerly Francis Conyngham) had strongly urged, and in so doing he had insulted Harriette. Harriette's power over himself, the government and the monarchy was a fact of which Brougham needed reminding. She appears nervously confident in her letter; she is on a winning streak and doesn't know how long it will last; she is hot-headed and breathless, shifting with ease between dire threats and the petulant recollection of personal slights.

Having been Brougham's lover she has a licence to address him without the formality even a blackmail letter requires, and it is clear by her style that Brougham and Harriette have crossed a vital threshold allowing her to give him the full weight of her raw emotion. 'I have so little fear of threats', she told him, 'that I have entreated Mr Canning to make amends to my husband for having refused to grant him his interest as to public employment – at the request of Lord Mountcharles by interceding with *that family* [the Conynghams] to do Mr R[ochfort] a private service – which will prevent the strong necessity I am . . . under to publish that which may be *displeasing to all parties*.' She threatened to reveal not only the Ponsonby and Conyngham business but also the time 'when you treated me in all (by *paying me*) with all the cold disrespect due to a *common prostitute*' and the occasions when she became the 'mere . . . instrument of your pleasure when you happened to be inclined to *commit adultery gratis*'. 'You can prevent all this,' she continued, 'and you know that the real well wishers of the Conynghams and Sir Robert Wilson would interfere to prevent the publication of their having *confessed* their vices adultery etc to Harriette Wilson. Do we bribe for the concealment of vices we never committed?' Harriette concluded by warning Brougham that she was keeping a copy of this and of his other letters, 'in case I am by *hard, very* hard necessity obliged to publish them', and informing him that an offer of £1,000 sterling had been made 'for the *Bought out* book'.[23]

Nine days later, George Canning died and Wellington formed the new government. That August, Knighton was again dispatched to see Granville in Paris. ('You have just received a visit from a *great person* in the State,' Dudley wrote to the British Ambassador. 'You need not be told how much importance is attached by a *still greater person* to the objects of his journey – particularly that with which you are best acquainted.'[24]) Two weeks later, Knighton called on Sir Charles Bagot, Ambassador to The Hague, with letters from Dudley and the King. Late in the evening on 3 October, one of Bagot's envoys knocked on the door of the Rochfort house in Tournai de St Rémy.

The envoy, who refused to give his name, asked to see Harriette. She was not there, Rochfort informed him; she was either in Paris or London and would not be back again until the following summer. The visitor was directed by Bagot to

acquaint Mrs Rochfort from me that from the moment of her first establishment in this country it had been, as she would readily conceive, a part of my duty to keep an eye fixed upon her proceedings – that the person with whom she was in connexion – the characters with whom she was in correspondence, and all the steps which she had taken, were intimately known to me – that I had no wish to proceed to any extremities, or to take any harsh measures in regard to her if I could avoid it, but that I must have some positive security that she would discontinue immediately and for ever those annoyances which she had long and particularly of late been in the practice of directing against a quarter which she would perfectly understand, and in which it was not possible that they should be endured – that I would be perfectly content to accept her word of honour given to myself that these annoyances should cease – but that unless she was prepared to give me such a pledge, it would be necessary for me, under the instructions with which I was furnished, to take without delay such measures with the

Government of this country in respect to her, and to those immediately connected with her, as would be infallibly attended with inconveniences to which she had probably never looked.

Rochfort feigned ignorance of Harriette's actions and their effects. He said that he knew the *Memoirs* had 'made Mrs Rochfort . . . many enemies among what are called the great people in England, and I will tell you besides that the same step which you are taking now has been tried with me before – it is nothing new – application was made to the French Government to turn *her* out of France and *they refused* . . . I know there is a determination to destroy her, and also know where they wish to send her to, but they never shall succeed . . . while I am able to protect her.' He went on to tell the envoy that 'the multiplicity of steps [Harriette] had taken for the last twelve months was so great that she could not by any possibility be certain of the quarter [i.e., the particular party] referred to – that she had been in correspondence with perhaps two hundred people, all in high quarters, for that she disdained the low ones'. Bagot, hearing the envoy's report, doubted 'whether our démarche will be attended with the success which is to be desired'.[25]

Rochfort sent the next day a lengthy letter to Bagot, telling him of the previous night's events and asking 'whether such a mission as herein described was actually sanctioned by your excellency'. 'I am free to avow', Rochfort wrote, with his usual sense of drama, 'that the visit appeared and still appears to me of a very mysterious nature; late in the evening and dark, the person muffled in a large cloak, absolute and repeated refusal to give me his name or leave your excellency's letter altogether induce me to doubt whether such a visit could really bear the sanction of your communication with such an anonymous visitor.' Rochfort's primary concern was the continuation of his furnace project, which he was told would be threatened if Harriette refused to stop annoying the King, and it was in an attempt to save his own skin that he tried to defend his wife. The envoy had told Rochfort that Harriette's 'connection' with General MacGregor was known about. 'Ill and ill placed as I considered this remark', Rochfort wrote to Bagot, 'I chose to correct the unknown erroneous idea on that head, and I told him what I now take the liberty frankly to repeat to your excellency; – in quality of ancient aide-de-camp to General MacGregor I possessed much of his confidence, and he was frequently at my house in Paris, and I at his. Mrs Rochfort never in her life saw General MacGregor before he came to my house, and never afterwards but in my presence . . .' Were Mrs Rochfort here, Rochfort continued, she would be as baffled as himself by the visitor and his demands. He expressed surprise at 'a poor weak woman having set the government in motion', and refused to believe 'that the British govnt would take upon themselves to interfere with my furnace and establishment under my protection'.[26]

Sir Charles Bagot never replied to Rochfort's letter, but he wrote to Knighton a day or so later, on 9 October, that 'it might not be attended with the effect which it is desired to produce if a secret intimation should be given from the highest authority of the police that the attention of this Government has been awakened to Mrs Rochfort's proceedings . . .'[27] Rochfort had also written to Harriette about the 'nefarious' visit, and she promptly wrote to Bagot laying out her terms and conditions. The letter, which no longer exists, was forwarded to Lord Dudley on 19 October, and its contents are made apparent in what Bagot had to say in his enclosure to Dudley. 'They who have had to deal with her upon the subject of her publications,' the Ambassador to The Hague wrote,

are the best judges of the degree of reliance which is to be placed upon her promises; but, for my own part, I confess that I should be disposed to trust to the engagements which she declares herself ready to take upon the conditions which she states in her letter, and to accept those conditions without hesitation . . . I am strongly tempted to submit to your consideration whether (assuming that H. Wilson is really in possession of facts the disclosure of which it may be an object to prevent) it might not be prudent to agree to her terms, and to accept her conditions precisely as she offers them. Her first object seems to be to obtain some situation for Mr Rochfort, but she appears to be quite aware that any appointment given to *him* would tell its own tale, and she therefore offers, in case no situation can be found for him, to accept £300 for what she calls her immediate difficulties, and £100 a year for her life conditionally – that is – so long only as the parties in question shall be no further troubled in any way by her letters, publications or otherwise, and so long only as the fact of her receiving such annuity shall be by her kept secret from all the world. Now it appears to me that these conditions, or some conditions *of this kind*, do afford the best and probably the only guarantee which can be obtained from a person of her character for her future silence, if there is any object in securing that silence. It seems evident from her letter that, unless she is to be defied, I must at last come to some arrangement of this nature. It is *very* doubtful whether I could carry into *complete* effect what it has been suggested to me . . . – and, if I could do so, it would be still more doubtful whether the result would be the prevention of all publication anywhere, anyhow, or at any time.[28]

Lord Dudley agreed that the best solution was to continue bribing Harriette. Knighton thought otherwise. Dudley wrote that Knighton 'seems inclined to defy the *heroine*, and for the present take no further steps about her . . . For my part I think I should rather have been disposed to try the effect of money given from time to time during good behaviour. If none had ever been given, the case would be different, but having already to say with truth that she has been bribed, I don't see any additional evil from a continuance of the same system.' Dudley continued that he had seen Ponsonby's letters to Lady Conyngham, and that he 'would not write on such a subject, even in cypher'.[29]

Knighton wrote on the same day, that 'under all circumstances nothing further should be done at present'. His advice won the Foreign Secretary round, and Dudley wrote to Bagot on 9 November, that 'When I saw Sir William Knighton last, he was still disposed to let the enemy do her worst. This is certainly the most courageous and the most prudent way.'[30] An advertisement in the *Morning Post* on 29 November announced that the new volumes of Harriette's *Memoirs* were now ready.

On 16 December, staying in Calais, Harriette wrote in desperation to Brougham who had ignored her previous letter. She reiterated her threat to reveal the continuation of their affair since his marriage and to '*publish* such truths as will sell'. She asked for £40 a year, or £30 if he could not afford more.[31]

Brougham sent Harriette £20 and an unsigned letter, both gestures clearly designed to irritate her. He knew she needed his advice and support too much for her to make an enemy of him. She acknowledged receipt of the bill on 9 January 1828.

– your letter without a signature can be good for nothing, and were you to die tomorrow, your heirs would laugh at my claiming 40 pounds a year from one unsigned note . . . This, or something to this effect, is all I require to be thankful and grateful to you:

I agree and engage myself to pay or cause to be paid to your order the sum of forty pounds annually in two half yearly payments of twenty pounds on each and every first of January and 1st of July in every year during your life time so long as you cause me no just or serious annoyance either by using my name or causing it to be used in any publication – or in any other way after this day the — 1828 and in the event of your [?survivance] I will make it a request that my heirs or executors keep up the payments regularly –

Signed —[32]

Brougham complied and began to send her six-monthly bills of £20. The next month he made the most celebrated speech of his political career, holding forth for six hours on law reform, sucking oranges as he spoke.

Harriette had still not settled with the King and on 19 January 1828 George wrote to Knighton from his sickbed that 'the Wilson business of yesterday has entirely knock'd me up & destroy'd almost all the little amount of strength I had . . .'[33] In early October, exactly a year since Rochfort's 'nefarious' visit, Knighton conceded defeat and Bagot was compelled again to send his envoy to Chimay. Rochfort was still living alone and the offer was made of an official situation for him and an annuity of £100 for Harriette, in return for her pledge not to disclose 'certain facts'. 'What can I do?' Bagot wrote to Knighton. 'I have of course not taken any notice of her letter, nor shall I now make any further move of any kind in the business until I hear again from you.'[34]

By June 1828 Harriette was living in Dieppe and wrote to Brougham – who had that year founded London University – to remind him to send his £20 'on the day it is due by your own agreement'. She was 'so miserably distressed, the least delay in my present very unfortunate circumstances will be severely felt, without being of the *slightest service* to you'. She added in a postscript that Lord Tankerville's payment to her was due on the same day as his own and that if Brougham should happen to see His Lordship, might he let him know that their mutual friend was 'much distressed and offer to forward me his £20'.[35] Harriette's next letters to Brougham are calmer and more businesslike. She had got what she wanted and while she never ceased to trouble him for more, she did not hold it against him when his door closed firmly against her.

Mr and Mrs Rochfort decided to return to England in late 1828. Rochfort's furnace project had gone disastrously wrong and he was looking elsewhere for employment. He wanted to become a clubbable part of the London elite and win the respect of the men who had once enjoyed his wife. That he remained unemployed suggests the King's dealings with Harriette had not gone well and, in August 1828, she wrote to Brougham to ask, not by way of a 'favour' but, 'in the name of common sense and common policy to turn over in your mind the talents of Rochfort and consider whether you can employ him in any way that may turn out useful to yourself or friends'. Rochfort might be a clerk, Harriette suggested; his 'extraordinary quickness of movement and resource in all manner of difficulty are rare and useful qualities; so active a mind – as fertile in invention and resources I never met with as [his]'. Her husband had 'extraordinary energies and abilities', was 'high flown and romantic', his word 'is more sacred than that of any persons I ever met with', and his 'style of quickness and cleverness' would suit Brougham's 'taste' entirely.[36]

On 25 May 1829, Rochfort sent Lord Aberdeen, who had the previous year replaced Dudley as Foreign Secretary, a copy of his letter to Bagot of three years before and told the Earl about 'the sequel' to the mysterious envoy's visit. It is typical of Rochfort to try to reap benefit out of past misfortunes and equally typical is the misfortune he has to relate. He had 'succeeded', he wrote, 'in erecting one of the most novel and best-working machineries in the country, and which was afterwards honoured by the visit of several ambassadors from Brussels', but he ran out of money and repaired to an address in Mayfair where he tried to get funding from several sources, including Brougham ('I can now only assure your lordship', Rochfort replied when Brougham refused the loan, 'that the said sum would have been *religiously* refunded before I left town. You have done and will do as you please about lending it – Circumstances of a nefarious nature added to the delay attendant on my visit to London, and my late arrest for debt, compel me to apply to you for the small loan of £25 or £30 . . .'[37]) Brougham, Rochfort said, warned him 'as to the dangers I should incure even in my Belgian establishment if I irritated in any manner the influential and almost omnipotent personages whose promises of support I bore, and calculated upon'.[38]

Rochfort had been reliant on the trust and patience of creditors in order to proceed with his furnace. His project was going well, he told Aberdeen, until:

my Lord the Ambassador's anonymous envoy arrived, and in very little better than a fortnight afterwards, the threat of this anonymous envoy began to be fulfilled! Creditors were induced to sue – my works were broken – and in less than six weeks I was declared a Bankrupt and consigned in the public points to Charleroi-jail, and if I was not conveyed there it was because I made my escape into France. The untouched stock on the premises was sold back to the very persons from which I had purchased it for little better than one half, and his Highness of Chimay paid me in August last year 8000 francs as a sort of indemnification for which I certainly felt so far grateful, that by law he was in no sense obliged to pay me anything, but I had expended forty five thousand!! . . . I now lay the case before your Lordship for such retribution as the wisdom of his majesty's government may consider right and tender.[39]

The Conyngham business having been kept secret and his not being one of Harriette's ex-lovers, Aberdeen had no idea who Rochfort was, what his letter was about or why he was trying to extort money from the government. He duly contacted Bagot, who told him that as he had been sworn to secrecy Aberdeen should consult Dudley in private about the matter. Bagot revealed only that Rochfort was the 'supposed husband' of Harriette Wilson and assured Aberdeen that 'no measures were taken or suggested or encouraged by me either directly or indirectly for the purpose, or which could possibly have the effect of injuring Mr Rochfort in any way publicly or privately in this country or elsewhere – [. . .] it is not within my knowledge that any such measures were taken by anyone else – and [. . .] to the best of my belief, they were never taken at all'.[40]

In November 1829, Ponsonby, returning home from three years in Argentina, stopped at Paris where he met with Sir Charles Stuart, Granville's predecessor as Ambassador. Stuart, he discovered, was buying Harriette's silence. Ponsonby wrote straightaway to Knighton, stressing his objection to 'the practice of any *concession* to her *demands*'. Paying blackmailers did nothing but encourage them, he argued. 'Nothing', he concluded, 'but my entire respect for Lady Conyngham could force me to abstain from instituting a prosecution against Mrs Wilson for attempting by letters menacing to bring false & foul charges against me, to extort money from me to buy her silence, and I avow myself unable to comprehend why her ladyship should submit, for one moment, to bear with the villainies of that woman. What can Lady Conyngham have to apprehend? She has her perfect innocence to support her, and, *if the accusations could be substantiated they go only to establish my villainy.* I alone could be branded.'[41]

As ever Ponsonby was irresolutely headstrong, conceding that while it would make Lady Conyngham uncomfortable, legal measures were the only way in which Harriette could be stopped. He informed Knighton that he had 'prepared everything & directed Counsel to be retained for prose-cution in that case'. Among the papers he had put in the hands of his lawyer was a letter from Harriette, 'in which she admits the injustice of what she had alleged against me and expresses her sorrow for what she had done'.[42]

Ponsonby described Harriette as an 'obscene harpy'.[43] In his reply, Knighton called her a 'vile woman', a 'wretched individual' a 'wretch' and a 'wicked monster'. He urged Ponsonby to 'adopt no legal proceedings. This is founded on the principle that you cannot relieve the feelings of the distinguished lady, mentioned in your letter, by dragging her name, and for ought you know, even her presence, into the court of Justice. The course to be pursued', Knighton concluded, 'was to take no notice what-ever of her wretched applications; to give her no money, and never to return the slightest answer to any of her letters.'[44] Ponsonby's response was that he must be expected to defend his character:

The calumnies which are threatened to be set forth are calumnies against *me*; if they could be substantiated they would fix upon me stigma of baseness and lying. I must not fail to guard myself against the appearance, at any future time, of having feared to meet those calumnies or of having been willingly accessory to any measures taken to prevent the calumnator carrying into effect *the threatening of a pub-lication* . . . I have had many letters from that woman threatening me to circulate the calumnies in question, I have never replied to any of them, nor had, directly or indirectly, the least communication with her. Contempt is her due – but when a printer divulged he had a publication almost ready to appear, I thought it neces-sary to let him know that I would try if the laws were not strong enough to protect me and to punish him. I have cause to believe that the man was afraid to venture further in his base intentions . . .[45]

He stressed once more that it was his intimate concern in the matter that led him to speak openly on it, that he would defend his name no matter what, and that he couldn't 'conceive how by doing so I can hurt anybody's feelings'. The traumatized Lady Conyngham would only respect his position. Nothing, Ponsonby concluded, had ever given him 'half of the pain I have felt from all that has happened . . . with this affair; I would willingly do anything to put an end to it forever were it possible to know what to do'.[46]

Ponsonby took Knighton's advice and said nothing, not answering Harriette's letters, eventually not opening them, and not taking her to court. His next diplomatic post was Constantinople, where Harriette continued to pester him. In the autumn of 1830, Brougham received the Great Seal and was elevated to the peerage. The King, increasingly delusional, had died in the summer – 'and on a Saturday, too', wrote Creevey. There was little mourning for George IV; in fact the London streets 'had more the appearance of rejoicing'.[47] The Marquis of Conyngham followed his monarch two years later, and Knighton breathed his last four years after that. Lady Conyngham, who had prayed for the King's recovery, looted Windsor Castle before leaving it. She died aged ninety-one in a country house in Kent.

It is there that the episode of Harriette's dealings with the King effectively comes to an end and the story folds back into silence. Since we do not know quite what hold she had on him, or what passed in the negotiations, it is impossible to judge whether in this, the apex of her blackmailing career, she was the winner or the loser. What we can say is that her demands, not just for money, but for a position for Rochfort, although not all were met, show her, as usual, astute in judging her power. The King's men paid heavily, in one way or another, for her silence. Harriette kept her secrets; the whole business was kept under wraps for over a century. The facts of the Conyngham crisis became known only when George IV's complete correspondence was published in 1938, and it is only now, after another seventy years, that the full extent of Harriette's threat to the crown has been revealed.

CHAPTER 24

Trevor Square

In the autumn of 1828, Harriette and Rochfort had returned to live in London. She claimed that she 'came to England with the best intentions and was endeavouring to write an unexceptionable book in quiet retirement', but she might well have been obliged to leave as part of the agreement with the French government.[1] Neither can have been enthusiastic about being back in England: Rochfort's latest venture had failed, he was without money or employment and had to face his creditors. Harriette's reception would, at the very best, be frosty. Despite protestations of dire poverty, she was wealthy enough to take a fourteen-year lease on a handsome corner house at 16 Trevor Square, a stone's throw from where Harrods now stands on the Brompton Road, and to furnish it extravagantly. Here the Rochforts lived with Julia la Toille, a pretty eighteen-year-old maid hired by Harriette in France.

Harriette was to move around Knightsbridge and its neighbouring Chelsea for the next sixteen years. When Harriette was growing up, Chelsea had been separated from Westminster by a marshy and derelict area called the Five Fields in which asparagus was grown. This swamp was now Belgravia and the two parishes were bridged, but Chelsea remained a village populated with nurseries and botanical gardens. Harriette, although not one 'for ruralising', found privacy here and a refuge from the harassment she would have endured in the West End, where

Regency Chairs, *The Book of Decorative Furniture*

Amy was working as a translator of Italian opera at the King's Theatre.[2]

Brougham, never out the picture for long, was informed by Harriette on her return of the sudden death of Mr Fermor. Fermor, an Irish relation of Mrs Fitzgerald, had been paying Harriette an annuity of £100 'on his life', the unexpected termination of which had 'reduced' her to 'such difficulty' that she was forced to ask for an advance on Brougham's own payment. 'No want of economy has been the cause,' Harriette stressed, '– I have endeavoured to avoid giving my friends trouble – but having brought a few necessary articles of furniture when Mr Fermor was in perfect health, I shall be forced to pay for them or be put immediately to endless expenses of law writs etc.' She had 'half finished a novel in the style of *Gil Blas*', she added, 'for which I have reason to expect profit'.[3]

Ten days later Harriette once more implored Brougham to employ Rochfort, for his 'method, love of order, knowledge of business, law' and his 'beautiful handwriting, free from blunders'. If Brougham was worried about Rochfort's infamy, she assured him that his face was not well known. Or, if it would lessen Brougham's embarrassment, Rochfort could easily go by 'Belville', his mother's name. Employing her husband would be the best way of getting rid of him, Harriette argued. 'If you had only employed Rochfort one week so as to be able to speak with truth of his excellent abilities you would be enabled to give him a few lines that would gain him employment elsewhere.'[4] Again, Brougham resisted.

In February 1829, Harriette was arrested for a physical assault on Julia la Toille. Her arrest was unusual – mistreatment of servants was not uncommon – and suggests that she was being closely observed. Harriette complained that La Toille, believing her employer owed her money, 'had applied to the French Ambassador as she would have done to a juge de Paris. The moment she used the name of Rochfort, they asked her if it was the author of the *Memoirs* – and then eagerly offered to assist her, and went with her to swear an assault to Miss Wilson, not Rochfort . . .'[5] When the police officers arrived at Trevor Square, Rochfort declared that there was no one in the house by the name of either Mrs Rochfort or Harriette Wilson; Harriette was discovered, however, making her exit, 'gliding – no, roll[ing], her gliding days [being] over – into a back room', and marched off to Marlborough Street.[6] La Toille swore that her mistress had pulled the chair from under her, thrown her on to her face, and threatened to lock her in her bedroom on a diet of bread and water. Harriette denied the charges, saying that she had merely shaken the chair while Julia was sitting doing needlework, and was surprised when the girl fell on to her face. She argued that she 'was renowned for her humanity and tenderness of heart' and had saved Julia from ruin after the maid gave birth to a bastard child.[7] She had tried, Harriette said, to instil religious principles into her employee but without success; Julia had stayed out in an improper fashion with Harriette's brother until four in the morning.

Harriette was again the focus of a delighted media. 'Harriette Wilson Once More!' trumpeted *Bell's Life in London*. She had not been seen in public for years and all eyes were upon her. She arrived at the Magistrate's Court wearing, it was reported, 'a fashionable black silk dress, with a rich cashmere shawl flung negligently over her shoulders, and her head surmounted by a huge French many-coloured bonnet, from the point of which hung a rich white silk veil, but of a texture delicate enough to afford a perfect and distinct view of the features of its owner'.[8] The defendant was dressed, wrote the *New Rambler's Magazine*, 'in the extreme of Gallic fashion, but oh! how changed – her manners were vulgar, her face hideously ugly, and she seemed to be about 55 years of age'.[9] 'The present appearance of this unfortunate lady', agreed *Bell's Life*, 'makes it difficult to conceive that she could ever have been attractive either as to person or manner; her features are now ugly and coarse, her person bad, and her manners vulgar, with a harsh, discordant voice. She appears now to be about 55 years of age'.[10] 'This notorious woman', continued the scurrilous hack, John Mitford, in the *New Rambler*

whose pen has laboriously recorded her own infamy, has after a lapse of years, again appeared in her proper sphere – a police office . . . If she had a relic of feeling left, she would rather have endured the insolence of ten servants, than expose her grey hairs and furrowed cheeks to the gaze of the mob who frequent police offices . . . but severe service, debauching by day, and bivouaking in Leicester Fields by night, have worn down her frame and hardened her . . .[11]

Following Harriette's re-entry to public life, *Bell's Life* published an *Ode to Harriette Wilson, alias Made. De Bouchère, alias Made. Rochfort, on her late appearance at the Marlborough Street Police Office*, which reveals how far she had fallen. The final verse ran:

No wonder when now fifty-five
You're better than when but fifteen
'Tis a pity you cannot contrive
To make yourself fit to be seen.
To Police Office when you were brought
By warrant, refusing to trot,
There was no one that saw you but thought,
'The sooner the better forgot.'[12]

The magistrate ordered Harriette to find bail and newspapers reported her boast that 'there were plenty of persons of the first consequence who would be happy to come forward' and that she would apply to Brougham and Lord Robert Manners. Harriette later assured Brougham that she had only muttered to Rochfort, in a 'low voice', that, 'perhaps Mr Brougham and Lord R. Manners might oblige me but I should not wish to ask them – I have nothing to reproach myself with in this matter and am disposed to take my chance', and that her private remark had been overheard and distorted.[13] Rochfort said he had extensive estates in Ireland and swore that he and Harriette were worth only £40 each. It was agreed that he could stand bail in jointure with Harriette, who lost her personal security and the elegant furniture Mr Fermor and Brougham had helped her to buy. Harriette was not, Rochfort told the court, strictly his wife. The couple then 'departed in a hackney coach, as they came'. The next day Rochfort appeared in court again, '"to eat his words" as to his possessions in Ireland. He denied that he said the estates were his – but asserted that he merely represented them to be his mother's. The recollection of the magistrates and the clerk was however, clear, that he had claimed the estates as his own, whatever might be the fact.'[14]

Panicked by the La Toille scandal and besieged by abusive and anonymous letters, Harriette leaned on Brougham. And, once more, she used Lady Conyngham as collateral. 'Perhaps, as my counsel,' she asked Brougham, 'you will not object to state in writing your candid opinion of the *justice* of my late arrest . . . It would be a hard case if insult is *ever* to be heaped on me, because the Conyngham's *dread* the publication of a comedy for which I have refused £1,000, desiring to have a harmless quiet life.' She was being persecuted because of her *Memoirs*, Harriette told Brougham, and since this I am to be held up to the public as an object disgusting old hideous and infamous the next time I am dragged out of my house for *nothing* I shall produce these private letters and send for Lord Mountcharles [Francis Conyngham] to back me – I may as well also hand over the Comedy to Stockdale for publication since I cannot fare worse . . . vainly should I say '*I would not publish*' for while I live they will *dread*, and . . . outlaw me – unless someone will settle the thing by making it our interest not to publish the play – as their friend could you point out any other way of settling their minds at rest? If not, I think you would recommend some fair arrangement to set the matter at rest *for ever*.

I am disposed to renounce for ever *all writings of a personal nature* – either of the Conynghams or any other family so that I am secure from being insulted and out-law'd – and so that I am decently provided for – if you think that it is not to the interests of all parties and particularly your friends Duke and Duchess of Argyle that some final settlement should be managed – you will of course act accordingly and I have only humbly to beg pardon for this trouble –[15]

Rochfort's battles with his mother were exacerbated by her disapproval of his relationship with Harriette. As he was dependent on maternal good will in the never-ending pursuit of his inheritance, Rochfort and Harriette agreed to live at separate addresses. 'All Rochfort's *hopes* with his mother, who is 90 years old, *depend* on her believing me not married and therefore I am willing to be *single*,' Harriette told Brougham in February 1829, just after the La Toille case.[16] Harriette stayed in Trevor Square until 1830 after which she never returned. Rochfort rented rooms on Berkeley Street West, Connaught Square.

Rochfort had stood by Harriette when she needed a husband and it suit-ed him now to be without her as a wife. The separation paid off. Harriette informed Brougham in August that 'Rochfort is now quite friends with his parent who I hope will in due time do something for him, probably pay the debts on his Irish estates'. She concluded her letter by asking for her annuity a few months early and reassuring him that she would 'never again be so distressed for it, since Rochfort has acquired economy by expe-rience and also a parent who can take care of him, as soon as she is *sure* of his reform'. In 1830, Rochfort asked Brougham to bring his case to the Commons in the next parliamentary term.

Rochfort's need for money had become desperate. His letter to Lord Aberdeen asking to be compensated for the 'nefarious' events of three years earlier having borne no fruit, that September Rochfort put pen to paper again, this time in a 'statement of facts' addressed to the Duke of Wellington. He told the Duke about the police raid at his and Harriette's home on grande rue de Chaillot in September 1825, which he believed was related to his association with the imprisoned General MacGregor. The police removed 'seals, books, charts, silver boxes, title deeds, portraits, about 500 or 100 small brass eagles (which, by the bye they said would turn out convicting evidence against me), as many buttons, sundry papers, and various other articles now out of my recollection, in all amounting to from £150–£200 in value'. Might the Duke, Rochfort asked, 'obtain . . . restitution of my property, with such redress as in your wisdom you may consider me entitled to receive'?[17] Wellington replied drily that while he was not the Secretary of State for Foreign Affairs, he 'would beg leave to observe to Mr Rochfort that before he applies to the offices in London on such a subject, five years after the cause of complaint had occurred, and after a revolution which had put an end to the Government under whose auspices the injury complained of had been done, he should have applied to the King's Ambassador in Paris'.[18]

Now that she and Rochfort were no longer keeping up appearances, Harriette was once more keen to test her powers of attraction. On 30 August 1829, she had begun to read Edward Bulwer Lytton's *Devereux*, and the next day she wrote to introduce herself to the lead player of the new genre, the 'fashionable novel'. Bulwer was very much to her taste; he was young (sixteen years Harriette's junior), handsome – a 'finished dandy' – and about to conquer society. He was an admirer of Byron, recently a part of Mayfair society (he had just moved into 36 Hertford Street) and from an ancient family. Five years earlier, aged twenty-one, he had an affair with the thirty-nine-year-old Lady Caroline Lamb. Bulwer was, like Harriette, fascinated by the disappearing world of which Byron and she had been a part. He wrote for money and produced a book each year; *Pelham* was published in June 1828, *The Disowned* in December 1828, *Devereux* in June 1829, *Paul Clifford* in 1830, *Eugene Aram* in 1832 and *Godolphin* in 1833. Four of the letters Harriette wrote to Bulwer survive, and for posterity he inscribed them with the following: 'These letters were written to me when I first came up to town, after my marriage and in my second year of authorship. Of course I never acceded to her wish to know me.'

It would be hard to imagine a more engaging fan letter than the one Bulwer received through his publisher, Henry Colburn, on 31 August 1829. Harriette was always at her best in her introductory letters; she enjoyed the challenge of writing to people she didn't know, teasing them out of formality, charming them into making her acquaintance. She also enjoyed the drama of self-presentation, playing the myth of 'Harriette Wilson' off against the reality. She writes here as one author to another; as ever, she assumes equality. She plays on Bulwer's fantasy that he is the new Byron, she flatters and teases as though she hasn't a care in the world, as though she is unaffected by the events of the previous four years and her bilious public reception. She has a sense of her own power, and her charm is strikingly more powerful than her rage.

None the less, this first letter is a complex document. While it seems on first glance that Harriette has lost none of her *joie de vivre* or her sexual confidence, a more concentrated read suggests precisely the opposite. She enjoys celebrated men and was at one time used to their company, but in trying her luck with current celebrities, twenty-nine years after running away with Lord Craven, seventeen years after first writing to Byron, she is showing her naivety. She has not yet accepted the passing of time. In the past she could rest on her reputation as the favourite of the fashionables when she wrote to strangers; what could she use as her selling point now that she was reviled? She cannot decide how to present herself to Bulwer; she is a fan, just like any fan, but she is also, she immediately lets him know, a fellow writer as well. She says she is an elderly lady (she is forty-three), but she wants to be seen as a girl. She lets him know that she is funny and smart, but also that she is lonely and disappointed, engaged in an unrequited epistolary love affair with an ugly and elderly man. She suggests that on meeting him she might not like Bulwer, but her worry is that he will not like her; she knows that she would enjoy his company regardless. In case he is repelled by her, she tells him that she is unavailable, and in the event that he is attracted to her, she suggests that her husband is pretty amenable. She is so used to drawing on her sexuality that she does not know how else to present herself, what other terms she can employ; rather than avoid the subject of her physical appeal altogether and play instead on her intellect, she lets him know that she is no longer sexually attractive. Harriette's letter gives us such a rich sense of her state of mind that it is worth quoting in full.

Sir

Though I have disliked reading all my life unless it was Shakespear's plays, yet I got to the end of Pelham. It was not a book to my taste either, for I thought the writer was a cold-hearted man, and his light chit-chat was pedantic, smelling of the *Lamp* – not so good as my own. But then it was a sensible book, the fancies brilliant, the thought deep, the language very expressive. In short, I got to the end of it. *The Disowned* I liked better still, and felt *very much* obliged to you for writing one of the few books I *can* come to the end of, with all my desire for amusement. But that imbecile [Mordaunt] who allow'd his wife to be starved like a helpless blockhead, *his* want of French philosophy made me *sick*. Do you consider that man virtuous or sensible whose *little* soul makes him ashamed of doing his duty in that state of life into which it may please God to call him? He had arms, legs, health and intelligence – why did he not clean his wife's room and white-wash the wall, earn her by his daily work a mutton chop, and then fry it for her à la Maintenon? . . .

Now for *Deveraux,* I have nearly finished the first vol and am so charmed with it, that I have laid it aside to tell you how proud I should be if you felt disposed to honour me your acquaintance. I merely *suggest* this to you because life is too short and too miserable for us to afford prudently to risk the loss of a possible pleasure for want of asking for it, and it is just *possible* that we might derive pleasure from being acquainted – not very probable, however, because I am not a bit agreeable except to those who are predisposed to like me and who appear to feel and understand all that is original or eccentric or amusing or likeable in my character at once. I am very shy, and when people do not flatter and encourage me by making me feel sure of their predisposition to like me, I am not a bit *amiable* because I am *gênée.* I am *not,* and never was, a general favourite; but nobody likes me a *little* or forgets me when they have once liked, understood and been liked by me. I am very ignorant and can't spell, but there is this advantage in not reading, you are all copies and I am the thing itself. You are sure if I say anything to strike or please you that it came out of my own little head.

What do you think about it? Perhaps you would like my society better than I should like yours, after all, entre nous, I *like contemplative people,* and so far you would suit my taste – but if there is no *comedy* in your composition, no genuine *Falstaff* (and I doubt it) none of the amiable folly of romance, without which no man has a good heart – we should bore each other – I could write you a much neater scrawl by copying, thinking, and using my *dictionary* but I can't take the trouble. It's such a *forlorn hope* that of your chusing to make my acquaintance. The chances are five hundred to one against me. I am *not,* however, ugly, as they describe me in the papers; but on the contrary rather handsome, particularly by candlelight when I am amused – although I was born at ten minutes before eight o'clock, the 22 February 1786 and christened at St George's Church – I love to be particular.

The beginning of *Devereux* is quite perfect in my humble opinion. I would not change a *line*, and I believe firmly that Walter Scott could not improve *one line* or thought up to page 266. You always fall off in love scenes, perhaps because your heart is dry and you want the romance, the thrill, the *body* of the thing to mix up with your visions; therefore you don't excite desire for your *heroines*, no man wants their sweet favours. Matilde (of Malechade) is *pure enough* for *your high flown notions*, yet she is drawn *the woman* and she excites passion. No matter, the fault (as I said to the Duke of Beaufort) 'is not in your heart but in your *want of heart*'.

I never heard your person described, but can fancy you a little fright just like Lord Dudley and Ward. No matter, I am sick of beauty, and the only small caprice I have encouraged for some time past is for a little fat, snub-nosed old gentleman of *high degree*, high in place too, whom I never beheld but once and that was 12 years ago. He was then at least five and forty, but his public character has *tête-monded* me, and me *only* perhaps. You would be surprised that his lordship should make any woman's dream of love, and yet I am *always* dreaming of the dear little fat old gentleman. I have told him in more charming letters than this that I adore him, and he only answers thus:–

'My dear Madam – Yours of the date of . . . came to hand on the 30th of . . . and I return you my sincere thanks for the many obliging expressions it contains, etc.'

Cut me, Mr Pelham, if you will, but give me no cut and dried '*dates of*' Oh!! To think that an ever tender enthusiastic elderly gentlewoman should be doom'd to love a little *fat man*, who in return gives her nothing but 'Yours Madam of the date of . . .'!!! However, I shall take a voyage to . . . where he resides and make an attack on him, unless you make me like you better. At present I have not a distant *presentiment* that it would be possible: I am only in love with your *last* work as far as I have read it, and have pleasure in expressing to the author my perfect glowing admiration of every line up to page 266. I have not begun the 2nd vol yet, as I only got the work yesterday.

I am not my own mistress, but if *entout bien et tout honneur* you were to write me word that you would not object to favour me with a visit some day – or will you take a walk with me some evening? I am much pleasanter to *begin with* when I am walking, because it is dark I thus get rid of my shyness or nervousness which is constitutional with me and renders me a bore to strangers until I am encouraged delightfully by a certain inward conviction that they like me enough to be indulgent.

Yours truly, and with high respects for your superior talents,
Harriette Rochfort
Author of the *Memoirs of Harriette Wilson*[19]

Harriette always exposed her most raw and vulnerable self in her postscripts, and in this case the anxieties expressed at the very end of her letter undermine the *laissez-faire* confidence she has spent the previous pages trying to present.

As a sensible man who can use your own excellent judgement I know that you will not like me *more* or less because I am abused – nor will you cause me any unpleasant tracasseries by the little vulgar trick of talking about me to others – Mr Rochfort would not mind my trying to make your *acquaintance* because he would know my *motive* to be really innocent and so it was with Lord Byron, who did not refuse my bold request except in the *first* instant, but I shall not ask *you* a second time – although if we never meet I shall always think of you with a feeling of such high respect as nobody but you and my little fat old gentleman of '*the date of +*' can inspire – I love *solitude* luckily, therefore shall not *die* though both of you are cruel –[20]

'From the Notorious Harriette Wilson', Bulwer wrote on the envelope, too conscious of his image to meet her, too flattered by her attentions to throw the letter away: '– I never saw her . . .'

A month later Bulwer sent what seems to have been a stuffy reply, saying that while he enjoyed her letter, they would not be meeting. He declined also to read her draft of *Clara Gazul,* the novel she had been writing since her return to England. Harriette responded immediately. Despite his '*dead cut*', she was determined to push their relationship forward and having licked her wounds she continued to joust with him. 'I know from your writing that you are thin and bilious and severe,' she teased. 'I should say dry, not graceful; but one wants variety, I should like your shrewd wisdom for a change; harsh it might sound to a lady's ear, after the gentle, voluptuous graceful luxurious Argyles or Ponsonbys . . . I will tell you what would make a perfect novel – you write all but the love scenes and send them for me to draw.' She now writes as a friend, she tells him, rather than a prospective lover, 'Believing you married, I only desired the honour of your acquaintance under the impression that love or desire for me *now* was entirely out of the chapter of possibilities, and that no wife would pay me the compliment to object to my occasionally enjoying the benefit of a little chat with her husband.' But what is most striking in these letters is the force of Harriette's fantasy about Bulwer, the extraordinary strength of her imaginative engagement with a man she does not know at all. She projects on to him great waves of trust and affection, offering him her most fragile thoughts and feelings.

I have many causes of melancholy just now, from the circumstance of the probable necessity that will exist (for Mr Rochfort's interests with his parents, who are *methodists*) for our seeming to [have] separated and living in separate homes – all this so very dull for us both, but my first object is his success. I would live to see him exerting his brilliant talents *usefully* and beautiful as he is, his real friend (c'est moi) his little merry companion in a prison will *never* be forgotten – though all the noble dames in Europe should woo him to their arms. I could really . . . amuse you with the desperate attacks that ladies are constantly making on the heart of Rochfort – his charms drive them mad!! And for his blue eye they lay aside all delicacy . . .[21]

It is doubtful that Harriette thought about Bulwer at all between letters, but while she was writing to him he utterly absorbed her. And, as with Byron, she wished to make the socially ambitious, vain young writer feel as if he were the only man in the world.

In January 1830, *Clara Gazul* appeared anonymously in three volumes. While publishers in general might well have been cautious about touching Harriette's work, Stockdale, despite the risk involved and losses he had already suffered through his relations with her, was still willing. Harriette, however, wanted to be free from any more of his interference and general mischief-making, and published the book herself from Trevor Square. She prefaced *Clara Gazul* with a *Notice to the Public* warning of Stockdale's editorial habits, confirming that much of what appeared in Parts 13 onwards of her *Memoirs* was not her composition, and stating that any *Memoirs* that might subsequently appear in her name will now be her own work. 'I give this information very reluctantly, as I should be sorry to injure the father of a family of whom with the above exception I have no cause to complain.'[22]

Clara Gazul also included an Introduction containing an account of Harriette's early life, and a Preface in which she told how 'an illustrious and in my opinion very amiable nobleman' (most likely to be George Lamb) recommended that she write a light novel, and how a 'gentleman belonging to the company of Edinburgh reviewers' (most likely to be

Henry Brougham), 'a well-known Whig from principle, a poet by inclination, a dramatist from taste . . . an athiest *par excellence* and a very gouty subject *malgré lui*' had reassurred her that 'the knowledge that it was written by
you would ensure a sale so that at least people would be forced to pay you
before they could abuse'. Harriette's eponymous heroine seems to be unrelated to the Spanish actress of Prosper Mérimée's invention; but as
Harriette was living in Paris during 1825, when Mérimée's *Théâtre de
Clara Gazul* was popular, the choice of name cannot have been fortuitous.

Plot, something in which Harriette had little interest, does not make an
appearance in *Clara Gazul*. 'It is what I fear I have no sort of taste or talent
for, and the reader may despise my brief attempt in that department, without the possibility of making me think worse of myself than I have done
hitherto.' Stockdale, on the other hand, saw plots everywhere and had he
been able to advise her on the novel he might have improved it. Stockdale
had his faults but he recognized where Harriette's skills lay, and as far as
generating publicity goes he was without peer.

Clara Gazul, which draws on Harriette's skills of caricature, is a *roman à
clef* of sorts, where the Duke of Inveraray stands for Argyll, Canwin for
Canning, Birch for Brougham, and General MacGregor is wittily represented
as the Cazique, the ludicrous King of Poyais. Harriette's representations
are fond and tame; there seems to have been no extortion involved and
besides, on this occasion she wanted to be taken seriously as a writer. In
eight of the book's best pages, Harriette dramatizes herself as the incom-
parable 'Harriette *Memoirs*', a woman of refinement, modesty and truth,
with gleaming eyes and a voice like music. Here Harriette reveals the
strength of her self-esteem and some of the secrets of her success:

Observe Harriette *Memoirs* in the society of a man she respects and desires to
attach, you will then see one of the most pleasant and amiable unlearned women
in England; playful in her wit, which is the more piquant from the almost imper-
ceptible dash of libertinage which serves but to excite curiosity; – respectful in her
address, she has the knack of inspiring those whom she would please, with esteem,
as well as love. No one knows how to flatter more agreeably, and when a person
feels convinced that she is deeply impressed with his merits, can he fail to respect
her for her superior understanding?

. . . During her whole career, she has honourably discharged every debt she has
ever contracted, and when in the hurry of leaving a foreign country, anything was

forgotten, she never failed to forward the sum due to her creditor after her arrival in England.

. . . Harriette's misfortune is ill health; her best qualities are her love of truth and singleness of heart. At this period, when her youth has passed away, she is infinitely more refined in her taste, and more difficult in her choice of society, than she was formally.

If her face has lost its youthful beauty, perhaps it has gained something in character and expression; and with regard to her talents for conversation, these are unquestionably improved by time and reflection, aided by her good sense.

. . . If her person is pretty, her clothes are hung about it so loosely, that it is difficult to guess what they conceal or disguise.

. . . Romantic to excess, with an imagination that can create a busy little world of her own, she prefers solitude to the society of persons who fall short of high superiority in her opinion.

I take Harriette to be a very high-couraged person whose strength of mind would be found equal to any sudden emergency. Though the world call her profligate, she is strict and severe in her principles of candour and honesty . . . Her temper and disposition are happy, for she can amuse herself harmlessly in solitude and never find the day long enough for her occupations.[23]

Harriette had great hopes for *Clara Gazul*, but it sank like a stone. She had imagined that it would reward her with money and reputation. She wanted the book to be a female *Gil Blas*, full of the unsentimental pace and variety of the picaresque. Usually so grounded in her estimation of her talents, Harriette had no sense of where her merits as a writer lay. She was unaware of the difference in quality between her autobiographical writing – in which she shone – and her attempts at formal literature. She was unaware that she had already produced the female *Gil Blas* in her *Memoirs*. Harriette Wilson's name alone was not enough to promote the sales of a mostly lifeless novel.

Rochfort, meanwhile, continued to write to those running the country, offering his help and asking for theirs. He had drawn Brougham into his inheritance sagas and reminded him on 16 November 1830, to 'consider his case' in Parliament.[24] As Brougham that month took on the office of Lord Chancellor and became a Cabinet Minister in Grey's Coalition Government, he might have been too busy to reply. If this was the problem, Rochfort had the solution; on 26 November, he suggested that he become the Chancellor's secretary. Passing his house on Hill Street the previous day, Rochfort had been struck by the 'mountain almost' of post that Brougham was expected to 'wade through'. Rochfort's duties might be, he suggested without irony, to read through all Brougham's confidential letters and report on them. The next day Rochfort wrote again to Brougham, offering his mother as surety.[25] Brougham suggested, with a certain amount of self-interest, that Rochfort might find employment in Ceylon and he offered to use his influence with the Governor there. Rochfort was excited, believing that he would make a good 'supernumary to any office or duty of his household',[26] but nothing came of the plan. Rochfort then spent the spring of 1831 inventing a secret writing which he showed to Brougham. His code, he said, was 'so simply contrived that a child with the key may in a minute work it, at the same time so complex and combined that without the key and instruction, I can defy the most ingenious decypherer to read a syllable of any Government despatch or other document so transmitted'.[27] Brougham praised it as 'a masterpiece of simplicity and complexity combined' and introduced Rochfort to Palmerston, now Foreign Secretary. Palmerston left Rochfort's code with his decyphering bureau for three months and then 'admitted that it quite surpassed the ingenuity of his "clever fellows" and pronounced the system "inscrutable".'[28] Rochfort's scheme was not adopted by the government but he eventually published it in 1836 as *A Treatise upon Archanography*.

Stockdale spent part of 1830 in the Whitecross Street Prison in the City, and his family moved to 8 Carlton Street in St James's. In the autumn of 1831, following his release, he brought out the eight-volume edition of Harriette's *Memoirs*. This included the full transcript of the *Blore* v. *Stockdale* trial, a detailed justification of his mistreatment in the *Fisher* v. *Stockdale* trial, a long account of the *Onwhyn* v. *Stockdale* piracy trial, copies of aggressive letters he had sent to the press, *An Introduction and A Non-Dedicatory Epistle to My Lords the King's Justices, The King's Sergeants, The King's Counsel, and Others, Whom it may Concern* (which he reproduced from his *Budget*), an account of the *Seduction and Attempted Suicide of one Eliza Eliot*, a case in which Stockdale involved himself in his usual heroic style (which story, he said, would have appeared in his *Budget* were that publication still in circulation), the letters exchanged with his wife while in the Fleet (four hundred pages alone, entitled *Persecution*), an account of Harriette's early life, written by Stockdale and lifted from her Introduction to *Clara Gazul*, and various other pieces of Stockdaleiana which he felt would benefit the public. Harriette's 1825 novel, *Paris Lions and London Tigers*, is given a volume to itself, and one-and-a-half volumes are taken up with Stockdale's eccentric index to the new *Memoirs*. His entry on Fisher takes up six pages alone and refers readers to examples of Fisher's being 'A hungry scoundrel', 'A blood sucker', and 'A lean-gutted voracious harpy'. References to Stockdale and his family consume thirty-six pages; 'To bear all blame' is a typical allusion to himself, as are 'Indulgent', 'courtesy to the Countess of Clare', 'Why', 'wronged by the Judge', and 'One law for him being publisher of Harriette Wilson and another for all the world besides'. For those interested in Julia Johnstone (who gets only eight pages), they are referred to the occasion on which she 'first submitted to Cotton, on a stone-stair-case'. Also included in the eight-volume edition, almost as an afterthought, are Harriette's now complete *Memoirs*, including Parts 13 onwards.

Stockdale was as blind to his talents as Harriette was to hers, and never doubted that his persecution would grip the public imagination as much as Harriette's revelations had done. It is one of Stockdale's most remarkable characteristics that while he persisted in believing in the power of the press to effect change, he had no awareness of the vital role played by his readers in achieving this end. Stockdale had no vision at all of his audience, of who they were, of what might interest them, what their boredom levels might be, or where their sympathies might lie. Nor had he any idea of how to present himself or his story in an appealing way. Despite proclaiming that the nation would be improved by hearing of his plight, Stockdale wrote for himself and 'posterity' and not for those who parted with money to read his publications, those without whom the press had no power at all.

The additional two volumes of *Memoirs* in the 1831 edition were mainly composed from those instalments published in 1827–28. Not only were these supplementary volumes unevenly and rather aimlessly written by Harriette in the first place, but in Stockdale's hands they were lumpenly rewritten and poorly edited. Stockdale's and Harriette's styles differ so markedly that it is not hard to see where he may have tried to influence the book. As Harriette puts it, 'Whenever a sentence occurs, duller than the rest, be assured that he has spoiled it by the substitution of his dullness for my vivacity.'[29]

Some of what Stockdale published in the final volumes Harriette had produced in 1825, but he added more recent material as well, such as a preview of Harriette's comedy *Bought in and Bought out*, which was begun in 1829 and in which she threatens to expose Lady Conyngham among others.[30] Because Harriette frequently interrupts her accounts of the past with reference to contemporary events (letters just received, news just heard), notice has to be paid to chronology. But Stockdale ignores dates and jiggles about with Harriette's text, clumsily cutting and stitching pages together until he makes from her prose as disfigured and unpresentable a monster as the author was seen to be herself.

His postscript to this edition confirmed Stockdale's ongoing commitment to blackmail as a profession. Those anecdotes which did not appear in the *Memoirs* would be published in '"Holly-Grove",' he declared, 'of which it will only be necessary for him to state that the first, and by far, least amusing part has already gone through eleven editions, and that what remains of publication will include not only the members of both houses of parliament, but directly and indirectly, almost every family of consequence in the United Kingdom. Lord Ponsonby, the Dowager Duchess of Clare, and the Marchioness of Conyngham etc.' Any further revelations of Harriette's will be published here as well.[31] There are no surviving copies of *Holly-grove*.

Stockdale's next project was *Mad-houses*, written under the *nom de plume* of Thomas Little and concerned with the maltreatment of a prostitute by both her protector and her doctor. On 4 October 1831, Stockdale wrote to Ferdinand Jeyes, an attorney of Chancery Lane: 'Sir – Having this day completed the *Memoirs* of Harriette Wilson, which now extends to eight volumes, before I consign to the same Editor, those papers which detail your flagrant seduction of Elizabeth Stabback, I think it right to communicate such intention to you.'

John North, the doctor concerned who lived in Upper Berkeley Street, received a similar threat. Several other 'gentlemen of distinction' were then informed that 'Stockdale has printed a shilling book, under the title of Mad-houses. Its contents are such as cannot possibly escape notice, therefore the sooner you take your steps the better, and the more particularly from the way in which your name has been introduced into the late volumes of Harriette Wilson.' There was no signature. One recipient placed his letter in the hands of magistrates and wrote to *The Times*. 'One of our correspondents', the paper's editor informed the public, 'writing to us on this subject, says, "I took no notice of the receipt of this letter, but the day before yesterday a shabby fellow called at my office, to know if I had received such an epistle. I happened, unfortunately, not to be in, and he left a message, stating that it would be much better for me to see Mr Stockdale on the subject, or to write to him, as he was not to be intimidated." Our correspondent acted very properly in taking no notice of this disgraceful attempt to extort money; but let him know, and others who are situated like him, give directions that the "shabby fellow" be laid by the heels the next time he calls.'[32]

Stockdale then applied to the Literary Fund for help to finance his new journal, *The Probe*. The 'objects of the present hebdomadal' were 'to establish RIGHTS, to redress WRONGS, to probe WOUNDS, whether of the BODY or the MIND, to correct ABUSES, public and PRIVATE . . .'[33] The Literary Fund ignored his request. Stockdale returned to prison in 1833 for 'conspiracy to extort money', following which he sued the authorities for wrongful imprisonment. At the end of the year he sent a petition to the House of Lords to set aside the judgment of the Lord Chief Justice in the Onwhyn trial seven years before, and swore at the public office that he was not worth more than five pounds. He was imprisoned again and on his release in 1835 wrote to Brougham about his new set of revelations, the 'Secret Memoirs of George IV'. He continued to write to Brougham all year, sending him copies of the latest petition he had drawn up, filling him in on Elizabeth Stabback, the victim of *Mad-houses*, informing him of any worthy cause His Lordship might support, asking if he could dedicate to Brougham his forthcoming memoir of the early days of Percy Bysshe Shelley. Stockdale then began a long legal battle with the Hansard family, using Brougham as his attorney, when they described as 'obscene' the book he had published of anatomical prints. The case, which turned on more interesting points of law than his previous trials had done, continued to entertain Stockdale until almost the end of his life.[34]

Following the 1831 *Memoirs*, Stockdale's relationship with Harriette Wilson clouds over and is blotted from view. Theirs had been one of the great literary partnerships of the nineteenth century; Stockdale had marketed Harriette and himself with unprecedented style. Although they were never, so far as we know, to meet again, Stockdale's investment in Harriette was not quite over.

CHAPTER 25

Mary Magdalen

Harriette's life changed dramatically in December 1831. Rochfort fell in love with the wife of Mr Thomas Wyatt of the Bengal Civil Service and the couple began living together, thus scuppering Rochfort's hopes for improved relations with his mother. Mrs Wyatt was 'destitute' following the demise of her marriage and she and Rochfort were penniless.[1] The following year, he at last found a vocation: Dom Pedro of Brazil was trying to oust his brother, Dom Miguel, from the throne of Portugal, and Rochfort went out as commander of an artillery brigade to help Dom Pedro's cause. When he returned to London, having now attained the colonelcy it had been presumed for the last ten years he already had, it was Mrs Wyatt's arms and not Harriette's into which Rochfort fell.

Writing to Ponsonby in March 1832, Harriette complained that as 'Mr Rochfort was abroad' she was, in her 'difficulties alone in your mercy',[2] and in a letter to Bulwer that November, she referred to Rochfort's trip to 'Dom Pedro' and called herself a 'grass widow'.[3] Did Harriette not want it known that the man whom she had boasted to Bulwer would never be 'wooed into the arms of another woman' had done precisely that? Or did she continue to describe Rochfort as her husband because it was still useful to pass herself off, as she had done for the previous nine years, as a respectable married woman? Either way, she never mentioned Rochfort

Patent Bread Works, Pimlico, *Views of London*

again – Harriette tended to erase those episodes which wounded her – and the following year she reverted to her original name of Dubouchet.

The year 1832 was bad for Harriette, and her unhappiness cannot have been unrelated to Rochfort's departure. Theirs had been a relationship of financial convenience but Rochfort had also been her friend and defender and it was their closeness and his support she was missing. Harriette was now living near the Thames in Pimlico, at 69 Vauxhall Bridge Road. That she was more than ever locked in the past suggests her present life was empty and she had nothing to hope for in the future. She wrote passionate letters to Ponsonby on a regular basis, probably after quite a bit of gin, probably at night when she could not sleep. Harriette had shone in her blackmail campaign; the sharp focus of her mission made all else fall away and she emerged from her letters crystal with precision. There is no such pleasure or precision in the following letter to Ponsonby; she feigns a toughness and a purpose that she lacks, and the rage that had previously given her polish is now the cause of her disintegration. She describes the hurt caused by Ponsonby's leaving her for Sophia as if she had not even begun to recover from it. The loss of Rochfort, who always reminded her of his Ponsonby cousin, had opened Harriette's old wounds, piling grief on grief, making it no longer clear who or what it was being mourned. Her letter lashes out in all directions and so misses its target; she knows that she is striking the wrong note, that she is unrecognizable as the 'little fellow' Ponsonby once teased or the 'angelick Harriette' he adored, but she is beyond control. In wanting him to return the money she had refused to accept twenty-five years before, Harriette is asking for a sign that Ponsonby had at least once cared for her, that the past has some significance for him, and that she has something of her old appeal. His refusal to meet her demands does more than undermine Harriette's version of their history; it undermines her version of herself and strips her life story of its meaning. If she was a good person it was because Ponsonby had thought so, if she was lovable it was because he had loved her. Ponsonby was Harriette's turning point and the yardstick against which all her other relationships, before and after, were measured and found wanting. And Harriette's life was the sum of her relationships. It became a matter of principle to her that Ponsonby acknowledge her present financial need just as she had once acknowledged his, 'I don't see how you, with your high pride can refuse me the sum you received from me after you had bestow'd it on me – particularly as you know my generous motive for not accepting it at the time –' Her letter ends with a threat, but now that the King was dead there was no remaining interest in an affair between the old royal mistress and another man that took place over thirty years before. Besides, Harriette is not writing to blackmail Ponsonby; she wants him to give her the money *willingly*, because he understands her. She wants the understanding between the two of them to return.

I was vilely brought up, my nature was disguised; from under the mark of profligacy, false pride, shyness, and bad habits – you never read my heart – you thought me what false childish pride – error in judgement and taste made me affect to be – could you have understood what in truth was noble in my character – had you known what really was the case – that H. Wilson's attachment for you would have been equal to the sacrifice of her life a thousand times over, that neither age or poverty or any wretchedness of yours, or future temptation falling in my way, could have made me waver in my faith, supposing you had but told me you wished me to be yours only – or that my constancy could make you happy – *perhaps* (so I reflected) if this man had known the stirling natural steadiness of my affections he would have felt *some* friendship for me. If your conduct was profligate and heartless as regards Sophia, if it was somewhat unfeeling as regarded the pecuniary difficulties you left me to struggle with – while my health and spirits were subdued by your desertion – still it may be said in extenuation that my high spirit and false pride were all exerted to blind you and conceal from me my distress both of mind and pocket. You *never understood me* – let me hope that if you *had* known me well and *truly*, I should not have had course to think so ill of you –

. . . It was hardly fair to leave even a common acquaintance of years without a guinea – and I have never received one from you since I returned your last donation – I leave it now to your good feelings, assuring you in truth that much as I have enjoyed abusing you myself I never can endure to hear of the German's [*sic*] doing it, considering myself the only privileged person in that particular.[4]

Three months later, on 26 June 1832, just after he had seen his Reform Bill approved by Parliament, Brougham received a long and desperate letter from Harriette. It is the last he preserved from her. She was irritated that he had sent Lord Tankerville to negotiate with her in the hope that she would 'annoy' him no further. She was ill with gout, the bailiffs had removed much of her furniture and she had been forced to sell other possessions in order to pay the rent. Brougham had sent her money but Harriette wanted confirmation that he was acting not out of fear but from genuine affection and concern. As with Ponsonby, Harriette brings up their past relationship of which she has vivid and bitter memories, reminding Brougham of how he ill-treated her and cut her when he married, chastizing him for having never 'understood' her. 'You were attentive to my wishes when I had *no great affection for you in Paris* . . . instead of treating me as a clever ignorant friend who would have liked to have grown wise by your knowledge and reasons, you thought it necessary *de faire l'aimable* and talk small talk to me as if you had made a fool of the soft sex to please . . .' She resumes her blackmail threats; she will *have* to publish her anecdotes if this is the only way to make a living, and she takes him to task for his self-serving 'support' of her in the Conyngham affair. 'If I must show you up my preface shall contain a copy of this and one or two other of my letters to you lately in which I declare I mean "that the *poverty you* subject me to, and *not* my will consents".' Finally, she wants his payments to her dramatically increased, from £40 a year to £40 a quarter.[5]

Lord Berwick died in Naples inthe autumn of 1832. From Paris, Harriette sent her consolations to his brother and heir, William Noel Hill. She also took the opportunity to ask the new Lord Berwick for money. 'I am desperately ill,' she told Bulwer later that month, back now in Pimlico, 'and the mind wears out with body, but I fear you will be so unhappy if you don't hear from me now and then before I die.' Writing to Bulwer, Harriette was again sharp, shrewd and amusing. She continued to praise his novels, teasing him that *Pelham* was 'but a bad edition of H. Wilson's *Memoirs* after all', before hitting on some home truths. 'Don't be such a *pedant*,' she joked, drawing on his priggishness towards her. 'Condescend to exert your playfulness and humour if you have any, in order that we may digest your dry solids. Be agreeable as well as wise and musty. Goodbye.'[6] Bulwer most probably feared Harriette's mockery and this was one reason he resisted a meeting; she had, after all, made fun to him of her 'short fat man with the snub nose' and it had not taken her long to pick up on Bulwer's own less attractive qualities: his stuffiness, pride and pedantry.

In the postscript to her letter, Harriette, as usual, shifts gear. Having got the better of Bulwer with her intellect and wit, she now loses her poise, ridicules herself, hands him all the power and puts him in a position to reject her. 'When shall we swear eternal love?' she suddenly asks. 'Still, up to the date hereof, my passion is quite a fervour grown. It attracts elderly ladies . . . I suppose, when the lover is hot blooded and yet cold in imagination. *We* . . . don't know what the duce to make of him, he charms and puzzles us with his calm head and sensitive passions, till he drives us mad!'[7] Harriette was hell-bent on sabotaging herself.

William Lamb, now Lord Melbourne, took over Lord Grey's Whig ministry in 1834. In the same year he began an affair with Caroline Norton, the daughter of Tom Sheridan, which became a national scandal. Harriette Wilson, who was rumoured to have been Melbourne's mistress, had been protected by his brother, Frederic, and Grey's brother-in-law, Ponsonby. She had also been the courtesan of two of the previous Tory prime ministers, Wellington and Canning, and Palmerston's ministry was yet to come. The lives of Harriette's old friends were increasingly gaining the definition that hers had lost. Even Rochfort's life was more purposeful than her own; he had been recommended by Brougham for a secret mission to Brussels, the object of which was a 'tortuous domestic affair of inheritance, adultery and lunacy' in the Wellesley family,[8] most probably concerning the Duke of Wellington's dissolute nephew, 'Wicked William' Long Wellesley, whose public and private behaviour was rarely out of the papers. By the end of the year, Wellesley and Rochfort were at one another's throats. In September, Wellesley wrote to Palmerston, then Foreign Secretary, calling Rochfort 'a man of infamous refute'. Rochfort demanded a public apology, which Wellesley refused to give. Captain Close, a friend of Rochfort's, then asked for a meeting with a friend of Wellesley's. Wellesley was denounced as a 'coward' by another party, leading Rochfort to refuse to fight with him; Rochfort was called a 'delinquent' by Wellesley, who refused a meeting on those grounds. Rochfort wrote to Wellesley saying that he was determined to communicate with him, but only 'through the medium of an ash plant or a double thronged Crowther horse-whip'.[9] Rochfort later recalled with pride his role in the secret mission, reminding Brougham in years to come (at the same time as asking to be recommended for an office in Ireland under the newly appointed Secretary, Sir William Somerville) of 'the long standing acquaintance subsisting between us' and of the professionalism with which he had dealt with the Brussels trip.[10] The mission 'did not terminate successfully', Rochfort conceded, but it 'failed from no fault or remissness on my part as both Lord Devon and I think the Duke of Wellington will admit'.[11] Both Devon and Wellington, Rochfort again reminded Brougham in 1846, 'say how faithfully I discharged their trust, and at a recent trial in the Court of Chancery in London, Lord Wellesley . . . has bourne out faithfully everything forecast by me . . .'[12]

Harriette, meanwhile, who had begun calling herself Mrs Du Bouchet, was following the career path of a retired prostitute by procuring young women for gentlemen of the 'first nobility'. In August 1834, she wrote to Ponsonby from her present address at 2 Park Row, Knightsbridge, reminding him again of the annuity she had turned down and suggesting that his refusal to return the money was because she had once suggested that he was not handsome enough. At this point in the letter she sounds drunk, and while she recovers some dignity later there is no sign of her old spark. She was, Harriette told him, 'still cheerful, thank God, though slowly but surely *dying*, and too weak to walk half a mile; looking so *fair* and *delicate* that I am quite a different person to the H. Wilson you knew me – some say the fairness became me – I certainly do not look so *ugly* as might be expected which signifies but little to one who leads the life of a hermit'. The purpose of her letter, Harriette continued, was to inform him of a young lady, Miss Buchan, 'in love with my [Harriette's] mind and memories', who had applied to her to be 'set up in trade' as a 'fashionable whore'. Would Ponsonby, as a man of 'honour', 'good taste', 'morals' and 'manners', be interested in an introduction? If so, he could save the child from 'the Dogs'.[13]

Had Ponsonby read Harriette's letter (he kept it unopened and it was found in this state in 1984), he would have seen how little its content differed from the previous letters she had sent him. Harriette's subject was still the past; what, if anything, it had meant to him, how they could return there. Ponsonby would have seen that the 'handsome' dark-haired girl described, with the 'delicate white skin', who wore only white and was quite 'mad', represented to Harriette her younger self. By asking him to 'save this person' whose life was in the balance, Harriette was asking if he had once been willing to save *her*, if he blamed himself for her demise, if he at all remembered Harriette's *own* charms. The analogies between Harriette and Miss Buchan continue; this is a girl, she told Ponsonby, whose 'bad taste' a 'man of real good taste could entirely change', who could be induced 'to read and improve', who had '*vow'd* [to] never marry' and to 'lead a public not a *private* life', who insisted she was 'shy' and that men 'ought to understand' her, who was 'obstinate' as 'the wind' and wanted to 'enjoy life for a few years now instead of being buried alive with her mother'.[14] Her life could go either way, and her fate was up to Ponsonby. Harriette's charge for the introduction would be £100. She might have continued writing to him, but there are no other letters from Harriette in the Ponsonby archive.

Sometime after 1834, Harriette moved to 2 North Cottages, Princes's Street, south of the Brompton Road. Her house looked out over fourteen acres of land owned by the Smith Charity Estate and a large market garden called the Quail Field. Beyond that could be seen the Chelsea Pavilion. In thirty years' time, Harriette's cottage would be razed to make way for the expansion of Chelsea; the barley fields, hawthorne hedges, shrubs and clover would be paved over by Lennox Square, and Princes's Street would become Rawlings Street. By the end of the decade, the young Queen Victoria would be installed less than a mile away in Buckingham Palace. By the end of the century the Metropolitan and District underground line would run beneath the site where Harriette's cottage had been.

Many years before, Harriette had fantasized about her old age. She relished the idea of settling into her eccentricities and describes herself in a letter to Byron as a benign witch, toothless and unrecognizable, full of nostalgia and without regret. 'I . . . hope that we shall one day (some twenty years hence) take a pinch of snuff together before we die; and as you watch me, in my little pointed cap, *spectacles*, bony ankles and thread stockings, stirring up and tasting my *pot au feu*, you'll imagine Ponsonby's Worcester's and Argyle's *Angelick Harriette*.'[15] According to the one account there is of Harriette Wilson during her years in Chelsea, her vision was not far from the truth. She and Byron were never to share their pinch of snuff, but her famous features had taken on the almost preternatural gleam of the sorceress. George Sala, son of the once famous operatic singer, Madame Sala, remembered Harriette in her fifties as 'a wonderful old hag, who lived on lucifer matches and gin in a little hovel at Chelsea, but with a bright eye and a skin as white as milk'.[16]

Berkeley Craven shot himself in 1836 after losing at the races, and the Duke of Argyll died in 1839. Amy's husband, Bochsa, created another scandal that year when he eloped with the soprano Anna Bishop. It is not known if he was still married to Amy at the time; nor do we know how long Amy lived or what became of either her or her children. In 1841, Frederic Lamb at last married, taking as his bride Alexandrina, Countess von Mahltzahn, the daughter of the Prussian Envoy to the Court of Vienna. She was thirty-six years his junior and their relationship had caused quite a stir. For many people, Harriette was still a heroine; she had proved what they suspected to be true about the moribund morality of the landed aristocracy. In 1838, an anonymous novel appeared called *Eliza Grimwood, A Domestic Legend of Waterloo Road*, which fictionalized the much discussed case of the murder of a prostitute at Wellington Terrace, Lambeth. Popular rumour had it that she was killed by one of her aristocratic clients – supposed by the majority to be the Duke of Cumberland – who feared that Eliza might 'do' a Harriette Wilson and expose him. In the novel, Eliza falls into prostitution when a libertine lord plots to deprive her of her fortune. It is in her new life that she first reads *The Memoirs of Harriette Wilson*:

She had heard this work spoken of on more than one occasion. The Earl had mentioned it, and spoke contemptuously of its contents, as neither containing wit, wisdom, nor the reverse; he declared it to be nothing but vapid scandal, which had not even the merit of being entertaining. To this, Davidson and another gentleman, who were present at the time, had given a different opinion; and rallied the Earl on his dislike of the *Memoirs*, by alleging that he himself figured in them; and that it was his youthful rakishness therein exposed which made him decry the book. His lordship did not deny that he had once felt annoyed at seeing himself exposed in such a work, but that he had long since ceased to have any uneasiness on the subject, while his opinion of its silliness was still the same. Some apology was made to Eliza for having spoken of such a work in her hearing; the consequence was that she could not rest satisfied until she had procured the *Memoirs* and read them.

She saw nothing so very reprehensible as the Earl declared the work to be! While many portions of the heroine's life affected her with much interest. She felt a sympathy which was perhaps peculiar to herself. Harriette Wilson had not been married to any of the noblemen who sought and gained her society, as she, Eliza, was to the Earl; but the snare that had been laid by noble, rich, middle-aged men, was the same in both cases.[17]

The great Brummell died in a madhouse in Caen in 1840, aged sixty-one. He had lost first his style and then his mind; elegance and reason had always been inseparable in his philosophy. 'Like the orator, the great actor, the conversationalist,' wrote Barbey d'Aurevilly, 'Brummell left nothing but a name mysteriously sparkling in all the *Memoirs* of his time.'

Mrs Wyatt's poverty made it necessary that she and Rochfort live abroad and, in January 1841, Rochfort wrote to Brougham from Ostende. Four years earlier, Mrs Wyatt's husband had brought an action against Rochfort and was awarded damages of £230, following which Wyatt began proceedings against his wife and a divorce was pronounced on 27 June 1839. The divorce case was to be brought before the House of Lords and Rochfort was anxious that his mistress would see nothing of her husband's income, the details of which he painstakingly documented to Brougham. Rochfort's letter reads more like an order than a request for help; he lists the points to which Brougham is to pay particular attention, he covers every possible angle of the case. So desperate was Rochfort for Brougham to 'stand forward in the House as defender of the lady's interests' and to use his influence to 'obtain for her the best provision from her husband', that he uncharacteristically – Rochfort saw himself as a gentleman – reminded the lawyer of how, 'upon your slightest bidding in former days I was always attentive to and mindful of your every request and wish, as long as ever any power existed with me to influence or control the actions of another person who shall now be nameless . . .'[18]

A few minutes away from Harriette's home, on Cadogan Street, was the Chelsea Catholic Chapel (now St Mary's), founded in 1811 by Abbé Voyaux de Franous for the use of soldiers and veterans from the Chelsea Hospital. It had always been thought of as principally a French chapel and here, at around 1840, Harriette was received into the Catholic Church, confirmed with the name of Mary Magdalen. The doggerel published ten years before by *Bell's Life in London* was correct in all but the finer details.

> It seems you're grown moral at last,
> Though still you wear patches and paint;
> And you'll die, like the rest of your cast,
> A mortified Methodist Saint.

Renouncing her ways, Harriette did the one conventional – or rather clichéd – action of her life. But in becoming a Catholic she was neither acting out of character nor trying to step back over from the far side of the sword. She was getting older and wanted to ensure eternity in the next life, but she was also bent on amusing herself for her remaining years in this one. Catholicism was Harriette's final project. She had always thrown herself into whatever she happened to be pursuing, and the study required for her conversion satisfied her enquiring mind and love of learning. The Catholic Church was her new world; she liked cultures that were strange to her – she had, after all, mixed for years in male aristocratic society – and she liked the challenge of studying new codes and customs. And she enjoyed love affairs; Harriette's engagement with her new religion took the place of the passionate relationships to which she had otherwise been addicted. It enabled her to return to what she was made for. 'I can do nothing and love nothing *coldly*,' she explained. 'I was created for love, and now [. . .] all the love which my heart is capable of has turned towards God.'[19]

In the last of her surviving letters, which is undated, Harriette told Edward Bulwer Lytton about her conversion. She had not been in touch with the writer for years but continued to hope they might one day meet, although her commitment to God meant that she was not available for 'love' should he think this her intention. She was clearly happier than she had been for a long time; she still had the dash and go that had defined her in her youth and she employed the same good-humoured, impetuous and impudent voice she reserved for those to whom she was still hoping to be introduced. Catholicism entertained her and she enjoyed her present role of reformed sinner, which she adopted without in any way repenting of her youth. Harriette's life seems back on track again; her flirtations with the priests recall her behaviour as a wayward child in the French convent, and her account of studying the various Church denominations recalls her sojourn at Salt Hill over thirty years before, where she spent ten days wading through the speeches of the Whigs and Tories, wondering where her own sympathies lay. It is easy to see Harriette enjoying her Catholic companions; she always loved being with people she regarded as 'good', those like Fanny, Ponsonby and her mother, and presenting herself as bad by comparison. She had always enjoyed being shocking, and now she had a new audience to regale with stories of her wicked past. Her reform would be a continual topic for discussion in the Church and make her the focus of admiration and attention. Catholicism gave her a stage that allowed her to be her best self once more. 'When I was a sinner, and a *good looking* one', she wrote to Bulwer,

I thought you were right to refuse me the honour of your acquaintance; but I have been 'born again', as the Methodists say, and am now a Saint!!! What's more, I am *very sick, very old* and shall soon die. I was duly received into the Catholic Church by baptism, confessions with confirmation, etc, nearly a year ago, after six months' hard study. I did not think I could have read so hard or so many books of controversy, Protestant or Catholic. So intense was my curiosity that I neither slept nor dined for many months without a pile of Catholic books on one side of me and one of Protestant, *larger still*, on my left. Once or twice a week a most amiable Catholic Priest and preacher came to hear and answer all my objections by the hour together with the patience of a *true Saint*. Our interviews lasted three or four hours. To conclude, I am now a strict Catholic on conviction . . .

I think you are too clever to be a genuine Protestant, but if you are I should like to know *why*. Will you let me have the honour of a little chat with you with your lady's consent? You will find me intelligent and lively, though quite old and sick. I would run no risk of sin, but I was always firm and I *know* that there *is* no risk of my ever being unchaste again even by the encouragement of *thoughts*. This you will say is being too bold, but when was I unfaithful to my love? and I never loved any of you as I love God. I will not believe that any can wilfully offend what they *perfectly* love . . .

But you'll say you've no time; well, it is very shabby of you, for you may appoint any hour on any day after twelve, and I will wait your leisure. I have no object but the gratification I know I should feel in talking to a person who could understand me, and as to *regard*, if we are both honest and single-hearted we must command the goodwill and respect of each other; but as to love ! ! if I felt a spark stealing over me for any man alive I would avoid him from that hour. *Nothing* shall induce me to go into temptation again . . .[20]

And ever the imperious queen of the *demi-monde*, Harriette added that she never saw 'anyone without an appointment'.

Her final address was 3 Draycott Place, on the other side of the Chelsea Catholic Chapel. Draycott Place is now one of London's bijou enclaves, home to an exclusive row of red-bricked Victorian mansion blocks, but as Harriette lay there dying it was the back of beyond, a far cry from the Mayfair of her childhood, where Mr Blore rubbed shoulders with Beau Brummell, and stockings and squabbles filled the house in Queen Street; where her father stormed over his sums and the straw was laid out each year for the birth of another sibling; where her sisters sat at the window making eyes at Berkeley Craven and Tom Sheridan, and from where, at the dawn of the century, Harriette had stolen away with Berkeley's elder brother.

On 10 March 1845, two weeks after her fifty-ninth birthday, the spangled curtain came down on the life of Harriette Wilson, the last of the great English courtesans. It had snowed all week and on her final day the sky was hidden behind a thick blanket of cloud. She was consistent to the end; she asked the Duke of Leinster and Frederic Lamb to pay her medical expenses and she left behind a note for Brougham, requesting that he, Leinster, and Worcester, now Duke of Beaufort, pay for her burial. She had added up the cost of a plain and straightforward funeral.

On 8 April, from his desk at the House of Lords, Brougham wrote a few lines to Beaufort.

My dear Duke,

Our old acquaintance, Mme de Bochet (Harriet Wilson) died the week before last and left a note says she hoped two or three of her former acquaintance would give the few pounds (fifteen) required to bury her – she having had an estimate price in with all the particulars of the church and struck off what was merely ornamental – which has reduced it as the above.

Duke of Leinster has given a little and I think as she also named you and me, we ought to contribute our might.

What say you?[21]

Four days later Brougham wrote to Beaufort again, saying that in addition to the burial there were 'some pounds due for care and medicine', so Harriette's death would cost her former acquaintance more than they had expected. 'What I have done', he explained, 'is to give £3 and £5 – and if you will send me either £5 or £7 – as you please – it will be quite enough and very handsome and I will mention to Mr D[ubouchet], the brother, who is a respectable man in poor circumstances – a *tuner of pianofortes* . . .'[22] Brougham appears moved by Harriette's death, and alone of her lovers may have mourned her. In his evident respect for the Dubouchet family and concern to have Harriette's final wishes realized it is possible to see his still lingering affection for the smart saucy girl who, thirty years before, burst into his life all guns blazing and kept him on his toes ever since.

Harriette's funeral was almost certainly held at the Chelsea Catholic Chapel with, we can imagine, the remaining members of her family in attendance. Lady Berwick, now a charitable Victorian widow, journeys down from her Shropshire estate, preparing to forgive her repentant sister her infamous ways. The respectable spinsters, Jane and Charlotte, walk to the Chapel from their modest home in Church Street, Paddington. Mary and her husband, Mr Boroughs, appear with a bevy of their grandchildren, along with Rose Dubouchet and the brother who tuned pianofortes. And if Amy is still alive, she may emerge from the shadows to kiss those once fine eyes goodnight.

The chapel was too small for a cemetery. It is not known where Harriotte Du Bochet, as she is called on her death certificate, a 'woman of independent means', lies buried, but no doubt the earth above her has been troubled and stirred during London's never-ending metamorphosis. She has vanished into the bowels of her restless city leaving behind a book and a bundle of letters, without which it might almost be thought that Harriette Wilson was no more than a figment of the Regency imagination.

CHAPTER 26

Afterwards: Sophie Stockdale's Offer

Brougham and Rochfort continued to communicate; they had gone a long way together since their introduction twenty years before. A relationship born of blackmail had turned into one of sympathy and occasional friendship. Rochfort was back at war with his mother and leaned on Brougham in his battle to get money out of his Irish estates. In December 1843, Brougham had assured him that an amendment of certain clauses in the law between debtor and creditor would be achieved in the next parliamentary term, after which Rochfort's letters became more and more urgent. 'I am really concerned to appear troublesome,' he wrote in March 1844, 'but the coming term (15 April) is so close at hand when I wish if possible to be doing something and getting on . . .'[1] Brougham advised him that a petition to the Lord Chancellor might hurry his case along, but it was without effect. He then advised Rochfort to petition the House of Lords, and this was without effect as well. 'You will admit', Rochfort despaired, 'I have exhibited both patient endurance of protracted grievance and strict obedience to your Lordship's recommendations . . . as yet however I sorrow to say without even the shadow of redress . . .'[2] By Feburary 1846, Rochfort was reminding Brougham through clenched teeth of his '*promise*' to remedy 'the unjust position under which I have been so long and am still labouring'.[3]

Cherubs

On a fine Saturday in early June 1847, two years after Harriette's death, Brougham paid a visit to Rochfort's home in Henriette Street, Brunswick Square, to examine the Colonel's latest invention, a wind gauge, which Rochfort hoped might be taken up by the Admiralty. With Brougham's support, Queen Victoria might also be convinced of its usefulness and install one at Windsor and at Osborne. Nothing came of Rochfort's dream, but today the two men put aside their uneasy, shifting dance of powerful and powerless and became elderly Victorian mavericks exchanging ideas. Rochfort related to Brougham as one man of science to another.

His appeal was eventually heard in the House of Lords in 1849, where all agreed that Rochfort's 'was a case of peculiar hardship and that the law most decidedly required to be amended'.[4] But in the final letter Brougham preserved, written the following year, Rochfort's anguish was greater than ever as he repeated, 'for nearly the hundredth time the great injustice under which I have been so long labouring',[5] about which nothing had yet been done. Two years later, in 1852, William Henry Rochfort died, leaving a 'wife' (his death certificate says he was a bachelor) called Elizabeth, who was probably Mrs Wyatt, and a son, who he hoped would eventually inherit the Irish estates. Rochfort, who was fifty-seven and had been insolvent all his adult life, was survived by his mother. Had he lived for another two years he would have outlasted her and seen the eventual sale of the Irish estates reach £20,000. Even after his numerous creditors had been paid off there would have been enough left over to bestow on him the dignity he felt he was owed and to keep his wife and son from poverty.

On 5 May 1854 Brougham received a letter from Rochfort's widow, now living at Wellington Road, St John's Wood, reminding him of the years of friendship between his Lordship and the 'late lamented Mr Rochfort' who 'we proudly believe . . . triumphed in your good esteem'. She was griefstricken, careworn and impoverished. Wanting to set her son up as an estate agent, she wondered if Brougham might send them some money; a cheque for a few shillings would do. Two years later, Brougham heard again from Elizabeth Rochfort, thanking him for his gift of one pound and telling him that her mother-in-law had at last died and the property sold. Rochfort's heir received nothing.[6]

Wellington died in the same year as Rochfort; Harriette's Worcester and Frederic Lamb followed him in 1853. Ponsonby died in 1855, his last post being Ambassador to Vienna. Ebrington became Lord Steward to the Queen's Household and died in 1861. Lady Berwick lived in Leamington Spa until in 1875 when she died, aged eighty-one. Brougham outlived them all, striding through the years of Victoria's reign, which saw his wife, his daughter, his friends and his enemies all buried. He withdrew from politics and immersed himself in law reform and the scientific study of light, spending more and more time after 1838 in the chateau he built in a small French hideaway near Nice. In 1839 he had the pleasure of reading his obituaries in the London newspapers; the rumours of his death originated, most people believed, from the mouth of Brougham himself. It was in his French home, on 7 May 1868, that Henry Brougham eventually did die, having reached his ninetieth year. By now, his residence in Cannes had attracted so many visitors that the sleepy fishing village was transformed into a fashionable resort. He was influential to the last.

But we have not quite reached the end of the story; nothing involving Harriette Wilson could end so neatly. How much more fitting that the story of her life should close in mystery and melodrama, or that it shouldn't close at all but beckon a further instalment. Two years after Harriette's death, the inexhaustible Stockdale breathed his last. A few weeks later, on 27 November 1847, Brougham received a letter from the publisher's widow, now living in Cardiff where her eldest son, Jeremiah Box, was the city's first police chief. It is a document of which her late husband would be proud.

My Lord

Pardon the liberty I take in writing to your Lordship.

In looking over my late husband's papers I find that the MSS of Harriette Wilson is quite perfect, and more than appeared in print, for there are all those who withheld their names merely crossed out with the pen. In offering the MSS to your Lordship, I was recollecting the circumstance of the late Lord Spencer's father applying for it, should it be sold, that had induced me to offer it to you. It is undoubtedly a true history of our times, and there are also the numerous letters, of who shall be in print and who shall not, for in years to come who would suppose that the greatest men of any age appear in the MSS.

I am not like Junius, I cannot afford to commit my MSS to the flames.

Sophie Stockdale[7]

Did Brougham take up her challenge? If not, the manuscript was most probably bought up by another of those, the 'greatest men of any age', whose name had been crossed out; another who, when the century was in its teens, fell for 'some flash of those fine dark eyes, some fling of those wild school boy manners'.[8] It was probably then destroyed; Harriette's words, like those of Junius and Byron, were no doubt thought too frank to survive. But it would have been hard for those whom Harriette had held enthralled to say a final goodbye to the Mayfair girl who was worth £50 for an introduction alone. Even if the manuscripts could no longer extort money from the aristocracy, they might raise a guinea or two from a publisher. We can only wait and hope; one day they may still come to light and we might learn who bought themselves out, what it was that the Marchioness of Conyngham wrote to Lord Ponsonby and that the King of England had to say to the King of France. We may discover even more of the true history of those times.

Psyche, Borne by the Zephyrs
to the Island of Pleasure

Bibliography

Primary Sources

WORKS BY HARRIETTE WILSON

Editions of Harriette Wilson's *Memoirs*
As with most aspects of Harriette Wilson's life, the existing accounts of the publishing history of the *Memoirs* are unreliable. The following list brings together scattered information gathered from library catalogues, references in court proceedings, and the evidence of surviving copies, but until more copies are found it remains provisional.

The Memoirs of Harriette Wilson written by herself
Published by J. J. Stockdale, with 28 engravings 'sketched and coloured from the life', 1825. Sold in parts and then together in four volumes. Stockdale printed 7,000 copies of one part which was expected to be particularly popular. He claimed to have produced thirty-five editions, and copies exist with various edition numbers noted on the title pages, but many are evidently not true editions but unsold sheets reissued.

The Memoirs of Harriette Wilson written by herself
Printed by John Mitford; sold by R. P. Stockdale
No date. John Mitford was a hack pornographer. R. P. Stockdale is unidentified.

The Memoirs of Harriette Wilson
Onwhyn, 1825. A word-for-word pirated copy of Stockdale's edition. Although Onwhyn admitted to having printed 5,000 copies, no copy is known to have survived.

The Memoirs of Harriette Wilson
Benbow, 1825. No copy known to have survived.

The Memoirs of Harriette Wilson written by herself
Printed and published by T. Dunbar, 1825, 4 vols, with coloured engravings.

Harriette Wilson's Memoirs of Herself and Others
T. Douglas, 1825, 3 vols, with lithograph illustrations.

Harriette Wilson's Memoirs of Herself and Others
T. Douglas, 1825, 4 vols, with colour engravings.

The Interesting Memoirs of Harriette Wilson, One of the Most Celebrated Women of the Present Day, Interspersed with Numerous Anecdotes of Illustrious Persons; Her First Introduction into Public Life . . .
Edward Duncombe, no date [?1825]

Memoirs of Harriette Wilson, A celebrated Courtezan, interspersed with Curious and Amatory Anecdotes of Illustrious Persons
Another Duncombe edition, no date, 4 vols.

Memoirs of Harriette Wilson
W. Dugdale, 1825, illustrated with engravings; reprinted, 1839. An abridgement.

The Interesting Memoirs and Amorous Adventures of Harriette Wilson, one of the most celebrated women of the present day
W. Chubb, 1825. An abridgement.

Memoirs of Harriette Wilson, Paris Lions and London Tigers, an account of the action for libel brought by Blore against the publisher etc. [*Memoirs* 1831]
J. J. Stockdale, 8 vols. including Index, 1831.

Contemporary Translations

Mémoires d'Henriette Wilson . . . Traduction de l'Anglais, revue et corrigée par l'auteur
Paris, 6 vols, 1825

Mémoires d'Henriette Wilson . . . Traduction de l'anglais . . . Deuxième édition. Les Lions de Paris et les Tigres de Londres
Brussels, 8 vols, 1825

Denkwürdigkeiten der Miss Henriette Wilson, Englands Ninon. Nach dem Englischen
Stuttgart, 3 vols, 1825
The repetition of the mistake in the name suggests that the translation was made from the French version.

Later Editions

The Memoirs of Harriette Wilson, written by Herself
2 vols, London: Eveleigh Nash, 1909

The Memoirs of Harriette Wilson
2 vols, illustrated with 32 portraits, privately printed for the Navarre Society, 1924

Harriette Wilson's Memoirs of Herself and Others [*Memoirs*]
With a preface by James Laver, London: Peter Davies, 1929

Mistress of Many: Harriette Wilson. The Memoirs of a Beautiful Woman who lived for love
Edited by Max Marquis, London: Bestseller Library, 1960

The Game of Hearts: Harriette Wilson and her Memoirs
Selected and with an introduction by Leslie Blanch, illustrated with plates and portraits.
Gryphon Books, 1937; reprinted as *Harriette Wilson's Memoirs*, The Folio Society, 1964; reprinted Century, 1985; reprinted Phoenix, 2003

Other Works

Paris Lions and London Tigers
Stockdale, 1825. The BL copy claims to be a fifth edition.

Paris Lions and London Tigers
Edited with an introduction by Heywood Hill, London: The Navarre Society, 1931

Clara Gazul; or Honi soit qui mal y pense [*Clara Gazul*]
London: published by the author, Trevor Square, 3 vols, 1830

WORKS BY JULIA JOHNSTONE

Confessions of Julia Johnstone, written by herself, in contradiction to the fables of Harriette Wilson
[*Confessions*]
London: Benbow, 1825

Archival and Manuscript Sources

Badminton	Letters of Lord Edward Somerset, the Marquis of Worcester, and Mr Robinson to the Sixth Duke of Beaufort, and from Henry Brougham to Seventh Duke of Beaufort; HW's financial receipts; preserved at Badminton, Gloucestershire.
BL	Letters of Rochfort to Lord Aberdeen, Sir Charles Bagot, Duke of Wellington, Sir William Huskisson; British Library
Brougham	Letters of HW and Rochfort to Henry Brougham; HW's financial receipts; Brougham Papers, Special Collections, University College London Library Services
Bulwer Lytton	HW's letters to Sir Edward Bulwer Lytton; Hertfordshire Archives and Local Studies, Hertford
Granville	Drafts of correspondence relating to HW conducted by the British Ambassador in Paris; Public Record Office, Kew
Murray	HW's letters to Lord Byron. John Murray archive, London
Ponsonby	HW's letters to Viscount Ponsonby, reproduced by permission of Durham University Library, Earl Grey Papers, GRE/E/673

Newspaper and Magazine Sources

The Bath Chronicle
Bell's Life in London
British Lion
Country Life
The Gentleman's Magazine
Morning Chronicle
Morning Herald
New Rambler's Magazine
Stockdale's Budget
The Times

Secondary Sources

Ackroyd, Peter, *London: The Biography*, London: Chatto and Windus, 2000
Addison, W., *English Fairs and Markets*, London: Batsford, 1953
Airlee, Mabell, Countess of, *In Whig Society*, London: Hodder and Stoughton, 1921
– *Lady Palmerston and her Times*, London: Hodder and Stoughton, 1922
Anon., *Characters of the Most Celebrated Courtesans*, London: 1788
Anon., *Eliza Grimwood, A Domestic Legend of Waterloo Road*, London: D. B. Cousins, *c.*1845
Anon., *The Englishman's Mentor*, 1819
Archenholz, J. W. von, *A Picture of England*, Dublin: 1790
Argyll, Dowager Duchess of (ed.), *George Douglas, 8th Duke of Argyll, Autobiography and Memoirs*,
    London: John Murray, 1906
Argyll, Duke of (ed.) *Intimate Letters of the Eighteenth Century*, London: Stanley Paul and Co., 1909
Army Lists, 1790–1840
Aspinall, A. (ed.) *The Letters of King George IV, 1812–1830*, 3 vols, Cambridge: Cambridge
    University Press, 1938
– *The Later Correspondence of George III*, 5 vols, Cambridge: Cambridge University Press, 1970
Austen, Jane, *Persuasion*, London: Hamish Hamilton, 1946
– *Emma*, London: Dent, 1961
Baily, F. E., *The Love Story of Lady Palmerston*, London: Hutchinson and Co., 1938
Bamford, Francis, and the Duke of Wellington, *Journal of Mrs Arbuthnot, 1820–1832*, 2 vols,
    London: Macmillan, 1950
Baxter's Stranger in Brighton, Brighton: Baxter, 1826
Benbow, William [attrib.], *Memoirs of the Life of the Celebrated Mrs Q*, London: Benbow, 1822
Berant, Sir John, *Narrative of the Expedition under General MacGregor against Portobello*, London:
    C. & J. Ollier, 1820
Berkeley, The Hon. Grantley F., *My Life and Recollections*, 4 vols, London: Hurst and Blackett, 1866
Berry, Paul, *By Royal Appointment: A Biography of Mary Anne Clarke, Mistress of the Duke of York*,
    London: Femina, 1970
[Blackmantle, Bernard, pseud.], *The English Spy, drawn from the life by Bernard Blackmantle*, 2 vols,
    London: Sherwood, Neely, 1826 [*The English Spy*]
Bleakley, Horace, *Ladies Fair and Frail: Sketches of the Demi-monde during the Eighteenth Century*,
    London: The Bodley Head, 1909
Borer, Mary Cathcart, *The Years of Grandeur: The Story of Mayfair*. London: W. H. Allen, 1975
Bourne, Kenneth, *The Blackmailing of the Chancellor. Some intimate and hitherto unpublished letters from
    Harriette Wilson to her friend, Henry Brougham*, London: Lemon Tree Press, 1975
– *Palmerston: The Early Years, 1784–1841*, London: Allen Lane, 1982
Boyles Court Guides, 1792–1816
Brewer, John, *The Pleasures of the Imagination: English Culture in the Eighteenth Century*, London:
    Harper Collins, 1997
Bridgeman, H., and E. Dury, *Society Scandals*, London: David and Charles, 1977
Broadley, A. M., and Lewis Melville, *The Beautiful Lady Craven. The Original Memoirs of Elizabeth
    Craven etc.* London: The Bodley Head, 1913
Brougham, Henry, *The Life and Times of Henry Brougham*, 3 vols, London: Blackwood, 1871
Brown, Roger Lee, *History of the Fleet Prison, London: The Anatomy of the Fleet*, Lewiston, NY: The
    Edwin Mellon Press, 1996

BIBLIOGRAPHY

Brownlow, Emma Sophia, Countess of, *The Eve of Victorianism: Reminiscences of the Years 1802–1834*, London: John Murray, 1940

Burn, John Southerden, *History of the Fleet Marriages, etc.*, London: Rivington, 1834

Bushell, S. A. (ed.), *Grand National Holiday*, London: Pelagrian Press, 1996

Butler, E. M. (ed.), *A Regency Visitor: The English Tour of Prince Pückler-Muskau described in his letters 1826–1828*, translated by Sarah Austen, London: Collins, 1957

Butler, Iris, *The Eldest Brother: The Marquess Wellesley, the Duke of Wellington's Eldest Brother*, London: Hodder, 1973

Burford, E. J., *Wits, Wenchers and Wantons: London's Lowlife, Covent Garden in the Eighteenth Century*, London: Robert Hale, 1986

– *Royal St James's, Being a Story of Kings, Clubmen and Courtesans*. London: Robert Hale, 1988

Burnett, T. A. J., *The Rise and Fall of a Regency Dandy: The Life and Times of Srope Berdmore Davis*, London: John Murray, 1981

Byron, George Gordon, Lord, *Don Juan*, Harmondworth: Penguin, 1973

Cameron, David Kerr, *London's Pleasures, From Restoration to Regency*, Stroud: Sutton Publishing, 2001

Castalia, Countess Granville (ed.) *Lord Granville Leveson Gower: Private Correspondence*, London: John Murray, 1916

Cecil, Lord David, *Melbourne*, New York: The Bobs-Merrill Company Inc., 1939

Chancellor, E. B., *The Eighteenth Century in London: An Account of its Social Life and Arts*, London: Batsford, 1920

– *Life in Regency and Victorian Times, 1800-50*, London: Batsford, 1927

Chandre Moti, *The World of Courtesans*, Delhi: Vikas Publishing House, 1973

Chapman, R. W. (ed.), *Jane Austen's Letters*, Oxford: Oxford University Press, 1952

Clarke, Anna, 'Whores and Gossips: Sexual Reputation in London 1770–1825', in Angerman et al., *Current Issues in Women's History*, London: Routledge, 1989

Clarke, Mary Anne [attrib.], *Biographical Memoirs and Anecdotes of the Celebrated Mary Anne Clarke*, London: Wilson and Herbert, 1804

– [attrib.] *Memoirs of Mrs Mary Anne Clarke, from the age of fifteen to the present time*, London, C. Chapple, 1809

– *The Rival Princes*, 2 vols, London: Chapple, 1810

Clinch, George, *Mayfair and Belgravia: Being an Historical account of the Parish of St George, Hanover Square*, London: Truslove and Shirley, 1892

Colby, Reginald, *Mayfair: A Town within a Town*, London: Country Life, 1966

Cole, Hubert, *Beau Brummell*, London: Granada, 1977

Colquhoun, Patrick, *A Treatise on the Police of the Metropolis*, London: C. Dilly, 1797

Dallas, Gregor, *The Final Act: The Roads to Waterloo*, New York: Henry Holt, 1996

Darnton, Robert, *The Forbidden Best-Sellers of Pre-Revolutionary France*, London: Harper Collins, 1996

Davidoff, Leonora, *The Best Circles: Society Etiquette and the Season*, London: Croom Helm, 1973

Davis, I. M., *The Harlot and the Statesman: The Story of Mrs Armistead and Charles James Fox*, Buckinghamshire: Kensal Press, 1986

Debrett's Peerage

Du Maurier, Daphne, *Mary-Anne*, Harmondsworth: Penguin, 1954

Durant, Horatia, *The Somerset Sequence*, London: Newman Neame, 1951

Dury, Elizabeth, 'The Outrage of a Fashionable Impure: The Memoirs of Harriette Wilson', in Dury and Bridgeman (eds.), *Society Scandals*, 1977

Edgecombe, Richard (ed.), *The Diary of Lady Frances Shelley, 1787–1817*, London: John Murray, 1912

Egan, Pierce, *Life in London*, London: Sherwood, Jones and Co., 1823

Fitzgerald, Percy, *Memoirs of an Author*, 2 vols, London: 1894

Ford, Trowbridge, *Henry Brougham and His World*, London: Barry Rose, 1995

– *Chancellor Brougham and his World*, London: Barry Rose Law, 2001

Fraser, Flora, *The Unruly Queen: The Life of Queen Caroline*, Basingstoke: Macmillan, 1996

Furlong, R. Rochfort, *Notes on the History of the Family of Rochfort or Rochefort*, Oxford: 1890

Garratt, G. T., *Lord Brougham*, London: Macmillan, 1935

George, M. Dorothy, *Catalogue of Political and Personal Satires preserved in the Department of Prints and Drawings in the British Museum*, vol x, 1820–27, London: British Museum, 1952

– *London Life in the Eighteenth Century*, London: Peregrine, 1966

Gore, John (ed.), *The Creevey Papers*, London: Batsford, 1963

Grierson, H. J. C. (ed.), *The Letters of Sir Walter Scott*, 12 vols, London: Constable and Co., 1935

Gronow, Captain, *Last Recollections*, London: Smith, Elder and Co., 1866

Gross, Jonathan, *Byron's 'Corbeau Blanc' – The Life and Letters of Lady Melbourne*, Houston, Texas: Rice University Press, 1997

Grosvenor Myer, Valerie, *Harriette Wilson: Lady of Pleasure*, London: Fern House, 1999

Harvey, A. D., *Sex in Georgian England*, London: Phoenix, 1994

Haggard, Captain D. J. (ed.), 'With the Tenth Hussars in Spain: Letters of Edward Fox Fitzgerald', *Journal of the Society for Army Historical Research*, vol. 44, 1966

Harris's List of Covent Garden Ladies: Or, Man of Pleasure's Kalender for the Year 1773

Hartcup, Adeline, *Love and Marriage in the Great Country Houses*, London: Sidgwick and Jackson, 1984

Henderson, Tony, *Disorderly Women in Eighteenth Century London: Prostitution and Control in the Metropolis, 1730-1830*, London: Longman, 1999

Henriques, F., *Prostitution and Society*, 3 vols, London: 1963

Hibbert, Christopher (ed.), *George IV: Prince of Wales 1762–1811*, Harmondsworth, Penguin, 1972

– *Captain Gronow: His Reminiscences of Regency and Victorian Life 1810–60*, London: Kyle Cathie, 1991

– *Wellington: A Personal History*, London: Harper Collins, 1998

Hill, Anne, *Trelawny's Strange Relations. An Account of the Domestic Life of Edward John Trelawny's Mother & Sisters in Paris and London, 1818–1829*, Stanford Dingley: The Mill House Press, 1956

Hinde, Wendy, *George Canning*, Oxford: Blackwell, 1989

Hufton, Olwyn (ed.), *The Prospect Before Her: A History of Women in Western Europe*, vol. 1: *1500–1800*, New York: Alfred A. Knopf, 1996

Hyde, H. Montgomery, *A Tangled Web: Sex Scandals in British Politics and Society*, London: Futura, 1987

Ilchester, the Earl of (ed.), *The Journal of Elizabeth Holland*, vol. 1, London: 1908

– *The Journal of Henry James Fox, 1818–30*, London: 1923

Jesse, Captain, *The Life of Beau Brummell*, London: 1844

Jones, Frederick L. (ed.), *The Letters of Percy Bysshe Shelley*, 2 vols, Oxford: Oxford University Press, 1964

Kelly, Linda, *Richard Brinsley Sheridan: A Life*, London: Sinclair Stevenson, 1977

Kennedy, Carol, *Mayfair: A Social History*, London: Hutchinson, 1986

La Roche, Sophie v., *Sophie in London, 1786. Being the Diary of Sophie v la Roche,* London: Cape, 1933

Lane, Maggie, *Jane Austen's England,* London: Hale, 1986

Larsen, Egon, *The Deceivers,* London: John Baker, 1966

Leveson Gower, The Hon. F. (ed.), *Letters of Harriette, Lady Granville, 1810–1845,* 2 vols, London and New York, 1894

Lindsay, Ian G. and Mary Cosh, *Inverary and the Dukes of Argyll,* Edinburgh University Press, 1973

Lockhart, J. G., *Memoirs of the Life of Sir Walter Scott,* 3 vols, Paris: Baudry's European Library, 1838

Longford, Elizabeth, *Wellington: The Years of the Sword,* London: World Books, 1971

Low, Donald A., *The Regency Underworld,* London: Dent, 1982

McCalman, I., *Radical Underworld: Prophets, Revolutionaries and Pornographers in London 1795–1840,* Cambridge: Cambridge University Press, 1988

Mansell, Philip, *Paris between Empires,* London: John Murray, 2001

Marchand, Leslie, *Byron: A Biography,* 3 vols, London: John Murray, 1957

– (ed.), *Byron's Letters and Journals,* 12 vols, London: John Murray, 1973–82

Margetson, Stella, *Leisure and Pleasure in the Nineteenth Century,* London: Cassell, 1969

– *Regency London,* London: Cassell, 1971

Maxwell, Sir H., *The Creevey Papers, A Selection from the Correspondence and Diaries of the Late Thomas Creevey MP,* London: John Murray, 1923

Melville, Lewis, *Beaux of the Regency,* London: Chapman and Hall, 1909

– *Brighton: Its history, its follies and its fashions,* London: Chapman and Hall, 1909

– *Regency Ladies,* London: Chapman and Hall, 1926

Mitchell, L. G., *Lord Melborne, 1779–1848,* Oxford: Oxford University Press, 1997

Mitchell, R. J., and M. D. R. Leys, *A History of London Life,* London: Pelican, 1958

Mollo, John, *The Prince's Dolls: Scandals, Skirmishes and Splendours of the First British Hussars 1793–1815,* London: Leo Cooper, 1977

Montague, Matthew, ed., *The Letters of Elizabeth Montague,* London, 1813

Montgomery, Robert [attrib.], *The Age Reviewed,* 2nd edn, London: 1828

Moore, Doris Langley, *The Late Lord Byron,* London: John Murray, 1966

Mudge, B. K., *The Whore's Story: Women, Pornography and the British Novel 1684–1830,* Oxford: Oxford University Press, 2000

Murray, Fanny [attrib.], *Memoirs of the Celebrated Miss Fanny Murray,* London: 1776

Murray, Venetia, *High Society: A Social History of the Regency Period, 1788–1830,* London: Viking, 1998

Nightingale, Joseph, *Memoirs of the Public and Private Life of Queen Caroline,* edited by Christopher Hibbert, London: Folio Society, 1983

Parreaux, A., *Daily Life in England in the Reign of George III,* London: 1966

Paston, George, and Peter Quennell, *'To Lord Byron': Feminine Profiles, based upon unpublished letters 1807–1824,* London: John Murray, 1939

Perrot, Michelle (ed.) *A History of Private Life: From the Fires of Revolution to the Great War,* Cambridge, Mass.: Belknap Press, 1990

Ponsonby, Sir John, KCB, *The Ponsonby Family 1771–1855,* London: Medici Society, 1929

Priestley, J. B., *The Prince of Pleasure and His Regency 1811–1820,* London: Sphere Books, 1971

Pückler-Muskau, Prince, *A Regency Visitor: The English Tour of Prince Pückler-Muskau Described in his Letters, 1826–1828,* London: Collins, 1957

Pugh, Edward [David Hughson, pseud.], *London*, 6 vols, London: 1805–9

Quennell, Peter, (ed.), *The Private Letters of Princess Lieven to Prince Metternich 1820–1826,* London: John Murray, 1937

– *Byron: The Years of Fame*, London: Book Club Associates, 1974

– *Memoirs of William Hickey*, London and Boston: Routledge and Kegan Paul, 1975

Raikes, Tom, *Personal Reminiscences*, edited by R. H. Stoddard, New York: Scribner, Armstrong and Co., 1875

Richardson, Joanna, *The Courtesans: The Demi-monde in Nineteenth Century France*, London: Phoenix Press, 2000

Rochfort, William Henry, *A Treatise Upon Archanography*, London: De la Rue, 1836

Rosenthal, Margaret F., *The Honest Courtesan: Veronica Franco, Citizen and Writer in Sixteenth Century Venice*, Chicago: University of Chicago Press, 1992

Rousseau, George, and Roy Porter, *Sexual Underworlds of the Enlightenment*, Manchester: Manchester University Press, 1987

Rudé, George, *Hanoverian London, 1774–1808*, London: Secker and Warburg, 1971

Ruter, A. J. C., 'William Benbow's *Grand National Holiday* and *Congress of the Productive Classes*', *International Review for Social History*, Amsterdam/Leiden: E. J. Brill, 1986

Sadler, Michael, *Bulwer: A Panorama. Edward and Rosina, 1803–1836*, London: Constable, 1936

Schwartz, Richard B., *Daily Life in Johnson's London,* London: University of Wisconsin Press, 1983

Simmond, Louis, *An American in Regency London: The Journal of a Tour in 1810 –1811*, edited by Christopher Hibbert, London: Robert Maxwell, 1968

Smith, E. A., *A Queen on Trial: The Affair of Queen Caroline*, Stroud: Alan Sutton, 1993

Smyth, William, *Memoir of Mr Sheridan*, Leeds: J. Cross, 1840

Steele, Mrs Elizabeth*, The Memoirs of Mrs Sophia Baddeley, Late of Dury Lane Theatre*, London: 1787

Stockdale, Eric, 'John Almon and the Stockdales 1760-1840', typewritten copy, BL Add. mss. 71220

Stone, Lawrence, *The Family, Sex and Marriage in England, 1500–1800*, London: Weidenfeld and Nicholson, 1977

Strachey, Lytton, and Roger Fulford, *The Greville Memoirs*, 8 vols, London: Macmillan, 1938

Surtees, Virginia, *The Second Self: The Letters of Harriet Granville, 1810–1845*, Hampshire: Michael Russell, 1990

Tannahill, Reay, *Regency England: The Great Age of the Colour Print*, London: The Folio Society, 1964

Temperley, Harold (ed.), *The Unpublished Diary and Political Sketches of Princess Lieven together with some of her letters*, London: Jonathan Cape, 1925

Thale, Mary (ed.), *The Autobiography of Francis Place*, Cambridge: Cambridge University Press, 1972

Thirkell, Angela, *The Fortunes of Harriette: The Surprising Career of Harriette Wilson*, London: Hamish Hamilton, 1936

Thompson, F. M. L., *English Landed Society in the Nineteenth Century*, London: Routledge & Kegan Paul, 1963

Thompson, Lynda M., *The 'Scandalous Memoirists': Constantia Phillips, Laetitia Pilkington and the shame of 'public fame'*, Manchester: Manchester University Press, 2000

Thorne, R. G., *The Commons 1790–1820*, London: Secker and Warburg, 1986

Thorold, Peter, *The London Rich: The Creation of a Great City from 1666 to the Present,* London: Viking, 1999

Vincent, James Edmund, *Highways and Byways in Berkshire*, London: Macmillan, 1906

Walford, Edward, *Old London and New: A Narrative of its History, its People and its Places*. vol IV, Westminster and the Western Suburbs. London: Cassell, 1877

Wallace, Irving, *The Nympho and Other Maniacs*, New York: Simon and Schuster, 1981

Watson, H. C., *A Sketch of the Life of N. C. Bochsa*, Sydney: Paisey and Fryer, 1855

Weinreb, Ben, and Christopher Hibbert (eds.), *The London Encyclopedia*, London: Macmillan, 1983

Wheatley, H. B., *Round about Piccadilly and Pall Mall*, London: Smith, Elder and Co., 1870

White, T. H., *The Age of Scandal*, London: The Folio Society, 1993

Wight, John. *Mornings at Bow Street*, London: Charles Baldwyn, 1824

Woolf, Virginia, *Beau Brummell*, New York: Rimmington and Hooper, 1930

– 'Harriette Wilson', in *The Moment and Other Essays*, London: Hogarth Press, 1947

Woods, Joanna, *The Commissioner's Daughter: The Story of Elizabeth Proby and Admiral Chichogav*, Witney: The Stonesfield Press, 2000

Wyatt, Stanley Charles, *Cheneys and Wyatts: A Brief History in Two Parts*, London: Carey and Claridge, 1959

Notes

1 MAYFAIR

1 *Harriette Wilson's Memoirs of Herself and Others*, with a preface by James Laver, London: Peter Davies, 1929, p. 26. Hereafter cited as *Memoirs*.

2 Horace Walpole, quoted in Peter Thorold, *The London Rich: The Creation of a Great City from 1666 to the Present*, London: Viking, 1999, p. 134.

3 Quoted in Reginald Colby, *Mayfair: A Town within a Town*, London: Country Life, 1966, p. 15.

4 The consumption of rich households in the late eighteenth century was phenomenal, so it is not surprising that the number of tradesmen living in the Parish of St George, Hanover Square, outnumbered the quantity of customers: a tax collector's survey of 1790 reveals that nearly 60 per cent of the inhabitants were tradesmen and artisans, compared with 8.5 per cent titled residents, 7.5 per cent professional men and 22.5 per cent 'no occupation', which included the leisured classes. See Carol Kennedy, *Mayfair: A Social History*, London: Hutchinson, 1986, p. 81.

5 The comment is made by Julia Johnstone in *Confessions of Julia Johnstone, written by herself, in contradiction to the fables of Harriette Wilson*, London: Benbow, 1825, p. 14. Hereafter cited as *Confessions*.

6 Letter from Tom Bowlby, quoted in Horace Bleakley, *Ladies Fair and Frail: Sketches of the Demimonde during the Eighteenth Century*, London: The Bodley Head, 1909, p. 112.

7 Lord Byron, *Don Juan*, XIII, 49, Harmondsworth: Penguin, 1973, p. 455.

8 *Confessions*, pp. 15 and 93.

9 The notoriety of the Dubouchet girls was such that not even Harriette's sister Sophia, when she traded in her career as a courtesan to become Lady Berwick, had a painting of her displayed at Attingham, her country house.

10 J. G. Lockhart, *Memoirs of the Life of Sir Walter Scott*, vol. 3, Paris: Baudry's European Library, 1838, p. 338.

11 *Confessions*, p. 93.

12 Lockhart, op. cit., p. 338.

13 H. J. C. Grierson (ed.), *The Letters of Sir Walter Scott*, vol. IX, *1825–1826*, London: Constable and Co., 1935, p. 7.

14 Lockhart, op. cit., p. 338.

15 Letter from Harriette Wilson to Edward Bulwer Lytton, Bulwer Lytton, D/EK C1/18 3.

16 *Confessions*, p. 68.

17 Grierson, op. cit., p. 7.

18 [Bernard Blackmantle, pseud.], *The English Spy, drawn from the life by Bernard Blackmantle*, vol. 2, London: Sherwood, Neely, 1826, p. 51. Hereafter cited as *The English Spy*.

2 JOHN AND AMELIA DUBOUCHET

1 This rumour appeared in *Memoirs of the life of the Celebrated Mrs Q* (1822), a narrative published, and probably written, by William Benbow. Harriette Wilson is confused with the King's current mistress, Harriet Quentin, née Lawrell, who was married to Colonel Quentin of the 10th Hussars.

2 *The English Spy*, vol. 2, p. 31. Lord Chesterfield and Elizabeth Debouchette had one natural son already, born in 1732, to whom Chesterfield would write his famous daily letters. The assumption that Harriette's father was the unacknowledged bastard of Chesterfield is no doubt attractive and the dates certainly fit, but it is highly dubious. Dubouchet, who would have revelled in it, never mentioned the connection; his was a not uncommon Genevan name, and why would Chesterfield trumpet to the world his acknowledgement of one son, for whom he would procure a parliamentary seat and a diplomatic post, while keeping entirely secret the existence of the other?

3 See Valerie Grosvenor Myer, *Harriette Wilson, Lady of Pleasure*, Ely: Fern House, 1999, p. 8, and Leslie Blanch, introduction to *Harriette Wilson's Memoirs*, London: The Folio Society, 1964, p. 8.

4 *Memoirs*, p. 371.

5 Harriette Wilson, *Clara Gazul, or, Honi soit qui mal y pense*, London: Trevor Square, 1830, p. v. Hereafter cited as *Clara Gazul*.

6 General Burgoyne left for America in April 1775, returned again in March 1776, and left again in the spring of 1777. The Dubouchets were married in early 1777 and their first child was born in October of that year, two weeks before Burgoyne's surrender to General Gates in Saratoga Springs. Dubouchet could have married, impregnated his wife, and returned to America with Burgoyne, but it seems unlikely that such a chancer, having secured a home to return to after a day of leisure, would bother to up and cross the Atlantic to live in discomfort. But it is possible that he did have some dealings with Burgoyne, perhaps in the General's initial journey to America in 1775, not least because Burgoyne returned to London to live the rest of his life at 10 Hertford Street, a moment away from the Dubouchet's home in Carrington Street, and it would have been difficult for Dubouchet to carry off the story had he been completely unknown to his famous neighbour. But on the other hand, after Burgoyne's death in August 1792, the General was no longer around to confirm or deny his part in John Dubouchet's career.

7 *Memoirs of Harriette Wilson: written by Herself*, London: J. J. Stockdale, 1831, vol. 5, p. 374. This later, extended edition of Harriette Wilson's *Memoirs* will hereafter be cited as *Memoirs 1831*.

8 Robert Henry Cheney, the eldest son, was an accomplished watercolourist and a favourite pupil of the landscape painter Peter de Wint. His friendship with Lord Holland introduced him to the exclusive Holland House set, the centre of Whig society. Edward Cheney, the second son, was an authoritative collector of Old Master drawings, contemporary water-colours, Venetian pictures and Rembrandt etchings.

9 This information was very kindly given to me in conversation with Michael Capel Cure, a descendant of the Cheney family.

10 *Memoirs 1831*, vol. 5, p. 372.

11 See Angela Thirkell, *The Fortunes of Harriette: The Surprising Career of Harriette Wilson*, London:

Hamish Hamilton, 1936, p. 12, and Grosvenor Myer, op. cit., p. 8.

12 *Memoirs* 1831, vol. 5, p. 366.

13 Ibid., p. 372.

14 George Rudé, *Hanoverian London, 1774–1808*, London: Secker and Warburg, 1971, p. 38.

15 *Memoirs* 1831, vol. 5, p. 373. In 1755 Mary Meredith married the eccentric Fourth Earl of Ferrars. After he threatened to kill her, she managed to get a separation by Act of Parliament. The Earl then killed his steward instead and was hanged at Tyburn in 1760. He went to the gallows in his silver-braided wedding suit, saying that the day of his marriage and the day of his death were the worst of his life.

16 Ibid.

17 Ibid., p. 381.

18 Ibid., p. 375.

19 Ibid., p. 378.

20 Ibid., p. 380.

21 Ibid., p. 378.

22 *Clara Gazul*, p. x.

23 *Memoirs* 1831, vol. 5, p. 377.

24 *Memoirs*, p. 19.

25 Ibid., p. 472.

3   QUEEN STREET

1 *Memoirs* 1831, vol. 5, p. 379.

2 Ibid.

3 Ibid., p. 263.

4 *Confessions*, p. 55.

5 *Memoirs*, p. 31.

6 *The English Spy*, vol. 2, p. 47.

7 *Memoirs*, p. 29.

8 *Confessions*, p. 5.

9 *Clara Gazul*, p. xii.

10 Ibid., p. xvii.

11 Ibid.

12 *Memoirs*, p. 19.

13 *Clara Gazul*, pp. xxiv–xxv, xxii.

14 Ibid., p. xxv.

15 Ibid., pp. xxvi–xxvii.

16 *Bell's Life in London*, 20 March 1825.

17 *Clara Gazul*, p. xxvii.

18 Ibid., p. xxii.

19 Ibid., p. xxviii.

20 Ibid., p. xli.

21 Ibid., p. l.

4 COURTESANS

1 *Clara Gazul*, p. lix.
2 *The Autobiography of Francis Place*, edited with an introduction and notes by Mary Thale, Cambridge: Cambridge University Press, 1972, p. 81.
3 Ibid., p. 78n.
4 Ibid., p. 71.
5 Patrick Colquhoun, *A Treatise on the Police of the Metropolis*, London: C. Dilly, 1797, p. 313.
6 *Bell's Life in London*, 3 April 1825.
7 *Confessions*, p. 171.
8 An article in *The English Spy* (vol. 2, p. 48) suggests that Harriette had a child by 'a certain dashing solicitor's clerk' who preceded Lord Craven in her affections, but that the baby died and was buried in an unmarked grave in Chelsea. There is no evidence for this; nor is there evidence for Julia Johnstone's claim that Harriette gave birth to the child of a soldier while living in Charmouth. An exhibition of Regency Lyme at the Lyme Regis museum claims that when Harriette was living in Charmouth in 1815 she had two children. Baptism records show that the curator has confused records of the children of Harriet Wilson Lowndes, the wife of William Lowndes, who went on to develop areas of Knightsbridge, with Harriette Wilson.
9 See I. M. Davis, *The Harlot and the Statesman: The Story of Mrs Armistead and Charles James Fox*, Buckinghamshire: Kensal Press, 1986, p. 91.
10 *Memoirs of the Celebrated Miss Fanny Murray*, London: J. Scott, 1759.
11 See E. J. Burford, *Wits, Wenchers and Wantons: London's Lowlife, Covent Garden in the Eighteenth Century*, London, Robert Hale, 1986, pp. 103–4.
12 *Memoirs* 1831, vol. 5, p. 291.
13 Peter Quennell (ed.), *Memoirs of William Hickey*, London: Hutchinson, 1960, p. 69.
14 Quoted in Elizabeth Longford, *Wellington: The Years of the Sword*, London: World Books, 1971, p. 230.
15 Richard Edgecumbe (ed.), *The Diary of Lady Frances Shelley, 1787–1817*, London: John Murray, 1912, p. 39.
16 Quoted in Adeline Hartcup, *Love and Marriage in the Great Country Houses*, London: Sidgwick and Jackson, 1984, p. 17.
17 *Memoirs*, p. 31.
18 Ibid., p. 30.
19 *Clara Gazul*, p. lv.
20 William Smyth, *Memoir of Mr Sheridan*, Leeds: J. Cross, 1840, p. 65.
21 *Clara Gazul*, pp. lxi–lxii.
22 *Memoirs*, p. 15.
23 Louis Simmond, *An American in Regency London: The Journal of a Tour in 1810–1811*, edited with an introduction and notes by Christopher Hibbert, London: Robert Maxwell, 1968, p. 30.
24 *Clara Gazul*, p. lxiv.
25 Ibid., p. lxviii.
26 Ibid., p. lxxviii.
27 Matthew Montague (ed.), *The Letters of Elizabeth Montague*, London: 1813, p. 96.

28 *Clara Gazul*, p. lxxx.
29 Ibid., pp. lxxx–lxxxi.
30 Ibid., pp. lxxxiii–lxxxiv.

5 LORD CRAVEN

1 James Edmund Vincent, *Highways and Byways in Berkshire*, London: Macmillan, 1906, p. 33.
2 *Memoirs*, p. 108.
3 Jane Austen to Cassandra Austen, 8 January 1801, in *Jane Austen's Letters*, collected and edited by R. W. Chapman, Oxford: OUP, 1952.
4 *Memoirs*, p. 1.
5 Ibid., pp. 2–3.
6 Ibid., p. 2.
7 Ibid., pp. 1–2.
8 Ibid., p. 3.
9 Ibid.

6 FREDERIC LAMB

1 'I was not depraved enough to determine immediately on a new choice, though I often thought about it.' *Memoirs*, p. 2.
2 Ibid.
3 Ibid. William Hickey recalls in his *Memoirs* being introduced to courtesans who, 'as is almost always the case, were unfaithful to their immediate patrons, always having one or more gallants for their own private gratification'. Peter Quennell (ed.), *Memoirs of William Hickey*, London and Boston: Routledge and Kegan Paul, 1975, p. 162.
4 *Memoirs*, p. 6.
5 Ibid., p. 7.
6 Ibid.
7 L. G. Mitchell, *Lord Melbourne 1779–1848*, Oxford: OUP, 1997, p. 53.
8 *Memoirs* 1831, vol. 5, p. 426.
9 Mabel, Countess of Airlee, *Lady Palmerston and her Times*, London: Hodder and Stoughton, 1922, vol. 1, p. 2.
10 *Memoirs*, p. 2.
11 Ibid.
12 Lord David Cecil, *Melbourne*, New York: The Bobs-Merrill Company Inc., 1939, p. 39.
13 Ibid.
14 Ibid.
15 30 August 1819. The Hon. F. Leveson-Gower (ed.), *Letters of Harriette, Lady Granville, 1810–1845*, 2 vols., London and New York: 1894, p. 144.
16 Jonathan David Gross, *Byron's 'Corbeau Blanc' – The Life and Letters of Lady Melbourne*, Houston, Texas: Rice University Press, 1997, p. 26.
17 L. G. Mitchell, op. cit., p. 7.
18 Peter Quennell, op. cit., p. 270.
19 Julia Johnstone claims that Harriette wrote to the Prince only to make Lamb jealous and to

extort money from him. The Prince's reply, Julia says, was in fact written by Colonel Thomas, his secretary: the Prince knew nothing of the letter, and Frederic was so jealous that, as Harriette had hoped, he gave her £200.

20 *Memoirs*, pp. 19–20. Byron was of course scarcely known until 1810, eight years after Harriette's relationship with Lamb ended.

21 Ibid., p. 192.

22 Ibid., pp. 7–8.

23 Ibid., p. 126.

24 Jane Austen, *Emma*, London: Dent, 1961, p. 90.

25 Edward Pugh [David Hughson, pseud.], *London*, London: 1805–9, vol. 4, p. 384.

7 JULIA JOHNSTONE

1 Quoted in Valerie Grosvenor Myer, *Harriette Wilson: Lady of Pleasure*, p. 71.

2 *Confessions*, p. 27.

3 *Memoirs*, p. 21.

4 *Confessions*, p. 9.

5 Ibid., p. 10.

6 Ibid., p. 12.

7 Ibid.

8 Ibid., p. 16.

9 Ibid., pp. 52–3.

10 *Memoirs*, p. 20.

11 Ibid., p. 21.

12 Ibid., pp. 20–21.

13 *Confessions*, p. 14.

14 Ibid.

15 Ibid., p. 21.

16 *Memoirs*, p. 30.

8 THE MARQUIS OF LORNE

1 *Memoirs*, p. 11.

2 Captain Gronow, quoted in Lewis Melville, *Beaux of the Regency*, London: Chapman and Hall, 1909, p. 70.

3 *Memoirs*, p. 29.

4 The Earl of Ilchester (ed.), *The Journal of Elizabeth Holland*, vol. 1, London, 1908, p. 233; 25 March 1799.

5 The Earl of Ilchester (ed.), *The Journal of Henry James Fox, 1818–30*, London, 1923, p. 34; 23 July 1820.

6 George Douglas, Eighth Duke of Argyll, *Autobiography and Memoirs*, edited by Dowager Duchess of Argyll, London: John Murray, 1906.

7 Duke of Argyll (ed.), *Intimate Letters of the Eighteenth Century*, London: Stanley Paul and Co., 1909, pp. 455–6.

8 *Memoirs*, p. 8.

9 Ibid.

10 Ibid., pp. 8–9.

11 Ibid., p. 9.

12 Ibid., p. 10.

13 Ibid., p. 11.

14 Ibid., p. 13.

15 Ibid., pp. 16–17.

16 Ibid., p. 18.

17 Ibid., p. 19.

18 Ibid., p. 25.

19 Ibid., p. 26.

20 Ibid., p. 27.

21 Ibid., p. 209.

9 SIR ARTHUR WELLESLEY

1 *Memoirs*, p. 27.

2 Ibid.

3 Quoted in Stella Margetson, *Regency London*, London: Cassell, 1971, p. 76.

4 John Brewer, *The Pleasures of the Imagination: English Culture in the Eighteenth Century*, London: HarperCollins, 1997, p. 348.

5 Quoted in Hubert Cole, *Beau Brummel*, London: Granada, 1977, p. 53.

6 E. M. Butler (ed.), *A Regency Visitor: The English Tour of Prince Pückler-Muskau described in his letters 1826–1828*, translated by Sarah Austen, London: Collins, 1957, p. 178.

7 *Memoirs*, p. 206.

8 Ibid., pp. 36–7.

9 Ibid., p. 37.

10 After the birth of Julia's first child, Brummell wrote her the following lines in his commonplace book:

Unhappy child of indiscretion,
Poor slumberer on a breast forlorn!
Pledge and reproof of past transgression,
Dear, though unwelcome to be born . . .

Quoted in Captain Jesse, *The Life of Beau Brummell*, London, 1844. Jesse says that 'the unfortunate Julia Storer' died a few years after these lines were written.

11 *Confessions*, p. 59.

12 *Memoirs*, p. 70.

13 Ibid., p. 34.

14 Ibid., pp. 34–5.

15 *Confessions*, p. 61.

16 Quoted in Margetson, op. cit., pp. 72–3.

17 *Confessions*, p. 76.

18 *Memoirs*, pp. 243–4.

19 Ibid., p. 111.

20 Ibid., p. 32.

21 A letter among the Creevy papers from Lord Kinnaird, dated 1819, says that 'Lord

Lascelles's son has married Harriette Wilson's sister.' Kinnaird knew the Dubouchet girls well. There is no material to show that this marriage did take place, but the records of Edward, Lascelles's eldest son and the most likely candidate, are sufficiently ambivalent to suggest that no one had much idea what he was up to. *The Complete Peerage* says that he is thought to have married a woman called Louisa Rowley in 1821, and *Burke's Peerage* says that he married Ann Elizabeth Rosser in that year. It is possible that one of the Dubouchet sisters, possibly Rose, who was then aged twenty, may have lived with Edward for a year or two as his common-law wife. Further, a letter in *Bell's Life in London*, dated 1825, from an anonymous correspondent who was intimate with the family, says that Julia Dubouchet was kept by a younger son of the Earl of Coventry, and bore him several children.

22 *Memoirs*, p. 58.
23 *The English Spy*, vol. 2, p. 47.
24 Ibid.
25 Elizabeth Longford, Wellington, *The Years of the Sword*, London: World Books, 1971, p. 15.
26 Ibid., p. 18.
27 Ibid., p. 141.
28 Ibid., p. 192.
29 *Memoirs*, p. 59.
30 Ibid., p. 60.
31 Ibid, pp. 74–5.
32 Ibid., p. 195.
33 Longford, op. cit., p. 195.
34 *Memoirs*, p. 127.
35 Longford, op. cit., p. 201.
36 *Confessions*, p. 127.
37 Longford, op. cit., p. 152.
38 Iris Butler, *The Eldest Brother, The Marquess Wellesley, the Duke of Wellington's Eldest Brother*, London: Hodder and Stoughton, 1973, p. 465.
39 *Memoirs*, pp. 90–91.
40 Ibid., p. 76.

10 LORD PONSONBY

1 *Memoirs*, p. 61.
2 *Memoirs* 1831, vol. 7, p. 138.
3 *Memoirs*, p. 61.
4 Ibid.
5 Ibid., p. 64.
6 Ibid., p. 72.
7 Ibid., p. 198.
8 Sir John Ponsonby, KCB, *The Ponsonby Family, 1771–1855*, London: The Medici Society, 1929, p. 75.
9 *Memoirs*, p. 96.
10 Ponsonby, op. cit., pp. 78–9.

11 *Memoirs*, p. 639.

12 Ibid., p. 73.

13 The Hon. F. Leveson-Gower (ed.), *Letters of Harriette, Lady Granville, 1810–1845*, London and New York: Longman, 1894, vol. 1, p. 43.

14 *Memoirs*, p. 80.

15 Ibid., p. 81.

16 Ibid., p. 89.

17 Ibid., p. 83.

18 Ibid., p. 164.

19 Ibid., p. 84.

20 Ibid.

21 Ibid., p. 90.

22 Ibid., p. 121.

23 Ibid., p. 96.

24 Ibid., p. 120.

25 Ibid., p. 98.

26 Ibid., p. 96.

27 Ibid., p. 106.

28 Ibid., p. 107.

29 Ibid., p. 108.

30 Ibid., p. 110.

31 Ibid., p. 126.

32 Ponsonby: GRE/E/673/3.

33 *Memoirs*, p. 126.

34 Ibid., p. 221.

35 Julia Johnstone's version of Harriette's affair with Ponsonby differs in every detail. According to Julia, 'Harriette was never connected with Lord Ponsonby, and never spoke to him above twenty times in her life.' It is possible that Julia knew very little about their relationship; it is equally possible that she knew all about it and was envious. Ponsonby first saw Harriette, she says, when the two women were living together in Bloomsbury and he came to the house drunk one evening, in the company of Argyll and some others. 'He selected Harriette for his friend and till twelve at night talked her into the belief that he was really smitten with her charms.' Any contact Ponsonby continued to have with Harriette was charitable rather than amatory; he had offered to help her brother George, who was in financial trouble. Ponsonby helped to get him bound on a ship for the West Indies. This is where Harriette's and Ponsonby's relationship began and ended. Problems in credibility arise from George Dubouchet's being born in 1796, which would have made him ten years old at the time of his bankruptcy. There are no Dubouchets named in any of the army lists, which puts paid also to Julia's account of Harriette's other brother, 'the Major', who she describes as being 'manly, open hearted, and free, much readier to censure his sister for her faults than throw away money to pamper her frivolous disposition'. And of course any remaining doubts can be assuaged by reading Harriette's surviving letters to Ponsonby.

36 Ponsonby appears to have left Harriette in 1809, but a letter from Lady Granville to Lady Morpeth, written on 12 December 1812, says that he and his wife had come to 'an understanding' whereby 'he is to give up Miss Wilson and all that sort of thing . . .'

Leveson-Gower, op. cit., p. 43. The most plausible interpretation of the discrepancy in dates is that 'Miss Wilson' had become a byword for courtesans.

37 *Memoirs*, p. 106.

38 Harriette Wilson to Lord Byron, in George Paston and Peter Quennell (eds), *'To Lord Byron':Feminine Profiles, based upon unpublished letters 1807–1824*, London: John Murray, 1939, pp. 160–61. Hereafter cited as *'To Lord Byron'*.

39 Ibid.

40 *Memoirs*, p. 254.

41 Ponsonby: GRE/E/673/3.

42 *Memoirs*, p. 151.

43 Ibid., p. 182.

11 THE MARY ANNE CLARKE AFFAIR

1 Paul Berry, *By Royal Appointment: A Biography of Mary Anne Clarke, Mistress of the Duke of York*, London: Femina, 1970, p. 42.

2 Ibid., p. 43.

3 Ibid., p. 14.

4 Ibid., p. 18.

5 Ibid., p. 171.

6 Ibid., p. 136.

7 Ibid., p. 171.

8 Ibid., p. 164.

9 Mary Anne Clarke, *The Rival Princes*, 2 vols., London: Chapple, 1810.

12 SOPHIA

1 *Memoirs*, p. 445.

2 Captain Gronow, *Last Recollections*, London: Smith, Elder and Co., 1866, pp. 163–4.

3 Ibid., p. 163.

4 *Memoirs*, p. 112.

5 Ibid., p. 133.

6 Ibid.

7 Ibid., p. 230.

8 Ibid., p. 231.

9 Ibid., p. 233.

10 Ibid., pp. 234–5.

11 Ibid., p. 241.

12 Ibid., p. 174.

13 Ibid., p. 177.

14 Ibid., p. 173.

15 *Bell's Life in London*, 3 April 1825.

16 The Hon. Grantley F. Berkeley, *My Life and Recollections*, London: Hurst and Blackett, 1866, p. 46.

17 *Memoirs*, p. 191.

18 Ibid., p. 296.

19 Ibid., p. 310.
20 Ibid., p. 311.
21 Ibid., p. 312.
22 Ibid., p. 348.
23 Ibid.
24 Ibid., p. 372.
25 Ibid., p. 374.
26 Ibid.
27 Ibid., p. 376.
28 Ibid., p. 374.
29 Ibid., p. 376.

13 THE MARQUIS OF WORCESTER

1 *Memoirs*, p. 244.
2 Badminton: Fm M4/1/16; 3 May 1816.
3 *Memoirs*, p. 312.
4 Ibid., p. 313.
5 Ibid., p. 242.
6 Ibid., p. 263.
7 Ibid., p. 301.
8 Ibid., p. 323.
9 Ibid., p. 324.
10 Ibid., p. 312.
11 Ibid., p. 320.
12 Ibid., p. 323.
13 Ibid., p. 363.
14 Ibid., p. 329.
15 Ibid., p. 345.
16 Ibid., p. 331.
17 Ibid.
18 Ibid., p. 353.
19 Ibid., p. 398.
20 Ibid.
21 Ibid., p. 399.
22 Ibid., p. 428. Harriette's comments about Robinson are confirmed by Worcester in a letter to Beaufort dated 22 July 1813: 'I was very sorry to hear of Robinson but could hardly think him so great a rogue.' Badminton: Fm M4/1/18(7).
23 *Memoirs*, p. 428.
24 Ibid., p. 429.
25 Ibid., p. 432.
26 Badminton: Fm M4/1/13(2).
27 John Mollo, *The Prince's Dolls: Scandals, Skirmishes and Splendours of the First British Hussars 1793–1815*, London: Leo Cooper, 1977, p. 102.
28 *Memoirs*, p. 433.
29 Ibid., pp. 433–7.

30 Ibid., p. 447.

31 Badminton: Fm M4/1/13(3).

32 *Memoirs*, p. 439.

33 Ibid.

34 Ibid., p. 441.

35 Ibid.

36 Badminton: Fm M4/1/13(4).

14 MEYLER

1 Christopher Hibbert (ed.), *Captain Gronow: His Reminiscences of Regency and Victorian Life 1810–60*, London: Kyle Cathie, p. 57.

2 *Memoirs*, p. 427.

3 Ibid., p. 426.

4 Ibid., pp. 426–7.

5 Ibid., p. 444.

6 Ibid.

7 Ibid., p. 426.

8 Ibid., pp. 426–7.

9 Badminton: Fm M4/1/13(5) and (6).

10 Badminton: Fm M4/1/13(7).

11 *Memoirs*, p. 459.

12 Ibid., p. 460.

13 Ibid., p. 457.

14 Ibid., p. 458.

15 Ben Weinreb and Christopher Hibbert (eds.), *The London Encyclopedia*, London: Macmillan, 1983, p. 119.

16 *Memoirs*, p. 200.

17 Mildmay's passion for his sister-in-law knew no bounds: 'The English language is too weak to express my love for you – sleeping or waking, you alone engross my thoughts,' he wrote in one of the letters that was eventually read out in court. When Lady Rosebery went to her husband's Scottish estate, Mildmay disguised himself as a sailor and stayed at the local inn, climbing in through her bedroom window every evening after supper. Here Sir Henry was discovered beside Lady Rosebery's bed, wearing a blue duffel jacket, red waistcoat and trousers and sporting a large false beard. The couple ran away together the next day, to the German kingdom of Württemberg, where marriage between a man and the sister of his deceased spouse was not considered, as it was in England, incestuous. There Sir Henry and Lady Mildmay remained for thirty years until his gambling debts became so great that he shot himself.

18 *Memoirs*, p. 199.

19 Ibid., p. 548.

20 Maggie Lane, *Jane Austen's England*, London: Hale, 1986, p. 94.

21 Jane Austen, *Persuasion*, London: Hamish Hamilton, 1946, pp. 94–5.

22 *Memoirs*, p. 464.

23 The Hon. F. Leveson-Gower (ed.), *Letters of Harriette, Lady Granville, 1810–1845*, London and New York: 1894; 24 September 1812.

24 Austen, op. cit., p. 95.

25 *Memoirs*, p. 464.

26 Ibid., p. 471.

27 Ibid., p. 479.

28 Ibid., p. 483.

29 Ibid., p. 484.

30 'To Lord Byron', p. 145.

31 Ibid., p. 146.

32 Ibid., pp. 147–8.

33 *Memoirs*, p. 476.

34 Badminton: Fm M4/2/8.

35 Ibid.

36 Badminton: Fm M5/4/1.

37 In *The Somerset Sequence* (London: Newman Neame, 1951), Horatia Durant doubts that the veracity of the story Harriette Wilson tells about her relationship with Worcester prior to his leaving to join Wellington. She uses as her source the memoirs of the 10th Hussars, which claim that Worcester ran away to Portugal in 1810, where he stayed until 1813 when the 10th Hussars landed at Lisbon and he joined them as lieutenant. 'We are confronted with the difficulty of making this account of Worcester's soldiering tally with Harriette Wilson's *Memoirs*. Someone must have lied, and we can scarcely accuse the historian of the 10th Hussars' (p. 180). If Harriette Wilson cannot be believed, then the letters in the Badminton archive confirm beyond measure that if anyone 'lied', it was in fact the military historian.

38 Badminton: Fm M4/1/16.

39 Ibid.

40 Ibid.

41 *Memoirs*, pp. 486–7.

42 Ibid., p. 488.

43 Badminton: Fm M4/1/16.

44 *Memoirs*, p. 488.

45 Ibid., p. 491.

46 Ibid., p. 493.

47 Ibid., p. 495.

48 Ibid.

49 Ibid., p. 496.

50 Badminton: Fm M4/1/18(7).

51 Badminton: Fm M4/1/18.

52 *Memoirs*, p. 498.

53 *The English Spy*, vol. 2, p. 49.

54 Badminton: Fm M5/4/1.

55 The Badminton archive contains a receipt written in Harriette's distinctive, sloping hand, stating: 'Received January 9th 1814 of his Grace the Duke of Beaufort by payment of Messrs Hoare, the sum of one hundred pounds being the amount of half a year's annuity due this day, Harriette Wilson.' Badminton: Fm M4/1/18(16).

56 Quoted in J. B. Priestley, *The Prince of Pleasure and His Regency 1811–1820*, London: Sphere Books, 1971, p. 126.

57 *Memoirs*, p. 597.

58 Richard Edgecumbe (ed.), *The Diary of Lady Frances Shelley 1787–1817*, London, John Murray, 1912, p. 70.

59 *Confessions*, p. 295.

15 PARIS

1 Gronow writes in his *Reminiscences* of Worcester's performance as aide-de-camp to Wellington, that he 'upon every occasion showed that he was worthy of the race of John of Gaunt, from which he sprang'.

2 *Memoirs*, p. 530.

3 Ibid., p. 500.

4 Ibid., pp. 500–501.

5 Ibid., p. 516.

6 Ibid., p. 520.

7 Ibid., p. 526.

8 Ibid.

9 Ibid.

10 Ibid., p. 501.

11 Ibid.

12 Ibid., p. 503.

13 Ibid., p. 504.

14 Ibid., p. 515.

15 Leslie Marchand, *Byron: A Biography,* London: John Murray, 1957, vol. 1, p. 459.

16 *Memoirs*, pp. 579–80.

17 Ibid., p. 582.

18 Ibid., p. 586.

19 Ibid., p. 588.

20 Ibid., p. 592.

21 'To Lord Byron', p. 157.

22 Murray.

23 'To Lord Byron', pp. 154–5.

24 *Memoirs*, p. 530.

25 Ibid., p. 526.

26 Ibid., p. 530.

27 Anon., *The Englishman's Mentor*, 1819, p. 186.

28 Philip Mansell, *Paris Between Empires,* London: John Murray, 2001, p. 48.

29 *Memoirs*, p. 531.

30 Elizabeth Longford, *Wellington: The Years of the Sword*, p. 436.

31 Lady Caroline's flirtation with the Duke formed one more connection between herself and Harriette: both had been involved with, and educated by, Lady Melbourne's sons and Harriette was intimate with other relations of Lady Caroline's, including her cousins the Duke of Devonshire and Earl Spencer. Harriette had at one time hired a maid who had been on the staff of Caroline Lamb, and the two gossiped about the behaviour of her former employer. Both Harriette and Caroline created sex scandals, wrote books to avenge their lovers, and each moralized about the other, Caroline Lamb writing a condemnatory poem about Harriette Wilson in the year that the *Memoirs* were published:

Harriette Wilson, shall I tell thee where,
Besides my being CLEVERER,
We differ? – thou wert hired to hold thy tongue,
Thou hast no right to do thy lovers wrong:
But I, whom none could buy or gain,
Who am as proud, girl, as thyself art vain,
And like thyself, or sooner like the wind
Blow raging ever free and unconfined.-
What should withhold my tongue with pen of steel
The faults of those who have wronged me to reveal?
Why should I hide men's follies, whilst my own
Blaze like the gas along this talking town?
Is it being bitter, to be too sincere?
Must we adulterate truth, as they do beer?
I'll tell thee why, then! As each has his price,
I have been bought at last – I am not ice,
Kindness and gratitude have chained my tongue,
From henceforth I will do no mortal wrong.
Prate those who please – laugh – censure who that will,
My mouth is sealed – my thoughts – my pen – are still.
In the meantime – we Lambs are seldom civil
I wish thy book – NOT THEE – at the Devil!

32 *Memoirs*, p. 574.
33 Ibid., p. 533.
34 Ibid.
35 Ibid., p. 537.
36 Ibid., p. 520.
37 Ibid., p. 538.
38 Ibid., p. 560.
39 Ibid., p. 520.
40 Ibid., p. 535.
41 Ibid., pp. 520–21.
42 Ibid., p. 538.
43 Ibid., p. 539.
44 Ibid., p. 569.
45 Ibid., p. 192.
46 Ibid., p. 639.
47 *Confessions*, p. 351.
48 Ibid., p. 343.
49 *Memoirs* 1831, vol. 7, p. 365.
50 *Memoirs*, p. 638.
51 *Memoirs* 1831, vol. 7, p. 366.

16 HENRY BROUGHAM

1 Henry Brougham, letter to Thomas Creevey MP, 25 August 1816; quoted in
  G. T. Garratt, *Lord Brougham*, London: Macmillan, 1935, p. 115.
2 See Leslie Marchand (ed.), *Byron's Letters and Journals*, London: John Murray, 1973, vol. 9,
  p. 29: 'When Brummell was obliged (by that affair of poor Meyler – who thence acquired
  the name of "Dick the Dandy-Killer" – it was about money and debt and all that) to retire
  to . . .' *Memoirs* also refers to Meyler as 'Dick the Dandy-Killer'.
3 Virginia Woolf, *Beau Brummell*, New York: Rimmington and Hooper, 1930, p. 5.
4 *Memoirs*, pp. 602–4.
5 Ibid., p. 604.
6 Woolf, op. cit., p. 1.
7 *Memoirs*, p. 609.
8 R. G. Thorne, *The Commons 1790–1820*, London: Secker and Warburg, 1986, vol. 4, p. 585.
9 Garratt, op. cit., preface, quoting Morley.
10 Lytton Strachey and Roger Fulford, *The Greville Memoirs*, London: Macmillan, 1938, vol. 1,
   p. 120.
11 Ibid.
12 *Edinburgh Review*, January 1808.
13 Doris Langley Moore, *The Late Lord Byron*, London: John Murray, 1966, p. 162.
14 *Confessions*, p. 336.
15 Quoted in Garratt, op. cit., p. 1.
16 Quoted in Flora Fraser, *The Unruly Queen: The Life of Queen Caroline*, Basingstoke: Macmillan,
   1996, p. 433.
17 Quoted in E. A. Smith, *A Queen on Trial: The Affair of Queen Caroline*, Stroud: Alan Sutton,
   1993, p. 118.
18 Ibid., p. 115.
19 Thomas Creevey, quoted in Fraser, op. cit., p. 465.
20 Lady Charlotte Bury, *The Diary of a Lady in Waiting*, quoted in Garratt, op. cit., p. 70.
21 Brougham's memoirs, quoted in Smith, op. cit., p. 33.
22 Smith, op. cit., p. 92.
23 Moore, op. cit., p. 125.
24 Quoted in Moore, op. cit., p. 52.
25 The evidence for this comes from the painter Benjamin Haydon's diary, and is quoted in
   Moore, op. cit., pp. 162–3.
26 *Memoirs*, p. 570.
27 Ibid., p. 636.
28 Ibid., p. 440.
29 'To Lord Byron', p. 154.

17 RETIREMENT

1 See Kenneth Bourne, *Palmerston: The Early Years, 1784–1841*, London: Allen Lane, 1982,
  pp. 195–6.
2 F. E. Baily, *The Love Story of Lady Palmerston*, London: Hutchinson and Co., 1938, p. 75.

3 *Memoirs* 1831, vol. 5, p. 359.
4 *'To Lord Byron'*, p. 155.
5 *Memoirs* 1831, vol. 4, p. 267.
6 Ibid., pp. 269–70.
7 Brougham: MS 14,535.
8 *Memoirs* 1831, vol. 4, p. 269.
9 Ibid., p. 240.
10 Virginia Surtees (ed.), *The Second Self: The Letters of Harriette Granville, 1810–1845*, Hampshire: Michael Russell, 1990, p. 20.
11 *Memoirs* 1831, vol. 7, p. 237.
12 Ibid., p. 251.
13 Ibid., p. 262.
14 Ibid., p. 263.
15 *'To Lord Byron'*, p. 150.
16 *Memoirs*, p. 611.
17 Ibid., p. 612.
18 Murray; 16 April 1818.
19 *Memoirs*, p. 614.
20 *'To Lord Byron'*, p. 154.
21 Ibid., pp. 151–2.
22 H. C. Watson, *A Sketch of the Life of N.C. Bochsa*, Sydney: Paisey and Fryer, 1855, p. 13.
23 *The English Spy*, vol. 2, p. 48.
24 *Memoirs*, p. 222.
25 Ibid.
26 *Memoirs* 1831, vol. 5, pp. 401–2.
27 Ibid., p. 361.
28 Ibid., p. 233.
29 Ibid., p. 241.
30 Ibid., p. 240.
31 Ibid., vol. 7, p. 42.
32 *'To Lord Byron'*, pp. 157–8.
33 *Memoirs* 1831, vol. 7, p. 104.
34 Ibid., vol. 5, p. 414.
35 Ibid., vol .7, pp. 373–4.
36 Ibid., p. 377.
37 *The English Spy*, vol. 2, p. 52.
38 *Memoirs* 1831, vol. 7, p. 375.
39 *Memoirs*, p. 118.

18 THE MOUSTACHE

1 *Memoirs* 1831, vol. 5, p. 423.
2 *The English Spy*, vol. 2, p. 50.
3 *Memoirs* 1831, vol. 5, p. 425.
4 Ibid., pp. 428–9.
5 Ibid., vol. 7, p. 7.

6 Ibid., p. 9.
7 Ibid., p. 10.
8 Ibid., p. 11.
9 Ibid., pp. 57–9.
10 See Roger Lee Brown, *History of the Fleet Prison, London: The Anatomy of the Fleet*, Lewiston, NY: The Edwin Mellon Press, 1996, p. 280.
11 *Memoirs* 1831, vol. 7, p. 126.
12 Ibid., p. 139.
13 Ibid., p. 318.
14 Ibid., p. 144.
15 Ibid., p. 145.
16 Ibid., p. 156.
17 Ibid., p. 159.
18 Ibid., p. 195.
19 Ibid., p. 205.
20 Ibid., p. 212.
21 Brougham: 21,680.
22 Brougham: 21,769.
23 Brougham: 21,680.
24 Sir John Berant, *Narrative of the Expedition under General MacGregor against Portobello*, London: C. & J. Ollier, 1820.
25 Egon Larsen, *The Deceivers*, London: John Baker, 1966, p. 78.
26 *The English Spy*, vol. 2, p. 52.

19 STOCKDALE

1 Brougham: 39,602.
2 'Court of King's Bench, Westminster, July 1, *Blore* v. *Stockdale*', *The Times*, 2 July 1825, p. 3.
3 A. Aspinall (ed.), *The Later Correspondence of George III*, Cambridge: Cambridge University Press, 1970, vol. 5, p. 189n.
4 *The Claims of Mr Wardle to the Thanks of the Country*, by A Citizen, London: J. J. Stockdale, 1809, p. 1.
5 *Stockdale's Budget*, 1827.
6 Frederick L. Jones (ed.), *The Letters of Percy Bysshe Shelley*, Oxford: Oxford University Press, 1964, vol. 1, p. 26.
7 *Stockdale's Budget*.
8 I. McCalman, *Radical Underworld: Prophets, Revolutionaries and Pornographers in London 1795–1840*, Cambridge: Cambridge University Press, 1988, p. 162.
9 Ibid., p. 163.
10 *Memoirs* 1831, vol. 4, Stockdale's postscript, dated 1 June 1825.
11 Ibid., p. 23.
12 *Bell's Life in London*, 20 February 1825.
13 Ibid., 6 March 1825.
14 *Memoirs of George Anne Bellamy*, by a Gentleman of Covent Garden Theatre, London: J. Walker, 1785, p. 1.
15 Letter to Edward Bulwer Lytton; Bulwer Lytton: D/EK C1/16.

16 *Memoirs* 1831, vol. 7, pp. 181–2.

17 Anne Hill, *Trelawny's Strange Relations. An Account of the Domestic Life of Edward John Trelawny's Mother & Sisters in Paris and London, 1818–1829*, Stanford Dingley: The Mill House Press, 1956.

18 See chapter 21 for an account of the blackmail campaign.

19 *Blore v. Stockdale*, *Memoirs* 1831, vol. 4, p. 10.

20 Recent additions to the genre have been Andrew Morton's biography of Diana, Princess of Wales, Jane Hawking's account of her marriage to the physicist Stephen Hawking, Margaret Cook's revelations about her marriage to the politician Robin Cook, Ulrika Jonsson's exposé of relations with, among others, the England football manager, Sven Goren Eriksson, and the revelation made by Edwina Curry of her affair with the then Tory minister, John Major.

21 Leslie Blanch (*Harriette Wilson's Memoirs*, London: The Folio Society, 1964, p. 9) sees Rochfort as more of an influence than he was. 'In the present writer's opinion,' Blanch writes, 'the *Memoirs* are not dictated so much by spite, revenge, or a desire for money on Harriette's part, as by the influence of Rochfort, frustrated, ruthless and bullying. It is he, I think, who is behind the phrase, "two hundred pounds by return of post, to be left out".' Julia Johnstone says that Rochfort wrote Harriette's extortion letters for her, which would not have been possible as he was in Brussels and she in Paris during the most heated moments of her campaign.

22 *Memoirs* 1831, vol. 7, p. 237.

23 Ibid., p. 364.

24 Lynda M. Thompson, *The 'Scandalous Memoirists': Constantia Phillips, Laetitia Pilkington and the shame of 'publick fame'*, Manchester: Manchester University Press, 2000, pp. 1–4.

20 THE *MEMOIRS* AND THE *CONFESSIONS*

1 *Bell's Life in London*, 6 March 1825.

2 H. J. C. Grierson (ed.), *The Letters of Sir Walter Scott*, London: Constable and Co., 1935, vol. IX: *1825–1826*, p. 7.

3 *Memoirs* 1831, vol. 4, p. 302.

4 Quoted in Angela Thirkell, *The Fortunes of Harriette: The Surprising Career of Harriette Wilson*, p. 216.

5 *Morning Chronicle*, 7 January 1825.

6 British Museum Print Room, 14828.

7 Robert Montgomery [attrib.], *The Age Reviewed*, 2nd edn, London: 1828.

8 *Bell's Life in London*, 20 February 1825.

9 Ibid., 6 March 1825.

10 Ibid., 13 March 1825.

11 Ibid., 4 December 1824.

12 Trowbridge H. Ford, *Henry Brougham and His World*, Chichester: Barry Rose, 1995, p. 396.

13 British Museum Print Room, 14831.

14 *Bell's Life in London*, 20 March 1825.

15 *Memoirs* 1831, vol. 7, pp. 327–8.

16 *Bell's Life in London*, 28 August 1825.

17 *Confessions*, p. 1.

18 Ibid., p. 156.

19 Ibid.
20 Ibid., p. 284.
21 Ibid., p. 353.
22 Ibid., p. 20.
23 The Public Record Office in Kew holds various documents relating to the bankruptcy of Colonel Cotton's uncle, John Cotton, of Broad Street, in the city of London, Merchant, Dealer and Chapman (B3/818,819, 820). He was in financial trouble in 1796, 1799, 1804, 1812, 1817, 1821 and 1824.
24 There is no knowing how long Julia continued to live with Cotton. He kept his rooms at Hampton Court until his death in 1848.
25 *Confessions*, p. 154.
26 Ibid., p. 139.
27 Ibid., p. 104.
28 Ibid., p. 213.
29 Valerie Grosvenor Myer and Angela Thirkell assume that Julia was correcting Harriette's fictions.
30 I have found no record of her death and she was certainly not buried in the family vault, as Harriette writes.
31 *Confessions*, p. 154.
32 John Wight, *Mornings at Bow Street*, London: Charles Baldwyn, 1824, p. 38.
33 *Confessions*, p. 97.
34 Ibid., p. 177.
35 Ibid., p. 93.
36 Ibid., p. 320.
37 Ibid., p. 353.
38 Ibid., p. 76.
39 Ibid.
40 Ibid., p. 6.
41 See *The Times*, 6 October 1824 and 9 October 1824, p. 3, col. d.
42 *Confessions*, p. 78.
43 *Memoirs* 1831, vol. 7, pp. 328–9.
44 Brougham: 14,535.
45 *Bell's Life in London*, 6 March 1825.
46 Sir Walter Scott to Lord Montagu, 18 February 1825; Grierson, op. cit.
47 *Memoirs* 1831, vol. 7, p. 304.
48 Ibid., vol. 5, p. 259.
49 J. G. Lockhart, *Memoirs of the Life of Sir Walter Scott*, Paris: Baudry's European Library, 1838, vol. 3, pp. 337–8.
50 *Bell's Life in London*, 6 March 1825.
51 *The Autobiography of Francis Place*, p. 81.
52 Prince Pückler-Muskau, *A Regency Visitor: The English Tour of Prince Pückler-Muskau Described in his Letters, 1826–1828*, London: Collins, 1957, p. 26. The treatment of Emma Hart, Lady Hamilton, is also worth considering. Her loose lifestyle had not stood in the way of her becoming British Ambassadress to Naples in 1805, but she was rejected by the nation following Nelson's death.
53 Ibid., p. 38.

54 Ibid., p. 335.

55 *Memoirs* 1831, vol. 5, p. 21.

56 Ibid., p. 72.

57 *British Lion*, 24 April 1825.

58 *Memoirs* 1831, vol. 4, p. 302.

59 Ibid., p. 300.

60 Ibid., p. 295.

61 *Bell's Life in London*, 20 March 1825.

62 *Memoirs* 1831, vol. 6, p. 271.

63 When Harriette saw the 'Old Rake's' letter in the *Morning Chronicle*, sent on to her by Stockdale in a package containing all the latest 'newspaper abuse', she said, 'I have twice spoken to that gentleman [Ambrose] in the course of my life, knew nothing about him, and cared nothing; but I thought him clever, and spoke of him as such to others.' Harriette and Ambrose were either being honest about their slight acquaintance or Ambrose had bought himself out of the *Memoirs* with a hefty sum; Harriette put him on her list of those who were to be exposed in her future *Memoirs* unless they paid up.

21 THE BLACKMAIL CAMPAIGN

1 Brougham: 39,602.

2 *Memoirs*, p. 626.

3 *Memoirs* 1831, vol. 5, p. xviii.

4 Ibid., p. 242.

5 Ibid., vol. 7, p. 243.

6 Venetia Murray, *High Society: A Social History of the Regency Period, 1788–1830*, London: Viking, 1998, p. 80.

7 *Memoirs*, p. 624.

8 Ibid.

9 Quoted in Elizabeth Longford, *Wellington: The Years of the Sword*, p. 192.

10 Ibid.

11 Brougham: 26,043.

12 *The Times*, 14 March 1825, p. 3.

13 British Museum Print Room, 14833. *Bell's Life in London* claimed on 20 March that the letter sent by Ellice was 'a pure *hoax* . . . first because Harriette can write in a much better style; and secondly, because this lady's name is not *Rochfort* but *Rochford*, and she could have no reason for misspelling her own name.' The editor of *Bell's Life* knew as little about Harriette as most of the public and confused Rochfort with the English noble family of Rochford.

14 *Bath Herald*, 8 October 1825, p. 3.

15 *The Times*, 14 November 1826, p. 2.

16 Ibid.

17 *Stockdale's Budget*, November 1826.

18 *Memoirs* 1831, vol. 5, p. 223.

19 Ibid.

20 Ponsonby: GRE/E/655/3.

21 Ponsonby: GRE/E/673/1.

22 Peter Quennell (ed.), *The Private Letters of Princess Lieven to Prince Metternich 1820–1826*,

London: John Murray, 1937, p. 355.

23 Lytton Strachey and Roger Fulford (eds.), *The Greville Memoirs*, London: Macmillan, 1938, vol. II, p. 175.

24 Francis Bamford and The Duke of Wellington, *The Journal of Mrs Arbuthnot 1820–1832*, vol. I, Macmillian: London, 1950, p. 410.

25 *Stockdale's Budget*, 27 December 1826.

22 STOCKDALE'S PERSECUTION

1 *Memoirs* 1831, vol. 7, p. 343.
2 Ibid., vol. 5, p. 157.
3 Ibid., p. 20.
4 Ibid.
5 Ibid., p. x.
6 Ibid.
7 Ibid., vol. 4, p. 308.
8 Ibid., p. 5.
9 Ibid., pp. 8–16.
10 Ibid., pp. 16–17.
11 Ibid., p. 22.
12 Ibid., p. 21.
13 British Museum Print Room: 14837.
14 *Memoirs* 1831, vol. 5, p. 83.
15 Ibid., p. 86.
16 Ibid., p. 112.
17 Brougham: 14,524.
18 Brougham: 14,525.
19 Harriette Wilson, *Paris Lions and London Tigers*, edited with an introduction by Heywood Hill, London: The Navarre Society, 1931, p. 12.
20 Ibid., pp. 36–7.
21 Ibid., Introduction, p. 10.
22 Ibid., p. 93.
23 Ibid., p. 155.
24 *Bell's Life in London*, 25 September 1825.
25 Wilson, *Paris Lions*, op. cit., p. 56.
26 Ibid., pp. 40–41.
27 Ibid., p. 114.
28 *Trelawny's Strange Relations*, p. 26.
29 *The Times*, 14 November 1825.
30 J. G. Lockhart, *Memoirs of the Life of Sir Walter Scott*, vol. 3, p. 337. 'Punk' was an Elizabethan word for prostitute.
31 *Memoirs* 1831, vol. 6, p. 71.
32 Ibid., p. 74.
33 Ibid., p. 119.
34 Leslie A. Marchand (ed.), *Byron's Letters and Journals*, London: John Murray, 1973–82, vol. 8, pp. 177 and 181.

35 For Byron's use of 'cicisbean' see, for example, Marchand, op. cit., vol. 6, p. 214; for 'cicisbeo', p. 226; and for Byron's protests to Murray that he will never make 'ladies' books', p. 106.

36 *The Times*, 22 May 1826, p. 3.

37 *Memoirs* 1831, vol. 6, p. 322.

38 Ibid., p. 190.

39 Ibid., p. 238.

40 Ibid., p. 638.

41 Ibid., p. 662.

42 Ibid., p. 606.

43 Ibid., p. 200.

44 Ibid., p. 201.

45 Ibid., pp. 211–12.

46 Ibid., p. 639.

47 Ibid., p. 593.

48 Ibid., p. 594.

49 *Bell's Life in London*, 1828.

50 Trowbridge Ford, *Henry Brougham and His World*, London: Barry Rose, 1995, p. 492.

51 *Memoirs* 1831, vol. 6, p. 574; 26 November 1826.

52 *Stockdale's Budget*, 13 December 1826.

53 Ibid., 20 December 1826.

54 Ibid.

55 *Bell's Life in London*, 10 February 1828.

56 *Memoirs* 1831, vol. 7, p. 366.

57 Ibid., vol. 5, p. 267.

58 Ibid., p. xx.

23 PANIC AT THE PALACE

1 Ponsonby to Sir Charles Bagot, in Wendy Hinde, *George Canning*, Oxford: Blackwell, 1989, p. 393.

2 *Stockdale's Budget*, 27 December 1826.

3 *Memoirs*, p. 549.

4 Brougham: 14,537.

5 Brougham: 14,535.

6 Ponsonby: GRE/E/342/2.

7 Granville: PLO 30/29/16/10 fs 16/20.

8 Ibid.

9 Granville: PRO 30/29/16/6. I am grateful to Frances Henderson for help with the transcription and translation of this document.

10 See Robert Darnton's *The Forbidden Best-Sellers of Pre-Revolutionary France*, London: Harper Collins, 1996, p. 153.

11 Aspinall (ed.), *The Letters of King George IV, 1812–1830*, p. 501.

12 Stockdale wrote to his wife, on 23 September 1826, 'They say Canning has gone to France on politics . . . I rather think that the real object of Canning's mission is to propitiate Mrs Rochfort. Ill as he has always treated me, I really can feel for him if he be reduced to such a dilemma!' *Memoirs* 1831, vol. 6, p. 382.

13 Aspinall, op. cit., p. 501.

14 Ibid.

15 Correspondence with the Duke of Wellington, 1830; BL Add. 43059, ff. 187–91.

16 Letter to Lord Aberdeen, 1829; BL Add. 43086 ff. 180–85v.

17 BL Add. 43059 ff. 187–91.

18 When MacGregor made a rash return to London in 1827 he was arrested for fraud and imprisoned in Tothill Fields, but charges were dropped. Not only were those who had been made fools of by him keen to avoid publicity but so too were those in high places who had helped MacGregor pull off his hoax, taking a skim of his earnings in return. The right strings were pulled and MacGregor got away with it. He happily continued his hoaxes for the next ten years.

19 Aspinall, op. cit., p. 177.

20 Ibid., pp. 177–8.

21 Brougham: 14,526; 16 May 1826.

22 See the correspondence in the British Library between Sir William Huskinson and Sir Charles Grant; Add. 40396 ff. 85, 99, 101.

23 Brougham: 14,527.

24 Aspinall, op. cit., p. 501.

25 Ibid., p. 502.

26 BL Add. 43086 ff. 180–85v.

27 Aspinall, op. cit., p. 502.

28 Ibid., p. 503.

29 Ibid.

30 Ibid., p. 504.

31 Brougham: 14,528.

32 Brougham: 14,529.

33 Aspinall, op. cit., p. 368.

34 Ibid., p. 504.

35 Brougham: 14,530.

36 Brougham: 14,531.

37 Brougham: 21,222.

38 BL Add. 43086 ff. 180–85v.

39 Ibid.

40 Aspinall, op. cit., p. 504.

41 Ponsonby: 14 November 1829, GRE/E/342/2.

42 Ibid.

43 Ibid. The phrase was used and then crossed out by Ponsonby in a letter written to Knighton.

44 Ponsonby: GRE/E/342/4.

45 Ponsonby: GRE/E/342/6.

46 Ibid.

47 Joseph Jeckyll, quoted in Christopher Hibbert, *George IV: Prince of Wales 1762–1811*, Harmondsworth: Penguin, 1972, p. 780.

24 TREVOR SQUARE

1 Brougham: 14,535.

2 *The Times*, 24 January 1828. 'Amy Wilson [*sic*], the gentle and excellent sister of the no less worthy Harriette, is actually engaged at the King's Theatre, as a translatress of operas. Now, to use a lordly phrase, "this is too bad" . . . in the *traduction* (an admirable word) of Meyerbeer's *Margherita d'Anjou*, we scarcely know which savours most strongly of the ridiculous – the utter ignorance displayed of the original Italian, or the execrable stupidity of the equally original English.'

3 Brougham: 14,533. Stockdale was in receipt of 'considerable information' about the Fermors.

4 Brougham: 14,534.

5 Brougham: 14,535.

6 *New Rambler's Magazine*, vol II, 1829.

7 Ibid.

8 *Bell's Life in London*, 15 February 1829.

9 *New Rambler's Magazine*, vol II, 1829.

10 *Bell's Life in London*, 15 February 1829.

11 *New Rambler's Magazine*, vol II, 1829.

12 *Bell's Life in London*, 22 February 1829.

13 Brougham: 14,523.

14 *Bell's Life in London*, 22 February 1829.

15 Brougham: 14,535.

16 Brougham: 14,523.

17 BL Add. 43059 ff. 187–9.

18 BL Add. 43059 ff. 187–9.

19 Bulwer Lytton, D/EK C1/15.

20 Ibid.

21 Bulwer Lytton: D/EK C1/16.

22 *Clara Gazul,* To the Public, p. lxxxvi.

23 Ibid., vol. 3, pp. 22–8.

24 Brougham: 21,223.

25 Brougham: 21,224 and 21,225.

26 Brougham: 23,496.

27 Brougham: 23,497.

28 Brougham: 21,682.

29 *Memoirs* 1831, vol. 7, p. 179.

30 Ibid., p. 372.

31 Ibid., p. 368.

32 *The Times*, 19 November 1831, p. 4. Stockdale presented himself at Marlborough Street on 15 November to say, 'I have no fault to find with *The Times*; on the contrary, I feel exceedingly obliged to the persons connected with that publication for having done me the justice to insert the report, as they have thereby afforded me an opportunity of publicly vindicating my character, and set me upon my guard against a secret enemy, who, I find, has been endeavouring to stab me in the dark. In the report I have just read, I find no name mentioned but my own. Now Sir, I do hope you will, as an act of justice, put me in possession of the

name of the person of distinction whom Mr Inspector Smith represented . . . I Sir, do not work in the dark; no, I am happy at being able to say that all my actions are done manfully and openly. I never shrink from any thing that I do, because I know that I only do what is creditable to me.' He was asked to leave the police station and refused. 'I am perfectly aware that I have rendered myself disagreeable to many persons, because I have laboured to expose vice in the censure of the world. They are a set of miscreants, who prowl about seeking whom they shall destroy. They insinuate themselves into the favour and confidence of kind and unsuspecting men, and afterwards testify their gratitude by the seduction of a beloved wife or a darling child. These are the reptiles with whom I make war. I tear the mask from their face, and hold them up to scorn and shame.' 'I beg you would desist,' the police officer replied.

33 Brougham: 46,105.
34 For a full report of the case see 'Copy of the Short-hand Writer's Notes of the Proceedings in the Case of *Stockdale* v. *Hansard*': *Accounts and Papers*, 1839, vol. XLIII, pp. 435–628.

25 MARY MAGDALEN

1 Brougham: 21,513.
2 Ponsonby: GRE/E/673/3.
3 Bulwer Lytton: D/EK C1/21.
4 Ponsonby: GRE/E/673/3.
5 Brougham: 14,537.
6 Bulwer Lytton: D/EK C1/21.
7 Ibid.
8 Kenneth Bourne, *The Blackmailing of the Chancellor: Some intimate and hitherto unpublished letters from Harriette Wilson to her friend, Henry Brougham*, London: Lemon Tree Press, 1975, p. 82.
9 The dispute was given full coverage in *Galignani's Messenger* at the end of December 1834, and summarized in *The Times* on 5 January 1835.
10 Brougham: 21,513.
11 Ibid.
12 Brougham: 21,800.
13 Ponsonby: GRE/E/673/6.
14 Ibid.
15 'To Lord Byron', p. 154.
16 Letter from G. A. Sala to Percy Fitzgerald, *Memoirs of an Author*, London: 1894, vol. 1, p. 109.
17 Anon., *Eliza Grimwood: A Domestic Legend of Waterloo Road*, London: B. D. Cousins, c.1845, p. 246.
18 Brougham: 21,513.
19 Bulwer Lytton: D/EK C1/19.
20 Ibid. Only the marriage and baptism records of the Chelsea Catholic Chapel now exist, making it impossible to ascertain the date of Harriette's confirmation.
21 Badminton: 3/3/23.
22 Ibid.

26 AFTERWARDS: SOPHIE STOCKDALE'S OFFER

1 Brougham: 21,790.
2 Brougham: 21,794.
3 Ibid.
4 Brougham: 21,688.
5 Ibid.
6 Brougham: 23,219.
7 Brougham: 22,918.
8 Virginia Woolf, 'Harriette Wilson', in *The Moment and Other Essays*, London: Hogarth Press, 1947, p. 134.

Index

Figures in italics indicate illustrations in the text